What's Left of Liberalism?

What's Left of Liberalism?

An Interpretation and Defense of Justice As Fairness

Jon Mandle

LEXINGTON BOOKS
Lanham • Boulder • New York • Oxford

LEXINGTON BOOKS

Published in the United States of America
by Lexington Books
4720 Boston Way, Lanham, Maryland 20706

12 Hid's Copse Road
Cumnor Hill, Oxford OX2 9JJ, England

British Library Cataloguing in Publication Information Available

Library of Congress Cataloging-in-Publication Data

Mandle, Jon, 1966–
    What's left of liberalism? : an interpretation and defense of justice as fairness / Jon
    Mandle.
       p.   cm.
    Includes bibliographical references and index.
    ISBN 0-7391-0103-x (cloth : alk. paper) — ISBN 0-7391-0104-8 (pbk. : alk. paper)
    1. Liberalism. 2. Justice. I. Title.

JC574.M36   2000
320'.01'1—dc21   99-050366

Printed in the United States of America

♾™ The paper used in this publication meets the minimum requirements of American
National Standard for Information Sciences—Permanence of Paper for Printed Library
Materials, ANSI/NISO Z39.48–1992.

for

Karen, Jay, Joan, and Adonal

Contents

Preface

A brief word of autobiography may help situate the concerns of this book. I initially read *A Theory of Justice* as a first-year graduate student in philosophy. Since I had grown up in a left-wing family, had participated in various progressive organizations in high school and college, and had been reinforced by like-minded graduate students, I already knew what I was supposed to think about such liberal academic treatises. Rawls's theory must be a mere apology for the existing capitalist order, detached from and unconcerned with the concrete lives of most real people. It certainly could not be useful to a self-defined leftist like me.

As I actually read the book however, I found myself, with alarming frequency, in agreement with what Rawls actually had to say. Three seemingly peripheral points were especially disconcerting to my initial image. The first was Rawls's robust defense of civil disobedience. Given the fact (as I discovered) that this material dated back at least to 1966, there could be no doubt that he had the Civil Rights movement in mind.[1] The second was a comment concerning the related topic of conscientious refusal: "given the tendency of nations, particularly great powers, to engage in war unjustifiably and to set in motion the apparatus of the state to suppress dissent, the respect accorded to pacifism serves the purpose of alerting citizens to the wrongs that governments are prone to commit in their name."[2] Published in 1971 at the height of the Vietnam War, the point was clear.

The third passage concerned what Rawls calls the "fair value of the political liberties." He writes:

> What is necessary is that political parties be autonomous with respect to private demands, that is, demands not expressed in the public forum and argued for openly by reference to a conception of the public good. If society does not bear the costs of organization, and party funds need to be solicited from the more advantaged social and economic interests, the pleadings of these groups are bound to receive excessive attention. And this is all the more likely when the less favored members of society,

---

1. See John Rawls, *A Theory of Justice* (Cambridge: Harvard University Press, 1971; revised edition, 1999), sections 55-59; and John Rawls, "The Justification of Civil Disobedience," in *Civil Disobedience: Theory and Practice*, Hugo Adam Bedau, ed. (New York: Pegasus, 1969).
2. Rawls, *A Theory of Justice*, 370 [325].

having been effectively prevented by their lack of means from exercising their fair degree of influence, withdraw into apathy and resentment.[3]

As I read this in the late 1980s, Rawls seemed absolutely prescient in his recognition that without political equality, we could only expect increasing apathy and resentment. Taking these passages together, I could almost conjure up an image of a knowing, smiling John Rawls quietly admonishing, "Don't prejudge me." I realized that the initial picture that I somehow received by osmosis was seriously defective. Yet, I seemed to be alone in this recognition.

Gradually, I discovered a few—very few—other authors who shared a left-wing interpretation of Rawls's theory. Ronald Dworkin's review of *A Theory of Justice* concludes by pointing out that to many critics Rawls's theory seems to be "a particularly subtle rationalization of the political status quo, which may safely be disregarded by those who want to offer a more radical critique of the liberal tradition." Dworkin replies: "If I am right, this point of view is foolish, and those who take it lose an opportunity, rare for them, to submit their own political views to some form of philosophical examination."[4] I felt that Dworkin was talking directly to me. The next year, Thomas Pogge's *Realizing Rawls* was published. It was thrilling to read precisely what I had been thinking: "This focus on the basic structure, combined with the priority concern for the least advantaged, makes Rawls a radical thinker."[5]

Unfortunately, it seems that prejudices similar to those I initially held remain dominant among many who identify themselves as progressives. I discuss the relationship between liberalism and the left in chapter one, but let me here suggest two brief explanations for the stubborn persistence of the left's negative attitude toward justice as fairness. First, the theory is complicated. Spread over two dense books, totaling over 1,000 pages, to say nothing of the secondary literature, it is easy to get lost. In chapters two and three, I provide an overview of justice as fairness that attempts to correct many common misunderstandings and to show how the various parts are related. Without an understanding of the overall structure, even the more familiar parts of the theory are easy to misinterpret. Second, Rawls does not self-identify or use the rhetoric typical of the left. This, I have gradually come to recognize, is a virtue. Rawls lets the arguments drive his conclusions; it is for others to label the theory, if they must. He aims simply to get it right. This is in sharp contrast to the two other families of political philosophies that I examine in this book. Both communitarianism and postmodernism often seem to be driven primarily by the desire to create something that is not liberalism. I argue in chapters four and five that these efforts fail to create a political philosophy more congenial to the left

---

3. Rawls, *A Theory of Justice*, 226 [198].

4. Ronald Dworkin, "The Original Position," in *Reading Rawls*, Norman Daniels, ed. (New York: Basic Books, 1975; reprint, Stanford: Stanford University Press, 1989), 52.

5. Thomas Pogge, *Realizing Rawls* (Ithaca, N.Y.: Cornell University Press, 1989), 9.

than liberalism itself. Either they end up as a form of conservatism, condemning critical reflection and unable to cope with diversity, or they are blinded by diversity, unable explicitly to endorse normative principles of evaluation. A left liberalism, such as justice as fairness, is therefore what is left—it is what remains and it is also what is politically progressive.

While still in graduate school, I wrote to John Rawls and asked whether my interpretation of his theory was on the right track. He did not have to take the time to write back to an unknown graduate student, but he did. Since then, Rawls has remained remarkably generous in his willingness to provide encouragement and assistance. I thank him first. Joan Mandle provided far more than her fair share of help and support in writing this book. I am grateful also to all those who contributed directly to this project, including: Mike Burke, Pat Burke, Alissa Hurwitz, Jay Mandle, Dale Miller, Laura Ruetsche, Ruth Sample, Karen Schupack, Bonnie Steinbock, Sergio Tenenbaum, and Adam Weinberg. Many other friends and colleagues have contributed indirectly, and I appreciate their help and encouragement, as well.

Finally, I thank Columbia University Press for permission to quote from *Political Liberalism*, by John Rawls. Copyright © 1993 Columbia University Press. Reprinted with the permission of the publisher.

Addendum

While this book was in the final stages of preparation, Rawls released a revised edition of *A Theory of Justice*. My citations remain to the original edition, but I have added page numbers in square brackets to indicate the corresponding page numbers in the revised edition. Where Rawls has changed the text, I have retained the quotes from the original edition, but have indicated the change in a footnote.

Chapter 1
Liberalism and the Left

For the past century-and-a-half, the left has sustained its optimism and faith by constantly identifying some aspect of society—economic, political, or social—as being "in crisis." Victory always seemed to be just one crisis away. Yet there can be no doubt that for some time it is the left itself that has been in crisis. This is clear enough to anyone willing to look. For some on the left who have been open to critical self-examination, the revolutions of 1989 and the collapse of the Marxist political program triggered this recognition.[1] For others, the crisis of progressive politics is the result of the left's excessive reliance on the identity politics that emerged in the late 1960s.[2] Ironically, the widespread alienation of the left from political relevance has occurred with little impact on the normal course of the left's academic life.[3] Self-identified leftists have flourished in many departments at many universities. To observe this is not to agree with those critics who, like Dinesh D'Souza, claim that our campuses have become so infected by left-wing ideologists that serious scholarship can hardly find fertile ground.[4] But the truth remains: the relative success that left-wing ideologies have enjoyed in the academy stands in stark contrast to the fact that they are largely discredited or ignored in the larger society. We should not allow the irony to escape us. The students of the New Left taunted and mocked their professors concerning their lack of "relevance." Now, having inherited the academy from their elders, this generation has become less politically relevant than almost any before. If the left is eventually to make a significant political difference outside the academy, there is an urgent need to reassess the fundamental principles of a progressive politics. Instead of defining itself as inevitably in opposition, the left must develop a positive vision of social justice.

In this book, I compare and assess the three dominant frameworks that are currently competing for the left's allegiance: liberalism, communitarianism, and postmodernism. None of these is especially unified or well defined, so at times I will simply have to stipulate what I include and exclude from each. The specific

---

1. See, for example, Ira Katznelson, *Liberalism's Crooked Circle* (Princeton: Princeton University Press, 1996).

2. Todd Gitlin, *The Twilight of Common Dreams* (New York: Metropolitan, 1995).

3. See the discussion in Russell Jacoby, *The Last Intellectuals* (New York: Noonday Press, 1987), chapters 5 and 6; and *Dogmatic Wisdom* (New York: Doubleday, 1994), chapter 6.

4. Dinesh D'Souza, *Illiberal Education* (New York: Free Press, 1991).

form of liberalism that I will consider is John Rawls's *justice as fairness*. The communitarian and postmodern doctrines that I examine define themselves, in large part, in opposition to perceived failures of liberalism. Both have proven to be attractive to the left as it searches for a congenial philosophical framework. In fact, I believe that in large part these approaches are attractive to the left precisely because of their oppositional stance with respect to liberalism. In this book, however, I argue that a more precise and accurate understanding of justice as fairness will reveal that the left's flirtation with communitarianism and postmodernism are destructive of what should be the left's most basic commitment to social justice. Specifically, I argue that a form of political liberalism such as justice as fairness best provides a basis for defending the fundamental values of the left.

Liberalism encompasses a diverse and heterogeneous family of views, and obviously it should not be embraced uncritically. Different forms of liberalism focus on disparate problems and attempt to solve them in various ways. Justice as fairness aims to develop a framework within which to evaluate the moral character of a society's basic institutional structure. It is especially important that this framework of evaluation not be identified with the actual institutional arrangement of any particular society. The history of societies attempting to implement liberal principles is checkered—though of course this is true of every social orientation. Political liberalism can provide a critical perspective even on those societies that are frequently identified as liberal. Justice as fairness is neither a defense of the excesses of possessive individualism (as the left often charges) nor an apology for "big government" welfare state programs (as the right claims). Prior to a careful empirical survey, justice as fairness is not committed to any particular view about the degree of justice or injustice in any given society, nor to any specific policy or social arrangement. Rather, it provides a framework within which these evaluations can be made.

It is worth emphasizing that justice as fairness (like any abstract normative framework) is of little practical value when considered by itself. As Thomas Pogge observes: "The specification of Rawls's conception of justice is a paradigmatically interdisciplinary enterprise."[5] Contrary to widespread belief, justice as fairness does not aim at providing a blueprint for an ideal society *ex nihilo*. Its normative framework only becomes useful when it is supplemented by detailed and accurate accounts of the particular society in question. When this information is available, justice as fairness provides a standard against which to assess existing and feasible alternative social arrangements. To be able to make and defend such judgments, in addition to empirical information we must adopt some kind of normative orientation, and this is what justice as fairness attempts to provide. The most accurate empirical data in the world alone cannot tell us which of various competing alternatives is the most attractive or

---

5. Thomas Pogge, *Realizing Rawls* (Ithaca, N.Y.: Cornell University Press, 1989), 7.

politically progressive. Rawls's theory is often charged with being too abstract and detached from concrete social and historical reality, but justice as fairness views itself as contributing to a larger interdisciplinary project. By itself, it does not provide (nor does it claim to provide) insight into historical developments or the structure of existing social arrangements. However, together with specific knowledge of the conditions of a particular society, it helps to identify existing injustices and to point the way to possible improvements.

Through a detailed examination of justice as fairness and two rival frameworks I hope to show not only that many of the most frequently repeated criticisms of liberalism simply do not apply to political liberalism, but also that this orientation is congenial to the most admirable ideals of the left. At one point, not long ago, the suggestion that the left should embrace a liberal philosophical framework would have been anathema—hardly worth serious consideration. But the time for easy ideological dismissal is long past. The left is in desperate straits from which, I believe, only a liberal philosophical orientation can have any hope of restoring it to credibility and relevance. This is not a rehabilitation that will be made quickly or easily. Within the left, many will be reluctant to part with old labels and stereotypes. Ira Katznelson speaks for many on the left, no doubt, when he recalls that in the 1960s:

> I forswore the label "liberal" as tainted by racism, imperialism, militarism, and class domination, as did so many members of my generation. We implicated liberalism in the destructive myth of progress, in the deployment of universalism to mask a Western capitalist particularism, and in the silencing of dissent. . . . We believed that liberalism as we experienced it lacked ethical content as it validated only pragmatic and short-term private interests and was too often tempted to treat social and political collectivities as heaps of individuals abstractly conceived.[6]

If the left were to embrace a liberal orientation, as I advocate, non-leftists would also, no doubt, be skeptical of the sincerity of this new position—and with good reason. Within the left, ideologies have too frequently competed over which is the most oppositional. Vindication came to whichever philosophy could provide the most radical attack on the existing order. What we need is not just destructive criticism, however, but principled grounds for appreciating the virtues of our existing societies together with an account of how they could be better. The left will be able to recover its political capital and its authority to speak with a moral voice only gradually. I believe that a serious reconsideration of political liberalism would be a crucial step in this process.

When *A Theory of Justice*[7] was first published in 1971, it was nearly universally recognized, by both the left and the right, to be a modern

---

6. Katznelson, *Liberalism's Crooked Circle*, 37. He continues: "I think we were substantially correct in each of these respects even now, though I have come to value politics grounded in the liberal tradition."

7. John Rawls, *A Theory of Justice* (Cambridge: Harvard University Press, 1971;

philosophical masterpiece. From the right, Robert Nozick wrote, "Political philosophers now must either work within Rawls's theory or explain why not."[8] For the most part, Nozick attempted to explain why not. A review by Bernard Crick in the *New Statesman* in 1972, set the tone for what would remain the left's response to justice as fairness for the following decades. Crick praised Rawls's project of constructing principles of justice and admired Rawls's break with the "nitpicking rut of modern analytic philosophy."[9] However, he believed that Rawls's conception of justice was ill-suited to a socialist like himself, and he concluded by calling for an alternative socialist theory of justice: "Rawls is *profoundly* wrong but almost perfectly relevant. Truly he forces us to see that theories of socialism without a critical moral philosophy are as undesirable as they are impossible. Who can answer him fully and go beyond?"[10] The left has rarely strayed from this picture of Rawls as an orthodox, but sophisticated threat, whose theory presents a challenge to be answered.[11] He does not call himself a socialist; therefore, although he can be learned from, he must be refuted in the end.

Within the academy, more frequently than not, the left continues to view liberalism, and justice as fairness specifically, as the enemy. Many on the left rely on a set of remarkably persistent stereotypes of Rawls that allows an easy dismissal of his work. Just prior to the publication of *A Theory of Justice*, C. B. Macpherson claimed, as most authors continue to do, that Rawls defends a system of "private capitalist enterprise." Macpherson, unlike most other commentators, actually noted that Rawls explicitly denies this. But Macpherson did not allow a minor point like that to shake his confidence that he knew the form of economic organization that Rawls must favor. Without further explanation, he asserts that Rawls's explicit denial merely "suggests an extraordinary misunderstanding" on the part of Rawls.[12] To choose a single additional contemporary example, Terry Eagleton has written recently that any scheme of liberal rights that "centrally include[s] property rights" will engender "inequality and exploitation" and undermine its pretensions at justice. Again,

---

revised edition, 1999).

8. Robert Nozick, *Anarchy, State, and Utopia* (New York: Basic Books, 1974), 183.

9. Bernard Crick, "On Justice," *New Statesman*, 5 May 1972, 601.

10. Crick, "On Justice," 602.

11. For exceptions, see R. G. Peffer, *Marxism, Morality, and Social Justice* (Princeton: Princeton University Press, 1990), 364-365; Robert Amdur, "Rawls and His Radical Critics," *Dissent* (summer 1980); Arthur DiQuattro, "Rawls and Left Criticism," *Political Theory* 11, no. 1 (Feb. 1983); and my "Rawls and the Left," *Socialist Review* 21, no. 3-4 (July-Dec. 1991).

12. C. B. Macpherson, *Democratic Theory: Essays in Retrieval* (New York: Oxford University Press, 1973), 90-91. Following the publication of *A Theory of Justice*, he continued to chastise Rawls for being guilty of "an extraordinary confusion" on this point. See his "Rawls's Models of Man and Society," *Philosophy of the Social Sciences* 3 (1973), 344.

unlike many others, Eagleton notes that Rawls's account does not, "it would seem," give priority to property rights. Nonetheless, Rawls is dismissed as follows: "suffice it to say that Rawls, in his magisterial *A Theory of Justice*, has a single reference to exploitation, and that in a footnote."[13] Since he does not use the word *exploitation*, it must be that Rawls is no more than a spineless defender of the status quo. Even while these commentators point to the very passages that would undermine their assertions, neither is able to shake the traditional picture of Rawls that the left has held now for decades.

In part, I believe, this blindness is a holdover from the days when Marxism was frequently believed to provide the only legitimate philosophical basis for an authentic left. At best, liberals were viewed as timid and insufficiently rigorous in their critique of existing arrangements, or more typically as hypocritical apologists for individualism, capitalism, and imperialism. To be sure, not all of the left was Marxist.[14] But to be on the left was to be against liberalism and capitalism; Marxism certainly was that, and powerfully so, and was therefore seductive to many. Reflecting on the revolutions of 1989, Bruce Ackerman observes:

> One of Marxism's most consequential acts of appropriation in 1917 (or earlier) was to seize the idea of revolution. Of course, there were many more non-Marxist than Marxist revolutions even at the height of Leninism's ascendancy. But the Leninists were remarkably successful in getting nearly everyone to believe that their kind of revolution was the genuine article and that others were sham or worse.[15]

The point is more general. Marxism, in one form or another, claimed for itself alone the mantle of authenticity and thus blinded the left to the elements of liberalism that could frame a progressive critique of society. Ira Katznelson accurately captures the subtle relationship between the left and Marxism:

> Most of the non-Communist left railed against Bolshevism and Stalinism from the moments of their appearance and sought to draw a sharp line between good and bad socialism. Nonetheless, it would be too self-congratulatory for us not to see that social democracy and Communism have not inhabited separate universes. Grounded in a common doctrinal lineage, even critics on the democratic left often have seen Communism as the wayward member of a single progressive family.[16]

Paul Berman portrays the left's attitude this way:

---

13. Terry Eagleton, *The Illusions of Postmodernism* (New York: Blackwell, 1996), 81.

14. See, for example, the discussion generated by Eugene Genovese, "The Question," *Dissent* (summer 1994). Mitchell Cohen accurately points out in response that *Dissent* itself was a consistent critic of communism.

15. Bruce Ackerman, *The Future of Liberal Revolution* (New Haven: Yale University Press, 1992), 1.

16. Katznelson, *Liberalism's Crooked Circle*, 70.

Life in the Soviet Union might be lamentable in almost every respect; but Communism in the Soviet Union was a kind of pregnancy, and out of the pregnancy would be born a second, better Communism, perhaps the direct democracy that almost everyone on the radical left expected to see. . . . Exploitation and imperialism were the essence of capitalism, but slave labor and prison camps were not the essence of Communism, and sooner or later, peacefully or violently, the labor camps and the prison system were going to be eliminated.[17]

To repeat: there *were* members of the left who embraced a vision of a liberal society, perhaps even a majority, but they were put on the defensive by Marxism's successful grab for authenticity.

To be sure, those who identified themselves as liberals must share the blame for the left's estrangement from liberalism. To take but a single, though central and powerful example: liberals certainly have not done any of us any favors in their advocacy of an imperialistic foreign policy. But the apportionment of blame for the alienation between the left and liberalism is not my point. Rather, my point is simply that there is an urgent need to leave such disputes behind and reconsider the grounds on which to project a vision of a just society.[18] We need to reassess the left's basic political and social commitments.

Today the left is struggling to find a principled way to combine its commitments to both diversity and commonality. Too often it seems as though choosing one excludes the other. As I will argue below, in one direction (roughly postmodernism) is the valorization of difference that denies the possibility of common principles at all. In the other (roughly communitarianism) direction is the denial of difference in the name of shared norms. It is easy to understand diversity and commonality in ways that preclude their reconciliation. In fact, I believe this is in part what leads the left to see no alternative to a fateful choice between communitarianism and postmodernism. There is, however, an alternative. The problem of finding common principles that do not deny or undermine an underlying social diversity is exactly the project that animates political liberalism. Justice as fairness "look[s] for possible bases of agreement where none seem to exist."[19]

The beginning of wisdom is to identify what, precisely, we can and cannot hope for in our politics and political philosophy. It is too much to expect that political philosophy will identify a single, determinate way of life that is the most rewarding or fulfilling for all and then be able to construct a social order from this conception. What we can do, however, is examine how to be fair in the

---

17. Paul Berman, *A Tale of Two Utopias* (New York: Norton, 1996), 276-277.

18. As Richard Rorty put the point recently: "We must repudiate the Marxists' insinuation that only those who are convinced capitalism must be overthrown can count as leftists, and that everybody else is a wimpy liberal, a self-deceiving bourgeois reformer." See Richard Rorty, *Achieving Our Country* (Cambridge: Harvard University Press, 1998), 41-42.

19. Rawls, *A Theory of Justice*, 582 [509].

face of this very diversity of ways of life, or, in Rawls's language, this diversity of "reasonable comprehensive doctrines."[20] Our attempt must aspire to be as inclusive as possible by finding principles that respect others, whether or not we fully share their values. But we must also recognize that not everything goes. A central task for liberalism, therefore, is to determine what is to be tolerated and what not, for there must be limits if we are to have any shared principles at all.[21] Still, consistent with the requirements of justice itself, we should strive to tolerate as many ways of life as possible. Someone, after all, thinks each of them worthwhile. The basis for this tolerance, I hasten to add, is not a global skepticism about the possibility of evaluating different comprehensive doctrines. Not all ways of life are as good as others and we can and should continue to argue about which ways of life are best. Political liberalism does not deny this. However, the identification of the (or a) best way of life is an activity distinct from political philosophy and the examination of the requirements of basic social justice. Or so I shall argue.

In the past few years, left-wing authors in various fields have expressed growing frustration with the left and have seen the need to reflect on the principles that guide our basic political commitments. Todd Gitlin, for example, has recently expressed such dissatisfaction. He has argued vigorously against an over-reliance on identity politics, which he believes has splintered the left and incapacitated it politically: "There is no *it* there. What we have instead [of a left] is an ill-fitting sum of groups overly concerned with protecting and purifying what they imagine to be their identities."[22] Gitlin calls for a broad-based coalition that transcends differences and appeals to universalistic principles. I am sympathetic to these efforts, but his call leaves serious philosophical problems unanswered. In part, the left has been attracted to various forms of identity politics because it recognizes the difficulty of establishing truly universalistic principles in the face of deep diversity. As Gitlin shows in detail, the left's response to this difficulty has frequently been one of despair. Often it rejects all universal claims as hypocritical masks for exclusion and oppression.

The problem is that this rejection of universal principles has resulted in the left's being splintered into the familiar groups of identity politics. Each group attempts to construct its identity so that it is internally homogeneous. Even if this could be done, the result would be that the groups would not share a principled basis for engagement in common political action. As Gitlin puts it: "The demand for the respect for difference—for what came to be called

---

20. John Rawls, *Political Liberalism* (New York: Columbia University Press, 1993; paperback edition, 1996), 13, 175.

21. Justice as fairness distinguishes between those comprehensive doctrines that are reasonable and those that are unreasonable. See *Political Liberalism*, 58-66, and the discussion in my "The Reasonable in Justice as Fairness," *Canadian Journal of Philosophy* 29, no. 1 (March 1999).

22. Gitlin, *The Twilight of Common Dreams*, 33.

multiculturalism—often swerved into the creation of parallel monocultures."[23] Gitlin calls for a rejuvenated left based on universalistic principles. However, he rightly worries about the stability of a broad-based coalition committed to such principles:

> To develop a political majority requires more than occasional coalitions knitted together by overlapping interests. It requires also, and urgently, a *culture* of commonality. If groups spend Monday through Saturday turned inward, separately cultivating their differences, consolidating their internal unities, practicing cordiality to the exclusivists in their midst, it will not do for them to gather together on Sunday morning to speak of commonalities. To be active citizens of the whole, they must also spend time Monday through Saturday fraternizing across the lines, cultivating cultural hybrids, criticizing the narrowness of the tribe, working up ideas that people "unlike" themselves might share. One may respect the democratic rights of distinct groups to organize as they choose and still argue vigorously against the aggrandizement of difference.[24]

Gitlin has the problem exactly right. The "aggrandizement of difference" is no basis on which to build a just society. Unfortunately, it is unclear exactly what alternative he advocates. If he is suggesting that we must generate a single "culture" so that we are more closely knit, he is in danger of falling into the communitarian denial of diversity. If, as seems more likely in Gitlin's case, something less than a full culture is to be shared,[25] what exactly is this? Which universal principles does he advocate, and how can we expect them to be shared in the face of sharp differences? Gitlin wants a form of universality that respects diversity, but it is unclear how we can get it or what its content would be.

Ira Katznelson has taken a different path from Gitlin's, but arrives at a similar assessment of the left's difficulty in combining its commitments to universal principles and to pluralism. He argues explicitly that a proper basis for progressive political action must be found in a re-invigorated left liberalism. Reflecting on the developments in Eastern Europe in 1989, he shows a genuine appreciation of the progressive potential of liberalism: "If 1989 is to prove genuinely revolutionary not only for having put Bolshevism to rest but for liberalism itself, I believe we need to focus on the issues of equality and pluralism and their relationship to the liberal tradition."[26] For Katznelson, only liberalism—or more precisely, some largely unspecified form of socialism within a liberal framework—can adequately combine these demands: "There is

---

23. Gitlin, *The Twilight of Common Dreams*, 148.

24. Gitlin, *The Twilight of Common Dreams*, 217-218.

25. In another context Gitlin criticizes those "who think that culture is politics." See "The Future of Progressive Politics" (speech in New York, 6 March 1997, "Alternative Radio").

26. Katznelson, *Liberalism's Crooked Circle*, xiii. Parenthetical references in this and the next paragraphs will be to this work.

no good alternative to an expansive liberalism as pluralism's best available resource." (104) The question for the post-Communist countries, as for the West, is "not whether it is desirable to have a liberal politics, economics, and social order, but how to judge and choose among contending kinds of liberalism." (15) Katznelson cites Rawls (along with Mill, Dewey, Mannheim, Russell, Walzer, and Bobbio) as having advocated some combination of "the best in liberal and socialist precepts." (57)

Nonetheless, he retains a striking suspicion of Rawls's work, repeating many of the frequent criticisms of it. Katznelson reads Rawls as little more than a defender of the welfare state (84) and insists on "going further [than Rawls] to press actively for the elimination of unwarrantable inequalities." (81) He repeats the common charges that the model of the citizen on which Rawls relies, and his theory generally are: "antiseptic" (107); "purified and hygienic" (108); "decontextualized, disembodied" (133); "exclusively rationalist" (153); and "too orderly and sanitized, downplaying the remarkable interlacings and amalgamations of human life, the rich varieties of cultural traditions, positions, and relationships, and ever-present possibilities for ugliness and unspeakable brutality exercised in the name of difference." (155)[27] This litany of charges, in one form or another, is repeated in almost every discussion of Rawls by the left. And yet, I shall argue they are groundless.

The left is deeply skeptical of liberalism's ability to balance its commitments to unity and diversity. Of course, it is easier to attack the alleged weaknesses of your (perceived) opponent than to construct a superior alternative, and the left has largely followed this easier path. It is a commonplace among left critics to charge that liberalism is biased in favor of a certain way of life—individualistic, selfish, capitalistic, male, phallocentric, logocentric, middle class, white, or whatever. The left is divided, however, concerning what follows once one or more of these alleged biases has been

---

27. More troubling than his misreading of Rawls, however, is his discussion of the fate of "Politically emancipated European Jews." On Katznelson's reading they "were asked, in effect, to divest themselves of their particularities in the name of universal human values; but having done so, the price of their acceptance was an embrace of specific national cultures they found themselves within, frequently by chance." (163) But how does Katznelson believe Europe "asked" them to do this; how were they "seduced"? (165) In his answer to this question, Katznelson betrays a profoundly conservative communitarianism similar to that which we will examine in chapter 4. He claims that the Jews "took advantage of the economic roles that opened to them with the decline of guilds, the importance of finance in periods of war, and the rapid increase in trade of various distances." As a result, he believes, the culture was transformed for the worse: "Life-styles liberalized. Rabbinic authority weakened. Religious observance, and respect for Jewish tradition declined." (163) Although Katznelson think that the Jews were "seduced" into making these changes, we might see them in a different light: when they were given a choice for the first time, they abandoned what they regarded as outmoded traditions.

identified. Some argue that all such biases must be eliminated in the name of a truly neutral social order, while others claim that a proper political order must continue to favor certain ways of life, but not the ones that liberalism favors.

Roughly, those on the left who are influenced by postmodernism argue that liberalism remains too narrow and intolerant, while communitarians argue for the substitution of a different set of values (although this position itself comes in two variants). Stephen White summarizes the postmodern criticism: "Liberal thought has often come in for heavy fire from postmodernists, as well as feminists, for endorsing, explicitly or implicitly, various ways of suppressing or marginalizing difference." Pointing out that liberals have emphasized toleration, he continues: "But the approach I am following does not so much contest this claim as question whether liberal tolerance alone is sufficient for grappling with the problem of difference or otherness in a social world where the pressures of rationalization and informationalization are so insistent."[28] A superior alternative, according to White, would be based on the following thought: "The positive valuation of difference, as opposed to mere tolerance, could give us grounds for a stronger commitment to public policies that do not merely *protect* the formal right of individual or collective concrete others to express themselves, but go further and do more to *empower* or to *foster* the emergence of such voices."[29] For defenders of postmodernism, any appeal to universal principles is already too exclusive and an illegitimate limitation on diversity. A proper postmodern politics, if there is such a thing,[30] would actively promote diversity without the limitations imposed by universal principles.

Critics influenced by communitarianism, on the other hand, agree that liberal toleration is inadequate. However, instead of attempting to achieve a more "positive valuation of difference," they argue that we must confront directly the question of which ways of life are superior. For these critics, liberal practice reveals what liberal theory conceals: that neutrality is a sham and every society must be based on a commitment to a particular system of values and ways of life. The only matter to be determined is which system of values is to be promoted and serve as the foundation of the social structure. As the sociologist Robert Bellah writes:

---

28. Stephen White, *Political Theory and Postmodernism* (New York: Cambridge University Press, 1991), 126.

29. White, *Political Theory and Postmodernism*, 110.

30. This is a significant qualification. Both defenders and critics of postmodernism have commented on the difficulty of pinning down postmodernists on their positive normative commitments. As White himself comments: "A thoroughly poststructuralist approach to political thinking would be one dominated by what is in effect a perpetual withholding gesture." (*Political Theory and Postmodernism*, 19) I will argue in chapter 5 that this "withholding gesture" is a central element of postmodernism itself and is not simply a gap or oversight that can easily be supplemented.

It is one of the oldest of sociological generalizations that any coherent and viable society rests on a common set of moral understandings about good and bad, right and wrong, in the realm of individual and social action. It is almost as widely held that these common moral understandings must also in turn rest upon a common set of religious understandings that provide a picture of the universe in terms of which the moral understandings make sense.[31]

Unlike those influenced by postmodernism, who argue for the promotion of diversity itself, these communitarians wish to substitute a more congenial set of particular values for those that they believe liberalism promotes.

Within this broadly communitarian approach, there are two alternatives. Some theorists present the specific form of the good life or values they favor, and argue that instead of promoting liberal ways of life, society should promote these values instead. Typically, the favored form of society involves a greater component of community involvement than these critics believe is found in liberal societies. Alternatively, some worry about the apparently undemocratic nature of such an imposition and argue that the specific values to be promoted should be drawn from the community itself. Liberalism, on this view, requires that a single way of life be imposed on a society "from the outside," instead of allowing each society the freedom to choose its own liberal or non-liberal way of life. Both of these approaches can be called "communitarian" in a certain sense: the first because it promotes a particular way of life, that of community involvement; the second because it promotes the values that the community holds, regardless of content.

To illustrate the first form of communitarianism recall that traditionally, under the banner of socialism the left has championed a citizenship that is actively involved in the political, social, and economic life of the community. Liberalism, on this view, is thought to covertly (or not so covertly) promote a form of competitive and possessive individualism and to neglect the value of community. Robert Paul Wolff, for example, reminds us: "The severest criticisms of liberal society, both from the left and from the right, focus on the absence of community in even the most efficient and affluent liberal capitalist state."[32] Liberal society, he claims, simply does not recognize the importance of achieving those values associated with mutual recognition and community. Wolff points to the long tradition on the left of advocating exactly these values, dating back to Marx's claim that humans find fulfillment not only in productive labor but in "*socially* productive labor."[33]

Another example of this type of criticism of liberalism comes from Ronald Beiner. He notes that some arguments for socialism have been based on

31. Robert Bellah, *The Broken Covenant*, second edition (Chicago: University of Chicago Press, 1975), xvi.

32. Robert Paul Wolff, *The Poverty of Liberalism* (Boston: Beacon, 1968), 183.

33. Wolff, *The Poverty of Liberalism*, 188.

egalitarian economic considerations, but his case for socialism "revolves around citizenship rather than social justice, around political enfranchisement rather than economic entitlements, and that substitutes the concept of solidarity for that of social equality as its pivotal term."[34] "In barest outline," he continues, "the claim would be that socialist arrangements would heighten political identity and enhance civic consciousness, and thereby reverse or at least mitigate the trend toward depoliticization and 'civil privatism' documented by Habermas among others. Socialism, in short, would make us better citizens."[35] Beiner is clear that this argument is not based on the requirements of social justice, but rather on his view of ideal citizenship: "social justice is sought to the extent that it promotes political citizenship."[36] On this first version of communitarianism, therefore, society should promote a lifestyle of active involvement in the community rather than the individualistic values that liberalism supposedly encourages.[37]

Finally, to come to the second form of communitarianism, some critics argue that liberals require that societies promote a certain (individualistic) way of life instead of allowing each society freely to choose its own values. These communitarians do not necessarily argue for the superiority of active community involvement, but say that a society can and should actively promote whichever way of life is most consistent with its own shared values. Michael Walzer is the leading theorist of this position. For Walzer, "Justice is relative to social meanings."[38] Justice requires distribution of goods according to the "shared meaning" of the good, and injustice occurs when there is a distribution of some good contrary to its social meaning. Since the social meaning of a good can vary from one society to another, any theory that does not rely on the specific meaning a good has in a particular society "presses its practitioners toward manipulation and compulsion."[39] The formulation of distributive principles not

---

34. Ronald Beiner, *What's the Matter with Liberalism?* (Berkeley: University of California Press, 1992), 143.

35. Beiner, *What's the Matter with Liberalism?* 146.

36. Beiner, *What's the Matter with Liberalism?* 151; cf. 161.

37. Beiner denies that he is a communitarian. This is because he takes communitarians to advocate the values endorsed by a particular community, whatever they happen to be. In contrast, he advocates "subject[ing] both the individual *and* the community to a more searching interrogation in a fully ambitious theoretical dimension—that is, with respect to judgments about the *substance* of a satisfying life." See Ronald Beiner, *Philosophy in a Time of Lost Spirit* (Toronto: University of Toronto Press, 1997), xiii. Beiner sees no need to specify the content of such a life and insists repeatedly that the social theorist must be a "gadfly," unconcerned with "offer[ing] sensible guidance on the conduct of social life." See *What's The Matter with Liberalism?* 190-192 and *Philosophy in a Time of Lost Spirit*, ix-xiii, 15.

38. Michael Walzer, *Spheres of Justice* (New York: Basic Books, 1983), 312.

39. Michael Walzer, *Interpretation and Social Criticism* (Cambridge: Harvard University Press, 1987), 64.

based on specific social meanings is "an authoritarian business."[40] In this form of communitarianism, the value of community participation is not necessarily central. Rather, the community determines which specific values are to be promoted.

Despite the chorus of accusations that identifies liberalism with individualism, we must be careful when we examine Rawls's views of community. There are important differences between liberals and communitarians, but they are not always what they are most commonly thought to be. The grain of truth in the communitarian charge that liberalism embraces a form of individualism is the fact that political liberalism is committed to justice in the face of reasonable diversity. Precisely because this diversity is reasonable, political liberalism insists that individuals not be compelled to embrace any particular comprehensive doctrine. If community is understood to require that all citizens share a single comprehensive system of values and ends, then the persistence of reasonable diversity in a just society would, indeed, preclude community in that sense. But justice as fairness develops a different account of the unity of society. Political liberalism insists that certain core principles of justice must be shared if society is to be stably just. But it does not require that everyone share a single comprehensive system of values and ends. The core principles of justice can be embedded in diverse and mutually incompatible comprehensive doctrines.

There is no reason to believe that liberal toleration of this diversity will necessarily result in the widespread selfishness or isolation that communitarians fear. Indeed, if communitarian claims about our social nature are correct, we would expect that in a society committed to political liberalism, most citizens would reject possessive individualism and embrace some form of social involvement. As Will Kymlicka has pointed out, "It is communitarians who seem to think that individuals will drift into anomic and detached isolation without the state actively bringing them together to collectively evaluate and pursue the good."[41] Justice as fairness does not say that only a life committed to possessive individualism is worth living; nor does it say that what really matters is an individual's act of choice in setting up or creating a new system of values. But justice as fairness is committed to the importance of each individual's being able to reflectively endorse, under non-coercive conditions, his or her own value commitments.

One lesson frequently taken from the left's past flirtation with Marxism is that we must be wary of "utopianism." The precise nature of utopianism in this sense may be unclear. For those on the left it simply cannot mean that we should stop projecting a vision of a better society; this would be to abandon the left's

---

40. Michael Walzer, "Philosophy and Democracy," *Political Theory* 9, no. 3 (Aug. 1981), 381.

41. Will Kymlicka, "Liberal Individualism and Liberal Neutrality," *Ethics* 99, no. 4 (July 1989), 904.

critical project of constructing a more just society. Without such a perspective from which to articulate the image of a better society, we would be condemned to a demoralized conservatism. When the term *utopian* is used pejoratively, what is being rejected is not simply the consideration of how things could be better. Rather, utopianism involves projecting an account of society in which there is a resolution of all conflicts and we find some form of ultimate salvation.[42] For the utopian, the only change worth making is a total revolution that will transform all aspects of human life. This is a millenarian vision that, in the end, can only destroy our ability to deal effectively with the conflicts that will inevitably arise in every diverse modern society. As Leszek Kolakowski writes: "We need a socialist tradition conscious of its own limitations, because the dream of final redemption is despair dressed in the cloak of hope, the greed of power clothed in the gown of justice."[43] The left should be properly chastened against this kind of utopianism. In large measure these days the left *is* reticent to project such a vision, largely, I suspect, due to the collapse of the Marxist program and a disillusionment arising from the perceived failures of the late 1960s.

It might be thought that Rawls's theory of justice is utopian in just this way, since Rawls proposes we start with so-called "ideal theory." But justice as fairness is not utopian in the sense just discussed.[44] Rawls takes the fundamental problem of justice to be designing institutions that are fair in the face of deep and pervasive disagreements and conflicts. Justice as fairness does not attempt to establish a unified view of the good life that would eliminate all conflict. What we need, and what justice as fairness helps us to identify, are institutions that are designed to manage the inevitable conflicts fairly and that themselves can command allegiance. What makes this a difficult project is that this allegiance must not depend on a denial of the very diversity that gives rise to the conflicts in the first place.

The left must not embrace the debilitating vision of a total revolution in which the conditions of conflict and diversity are completely transcended. As I indicated above, we should not expect political philosophy (or politics) to provide us with a complete vision of the single way of life that is best for all. But there is another important limitation on what we can expect from political philosophy. It is also too much to ask of political philosophy that it provide a mechanism that will make the change to a more just society inevitable. What it can do is provide a normative orientation, and when supplemented with empirical information about the specific society in question, it can generate a realistic picture of how things could go if they went well. We cannot ask of political philosophy that it guarantee that things will go this way. Philosophy

---

42. See Berman, *A Tale of Two Utopias*, 291-292.

43. Quoted in Katznelson, *Liberalism's Crooked Circle*, 54.

44. For a discussion and defense of ideal theory, see my "Justice, Desert, and Ideal Theory," *Social Theory and Practice* 23, no. 3 (fall 1997).

alone cannot make a society more just. This, obviously, takes people working to remake their institutions according to a vision of what social justice requires. Still, without the orientation and perspective that a political philosophy provides, there is no way to identify where changes are required, or to determine whether a proposed change is progressive, reactionary, or simply foolish. A progressive philosophy without a movement is empty; a movement without a philosophical framework is blind.

The left today has no mass movement to press our claims on the political institutions. But this is precisely the time to prepare ourselves by providing a philosophical grounding that will inform a left movement when it arises. When C. Wright Mills wrote in 1959, "Today in the United States, there is no Left,"[45] he was largely correct. The Civil Rights movement, however, was already beginning to transform race relations and within a decade the left was a powerful political force, even if never as close to dominant as popular myth would have it—Richard Nixon was elected in 1968, after all.[46] It is impossible to anticipate with any confidence where and when the next left will emerge. Few anticipated the democratic insurgencies of 1989. What we can do now, however, is attempt to generate the intellectual resources that will help that left stay on the tracks of constructing a just society. It is clear, I think, that the last left mass movement fell off the tracks in the late 1960s. In fact, in my conclusion, I will offer the hypothesis that part of the attraction of postmodernism comes from the left's perceived failure to make the total revolution to which so much of it aspired in the late 1960s. The left is still struggling to come to terms with the lessons of those successes and disappointments. It is important that when the next left emerges it have the intellectual resources at its disposal that can assist it in identifying which changes are progressive and which are regressive. I hope this study contributes to developing these resources.

Gitlin is correct that the left will only be able to become a major force for social justice if the "ill-fitting . . . groups overly concerned with protecting and purifying what they imagine to be their identities" can reach beyond themselves and enter a common struggle.[47] Some commentators, following Gitlin's lead, call for different groups of the left to form a coalition based on the identification of a common source of the various injustices they are fighting. Unfortunately, there are many ways for a society to be unjust, and so we will not always be able to find such a single enemy. Neither capitalism, patriarchy, racism, nor even logocentrism is the foundation of all injustice. Rather than attempting to forge a much-needed progressive coalition by searching for a single root of all evil, we

---

45. C. Wright Mills, "The Decline of the Left," in *Power, Politics and People*, Irving Horowitz, ed. (New York: Ballantine Books, 1963), 222.

46. For a valuable counterpoint to various mythologies of the 1960s, see Paul Lyons, *New Left, New Right and the Legacy of the Sixties* (Philadelphia: Temple University Press, 1996).

47. Gitlin, *The Twilight of Common Dreams*, 33.

should attempt to identify a vision of social justice that we all can share. Perhaps a clearer account of social justice—a positive model of a just society—may help members of the currently fragmented and demoralized left see themselves as part of a common struggle for social justice. The process of reflection on these issues, I hope, might even make a small and indirect contribution to building such a movement.

My presentation of justice as fairness is divided into two chapters. In the first of these, chapter two, I discuss the questions that justice as fairness asks and the resources it deploys in attempting to answer these questions. Of special concern will be problems that justice as fairness does not purport to solve. There are important limitations on its ambitions that are not always recognized by its critics. First, it is a philosophical theory. It is not, as Gitlin's book for example is, an analysis of political strategies and history. Rather, its hope is to present a philosophical framework within which more concrete analyses can proceed. The second limitation is that even though it is a philosophical theory, there are some important philosophical questions that it does not try to answer. For example, it does not attempt to identify which religion has the greatest support of reason, which metaphysical account of the self is most adequate, or which conception of the good will lead to the greatest satisfaction or happiness. As I indicated above, however, justice as fairness does not say that such projects are impossible or unimportant. It has sometimes been thought that political philosophy is impossible without first identifying an ideal of the good life. After all, it might be asked, what is the point of having just institutions if not to help individuals live good lives, and how can we know which institutions are likely to do this without a prior account of the good life? Justice as fairness, however, rejects this seemingly attractive approach to political philosophy. In chapter two, I will explain the reasons why, as well as identify precisely its goals and the resources on which it relies.

In chapter three, I discuss and defend the specific principles of justice that justice as fairness endorses. Both their content and the arguments for them have been subject to widespread misunderstanding. In part this is due to a few misleading remarks made by Rawls in his initial presentation of the principles. I develop an interpretation that reveals their content more clearly. This sets the stage for a clearer account of why they would be chosen from what Rawls calls "the original position." Even those who are sympathetic to the approach of political liberalism have generally been reluctant to embrace the specific principles that Rawls endorses. Considerably more can be said in their defense than is commonly assumed.

The fourth chapter deals with communitarianism. Many on the left feel themselves attracted to such a view. Communitarianism defines itself, in large measure, in opposition to liberalism, and this, I believe, partially explains its seductiveness for the left. Frequently this opposition is based on a mistaken characterization of liberalism. Before we can assess the extent to which communitarianism might serve as a proper basis for a progressive politics, we must clarify exactly how it differs from liberalism. I will argue that once the confusions and misinterpretations are cleared away, important differences between liberalism and communitarianism still remain. These differences, however, align communitarians with traditional conservatives.[48] This, of course, is not yet an argument against communitarians, although it should serve to weaken the left's infatuation with their theories. In fact, there are certain insights that a (moderate) conservatism offers that a non-utopian liberalism can easily and properly accommodate. However, communitarians and conservatives often attempt to draw more radical, anti-liberal conclusions that cannot be justified by these more moderate insights.

Finally, in the fifth chapter I continue my critical examination of the alternatives to liberalism by focussing on postmodernism. Postmodernism in its various forms valorizes differences and criticizes liberalism, often in blistering terms, for its reliance on universal principles. In doing so, however, it undercuts the grounds of its own normative critique and frequently ends up as a form of blind skepticism or nihilism. I make this case by focusing on the work of Jacques Derrida and Michel Foucault. Both of these theorists insist on the political relevance of their work. However, both are remarkably reluctant to make explicit the principles on which their normative evaluations are based, and there are important reasons for this. In the final section, I discuss the work of the foremost left-wing critic of postmodernism, Jürgen Habermas, focusing on his account of postmodernism and his alternative. Recently, there has been a growing interest in the relationship between Habermas and Rawls. Many commentators have suggested that Habermas's work is a more attractive model for the left than Rawls provides. I close chapter five by arguing that their theories actually complement each other very well.

I conclude by exploring some similarities between the postmodern and communitarian criticisms of liberalism, using Kant as a touchstone. I also offer hypotheses concerning why the left has been attracted to communitarianism and postmodernism. Both communitarianism and postmodernism reject the project of constructing principles of justice for a society characterized by deep and persistent diversity. In contrast, this is exactly the goal that political liberalism gives itself. There is a sense, then, in which political liberalism is a hopeful doctrine. This contrasts sharply with many theories recently embraced by the left. As Richard Rorty has recently observed, "Hopelessness has become fashionable on the Left—principled, theorized, philosophical hopelessness."[49]

In an unpublished manuscript, Rawls claims that justice as fairness aspires to be "realistically utopian." It considers the following question: "What would a perfectly just democratic society be like under reasonably favorable but still *possible* historical conditions, conditions allowed by the laws and tendencies of

---

48. "Traditional conservatives" as opposed to members of the libertarian right.
49. Rorty, *Achieving Our Country*, 37.

the social world?"[50] When we have an understanding of how things could go if they went well under favorable, but still realistic conditions, this may provide an antidote to the nihilistic abandon that has been a recent temptation to the left:

> No longer need [our social world] seem hopelessly hostile, a world in which the will to dominate and oppressive cruelties, abetted by prejudice and folly, must inevitably work their destruction. None of this may ease our loss, situated as we may be in a society for a time irredeemably corrupt. But we may reflect that the world is not in itself inhospitable to political justice and its good. Our social world might have been different and there is hope for those at another time and place.[51]

There is no guarantee, of course, that these alternatives will succeed or even be seriously pursued or considered. Political philosophy's contribution is limited, but it is important nonetheless. Some may object that philosophy is a needless abstraction that merely distracts from real-world injustice—injustice that cannot be fought through speculation alone. But political philosophy does not purport to take the place of social organizing and action. Rather, it provides normative orientation for such engagements. It helps to identify which existing institutions are unjust and which, among feasible alternatives, would be superior. In this sense, it is both eminently practical and hopeful: it provides a framework within which we can more clearly compare and assess various courses of practical political engagement.

---

50. John Rawls, "Justice As Fairness: A Brief Restatement" (unpublished, 1989), 3.
51. Rawls, "Justice As Fairness: A Brief Restatement," 31.

Chapter 2
Justice As Fairness I: Framework

In 1962, Isaiah Berlin published an essay entitled "Does Political Theory Still Exist?"[1] This was a serious question, for only a few years earlier Peter Laslett had declared, "For the moment, anyway, political philosophy is dead."[2] Berlin did not altogether disagree with Laslett concerning the state of political philosophy, but he concluded his essay this way: "So long as rational curiosity exists . . . political theory will not wholly perish from the earth," and despite political theory's current "shadowy existence" he looked forward to "new and unpredictable developments."[3] Berlin believed that part of the reason why the existence, or at least continued vitality of political philosophy, could seriously be doubted was the fact that "no commanding work of political philosophy has appeared in the twentieth century."[4] Ironically, John Rawls's article "Justice As Fairness," originally published in 1958, was reprinted in the same collection as Berlin's essay.[5] Rawls's article together with others that he published over the next decade were reworked and integrated into *A Theory of Justice*, and in 1971 the twentieth century had its commanding work of political philosophy.[6] Highly anticipated when it first appeared, it was recognized immediately as a modern classic. One commentator began his review (published in 1973) this way: "Rawls's book did not need to be completed to inspire dozens of seminars based on advance installments; it must have inspired dozens more since its completion, with hundreds yet to come."[7] An anonymous reviewer in the *Times Literary*

1. Isaiah Berlin, "Does Political Theory Still Exist?" in *Philosophy, Politics and Society* (second series), Peter Laslett and W. G. Runciman, eds. (New York: Blackwell, 1962). An earlier version of Berlin's paper was published in French in 1961.

2. Peter Laslett, introduction to *Philosophy, Politics and Society* (first series), Peter Laslett, ed. (New York: Blackwell, 1956), vii.

3. Berlin, "Does Political Theory Still Exist?" 33.

4. Berlin, "Does Political Theory Still Exist?" 1.

5. John Rawls, "Justice As Fairness," *The Philosophical Review* 67 (1958).

6. In this chapter and the next, citations to John Rawls, *A Theory of Justice* (Cambridge: Harvard University Press, 1971; revised edition, 1999), will be made parenthetically in the text as *TJ*. Citations to John Rawls, *Political Liberalism* (New York: Columbia University Press, 1993; paperback edition, 1996), will be made parenthetically in the text as *PL*. Note that in the paperback edition, which I cite, the introduction begins on page xv, while in the original hardback, it begins on page xiii.

7. David Braybrooke, "Utilitarianism with a Difference: Rawls's Position in Ethics," *Canadian Journal of Philosophy* 3, no. 2 (Dec. 1973), 303.

Supplement raved: "It is a convincing refutation, if one is needed, of any lingering suspicions that the tradition of English-speaking political philosophy might be dead. Indeed, his book might plausibly be claimed to be the most notable contribution to that tradition to have been published since Sidgwick and Mill."[8] Marshall Cohen echoed this thought in the *New York Times Book Review*: "It is frequently said in scholarly circles that Mr. Rawls has made the most penetrating contribution to systematic political philosophy since John Stuart Mill, and it is not unheard of for admirers to invoke the name of Immanuel Kant in the search for an adequate comparison."[9]

Over the next two decades, Rawls continued to develop his theory in another series of articles, leading to the publication of *Political Liberalism* in 1993, expanded in 1996. Few would doubt the vibrancy, let alone existence, of political philosophy today, and Rawls's justice as fairness has played a central role in this revitalization. The size of the secondary literature alone testifies to its centrality in contemporary political philosophy. The standard bibliography on Rawls, published in 1982, contained over 2500 entries.[10] Today, that number certainly has at least doubled.

Precisely because of the centrality of Rawls's work to the recent rejuvenation of political philosophy, criticisms of justice as fairness are often thought to cut to the heart of liberalism, if not political philosophy itself. Thomas Pogge assesses the contemporary scene in political philosophy this way:

> There is a widespread sense that Rawls's work is in shambles because his critics have shown its foundations to be essentially and irremediably flawed. Since Rawls's mistake is thought to be a deep one, the collapse of his theory is said to indicate something larger, to mark the end of an era, perhaps the death of liberalism, the demise of the Enlightenment tradition, or even the bankruptcy of systematic moral philosophy.[11]

Pogge wrote this in 1989, before *Political Liberalism* was published and the full effect of Rawls's "political interpretation" of justice as fairness was felt. I think it is safe to say, however, that recasting justice as fairness as a political conception (something we will discuss below) has done little to assuage the

---

8. Anonymous, "The Good of Justice As Fairness," *Times Literary Supplement*, 5 May 1972, no. 3662, 505.

9. Marshall Cohen, "Review of *A Theory of Justice*," *New York Times Book Review*, 16 July 1972, 18. Stuart Hampshire, in *New York Review of Books*, was more modest, claiming merely that *A Theory of Justice* was "the most substantial and interesting contribution to moral philosophy since the war, at least if one thinks only of works written in English." ("A New Philosophy of the Just Society," *New York Review of Books*, 24 Feb. 1972, 34.)

10. J. H. Wellbank, Denis Snook, and David Mason, *John Rawls and His Critics: An Annotated Bibliography* (New York: Garland Publishing, 1982).

11. Thomas Pogge, *Realizing Rawls* (Ithaca, N.Y.: Cornell University Press, 1989), 2.

widespread sense that justice as fairness and liberalism itself are in shambles. It is more common than ever for "political philosophers to make do with a brief reminder that Rawls's theory can be set aside because of its irremediable failure to come to terms with this or that fundamental difficulty."[12]

Despite the ubiquity of references to his theory, there remain remarkably persistent disagreements about what Rawls actually says. To a certain extent, this might be expected of any bold and controversial theory. However, although dense, Rawls's writing is not particularly obscure. As one commentator writes, the "clarity" of *A Theory of Justice* "puts it in a different universe from the suggestive murkiness of Foucault, Gadamer or Habermas; there is no suggestion that enlightenment can only be achieved after a prolonged groping in the dark."[13] Furthermore, it is interesting that criticisms of Rawls do not seem to track the political commitments of the interpreters. As we might expect, for many on the right, Rawls is a "radical egalitarian" whose theory is "just what is wanted by the New Left."[14] "It is obvious," another writes, "that a society attempting to implement Rawls' principles would have to submit to despotism."[15] On the other hand, Friedrich Hayek claims that the differences between his and Rawls's theory are "more verbal than substantial"—and he writes this in a book entitled *The Mirage of Social Justice*.[16] From the left, many critics believe that Rawls's theory is "deeply conservative,"[17] and that the principles that it generates are "not merely false but ideological."[18] Still, a few authors on the left, such as Pogge, recognize that Rawls's concern for those in the least advantaged social positions makes him a radical thinker. By carefully examining the structure of justice as fairness, I hope to vindicate this claim.[19]

Rawls is best known, of course, for his idea that we should think of principles of justice as being the result of a social contract made from the

---

12. Pogge, *Realizing Rawls*, 3.

13. Alan Ryan, "John Rawls," in *The Return of Grand Theory in the Human Sciences*, Quentin Skinner, ed. (New York: Cambridge University Press, 1985), 103.

14. Allan Bloom, "Justice: John Rawls versus the Tradition of Political Philosophy," in *Giants and Dwarfs* (New York: Simon and Schuster, 1990), 315, 318.

15. Robert Bork, *Slouching towards Gomorrah* (New York: Regan Books, 1996), 81.

16. Friedrich Hayek, *The Mirage of Social Justice*, vol. 2 of *Law Legislation and Liberty* (Chicago: University of Chicago Press, 1976), xiii; cf. 100.

17. Roberto Alejandro, *The Limits of Rawlsian Justice* (Baltimore: Johns Hopkins University Press, 1998), 9. Paradoxically, he also claims that justice as fairness is "a statist theory that requires a powerful state to regulate the inequalities that civil society produces." (8)

18. Robert Paul Wolff, *Understanding Rawls: A Reconstruction and Critique of "A Theory of Justice"* (Princeton: Princeton University Press, 1977), 208.

19. However, even Pogge claims that Rawls's more recent work exhibits a "trend . . . toward abstraction, vagueness, and conservatism." (*Realizing Rawls*, 4) I disagree, but I do not know whether Pogge would revise his assessment in light of the publication of *Political Liberalism*.

original position. Because this idea is so distinctive, the secondary literature has tended to focus rather narrowly on it alone.[20] Because of this exclusive focus, critics tend to neglect the purpose the original position is designed to serve and the basis on which Rawls defends its appropriateness for this task. This chapter will attempt to remedy this neglected background before discussing the details of the choice from the original position in the next chapter. In the first section, we will explore the subject that justice as fairness aims to address. Without this background firmly in mind, there is a temptation to use the theory for purposes for which it was not designed. In the second section, we consider Rawls's methodology of "reflective equilibrium." I argue that properly understood, reflective equilibrium represents a non-reductive, inclusive approach to normative questions of justice. What this reveals is that Rawls is not interested in a common philosophical project of reducing principles of justice to non-moral considerations or refuting skeptical worries about the possibility of objective moral claims. Rather, he is interested in *making* moral claims concerning justice, and he wants to get them right.

In the third section, we begin to identify the resources with which justice as fairness generates its principles of justice. Specifically, we consider the models of society and of the person (or the citizen) on which justice as fairness relies. These are crucial building blocks, but the secondary literature has not sufficiently considered how they are to be defended. When inordinate attention is placed on the choice from the original position, it may seem as though the constraints on choices made there rest on undefended assumptions. By examining the models of society and the person, we can better understand the appropriateness of the original position. When critics have turned their attention to Rawls's model of the person, they have often objected that it is too exclusive because it arbitrarily excludes certain individuals from consideration. Rawls has done little to defend this model, but I will attempt to provide such a defense. Finally, in the fourth section, we will consider Rawls's most recent work on the idea of "public reason." It is here that we can see most clearly how justice as fairness attempts to combine a proper respect for diversity with the goal of generating principles of justice that can be shared and endorsed as correct by all reasonable citizens. Only when this is done will we be able to continue the search for such principles in the next chapter.

---

20. At one point in *A Theory of Justice*, Rawls warns against interpretations of Kant's ethics that focus too narrowly on the universality of the categorical imperative and neglect the broader aspects of the theory in which the universality is embedded. (See *TJ*, 251 [221].) A similar fate, I am claiming, has befallen Rawls's theory.

The Basic Structure

Some of the wildly divergent interpretations of justice as fairness can be explained by inattention to a point that Rawls has stressed consistently in his work since at least 1963: justice as fairness is an attempt to work out principles of justice for a very specific subject in particular circumstances.[21] The subject with which justice as fairness is primarily concerned is what Rawls calls "the basic structure of society." Many different kinds of things can be evaluated as just or unjust including individual actions, character traits, people, and institutions, but justice as fairness is, in the first instance, a theory of the justice for the basic structure. Furthermore, the theory is only interested in generating principles of justice for this subject under certain conditions, namely, "modern democratic societies" which are characterized "by a pluralism of incompatible yet reasonable comprehensive doctrines." (*PL*, xviii) A theory of justice designed for this subject in these circumstances will certainly have implications for other subjects, including individual conduct, and some of the insights and techniques its develops may suggest ways to address other questions. Nevertheless, in order to avoid many of the most common misinterpretations of justice as fairness, we must begin where Rawls does—with the basic structure of a modern, pluralistic society.

For justice as fairness, "The primary subject of social justice is the basic structure of society, the arrangement of major social institutions into one scheme of cooperation. . . . The principles of justice for institutions must not be confused with the principles which apply to individuals and their actions in particular circumstances." (*TJ*, 54 [47]; cf. 7-11 [6-10]; *PL*, 11, 257-258) As examples of major institutions that may figure prominently in a society's basic structure, Rawls mentions "the political constitution, the legally recognized forms of property, and the organization of the economy, and the nature of the family." (*PL*, 258) Contrary to the impression given by some commentators, Rawls is not presupposing that these institutions are just. The point, rather, is that these familiar examples collectively are subject to evaluation from the point of view of basic social justice.

We can think of the basic structure as defining various social roles in the society.[22] The institutions of the basic structure publicly specify rights and

---

21. Rawls states that his concern will be "the fundamental structure of the social system" in "Constitutional Liberty and the Concept of Justice," in *Justice (NOMOS VI)*, C. J. Friedrich and John Chapman, eds. (New York: Atherton, 1963), 106. In his even earlier work, Rawls was explicitly concerned with the justice of institutions and practices. See, for example, "Two Concepts of Rules," *The Philosophical Review* 64 (1955).

22. Rawls often uses the formulation "representative persons" to indicate these various social positions. See, for example, *TJ*, 64, and section 16, "Relevant Social Positions." There is relevant material on how these positions are to be defined in Pogge, *Realizing Rawls*, 117-122, 204-205; and Walter Schaller, "Rawls, the Difference Principle, and

responsibilities (broadly understood) that are associated with these positions, and also how individuals come to occupy and leave these positions. Although Rawls is often assumed to hold a form of atomism or abstract individualism in which society is understood as the mere sum of individuals,[23] in fact, he rejects such a model. On the other hand, he also rejects an extreme form of functionalism in which individual agency plays no explanatory role. Justice as fairness accepts Alex Callinicos's observation: "To say that social structures have explanatory autonomy is to say that they cannot be eliminated from the explanation of social events. It is *not* to say that individuals and their attributes can, or should be eliminated."[24]

Institutions play a crucial role in our socialization, including the development of a sense of ourselves and of our values and ends, and Rawls has always been concerned with this process. An important part of *A Theory of Justice* is his discussion of the development of a sense of justice and how that process depends on the social environment.[25] In his Presidential Address to the American Philosophical Association, Rawls puts it plainly: "What sorts of persons we are is shaped by how we think of ourselves and this in turn is influenced by the social forms we live under."[26] This is most obviously true of the family, but Rawls also stresses the influence of other parts of the basic structure, including the political and economic institutions in shaping our self-conception.

The secondary literature has been extremely reluctant to acknowledge that Rawls takes socialization seriously. Instead, he is typically portrayed as neglecting this important role of the basic structure and evaluating it simply in terms of its ability to satisfy exogenously given preferences and ends. It is frequently asserted that Rawls's theory, like liberal theories generally, "is for the most part bounded by the supposed wants of man as a consumer";[27] that Rawls assumes that individuals "have wants, desires, and needs independent of social

---

Economic Inequality," *Pacific Philosophical Quarterly* 79, no. 4 (Dec. 1998).

23. For an influential discussion of atomism which does not mention Rawls but is commonly assumed to apply to him, see Charles Taylor, "Atomism," in *Philosophy and the Human Sciences*, vol. 2 of *Philosophical Papers* (New York: Cambridge University Press, 1985). Steven Lukes is explicit in claiming that justice as fairness is a form of "abstract individualism" in his *Individualism* (New York: Basil Blackwell, 1973), 139. Rawls cites Lukes and rejects this interpretation in "Fairness to Goodness," *The Philosophical Review* 84 (1975), 546-547.

24. Alex Callinicos, *Making History* (Ithaca, N.Y.: Cornell University Press, 1988), 83.

25. See *TJ*, chapter 8, "The Sense of Justice," which draws on his earlier paper, "The Sense of Justice," *The Philosophical Review* 72 (1963).

26. John Rawls, "The Independence of Moral Theory," *Proceedings and Addresses of the American Philosophical Association* 48 (1975), 20.

27. C. B. Macpherson, *Democratic Theory: Essays in Retrieval* (New York: Oxford University Press, 1973), 94.

context, relationships with others, or historical setting";[28] and that Rawls believes that "a rational choice framework [is] a descriptively adequate characterisation of modern societies and individuals."[29]

Contrary to the suggestions of these authors, even in his discussion of the economy Rawls does not simply take preferences as given, but considers the influence that institutions may have on their formation. Early in his discussion of justice in political economy he comments that the social system "determines in part the sort of persons [citizens] want to be as well as the sort of persons they are. Thus an economic system is not only an institutional device for satisfying existing wants and needs but a way of creating and fashioning wants in the future." (TJ, 259 [229]) Because of the importance of the basic structure in creating and shaping our preferences and values, it cannot be evaluated simply in terms of its efficiency at satisfying preexisting desires. We will see an important illustration of this when we turn to the issue of stability and how the basic structure encourages the development of a sense of justice among citizens.

The point that I want to emphasize now is that Rawls believes that the evaluation of the justice of institutions cannot be derived from a prior and independent moral evaluation of the conduct of individuals within those institutions. In the first instance, Rawls treats social justice as a virtue of institutions, not of individuals. To be sure, once we identify standards for assessing the justice of the basic structure, there will be implications for individual conduct and character. This is because, as Rawls puts it, "The social system is not an unchangeable order beyond human control but a pattern of human action." (TJ, 102 [88])

This means, on the one hand, that if we come to believe that our institutions should be changed, we can do this by collectively changing the public system of rules (both formal and informal) which guide the patterns of our interactions. On the other hand, even just institutions cannot be sustained—will not continue to be just—independently of the actions and attitudes of the individuals who shape them. Therefore, the requirements of a just basic structure certainly will have implications for the assessment of individual virtues and vices. Nonetheless, for Rawls, "the basic structure of society is the first subject of justice." (PL, 257) Justice as fairness begins by identifying the requirements of a just basic structure and deriving the implications for individual conduct and character. Notice that there is no thought that the institutional requirements of a just basic structure will generate an exhaustive list of individual virtues. Morality and individual virtue extend beyond the requirements of social justice.

At a certain level, no one would deny the importance of the basic structure since Rawls is so obviously correct that "its effects are so profound and present

---

28. Martha Minow, *Making All the Difference* (Ithaca, N.Y.: Cornell University Press, 1990), 151-152.

29. Elizabeth Frazer and Nicola Lacey, *The Politics of Community* (Toronto: University of Toronto Press, 1993), 56.

from the start." (*TJ*, 7 [7]) Every moral theory will grant the profound importance of the political, economic and social institutions within which people interact. However, by insisting that the moral evaluation of the basic structure of society cannot be reduced to the prior assessment of individual conduct or character, Rawls is going against the dominant trend in contemporary ethical thought. The vast majority of moral theories start by making moral assessments either of individual actions or of character. If they discuss the virtues of social institutions at all, they are derived from the assessment of the conduct of individuals who participate in them.[30] At first glance, this seems plausible enough. After all, if, as Rawls maintains, social institutions are patterns of human interaction, why not dispense with the evaluation of institutions as such and only make direct assessments of individual conduct?

I want to emphasize two answers to this question. First, it is a practical impossibility to require individuals to consider all of the possible moral implications of all of their actions—interactions in modern society are simply too complex and unpredictable. We must rely on institutions to preserve just background conditions within which individuals can act without the requirement that they consider all possible ways in which their actions may interact with all the possible actions of others. Institutions allow, in other words, a necessary division of moral labor. Second, given the ubiquity of institutional interactions, it is unsurprising that the moral character of individual conduct is often affected by the institutional context within which it takes place. What might be less obvious however, is that the moral status of an action is affected by the moral status of the institutional context. This implies that we need to be able to make a moral evaluation of the institutional context before we are able to evaluate the individual conduct that occurs within it. We will consider each of these points.

In modern societies, institutional schemes are necessary to stabilize and regularize exceedingly complex interactions among individuals and groups. There is simply no way that individuals can be expected to anticipate all of the likely moral consequences of their conduct without relying on institutions to make their interactions more predictable. The problem here is not that morality is too demanding, but rather that the informational requirements for the moral assessment of individual conduct would be overwhelming without institutions. Often the consequences of our actions are not only distant, but also unpredictable, since they are the joint product of interaction with other people.

Spending a dollar on certain groceries may be morally innocuous when we confine our view to the local context. But if, along with similar behavior on the part of many others, that purchase serves to enrich the owner of a farm which, in turn, gives him an unfair bargaining advantage over his workers whom he then exploits, it may not be as innocuous. Yet, we cannot expect individuals to

---

30. Or they derive moral principles for both individual conduct and institutions from a common foundation. Utilitarianism, for example, evaluates actions, characters, and institutions according to their production of happiness.

anticipate all of the ways in which their behavior might combine with that of others to generate undesired or unacceptable consequences. Instead we rely on background institutions to respond in a regular way to these kinds of complicated and unpredictable interactions. Suppose, for example, that a system of taxation were in place that would prevent accumulations from reaching the point at which such exploitation is likely. Then individuals could confine their attention to the local environment—spend their money on whichever groceries they prefer—confident that they were not unknowingly responsible for generating conditions of exploitation elsewhere. Of course, their concern still cannot be too local, since they will have to evaluate the institution itself, but in terms of their burden of information, this is an immense improvement.

As Pogge observes:

> We as individuals have no hope of coping with such complexity and interdependence if we take the existing ground rules for granted and merely ask "How should I act?" or "What should I do differently?" We can cope only by attending to this all-pervasive scheme of ground rules which shapes the way persons act and co-determines how their actions, together, affect the lives of others.[31]

It is, in part, for this reason that Rawls thinks of the basic structure this way: "The role of the institutions that belong to the basic structure is to secure just background conditions against which the actions of individuals and associations take place." (*PL*, 266) The institutions of the basic structure ensure that individuals have the resources and opportunities to enter non-exploitative relationships. Institutions are necessary to do this because:

> the conditions necessary for background justice can be undermined, even though nobody acts unfairly or is aware of how the overall result of many separate exchanges affects the opportunities of others. There are no feasible rules that it is practicable to require economic agents to follow in their day-to-day transactions that can prevent these undesirable consequences. These consequences are often so far in the future, or so indirect, that the attempt to forestall them by restrictive rules that apply to individuals would be an excessive if not an impossible burden.
> . . . fair background conditions may exist at one time and be gradually undermined even though no one acts unfairly when their conduct is judged by the rules that apply to transactions within the appropriately circumscribed local situation. . . . Therefore, we require special institutions to preserve background justice, and a special conception of justice to define how these institutions are to be set up. (*PL*, 266-267)

This suggests a conceptual split between those actions that occur within an institutional context and those which may serve to define or transform the institution itself. Once we assume that just background institutions are in place, individuals in their "day-to-day transactions" may act as they choose, confident

---

31. Pogge, *Realizing Rawls*, 9.

that the institutional context will maintain background justice. On the other hand, in rather more exceptional circumstances when the basic character of these background institutions is at stake, individuals must reflect on the very terms of their interactions with others and insure that they are just.

We must be careful at this point to avoid the impression that the focus on institutions absolves citizens of responsibility. On the contrary, instead of taking responsibility out of their hands, it allows them better to exercise it without requiring that they meet impossible burdens of knowledge. It is crucial that we recall that social institutions are sustained or transformed by a pattern of human conduct and attitudes. Typically, no one individual will be fully responsible for the character of the basic structure, but a group can be collectively responsible. Pogge explains the point well:

> Rawls's focus on basic social institutions and their effects makes it possible to clarify how injustice can be systemic, can exist without being traceable to any manifestly unjust actions by individuals or groups. Our causal contribution to the suffering of the poor is extremely indirect and intermixed with the causal contributions of others. It is quite infeasible for us to adjust our conduct so as to avoid such effects. And here again, Rawls's institutional approach is crucial for showing the alternative to such an (infeasible) adjustment of our conduct. We must initiate institutional reforms toward a scheme that, however differentiated and complex, does not tend to engender the severe poverty and oppression so typical of our current world.[32]

Since many of the more important moral consequences of our actions are indirect and there is no feasible way to anticipate and evaluate them in isolation, reliance on institutions provides a mechanism through which citizens can exercise collective responsibility. An emphasis on social institutions implies a division of moral responsibility between the individual and the society as a whole. Far from absolving citizens of responsibility, it shows how, together with our fellows, we can be collectively responsible for the background institutions within which we interact.

Consider now the second point concerning the influence of institutional context on the moral evaluation of individual conduct. Perhaps with an eye toward the criminal law, it is common to think of social institutions as restricting the permissibility of actions that would otherwise be morally acceptable. In fact, according to Anthony Giddens, "Most forms of structural sociology, from Durkheim onwards, have been inspired by the idea that structural properties of society form constraining influences over action."[33] This idea is mistaken, however, for in some cases participation in a social structure may permit an individual to act in ways that would be otherwise impermissible or unacceptable.

---

32. Pogge, *Realizing Rawls*, 11-12.
33. Anthony Giddens, *The Constitution of Society* (Berkeley: University of California Press, 1984), 169.

In cases where an institutional context changes the moral status of an action, a narrow assessment of the action without attention to the context will result in a mistaken moral judgment. Even more dramatically, participation in an institution may make new classes of actions conceptually possible for the first time. Saying "I do" only results in marriage when certain background institutional norms are in place.

When we participate in institutions, we take on institutional roles. Many of the moral decisions that we face engage us in these roles. As participants in economic institutions, we make decisions regarding our employers, employees, and co-workers; as family members, we make decisions regarding our parents, children, siblings, and loved ones; as participants in our political institutions, we consider how to vote, whom to lobby, and whether to demonstrate. Virginia Held may exaggerate, but she is not far off when she asserts that "nearly all morality is role morality."[34] If we fail to recognize the centrality of such contexts, we are unlikely to generate an adequate account of the morality of individual acts or character.

The key point for us is that in contexts in which social roles are central, we need an account of the justice or legitimacy of the institution before we can determine what morality requires of an individual occupying that position. The specific moral obligations that fall on a person occupying a certain social role depend, in part, on the legitimacy of the institution defining that position. Consider a single example. An individual is deciding whether it is morally permissible to spend her money on a vacation. Such a decision can only be made against a background scheme of property rights, and the nature of this scheme may have a decisive influence on the moral standing of her action. If the background scheme of property rights provides everyone a comparable opportunity, such an action may be perfectly acceptable. If, on the other hand, the scheme of property rights allowed her unjustly to exploit other members of her society and accumulate wealth on that basis, such an expenditure may be morally outrageous, although, we may assume, acceptable from a legal point of view. When we recognize the pervasive influence of the institutions of the basic structure, it becomes clear why their prior moral assessment is necessary in order to evaluate many if not most individual actions.

Institutions are necessary, then, in order to relieve individuals of burdens of information that are impossible to fulfill, without absolving them of responsibility. They do this by introducing an element of collective responsibility for the background terms of interaction. Once these institutional structures are in place, we typically need to know whether they are just or not in order to assess the morality of actions that take place within them. Rawls argues,

---

34. Virginia Held, *Rights and Goods* (Chicago: University of Chicago Press, 1984), 28. See also Michael Hardimon, "Role Obligations," *The Journal of Philosophy* 91, no. 7 (July 1994). For Rawls, "natural duties," unlike "obligations," are not institutional. See *TJ*, section 19.

therefore, that we must give explicit attention to the moral evaluation of institutions and not only of individual conduct. A moral theory that only evaluates individual actions and not the institutional contexts in which they occur is guilty of implicitly accepting whatever institutions happen to exist. Jeffrey Reiman criticizes the tendency of institutional contexts to fade into the background of moral discussions, claiming:

> That ignoring the social context in one's ordinary judgments of justice has the effect of conferring a positive judgment about the justice of the social structure is the core of what is called ideology. Ideology bestows its positive judgment precisely by our not noticing how the injustice of a social structure alters the justice of individual acts.[35]

If ideology is a failure to recognize the possibility of creating alternative social institutions, then it is also a kind of conservatism. Existing institutional structures are accepted by default because the possibility of an alternative is not even recognized. They are viewed simply as natural or inevitable, unchosen and beyond the control of citizens. Rawls, as we have seen, will have none of that. Social structures are human creations, sustained, changed or eliminated by the actions and attitudes of individuals and groups. "In their political thought, and in the discussion of political questions," Rawls writes, "citizens do not view the social order as a fixed natural order." (*PL*, 15)

This does not mean that all social institutions as they now stand are transparent to their participants. Indeed, some, we may surmise, depend for their survival on the fact that the majority of participants do not have a clear and accurate understanding of their operation. They depend on ideology in Reiman's sense for their continued existence. Rawls is surely right when he comments: "We often acquiesce without thinking in the moral and political conception implicit in the status quo, or leave things to be settled by how contending social and economic forces happen to work themselves out." (*TJ*, 260 [229]) Despite the existence of such ideological blinders, all social structures are the joint product of individuals and groups acting in various already existing social contexts. As such, there is always the possibility of deliberate, collective transformation, even if most change is not of this kind.

In addition to neglecting Rawls's concentration on the basic structure, the secondary literature also frequently loses sight of the fact that justice as fairness evaluates this object only in certain historical circumstances. Critics frequently assert that justice as fairness is "ahistorical." It is hard to know exactly why this criticism is so commonly accepted. Perhaps it is due to a misunderstanding of Rawls's idea of the original position, which, as we will see in the next chapter, is certainly not supposed to be historical. Some commentators seize on Rawls's

---

35. Jeffrey Reiman, *Justice and Modern Moral Philosophy* (New Haven: Yale University Press, 1990), 225.

suggestion that justice as fairness sets up a detached and independent "Archimedean point" from which to assess social justice.

In fact, when Rawls uses this phrase he is defending himself against precisely the charge we discussed earlier: that a social contract view like justice as fairness treats individuals as mere consumers and "relies upon the aims of existing individuals and regulates the social order by principles that persons guided by these aims would choose." (*TJ*, 260 [230]) The image of an Archimedean point is supposed to bring out the fact that "justice as fairness is not at the mercy, so to speak, of existing wants and interests." (*TJ*, 261 [231]) However, this does not mean that justice as fairness ignores social context, historical conditions, or other empirical contingencies. Indeed, in the very sentence in which he invokes the image of an Archimedean point, Rawls rejects the view that justice as fairness must be purely a priori: "It sets up an Archimedean point for assessing the social system *without invoking a priori considerations*." (*TJ*, 261 [231], my emphasis) It is true that parts of justice as fairness are very abstract, but the use of abstractions and abstract concepts is not a way for political philosophy to "withdraw from society and the world. . . . Rather, it is a way of continuing public discussion when shared understandings of lesser generality have broken down." (*PL*, 45-46)

Before considering more recent developments (which have partially served to alleviate the charge that Rawls's theory is ahistorical), we must recognize that justice as fairness is designed to apply to societies that meet certain historically specific conditions. Briefly summarized, these are the circumstances of moderate scarcity, in which social cooperation is both necessary and possible. This is an important point, and not only because it helps to dispel the myth that justice as fairness is ahistorical. More significantly, an appreciation of these circumstances is crucial to an understanding of the manner in which Rawls conceives the virtue of justice. Near the beginning of *A Theory of Justice*, Rawls comments:

> There is an identity of interests [among individuals in a well-ordered society] since social cooperation makes possible a better life for all than any would have if each were to live solely by his own efforts. There is a conflict of interests since persons are not indifferent as to how the greater benefits produced by their collaboration are distributed, for in order to pursue their ends they each prefer a larger to a lesser share. A set of principles is required for choosing among the various social arrangements which determine this division of advantages and for underwriting an agreement on the proper distributive shares. These principles are the principles of social justice: they provide a way of assigning rights and duties in the basic institutions of society and they define the appropriate distribution of the benefits and burdens of social cooperation. (*TJ*, 4 [4])

Adopting Hume's approach, therefore, Rawls explicitly limits his considerations to societies in which "the circumstances of justice" hold. "Unless these circumstances existed there would be no occasion for the virtue of justice, just as in the absence of threats to injury to life and limb there would be no occasion for physical courage." (*TJ*, 128 [110])

In *A Theory of Justice*, Rawls divides the circumstances of justice into objective conditions and subjective conditions. Among the objective circumstances, Rawls includes "moderate scarcity understood to cover a wide range of situations. Natural and other resources are not so abundant that schemes of cooperation become superfluous, nor are conditions so harsh that fruitful ventures must inevitably break down." (*TJ*, 127 [110]) In order to determine whether these objective circumstances obtain, we must also consider the subjective conditions. This is because, as used here, the concept of *abundance* makes implicit reference to the wants and desires of the individuals in question. The question is always the availability of resources relative to the goals and aspirations of citizens. Therefore, whether a scheme of cooperation is superfluous, impossible, or desirable depends not only on the available resources, but also in large part on the attitudes of the individuals concerned.

Justice is a relevant virtue when, in spite of the possibility and desirability of cooperation, different individuals have different "ends and purposes, and [therefore] make conflicting claims on the natural and social resources available." (*TJ*, 127 [110]) When citizens have divergent and conflicting ends, they will disagree with one another about which goals are most desirable and how social resources should be utilized in their pursuit. There are various possible resolutions to such conflicts. A society may permit diverse ends but force adherents to fight to claim their share of resources, or it might attempt to impose a single system of values on all of its citizens in an effort to reduce the occasions for conflict. Alternatively, it might attempt to design institutions based on principles of justice that aim to resolve these conflicts in a fair way. It can attempt to do this without dispelling the original diversity of ends. In such a society, citizens will recognize and act on the requirements of justice while continuing to affirm diverse and mutually incompatible value systems.

Immediately after noting that in the circumstances of justice there will be conflicts among ends, Rawls presents a warning that has frequently been ignored in the secondary literature. While the circumstances of justice obtain only when individuals have divergent ends, there is no assumption that these ends are self-interested (although for some individuals they may be): "Moreover, although the interests advanced by these plans are not assumed to be interests in the self, they are interests of a self that regards its conception of the good as worthy of recognition and that advances claims in its behalf as deserving satisfaction." (*TJ*, 127 [110]; cf. 129 [111]) In order to emphasize that he is not assuming that individuals are purely self-interested, as well as to point out that their ends are not whimsical but are often subject to lengthy and serious contemplation, Rawls observes that ends are typically embedded in broader frameworks: "As a consequence individuals not only have different plans of life but there exists a diversity of philosophical and religious belief, and of political and social doctrines." (*TJ*, 127 [110])

The core commitment of justice as fairness is the belief that we need principles of justice precisely where there are diverse and conflicting values. Over time however, Rawls's characterization of the diversity in question has changed. The assumption noted in the previous paragraph, that our ends and goals are typically embedded in more comprehensive systems of beliefs, foreshadows important developments in *Political Liberalism*. To bring this point out, and to show how diversity remains a central concern in both books, let me introduce two technical terms. A *conception of the good* is a system of goals or ends one believes worth pursuing:

> Such a conception [of the good] must not be understood narrowly but rather as including a conception of what is valuable in human life. Thus, a conception of the good normally consists of a more or less determinate scheme of final ends, that is, ends we want to realize for their own sake, as well as attachments to other persons and loyalties to various groups and associations. These attachments and loyalties give rise to devotions and affections, and so the flourishing of the persons and associations who are the objects of these sentiments is also part of our conception of the good. (*PL*, 19)

In contrast to a conception of the good, a *comprehensive doctrine* is a religious, philosophical, or moral view which includes, among other things, "conceptions of what is of value in human life, and ideals of personal character, as well as ideals of friendship and of familial and associational relationships, and much else that is to inform our conduct." (*PL*, 13) Thus, a conception of the good is typically embedded in, and is justified by a broader doctrine that is either partially or fully comprehensive in scope. (See *PL*, 175.) Although as we have seen, this idea was clearly present in *A Theory of Justice*, Rawls only introduced the idea of a comprehensive doctrine explicitly in *Political Liberalism*, and there it took center stage.[36] For reasons we will discuss below, in *Political Liberalism* Rawls emphasizes the importance not only of the diversity of conceptions of the good that gives rise to the circumstances of justice but also the diversity of comprehensive doctrines in which those conceptions of the good are embedded.

Reading *A Theory of Justice* one might get the impression that we might hope to move beyond the circumstances of justice. One might think that generating greater resources, for example, or narrowing the disagreements concerning which ends are valuable might eliminate fundamental conflicts and

---

36. In the "Introduction to the Paperback Edition" of *Political Liberalism*, Rawls indicates he now refers to "doctrines of the good" rather than "conceptions." This is to emphasize the connection between a doctrine of the good and comprehensive doctrines, while reserving the term *conception* for a political (rather than comprehensive) conception of justice. See *PL*, xxxvii n2; and xlvi n16. With care, the old terminology is adequate, even if not ideal.

vitiate the need for institutions to resolve individual and group conflicts. Rawls himself might have given this impression when he wrote: "In an association of saints agreeing on a common ideal, if such a community could exist, disputes about justice would not occur. Each would work selflessly for one end as determined by their common religion, and reference to this end (assuming it to be clearly defined) would settle every question of right." (*TJ*, 129 [112]) Even though he continues this passage by commenting that unlike a community of saints, "a human society is characterized by the circumstances of justice," one could get the impression that the circumstances of justice reflect a moral failure due to our insufficient selfless commitment to some ideal. This view, often associated with Marx, is held by some authors who believe that "The free society is one beyond justice."[37]

In his more recent work, Rawls has moved decisively to reject such a possibility. We cannot expect to move beyond the circumstances of justice for reasons unrelated to excessive selfishness or a lack of adequate fellow feeling. Rather, we simply cannot expect a modern democratic society to contain only a single comprehensive doctrine. We must assume that "the diversity of reasonable comprehensive religious, philosophical, and moral doctrines found in modern democratic societies is not a mere historical condition that may soon pass away; it is a permanent feature of the public culture of democracy." (*PL*, 36) In particular, this diversity is "the natural outcome of the activities of human reason under enduring free institutions." (*PL*, xxvi) Rawls calls this the "fact of reasonable pluralism."[38]

Even leaving aside "prejudice and bias, self- and group interest, blindness and willfulness," (*PL*, 58) we can identify many different commonsense reasons why we should not expect unanimity among all reasonable people. Our subjective experiences and the way they are interpreted, for example, differ from one person to another, and we construct our system of values in part based on such experiences and interpretations. Thus, we must recognize that "many of our most important judgments are made under conditions where it is not to be expected that conscientious persons with full powers of reason, even after free discussion, will all arrive at the same conclusion." (*PL*, 58) These "burdens of

---

37. Andrew Levine, "Beyond Justice: Rousseau against Rawls," *The Journal of Chinese Philosophy* 4, no. 2 (Aug. 1977), 140. On Marx, see the discussions in Allen Buchanan, *Marx and Justice* (Totowa, N.J.: Rowman & Allanheld, 1982), 169-170; and Jon Elster, *Making Sense of Marx* (New York: Cambridge University Press, 1985), 230-233, 453, 456-458, 526-527.

38. "Reasonable" because the claim concerns the diversity of *reasonable* comprehensive doctrines. We will discuss this qualification below. For now, note simply that not all comprehensive doctrines are reasonable in this sense. Rawls is assuming, then, that the diversity in question is not merely due to the inevitable presence of unreasonable comprehensive doctrines.

judgment"[39] and the resulting fact of reasonable pluralism mean that modern societies must abandon the hope that all significant conflicts can be fully transcended, even in the best of circumstances. We must learn to deal fairly with fundamental conflicts.

We must be careful not to confuse Rawls's reasonable pluralism thesis with another claim, which is itself often called "pluralism" and is defended by, among others, Isaiah Berlin. Although Berlin believes there are objective values, "The notion of the perfect whole, the ultimate solution, in which all good things coexist, seems to me to be not merely unattainable—that is a truism—but conceptually incoherent; I do not know what is meant by a harmony of this kind. Some among the Great Goods cannot live together. That is a conceptual truth."[40] He defines the pluralism that he defends as follows: "There are many objective ends, ultimate values, some incompatible with others . . . [resulting in] conflicting claims of uncombinable, yet equally ultimate and objective, ends."[41] The problem with such a view, from the point of view of justice as fairness, is that this doctrine of pluralism is exactly the kind of thing about which reasonable people disagree.[42] As we shall see, placing such an assumption at the base of justice as fairness would undermine its fundamental aspiration to provide justifications that all reasonable people can accept.

Rawls's commitment to reasonable pluralism is not a commitment to a plurality of fundamental objective values. In fact, as we will see below, unlike Berlin's doctrine, justice as fairness studiously avoids making any such pronouncements concerning the metaphysical status of fundamental values. Rawls is not committed to the truth or falsehood of any particular comprehensive doctrine. Instead of Berlin's metaphysical doctrine of pluralism, Rawls's claim concerns simply the diversity of reasonable comprehensive doctrines that, as a matter of fact, will be affirmed in an open society. He does not claim that they all capture some of (or all of) the underlying truth about values.

Although the fact of reasonable pluralism is not itself a moral fact, it is closely related to a moral claim: even assuming that there is a single true comprehensive doctrine (whether pluralistic or monistic), universal agreement concerning its truth could only be achieved (if at all) at an unacceptably high price. Although not quite making this moral claim explicit, Rawls certainly comes close: "a continuing shared understanding on one comprehensive

---

39. See *PL*, 54-58; and the discussion in Colin Bird, "Mutual Respect and Neutral Justification," *Ethics* 107, no. 1 (Oct. 1996).

40. Isaiah Berlin, *The Crooked Timber of Humanity*, Henry Hardy, ed. (New York: Knopf, 1991), 13. See also Berlin's "Two Concepts of Liberty" in his *Four Essays on Liberty* (New York: Oxford University Press, 1969), 169.

41. Berlin, *The Crooked Timber of Humanity*, 79-80.

42. See Charles Larmore, *The Morals of Modernity* (New York: Cambridge University Press, 1996), 12; and his discussion of these different senses of pluralism, 152-174.

religious, philosophical, or moral doctrine can be maintained only by the oppressive use of state power. . . . In the society of the Middle Ages, more or less united in affirming the Catholic faith, the Inquisition was not an accident; its suppression of heresy was needed to preserve that shared religious belief." (*PL*, 37)[43] Again, this observation is not an assertion that all (or even any) of the doctrines which flourish in a free society are in some sense true or objectively correct. Rather, it is to recognize with Charles Larmore that a "crucial element of modern experience" is that "on the meaning of life reasonable people tend naturally to disagree with one another."[44] We can explain this diversity without relying on any strong metaphysical assumptions about the underlying nature of value(s).

So, justice as fairness takes the virtue of justice to be a response to the diversity of conflicting, yet reasonable comprehensive doctrines that we must expect in modern society. Justice is a necessary virtue in order to negotiate fairly the conflicting goals and ends of different individuals and groups in a society characterized by a diversity of conceptions of the good and of comprehensive doctrines. Notice, then, that in the first instance it is not a response to immorality or a lack of virtue. Even if there were a very high level of virtue in society, we still must expect conflicting comprehensive doctrines and goals, and therefore the virtue of justice would be necessary in order to negotiate the inevitable conflicts. Of course, in such an idealized society, such conflicts would not generate deep animosity or strife since they would be tamed by a strong sense of justice. But that is the point: justice is the virtue that resolves such conflicts fairly. In discussing the basic structure, Rawls makes the following "obvious point: when our social world is pervaded by duplicity and deceit we are tempted to think that law and government are necessary only because of the propensity of individuals to act unfairly." (*PL*, 267) But this is not the only reason we need law and government, and the point holds for the virtue of justice itself.

Some critics of liberalism claim that justice is "a remedial virtue, whose moral advantage consists in the repair it works on fallen conditions."[45] Those who share this thought can take either a hard or a soft line. On the soft line, held for example by Michael Sandel, the conflicts which characterize the circumstances of justice are primarily due to insufficient identification with the community itself and potentially could be overcome. The circumstances of justice exist only in the absence of "the circumstances of benevolence, or

---

43. Rawls leaves no doubt concerning his moral assessment of this history of suppression: "A persecuting zeal has been the great curse of the Christian religion." (John Rawls, "The Idea of Public Reason Revisited," *University of Chicago Law Review* 64, no. 3 (summer 1997), 796n75)

44. Larmore, *The Morals of Modernity*, 12.

45. Michael Sandel, *Liberalism and the Limits of Justice*, second edition (New York: Cambridge University Press, 1998), 32.

fraternity, or of enlarged affections."[46] On the hard line, on the other hand, the fallen condition that characterizes the circumstances of justice is due to the inevitable presence of human evil. As John Kekes explains, in contrast to Socrates, "We recognize that the good may suffer and the wicked may flourish, even in the long run, even when all things are considered. The fundamental reason that underlies this attitude is that we do not believe in cosmic justice."[47] This potential divergence between moral merit and satisfaction—the fact that some evil individuals flourish while some virtuous individuals languish—is "a deplorable fact."[48] It is this fact that leads to the need for justice. Where once it was assumed that God would mete out punishments and rewards to avoid this outcome, now human justice must fill the void left by the death of God. Justice requires that we do what we can to punish the evil and reward the virtuous; hence, justice must be based on moral desert. "The purpose of justice," Kekes writes, "is to reduce this imbalance [between moral merit and satisfaction] by making them diverge less from each other."[49] Thus, if we were to imagine a situation of sufficient virtue and the absence of evil, we would be imagining a situation in which the virtue of justice would have no point. Justice, in our fallen human condition, is about "facing evil."[50]

In contrast, for Rawls the need for justice is generated neither by the presence of evil nor by insufficient public spiritedness. Even morally acceptable conceptions of the good and reasonable comprehensive doctrines will often generate conflicts, and we need a principled way to deal with them.[51] Kekes is correct that Rawls has relatively little to say about dealing with evil, but this is not because of a "liberal faith" in the natural goodness of all people.[52] Rawls treats justice as a response to the conflicts among reasonable comprehensive doctrines, rather than as a response to the presence of evil.

We can rely on the standard labels for these two problems, as long as we recognize the warnings I will give below. *Retributive* (or rectificatory) justice concerns the appropriate responses to evil, immorality, other ethical failures and lapses, and generally the fact that individuals achieve different

---

46. Sandel, *Liberalism and the Limits of Justice*, 32.

47. John Kekes, *Moral Wisdom and Good Lives* (Ithaca, N.Y.: Cornell University Press, 1995), 183.

48. John Kekes, *Against Liberalism* (Ithaca, N.Y.: Cornell University Press, 1997), 122.

49. John Kekes, *Moral Wisdom and Good Lives*, 189.

50. John Kekes, *Facing Evil* (Princeton: Princeton University Press, 1990).

51. To call a comprehensive doctrine "reasonable" in this sense does not mean that it is the correct view or even that we accept it. See the discussion below and in my "The Reasonable in Justice as Fairness," *Canadian Journal of Philosophy* 29, no. 1 (March 1999).

52. Kekes identifies "liberal faith" as the view that "if people were allowed to make choices without corrupting external influences . . . they would do what is good and they would not do what is evil." (Kekes, *Against Liberalism*, 38)

levels of moral virtue and moral desert. *Distributive* justice concerns the appropriate responses to conflicting goals among individuals and groups pursuing different plans and goals. It is important to remember that these are only labels defined by the problem they aim to solve. Distributive justice does not aspire to encompass all considerations relevant to matters of distribution of whatever kind of goods (or bads). Retributive justice certainly will involve "distributing" punishments and rewards. Moreover, as we will see below, there is no suggestion that distributive justice requires a central authority to distribute resources. With these precautions, we can rely on these labels and see that there is no reason to suppose ahead of time that the principles of distributive justice will be the same as or have any particular relationship to the principles of retributive justice. As Rawls points out: "To think of distributive and retributive justice as converses of one another is completely misleading." (*TJ*, 315 [277]) They are simply dealing with different problems. Nonetheless, for reasons I explain elsewhere, Rawls believes that we cannot develop an adequate account of either evil or retributive justice without first having available an account of distributive justice.[53]

Because of his emphasis on the basic structure, Rawls gives considerable attention to a concept rarely addressed explicitly in normative ethics and political philosophy: stability. Rawls notes "the problem of stability has played very little role in the history of moral philosophy," (*PL*, xix) but he believes that a proper appreciation of it has profound implications. In fact, many of the developments between *A Theory of Justice* and *Political Liberalism* result from Rawls's belief that his earlier discussion of stability was inadequate.[54] Ironically, this is one of the areas that largely escaped the attention of the secondary literature before the publication of *Political Liberalism*.[55]

A social structure is not the kind of thing that can be created once and continue to exist regardless of the attitudes and actions of the people living in it. Rather, it is dependent on them for its character and very existence. Now as we will discuss below, justice as fairness takes as fundamental a commitment to providing justifications of the basic structure that are acceptable to all

---

53. The point is not historical or sociological but conceptual. We must know what the virtue of justice demands as a response to diversity before we can determine how to respond to failures of these demands. This does not mean, however, that we can simply deduce an account of retributive justice from an account of distributive justice. See my "Justice, Desert, and Ideal Theory," *Social Theory and Practice* 23, no. 3 (fall 1997).

54. See Samuel Freeman, "Political Liberalism and the Possibility of a Just Constitution," *Chicago-Kent Law Review* 69, no. 3 (1994). See also the discussion in Joshua Cohen, "Democratic Equality," *Ethics* 99, no. 4 (July 1989), especially 744.

55. Exceptions include Brian Barry, *The Liberal Theory of Justice* (New York: Oxford University Press, 1973); Cohen, "Democratic Equality"; Edward McClennen, "Justice and the Problem of Stability," *Philosophy and Public Affairs* 18, no. 1 (winter 1989); and Anthony Laden, "Games, Fairness, and Rawls's *A Theory of Justice*," *Philosophy and Public Affairs* 20, no. 3 (summer 1991).

reasonable people who live within that structure. For now, notice that this implies that the basic structure of a well-ordered society can have no institutions that can only be defended on the basis of ideology (in the above sense). The full nature and justification of the basic social structure must be publicly available. (See *PL*, 66-67; and *TJ*, 16 [15], 175 [153].) This means that Plato's famous "noble lie" in Book III of the *Republic* and certain forms of utilitarianism that can only be imposed on citizens "behind their backs" so to speak are ruled out.[56] Now if the character of the basic structure depends on the actions and attitudes of citizens and these institutions must be transparent to them, the stability of the basic structure depends on the continuing free and willing support of citizens. Rawls assumes, therefore, that "an enduring and secure democratic regime . . . must be willingly and freely supported by at least a substantial majority of its politically active citizens." (*PL*, 38)

Although Rawls believes stability is a virtue, it would be a serious mistake to confuse this with conservatism. Justice as fairness takes stability to be a virtue only when just institutions are in place. The entrenchment of unjust institutions is certainly not a good thing. Thus, the assessment of stability depends on a prior assessment of the justice of the society in question. Many commentators have misunderstood the idea of an overlapping consensus (to be discussed below) to suggest that stability is now Rawls's primary concern. This simply is not true. Rawls thinks of justice as fairness as proceeding in two stages. (See *TJ*, 530-531 [465]; *PL*, 64-66, 133-134, 140-144.) At the first stage, we get a preliminary statement and defense of a particular conception of justice. At the second stage, we consider whether that conception would tend to generate its own support and thus be stable (relative to other conceptions). If we believe it would not be, we must reconsider the original choice. This is not only for practical reasons. The failure of a conception to be stable suggests that it is not acceptable to those living under its institutions. Even if stability could be bought at the price of deception or force, this would be unacceptable to justice as fairness. Thus, Rawls speaks of "stability for the right reasons." (See *PL*, xxxix, 391.)

There is another reason that it would be a serious mistake to confuse justice as fairness with a form of conservatism. Rawls is concerned with whether a scheme of institutions remains just over time, not with whether the institutions change. Stability requires that institutions track the requirements of justice as circumstances change. The following passage is especially valuable in showing, first, Rawls's view that just institutions must change in response to changing social circumstances, and second, that it is citizens who must bring about these responses:

---

56. See, for example, Henry Sidgwick, *The Methods of Ethics*, seventh edition (Indianapolis: Hackett, 1981), and the discussion of "Government House utilitarianism" in Bernard Williams, *Ethics and the Limits of Philosophy* (Cambridge: Harvard University Press, 1985), 108-110.

The stability of a conception of justice does not imply that the institutions and practices of the well-ordered society do not alter. In fact, such a society will presumably contain great diversity and adopt different arrangements from time to time. In this context stability means that however institutions are changed, they still remain just or approximately so, as adjustments are made in view of new social circumstances. The inevitable deviations from justice are effectively corrected or held within tolerable bounds by forces within the system. Among these forces I assume that the sense of justice shared by the members of the community has a fundamental role. (*TJ*, 457-458 [401])

The spontaneous generation of virtuous social arrangements without deliberate reflection on the possible existence of subjugation and exploitation is extremely implausible, especially in modern circumstances marked as they are by a plurality of conceptions of the good. Bernard Boxill puts the point this way:

To suppose that an unintended, unplanned change in such institutions will secure people's interests is as bizarre as to suppose that an unintended, unplanned change in a finely tuned engine will help it work better. . . . [I]nstitutions and practices that serve our larger, longer-term interests rarely happen by accident.[57]

As circumstances change, a just social structure will remain so only through the deliberate action of citizens. The failure to act in this way would suggest a lack of support for the principles underlying those institutions.

Rawls's insistence on the persistence of reasonable pluralism is resolutely anti-utopian. We cannot expect, and therefore cannot predicate our conception of justice on, a convergence of religious, moral, and philosophical comprehensive doctrines. Nonetheless, the achievement and stability of a just society requires the widespread support of citizens. How is this possible? As we will discuss below, while individuals will continue to disagree about their comprehensive doctrines and their associated conceptions of the good, Rawls hopes that they will be able to come to share a conception of justice (for the basic structure of society in circumstances of diversity). Indeed, justice as fairness attempts to make a practical contribution to achieving exactly this goal. This suggests a picture of what we should be aiming at: a society characterized by diverse comprehensive doctrines and conceptions of the good, in which individuals nonetheless share a common and effective sense of justice, and in which the basic structure satisfies their shared conception of justice. This is Rawls's idea of a well-ordered society. Notice that the idea of a well-ordered society does not itself specify a particular conception of justice. In theory, at least, a society could be well ordered by any one of many conceptions of justice.

Clearly the idea of a well-ordered society involves various idealizations from existing societies. The United States, for example, is not well ordered, at

---

57. Bernard Boxill, "The Culture of Poverty," *Social Philosophy and Policy* 11, no. 1 (winter 1994), 265-266.

least because there is not the required agreement on a conception of justice.[58] Nonetheless, the idea of a well-ordered society does not idealize beyond the circumstances of justice. It is therefore an appropriate model for determining the principles of distributive justice. As we have seen, even in such idealized conditions we will still have to deal with conflicts among reasonable comprehensive doctrines. On the other hand, by considering a well-ordered society, we will have abstracted away from (most of) the bases for retributive justice, which involves responding to immorality. Once we have an adequate understanding of the requirements of justice in this idealized case, we can go on to consider the more difficult case of justice in societies that either do not enjoy shared principles of justice or that have institutions that do not satisfy those principles.[59] This is not because retributive justice is unimportant, but simply because we will not be in a position to know how to deal with it unless we have a picture of what things would look like if they did go well.[60] As Rawls comments: "Obviously the problems of partial compliance theory are the pressing and urgent matters. These are the things that we are faced with in everyday life. The reason for beginning with ideal theory is that it provides, I believe, the only basis for the systematic grasp of these more pressing problems." (*TJ*, 8-9 [8])

Before moving on, I want to consider one final consequence of taking the institutions of the basic structure to be the first subject of social justice. Contrary to popular belief, Rawls's principles of justice do not require that resources be distributed to particular individuals in any particular pattern. Often discussions of distributive justice attempt to generalize from simplified cases, such as a case in which a cake is to be divided fairly among several individuals. In such scenarios, we are required to select among various principles that assign specific shares to particular individuals. This, however, is not the right model for understanding how Rawls thinks of distributive justice. Instead, his principles of justice (including the difference principle, which we will discuss in detail in the next chapter) work indirectly. Rather than requiring that particular individuals receive specific shares of resources, they select among institutional arrangements. These institutions, in turn, specify the background rules within which individuals pursuing their ends can legitimately claim shares of resources. Once we have set up the appropriate institutional structure, "the distribution that

---

58. Kurt Baier suggests that the U.S. does enjoy a "constitutional consensus," that is, a widespread agreement concerning the legitimacy of certain basic institutions, such as the Constitution, despite different conceptions of justice used to justify them. See Kurt Baier, "Justice and the Aims of Political Philosophy," *Ethics* 99, no. 4 (July 1989).

59. Pogge argues convincingly that justice as fairness must be able to go beyond the ideal case and at least assess the degree of failure in non-well-ordered societies. This would allow it to provide guidance concerning the urgency of needed reforms. See Pogge, *Realizing Rawls*, 127; 136-137; 143; 187n31; 206.

60. See the discussion in my "Justice, Desert, and Ideal Theory."

results will be just (or at least not unjust) whatever it is." (*TJ*, 304 [267]) The principles of justice, to repeat, work indirectly. There is no way ahead of time to know which individuals will be entitled to which shares of goods since these are determined by complex interactions with many contingencies.

This is a delicate point, however, because the principles of justice do require that we compare different institutional schemes in terms of the distribution of goods that each is likely to produce. But once we have made this comparison and selected the appropriate scheme, the principles of justice no longer have a direct role to play. The particular shares of resources that individuals can legitimately claim are the result of their choices, abilities, and fortune as specified by the institutional scheme. It is a matter of what Rawls calls "pure procedural justice." (*TJ*, 84-85 [74]) As he puts it in *Political Liberalism*:

> Again, the two principles of justice do not insist that the actual distribution conform at any given time (or over time) to any observable pattern, say equality, or that the degree of inequality computed from the distribution fall within a certain range, say of values of the Gini coefficient. What is enjoined is that (permissible) inequalities should make a certain functional contribution to the expectations of the least favored, where this functional contribution results from the working of the system of entitlements set up in public institutions. (*PL*, 283)

Justice as fairness does not require individuals to guide their day-to-day transactions by the difference principle, and therefore the particular allocation of goods in a just society is not dictated directly by that principle (or any other).[61] To be sure, there are limits to the permissible allocation of resources, since we may come to believe that our initial comparison among the feasible institutional arrangements was mistaken. But the fundamental point stands: depending on the actions of the citizens, a single set of just institutions can potentially produce very different allocations of goods, any one of which would be acceptable from the point of view of justice as fairness.

---

61. For explanation and elaboration of the difference principle, see the third section of chapter 3. When the character of the basic structure is at stake, citizens are required to act on the basis of their conception of justice. Recently, G. A. Cohen has challenged Rawls on whether this distinction can be sustained. See his "Incentives, Inequality, and Community" in *The Tanner Lectures on Human Values* 13, Grethe Peterson, ed. (Salt Lake City: University of Utah Press, 1992); "The Pareto Argument for Inequality," *Social Philosophy and Policy* 12, no. 1 (winter 1995); and "Where the Action Is: On the Site of Distributive Justice," *Philosophy and Public Affairs* 26, no. 1 (winter 1997). I am unable to respond to his critique here, but see the replies by David Estlund, "Liberalism, Equality, and Fraternity in Cohen's Critique of Rawls," *The Journal of Political Philosophy* 6, no. 1 (March 1998); Paul Smith, "Incentives and Justice: G. A. Cohen's Egalitarian Critique of Rawls," *Social Theory and Practice* 24, no. 2 (summer 1998); and Andrew Williams, "Incentives, Inequality, and Publicity," *Philosophy and Public Affairs* 27, no. 3 (summer 1998).

Some critics, especially from the left, have argued that a focus on distributive justice inevitably has the effect of limiting our understanding of justice. According to this criticism, principles of distributive justice fail to dig deeply enough into the structure of a society to uncover the sources of institutional injustice when they exist. These critics claim that distributive justice is only concerned with who ends up with how much wealth (or other goods) rather than with the underlying structures that generate this distribution. At best, they maintain, Rawls's principles identify the symptoms and not the causes of social injustice. "Inevitably," writes Robert Paul Wolff, "one finds oneself construing the difference principle as a pure distribution principle. One simply stops asking *how* the goods to be distributed actually come into existence."[62]

One stops asking this question, however, only by ignoring Rawls's repeated warnings against this mistake. In fact, Rawls already had rebutted this kind of misunderstanding in *A Theory of Justice*. In a neglected passage, remarkable for its anticipation of a line of criticism that has become commonplace, Rawls writes:

> A distribution cannot be judged in isolation from the system of which it is the outcome or from what individuals have done in good faith in the light of established expectations. If it is asked in the abstract whether one distribution of a given stock of things to definite individuals with known desires and preferences is better than another, then there is simply no answer to this question. The conception of the two principles does not interpret the primary problem of distributive justice as one of allocative justice. (*TJ*, 88 [76-77])

The problem of *allocative* justice arises when there is a fixed quantity of goods to be distributed among a known set of individuals. Rawls's principles are intended to be used at a higher level, namely the evaluation of the basic social institutions which themselves allocate the goods. In general, these institutions are not simply mechanisms for the allocation of a fixed supply of goods (like cake, in the example above), because the way they assign entitlements will often have profound effects on production of the very goods in question. Rawls's principles of justice require that we consider all of these possible effects. It is simply a gross distortion to claim, with Wolff, that "By focusing exclusively on distribution rather than on production, Rawls obscures the real roots of that distribution."[63]

It seems likely that the original source of this misinterpretation is to be found in Robert Nozick's critique of Rawls, which Wolff quotes approvingly.[64]

---

62. Robert Paul Wolff, *Understanding Rawls*, 200.

63. Wolff, *Understanding Rawls*, 210.

64. Compare Carol Gould, who writes: "Unlike Rawls, Nozick emphasizes production as well as distribution," in *Rethinking Democracy* (New York: Cambridge University Press, 1988), 12.

There seems to be a fairly well-established consensus that Nozick's criticisms of Rawls result in a standoff that reveals the futility of the project of establishing liberal principles of justice. Alasdair MacIntyre presents this view when he claims:

> Rawls makes primary what is in effect a principle of equality with respect to needs. . . . Nozick makes primary what is a principle of equality with respect to entitlements. For Rawls how those who are now in grave need came to be in grave need is irrelevant; justice is made into a matter of present patterns of distribution to which the past is irrelevant.[65]

On this common view, when Rawls's fundamental commitment to equality comes into conflict with Nozick's fundamental commitment to rights, there is no principled way to resolve the conflict, "For how can a claim that gives priority to equality of needs be rationally weighed against one which gives priority to entitlements?"[66] Nozick himself has encouraged this understanding with his characterization of justice as fairness as invoking a "patterned principle" of distribution. On this reading, Rawls's principles of justice require us to distribute goods according to a pattern dictated by the difference principle (and the other principles of justice). But, Nozick claims, "The likelihood is small that any actually freely-arrived-at set of holdings fits a given pattern; and the likelihood is nil that it will continue to fit the pattern as people exchange and give."[67] Thus, Rawls's critics conclude, the only way to preserve patterns is to use coercive measures designed to prevent people from disrupting the pattern of distribution. Thus, we have the familiar picture of Rawls, the defender of a pattern of equality, in a standoff with Nozick, the defender of individual rights and liberty.[68]

This picture depends on suppressing the fact that Rawlsian principles of justice are intended to evaluate the scheme of institutions that forms the basic structure. It is the institutions of the basic structure that assign entitlements and responsibilities to specific individuals in the society. Both Rawls and Nozick agree that particular goods ought to be distributed according to the entitlements arising from the actions individuals freely take within just institutional contexts. As we saw above, the basic structure is to establish a just institutional context within which "individuals and associations are then left free to advance their ends more effectively . . . secure in the knowledge that elsewhere in the social system the necessary corrections to preserve background justice are being

---

65. Alasdair MacIntyre, *After Virtue*, second edition (South Bend, Ind.: University of Notre Dame Press, 1984), 248.

66. MacIntyre, *After Virtue*, 249.

67. Robert Nozick, *Anarchy, State, and Utopia* (New York: Basic Books, 1974), 168.

68. This picture which has even made its way into the popular press. See Randall Rothenberg, "Philosopher Robert Nozick vs. Philosopher John Rawls: Give Me Liberty or Give Me Equality," *Esquire* (March 1983).

made." (*PL*, 269) The disagreement between Rawls and Nozick concerns which are the just institutions and procedures within which individuals and associations pursue their goals and acquire their specific entitlements.[69] As Rawls puts it: "We have a right to our natural abilities and a right to whatever we become entitled to by taking part in a fair social process. The problem is to characterize this process."[70] Nozick simply begs the question against Rawls when he asserts that "Patterned principles of distributive justice necessitate *re-distributive* activities."[71] Different institutional schemes will, of course, result in different allocations of goods, but they only *re*-distribute relative to some other distributive mechanism that is viewed as legitimate. While Rawls is explicitly concerned with the justice of these background institutional structures, Nozick does not confront this issue directly, assuming instead that a libertarian scheme is obviously correct.[72]

Reflective Equilibrium

One of the remarkable features of *A Theory of Justice* when it was published in 1971, was that it actually proposed and defended ground-level principles to be used in making certain moral judgments. It was not preoccupied, as so much moral philosophy was at the time, with linguistic, metaphysical and methodological concerns. Rawls wanted to make and defend moral judgments, not simply to analyze them from a detached point of view. In the preface, Rawls remarks: "I have avoided extensive methodological discussions. . . . Occasionally there are methodological comments and asides, but for the most part I try to work out a substantive theory of justice." (*TJ*, ix [xix]) Nonetheless, philosophers have often concentrated on Rawls's method, and the result has been confusion. Especially since the publication of *Political Liberalism*, the secondary literature has tended to lose sight of the relationship among the basic building blocks of justice as fairness. We need to clarify the relationship among

---

69. Brian Barry claims of Nozick's reading of Rawls on this point: "Seldom in the history of political philosophy can a criticism have been so hopelessly misdirected." (*Justice As Impartiality* [New York: Oxford University Press, 1995], 213.) See also Pogge, *Realizing Rawls*, chapter 1.

70. John Rawls, "A Well-Ordered Society" in *Philosophy, Politics and Society*, fifth series, Peter Laslett and James Fishkin, eds. (New Haven: Yale University Press, 1979), 16. See also Jeremy Waldron, *The Right to Private Property* (New York: Oxford University Press, 1988), 403-404.

71. Nozick, *Anarchy, State, and Utopia*, 168, my emphasis.

72. Many critics have pointed out that Nozick fails to make explicit the scheme on which his argument relies, apparently assuming that this can be done without controversy. See, for example, Thomas Nagel, "Libertarianism without Foundations," *The Yale Law Journal* 85, no. 136 (1975); and Thomas Scanlon, "Nozick on Rights, Liberty, and Property," *Philosophy and Public Affairs* 6, no. 1 (fall 1976).

reflective equilibrium, the original position, the model-conception of the person, the idea of an overlapping consensus, and public reason.

We can begin to sort out these elements by keeping firmly in mind the practical task of justice as fairness.[73] The goal has always been and continues to be to make proper and correct judgments about how the basic structure of society in modern circumstances should be arranged, or, more specifically, which principles we should rely on when making such judgments. The answer to this question, Rawls believes, is not obvious. From a philosophical point of view, there might seem to be two distinct reasons for the difficulty in identifying such principles. We might worry about the basis on which we can appropriately make any such normative judgments. We might think, for example, that the challenge of a global normative skepticism must be refuted before we can responsibly proceed. Alternatively, our worry might be exactly the opposite. Far from being concerned about the possibility that we will be unable to make any substantive judgments, we might think that the values, goals, and ideals that are relevant to such judgments are varied, complex, and difficult to reconcile with one another. Many considerations seem to pull in different directions. For Rawls, the source of difficulty in working out a conception of justice is emphatically the latter. Only if we were in the grip of a metaphysical theory, he suggests, would we worry about the very possibility of making normative judgments in the first place. Justice as fairness does not confront such normative skepticism directly at its own level. Instead, it relentlessly attempts a practical refutation: it ratchets down the discussion to the ground level of normative principles and asks what the practical implications are of various meta-ethical commitments at the level of substantive principles.

For Rawls, then, the difficulty of identifying the proper principles of justice for the basic structure is not a global skepticism but the relevance of many potentially conflicting considerations. He is particularly interested in the apparent conflict between two values that have figured prominently in the history of Western political philosophy: freedom and equality. Thus, Rawls writes that the point of justice as fairness "is to see whether we can resolve the impasse in our recent political history; namely, that there is no agreement on the way basic social institutions should be arranged if they are to conform to the freedom and equality of citizens as persons." (*PL*, 300; cf. *TJ*, 204 [179]) The problem is not simply that one individual is committed to freedom while another is attracted by equality. Each of us, he supposes, feels the pull of these two ideals. In this sense, the goal of justice as fairness is to generate a practical reconciliation of these values.[74]

---

73. Although I call this a "practical" task, it should not be confused with a different sense in which justice as fairness is sometimes thought to be "practical." Political liberalism does not aim to find a compromise among existing comprehensive doctrines. That would make it "political in the wrong way." (*PL*, 40)

74. Several authors have noticed how Rawls's project resembles Hegel's idea of

In the most general sense, Rawls's "method" is characterized by his attempt to reconcile these different commitments. It is an attempt to reach "reflective equilibrium." This is in a broad sense a coherentist project since there is no attempt to reduce moral claims to a self-evident and secure foundation: "A conception of justice cannot be deduced from self-evident premises or conditions on principles; instead, its justification is a matter of the mutual support of many considerations, of everything fitting together into one coherent view." (*TJ*, 21 [19]; cf. 578-579 [506-507]) The "everything" which is to fit together includes, but is not limited to, particular judgments concerning which actions and institutions are just or unjust, as well as more general principles and considerations, and still more abstract models of the person and society. We come to the project of identifying principles of justice with some provisional moral commitments and knowledge. The judgments about which we are most confident—Rawls mentions our belief that "religious intolerance and racial discrimination are unjust" as examples—are "provisional fixed points which we presume any conception of justice must fit." (*TJ*, 19-20 [17-18]) The idea, simply put, is that in the project of constructing our conception of justice, we should work from whichever relevant considerations have our highest level of confidence.

The common understanding of reflective equilibrium, I think, portrays it as asserting that moral truth is whatever fits our existing fixed points. On this understanding, we have essentially a curve-fitting problem: we attempt to identify a "covering law" that subsumes our particular moral intuitions, hopefully with simplicity and elegance. A few things Rawls says may encourage such a picture. For example, he writes: "There is a definite if limited class of facts against which conjectured principles can be checked, namely, our considered judgments in reflective equilibrium." (*TJ*, 51 [44])[75] Similarly, he compares the project of moral theory to that of a linguist attempting to describe the grammar of a natural language. (*TJ*, 47 [41]) This form of reflective equilibrium is open to two devastating objections. First, it suggests that the fixed points are to be understood on the model of observational data of a natural science. As Daniels points out, the term *moral intuition* suggests a kind of

---

reconciliation through reason, although without the metaphysical baggage. See Sybil Shwartzenbach, "Rawls, Hegel, and Communitarianism," *Political Theory* 19, no. 4 (Nov. 1991); Chandran Kukathas and Philip Pettit, *Rawls: A Theory of Justice and Its Critics* (Stanford: Stanford University Press, 1990), 144-148; Michael Hardimon, *Hegel's Social Philosophy: The Project of Reconciliation* (New York: Cambridge University Press, 1994), especially 6, 16; and Joshua Cohen, "A More Democratic Liberalism," *Michigan Law Review* 92, no. 6 (May 1994), 1507-1509.

75. As Norman Daniels cautions, however, this passage should be read to mean that "'the small but definite class' emerges *only when* reflective equilibrium is reached, and is still revisable in the light of further theory change." (Daniels, "Wide Reflective Equilibrium and Theory Acceptance in Ethics," in *Justice and Justification* [New York: Cambridge University Press, 1996], 43-44n17.)

perception into an independent moral realm, which Rawls wants to avoid.[76] Of course, even with such a perceptual model we might still revise our provisionally fixed points, as we do with our perceptual judgments when, for example, we are aware of an optical illusion. However, such revisions come about only when we cannot find a general principle that subsumes all of the fixed points and is simple enough.

This gives rise to the second objection since there seems to be no good reason to assume that a single, simple principle must be able to account for all of our fixed points. Why should we revise our beliefs just because things are complicated and we find it difficult to identify a simple covering law? Assuming that our fixed points are not logically inconsistent, we will be able to find *some* conception of justice to account for them if we allow it to be complicated enough. It looks, therefore, as though any revisions to the provisional fixed points are based on little more than aesthetic considerations: we prefer simple general principles rather than complicated conceptions. It is hard to see why such considerations should carry much (if any) weight, but there seem to be no further grounds on which to revise our fixed points.

In fact, however, this curve-fitting model does not adequately capture Rawls's considered understanding of reflective equilibrium. Using terminology that Rawls introduced in 1974,[77] this curve-fitting model captures the idea of *narrow* reflective equilibrium, in which we adjust our own general and specific moral judgments until they are brought into coherence with one another. With narrow reflective equilibrium, we select among the more general conceptions of justice "which more or less match one's existing judgments except for minor discrepancies." (*TJ*, 49)[78] *Wide* reflective equilibrium, in contrast, is not limited to systematizing our particular moral judgments. Instead, it allows us to incorporate whatever considerations may be related to our assessment of basic social justice. As Norman Daniels characterizes it, wide reflective equilibrium requires that we introduce "all the different moral and nonmoral beliefs and theories that arguably are relevant to our selection of principles or adherence to our moral judgments."[79] On this model, as Rawls points out,

> Moral philosophy is Socratic: we may want to change our present considered judgments once their regulative principles are brought to light. And we may want to

---

76. Daniels, *Justice and Justification*, 4-5, 30-31. Rawls quickly took steps to distance his account from this perceptual model: "Even the totality of particular judgments are not assigned a decisive role; thus these judgments do not have the status sometimes attributed to judgments of perception in theories of knowledge." ("The Independence of Moral Theory," 8.)

77. See Rawls, "The Independence of Moral Theory," 8. The contrast was implicit in *A Theory of Justice*, 49 [43].

78. In the revised edition of *TJ*, Rawls changes this passage slightly: "more or less as it is although allowing for the smoothing out of certain irregularities." [43]

79. Daniels, *Justice and Justification*, 2.

do this even though these principles are a perfect fit. A knowledge of these principles may suggest further reflections that lead us to revise our judgments. (*TJ*, 49)[80]

Thus, we are not taking our provisional fixed points as somehow foundational and attempting to find a covering law under which we can subsume them, but rather we are trying to *get them right* by assessing them against any other consideration we take to be relevant.

Although I have characterized wide reflective equilibrium as attempting to get our judgments right, justice as fairness is not a theory of truth for moral judgments. Rawls is not defining moral truth as whatever we believe in wide reflective equilibrium.[81] As we will see, in *A Theory of Justice* and especially more recently, Rawls has attempted to avoid metaphysical debates concerning what, if anything, makes a moral judgment true. Rather, his position is simply that the beliefs that we would hold in wide reflective equilibrium would be the beliefs that have the greatest support of the reasons available to us. Potentially, all considerations are relevant—none is ruled out ahead of time.

Understood in this way, who could possibly object to the idea of reflective equilibrium? In fact surprisingly many philosophers have objected, largely because they reject Rawls's treatment of philosophy as practical, in the sense characterized above. For example, if we thought that the (primary) goal of philosophy was to explain how it is possible to make moral judgments in the first place or to reduce moral judgments to some complicated statement of scientific fact, then we would insist on a prior exclusion of moral claims from our argument. If the skeptic must be defeated before proceeding to make any ground-level moral judgments, we must scrupulously avoid relying on any normative assumptions that the skeptic would reject. For authors pursuing this project, a logical reduction of moral claims into some secure foundation is the only way philosophy can proceed. As Richard Brandt puts it: "The fact that a person has a firm normative conviction gives that belief a status no better than fiction. Is one coherent set of fictions supposed to be better than another?"[82] If it is possible that our provisional fixed points are mistaken, the attempt to establish coherence among them will amount to "no more than a re-shuffling of moral prejudices."[83] Rather than accepting any of our moral beliefs as even provisional fixed points, Peter Singer asks, "Why should we not rather make the opposite

---

80. In the revised edition of *TJ*, Rawls changes this, but he continues to endorse the idea that moral philosophy is Socratic. See *TJ*, 578-579 [506-507].

81. This is contrary to the interpretation of Peter Singer, "Sidgwick and Reflective Equilibrium," *The Monist* 58, no. 3 (July 1974), 493, but in agreement with Norman Daniels, "Wide Reflective Equilibrium and Theory Acceptance in Ethics," 45n26.

82. Richard Brandt, *A Theory of the Good and the Right* (New York: Oxford University Press, 1979), 20.

83. Brandt, *A Theory of the Good and the Right*, 22.

assumption, that all the particular moral judgments we intuitively make are likely to derive from discarded religious systems, from warped views of sex and bodily functions, or from customs necessary for the survival of the group in social and economic circumstances that now lie in the distant past?"[84]

Critics of the idea of reflective equilibrium seek to inoculate their method from any possibly contaminated moral judgment while attempting to provide more secure foundations for their reconstruction of morality (or its superior replacement). This takes various forms but I will only mention three of them here.[85] In his review of *A Theory of Justice*, R. M. Hare chastises Rawls for not sticking to the "proper and peculiar" role for philosophers: analyzing and clarifying moral concepts and their logical properties. Rawls "run[s] the risk of doing no more for the topic of justice than journalists and politicians."[86] Instead of relying (in part) on substantial moral commitments, Hare attempts to base his moral philosophy "entirely on the formal properties of the moral concepts as revealed by the logical study of moral language."[87] In fact, Hare's method is even more restrictive, since he also rejects reliance on so-called "secondarily evaluative words" (sometimes called "thick" moral terms) such as "lazy," the use of which "commits us to substantial moral evaluations."[88] We must make do with analyses of the logic of "thin" moral terms like "ought" and "wrong." This is sufficient, Hare asserts, because a complete understanding of the formal logic of moral terms, together with all relevant non-moral facts, "constrain so severely the moral evaluations that we can make, that in practice we would be bound all to agree to the same ones."[89] This is the only way in which objective moral principles can be derived. Since Rawls does not stick to this method and instead depends on substantive moral judgments, his view is "a kind of subjectivism, in the narrowest and most old-fashioned sense."[90]

Richard Brandt agrees with Hare that we must reject Rawls's appeal to specific moral judgments. Indeed, "We must avoid intuitionism even if this were to mean (as it does not) that we must end up as complete sceptics in the area of practice."[91] However, against Hare, he argues that the linguistic analysis of

---

84. Peter Singer, "Sidgwick and Reflective Equilibrium," 516.

85. I am only considering these theories as alternative methods to reflective equilibrium. I do not take up the substantive principles that these authors endorse.

86. R. M. Hare, "Rawls' Theory of Justice," in *Reading Rawls*, Norman Daniels, ed. (New York: Basic Books, 1975; reprint, Stanford: Stanford University Press, 1989), 95.

87. R. M. Hare, "Ethical Theory and Intuitionism" in *Utilitarianism and Beyond*, Amartya Sen and Bernard Williams, eds. (New York: Cambridge University Press, 1982), 25.

88. R. M. Hare, *Moral Thinking: Its Levels, Method, and Point* (New York: Oxford University Press, 1981), 17.

89. Hare, *Moral Thinking*, 6.

90. Hare, "Rawls' Theory of Justice," 82.

91. Brandt, *A Theory of the Good and the Right*, 3. Parenthetical references in this paragraph will be to this work.

moral terms is an insufficient basis for moral theory. After all, Brandt points out, if moral philosophy is only concerned with linguistic analysis, then the most such a theory can do is to identify when a person is using a term like *ought* or *wrong* properly and when improperly. With such a theory in hand, the most we would be able to do would be to condemn a person of a linguistic infraction, and "Where is the sting of being denied the use of a certain English expression?" (9) More significantly for our purposes, however, Brandt observes that Hare's theory relies on appeals to linguistic intuitions, and there are two problems with this. First, contrary to Hare's assertions, Brandt worries that "normative words are so vague that reliance on 'linguistic intuitions' can reach no definite results." (6) Second, even if we could be assured that we have accurately identified the logic of our moral and normative terms, they "might well embody confusing distinctions, or fail to make distinctions it is important to make." (7) On reflection, we might find that our use of various terms stands in need of reformation. But on what grounds are we to propose such reforms? For Brandt, the answer comes from a theory of rational action. His idea is that it is rational to act on those beliefs and desires "which survive maximal criticism and correction by facts and logic." (10) Only if we identify which beliefs and desires are rational will we be able to identify the systems of moral principles that are rationally defensible, if any are. Brandt carefully distinguishes this project from reflective equilibrium because his "definition of 'rational', it is important to see, does not import any substantive value judgements into the concept of 'rational.'" (13) Thus, if all goes well, we will be able to defend certain moral codes as rational, based only on subjecting our existing beliefs and desires to the interrogation of non-moral facts and logic.

Finally, like Brandt, David Gauthier advocates a reconstruction of morality based on a theory of practical reason. He attempts to show "why an individual, reasoning from non-moral premises, would accept the constraints of morality on his choices."[92] He admits that the principles generated by rational choice theory may diverge to greater or lesser degrees from "the morality learned from parents and peers, priests and teachers."[93] Such a divergence should not lead us to revise the theory, however, but rather our particular moral judgments:

> If the reader is tempted to object to some part of this view, on the ground that his moral intuitions are violated, then he should ask what weight such an objection can have, if morality is to fit within the domain of rational choice. We should emphasize the radical difference between our approach, in which we ask what view of social relationships would rationally be accepted *ex ante* by individuals concerned to

---

92. David Gauthier, *Morals by Agreement* (New York: Oxford University Press, 1986), 5.

93. Gauthier, *Morals by Agreement*, 6.

maximize their utilities, from that of moral coherentists and defenders of "reflective equilibrium", who allow initial weight to our considered moral judgements.[94]

Thus, once again, a foundation for our reformed moral judgments can only be secured by excluding all of our prior moral commitments.

All three of these authors present their reductive methods as explicit alternatives to Rawls's idea of reflective equilibrium. Certainly, all three recommend methods in which we are not simply trying to identify a general rule that subsumes our particular moral judgments, and therefore they all reject narrow reflective equilibrium. There is a sense, however, in which these are not challenges to the idea of wide reflective equilibrium at all. Rather, they concern the weight to be assigned to various initial commitments in our effort to reach reflective equilibrium. Specifically, they claim, moral considerations should have no initial weight relative to other kinds of considerations such as judgments concerning the meaning of moral terms or the rationality of various beliefs and desires or the axioms of rational choice theory. As we have seen, unlike narrow reflective equilibrium, the effort to reach wide reflective equilibrium includes such judgments. These purported critics of reflective equilibrium, therefore, can be understood as advocating a particular resolution to (potential) conflicts that emerge within the effort to reach wide reflective equilibrium.

Understood in this way—as an inclusive, non-reductive approach— reflective equilibrium comes to seem rather trivial. It tells us little more than that we should attempt to determine which conception of justice has the greatest support of the reasons we can identify (of whatever kind) and that we should somehow attempt to resolve conflicts if they emerge. As far as his discussion of reflective equilibrium goes, Rawls says nothing about the weight of various considerations, and so he gives no advice ahead of time concerning the resolution of potential conflicts: "It is a mistake to think of abstract conceptions and general principles as always overriding our more particular judgments. These two sides of our practical thought (not to mention intermediate levels of generality in between) are complementary, and to be adjusted to one another so as to fit into a coherent view." (*PL*, 45)[95] If by a *method* we mean a procedure that will itself resolve conflicts, reflective equilibrium is no method at all. In fact, it is simply a statement of inclusion: a rejection of any and all prior restrictions on what is to count as relevant in attempting to reach our goal.

---

94. Gauthier, *Morals by Agreement*, 269.

95. Compare Gauthier, who advocates "Trusting theory rather than intuition" (*Morals by Agreement*, 269), and Thomas Nagel, who believes "one should trust . . . intuitions over argument, and pluralistic discord over systematic harmony. Simplicity and elegance are never reasons to think that a philosophical theory is true: on the contrary, they are usually grounds for thinking it false." (*Mortal Questions* [New York: Cambridge University Press, 1979], x)

Why, then, do critics think they are rejecting reflective equilibrium? I believe there are two reasons. First, if one is convinced that Rawls's idea of reflective equilibrium is supposed to be a more substantial procedure, one may be tempted to see it as a metaphysical thesis about the status of moral truth. The thought is that Rawls must be claiming that the fact that we hold a judgment in reflective equilibrium is itself what (metaphysically) makes that judgment true. But this is confused. The support for the judgment is to be found in the considerations that are relevant and relied on within the process of reaching reflective equilibrium, not in the fact of the reflective equilibrium itself. Hare complains that Rawls fails to understand "the essentially simple distinction . . . between the view that thinking something can make it so (which is in general false) and the view that if we are to say something sincerely, we must be able to accept it (which is a tautology)."[96] Hare gets the distinction precisely right. The mystery is why he thinks that Rawls is committed to the first rather than to the second claim. Nothing Rawls says suggests that our thinking something makes it so. Everything suggests that his concern is the practical one of identifying which conception has the greatest support of reason. Rawls makes no claims about the metaphysical conditions of moral truth.

The second reason that some reject reflective equilibrium is that, as we have seen, they want to rule out ahead of time the relevance of moral considerations. Contrary to Rawls, whose practical project is to identify which moral judgments are correct, they conceive moral philosophy as a reductive project. They are often convinced that for meta-ethical reasons the entire edifice of morality is in danger unless a secure foundation can be provided from the outside. This worry may be elicited by the thought that there is a fundamental problem understanding how values can fit into a scientific metaphysic. J. L. Mackie's famous argument that moral properties are too "queer" to fit into our basic picture of the world, and Gilbert Harman's claim that the attribution of moral properties carries no explanatory weight are examples of this type of argument.[97]

I have already suggested, however, that even these considerations, based on a kind of global skepticism, can be incorporated in the attempt to reach reflective equilibrium. There is no need to constrain the procedure from the outside. If it turned out that our best metaphysical theories made it impossible to understand how we could make (and defend) objective moral judgments, then we would have a problem, since we would not (yet) have achieved reflective equilibrium. However, it is not obvious what conclusion we should draw if that situation arose. One person's *modus ponens* is another's *modus tollens*. We could give up either our moral claims or our metaphysical understanding, if they

---

96. Hare, "Rawls' Theory of Justice," 83.

97. J. L. Mackie, *Ethics: Inventing Right and Wrong* (New York: Penguin, 1977); Gilbert Harman, *The Nature of Morality* (New York: Oxford University Press, 1977). See also Gauthier, *Morals by Agreement*, 55-59.

are incompatible. The choice we would make would depend, in part, on the strength and content of our commitments to each.

Suppose we had an apparently strong metaphysical argument the conclusion of which was that no moral judgments were, in fact, defensible. The conclusion of such a scorching skepticism, as Ronald Dworkin has recently pointed out, would come into conflict with the view, for example, that there is something morally objectionable about "exterminating an ethnic group or enslaving a race or torturing a young child, just for fun, in front of its captive mother." We would be forced to ask ourselves which of these views to abandon. Dworkin writes:

> That is not a question of where a burden of proof lies, but of what, considering each possibility as fully as we can, and noting its implications for the rest of what we think, we find that we believe. Of course I do not mean that our convictions are right just because we find them irresistible, or that our inability to think anything else is a reason or ground or argument supporting our judgment. On the contrary, these suggestions are forms of the skepticism I am opposing. I mean that any reason we think we have for abandoning a conviction is itself just another conviction, and that we can do no better for any claim, including the most sophisticated skeptical argument or thesis, than to see whether, after the best thought we find appropriate, we think it is so.[98]

We can put the point in terms of a dilemma: either meta-ethical considerations conflict with ground-level moral judgments or else they do not. If they do not, they are simply changing the subject since they are not relevant to our question of which principles of justice to endorse. On the other hand, if they do conflict with some moral judgments, we must decide which to abandon, and the attempt to resolve this conflict just is the attempt to reach reflective equilibrium. The only way to resolve such a conflict, of course, is to consider the arguments for and against the metaphysical view and for and against the moral judgment(s). However, we do not know what the best arguments for a moral judgment are until we identify our best moral theory. As Nagel observes: "Rawls believes that it will be more profitable to investigate the foundations of ethics when there are more substantive ethical results to seek the foundations of."[99] The claim, therefore, that our considered moral judgments should have no credibility is, as Daniels points out, "at best premature."[100]

The mistaken interpretation of reflective equilibrium as a new method of ethical investigation is a result of philosophers' obsession with one or another form of skepticism and reductionism. Only in a context in which the ability to make moral judgments in the first place was in question would the idea of reflective equilibrium seem to be anything but a triviality. Justice as fairness

---

98. Ronald Dworkin, "Objectivity and Truth: You'd Better Believe It," *Philosophy and Public Affairs* 25, no. 2 (spring 1996), 117-118.

99. Thomas Nagel, "Rawls on Justice," in *Reading Rawls*, Daniels, ed., 2.

100. Daniels, "Wide Reflective Equilibrium and Theory Acceptance in Ethics," 31.

does indeed take that ability for granted; Rawls is not proposing that the radical skeptic is somehow defeated by reflective equilibrium. Rather, reflective equilibrium is an expression of Rawls's attitude that the skeptic is to be ignored, at least until we have identified the most compelling case that we can for our favored conception of justice. As I noted at the beginning of this section, *A Theory of Justice* broke ground simply by attempting the practical task of identifying the ground-level principles to be used in making judgments concerning basic social justice. Reflective equilibrium does not tell us how to proceed in this search, only that we can proceed without first attempting to identify a self-evident or logically necessary foundation. The action of justice as fairness is found not in these broad methodological considerations, but rather in the reasons cited in attempting to work out a specific conception of justice.

The Model-Conceptions[101]

Recall, then, the circumstances for which we are considering the virtue of justice. Individuals are assumed to have diverse goals and interests that, although reasonable, may conflict with each other. Social institutions, on the one hand, mediate these conflicts and interactions, but on the other hand, these institutions are sustained and transformed only in virtue of attitudes and actions of individuals and groups. In a sense, all social institutions can be said to mediate the actions of individuals and groups, but *just* social institutions mediate these interactions *fairly*. Thus, Rawls characterizes a well-ordered society as "a fair system of cooperation over time, from one generation to the next." (*PL*, 15) This model of a just society is very abstract and may not appear to be helpful since we obviously must specify it further. Nonetheless, this characterization of society is "the fundamental organizing idea of justice as fairness, within which the other basic ideas are systematically connected." (*PL*, 15) This is because cooperation, as Rawls understands it, is not merely coordinated social activity. Cooperation, unlike mere coordination, "is guided by publicly recognized rules and procedures that those cooperating accept and regard as properly regulating their conduct." (*PL*, 16)

In addition to the rules of social interaction being public, cooperation implies that these rules are (in some sense still to be specified) acceptable to those subject to them. In a crucial passage, Rawls writes:

> Cooperation involves the idea of fair terms of cooperation: these are terms that each participant may reasonably accept, provided that everyone else likewise accepts them. Fair terms of cooperation specify an idea of reciprocity: all who are engaged

---

101. In his "Dewey Lectures," Rawls refers to the ideas of a well-ordered society and of a person as "model-conceptions." (See "Kantian Constructivism in Moral Theory: The Dewey Lectures 1980," *The Journal of Philosophy* 77, no. 9 [Sept. 1980], 520.) In *Political Liberalism*, however, he does not use this phrase.

in cooperation and who do their part as the rules and procedure require, are to benefit in an appropriate way as assessed by a suitable benchmark of comparison. (*PL*, 16)

The idea of reciprocity is central to justice as fairness. To begin to clarify this idea, let us contrast it with the approach which has dominated political and moral philosophy from Plato to contemporary accounts. On this dominant teleological approach, political theory proceeds by first attempting to provide an independent account of the good (or well-being or value or excellence) and then arguing that one or another institutional arrangement generates this good to a greater degree than others. There are two versions of this approach which are commonly thought to exhaust the possibilities.

According to the first version, the good that is to be maximized is objective and independent of the beliefs and subjective preferences of any individuals. J. Donald Moon calls this approach "the politics of virtue" and comments that "The idea that our political lives should be structured to realize a specific ideal of human well-being and/or excellence appears in many different guises, a commonality united such otherwise diverse thinkers as Aristotle and Hobbes, or John Stuart Mill and Marx."[102] Some theorists are skeptical of the existence of such a good and pursue the second version. They argue that the good is not a unified object that can be maximized, but rather consists in a plurality of goods, each tied to a distinct individual. On this approach, one's good may be more or less closely related to one's current preferences or desires, but in any case it is only one's own good that provides one with a reason to act. Each individual is responsible for making her own conception of the good internally coherent, but this does not eliminate the possibility, indeed the likelihood of conflicts among different individuals' conceptions of the good. Principles of justice are concerned with mediating the conflicts among the goods of different individuals. But why should individuals who only care about their own good be concerned with such an impersonal perspective and the principles of justice? The answer, on this approach, is that they will care about them only to the extent that they make an instrumental contribution to the pursuit of their own good. On this second version, then, principles of justice must be mutually advantageous as measured strictly by each individual's own good.

By starting with society as a fair system of cooperation, justice as fairness is committed to rejecting the traditional model in both its forms. Justice as fairness does not hold that there is a prior and independent good to be maximized. Instead, it recognizes that each individual has a conception of the good—a system of reasonable goals that the individual judges to be worth pursuing. Without such a conception of the good, justice would have no point, since individuals would be indifferent as to how social resources were used. (Without

---

102. J. Donald Moon, *Constructing Community* (Princeton: Princeton University Press, 1993), 6.

potentially conflicting conceptions of the good, recall, there would be no occasion for justice.) On the other hand, there is no thought that justice can be reduced to mutual advantage. As we have seen, the stability of a just society depends on an independent commitment to justice—independent of the specific content of the individual's conception of the good—and shared throughout a well-ordered society. Fairness and reciprocity depend on the existence of, but are not reducible to, the conceptions of the good held by various individuals.

We will return to the idea of "terms that each participant may reasonably accept," but let us now consider how we must conceive of individuals if society is to be a fair system of cooperation from one generation to the next. It is important to emphasize that this model is designed for the purpose of constructing principles of basic social justice. Obviously, other features will be relevant for other purposes. Rawls claims that for this purpose, we should rely on a model of the person that attributes to individuals two moral powers: a sense of justice and a capacity for a conception of the good. If society is to be a fair system of cooperation, then in addition to a specific conception of the good, individuals must also have these two moral powers.

The first moral power, a sense of justice, "is the capacity to understand, to apply, and to act from the public conception of justice which characterizes the fair terms of social cooperation." (*PL*, 19) As we have seen, a fair system of cooperation is based on the idea of reciprocity and requires that the terms of interaction be those that "each participant may reasonably accept." Therefore, having a sense of justice implies "a willingness, if not the desire, to act in relation to others on terms that they also can publicly endorse." (*PL*, 19) The second moral power consists in the "capacity to form, to revise, and rationally to pursue a conception of one's rational advantage or good." (*PL*, 19) As Sam Freeman has put it recently, this capacity means that we can "take responsibility for our lives."[103] In addition to this capacity, we assume that "persons also have at any given time a determinate conception of the good that they try to achieve." (*PL*, 19) Thus, as Rawls explains:

> Social cooperation is always for mutual benefit and this implies that it involves two elements: the first is a shared notion of fair terms of cooperation, which each participant may reasonably be expected to accept, provided that everyone else likewise accepts them. . . . This element in social cooperation I call "the reasonable." The other element corresponds to "the rational": it refers to each participant's rational advantage; what, as individuals, the participants are trying to advance. Whereas the notion of fair terms of cooperation is shared, participants' conceptions of their own rational advantage in general differ. The unity of social cooperation rests on persons agreeing to its notion of fair terms. (*PL*, 300-301)

---

103. See Samuel Freeman's contribution to the BEARS online symposium on John Kekes's "A Question for Egalitarians," <http://www.brown.edu/Departments/Philosophy/bears/9802free.html>.

We can label the two moral powers in this model by saying that persons are assumed to be both reasonable—because of their capacity to honor fair terms of cooperation—and rational—because of the capacity for a conception of the good.

Since justice as fairness requires that each individual benefit from cooperation in a fair institutional scheme, we need some way of assessing each individual's advantage. This is a serious problem because justice as fairness assumes that individuals hold diverse conceptions of the good, so there is no obvious metric with which to assess success across different individuals. We will return to this problem in the next chapter. Although this claim about diversity may seem to conflict with my earlier claim that justice as fairness does not take a position on the ultimate metaphysical structure of values—whether there is one or many—it does not. The assumption, here, as before, is that different individuals reasonably affirm diverse conceptions of the good. What we have now added is that the society is understood as a fair system of cooperation, that is, one that participants can reasonably accept from their own points of view. Therefore, regardless of what we take the ultimate structure of values to be, if justice requires reciprocity and people hold diverse conceptions of the good, then we must respect the diverse values that reasonable individuals will use when assessing the principles of justice from their own point of view. Even if we hold a position of value monism, if we view a just society as a fair system of cooperation, we must respect the diversity of reasonable comprehensive doctrines.

There are broadly two types of objections to this model of reasonable and rational persons: it might be thought to be too thick, because it includes too many undefended requirements; or it might be thought to be too thin, because it provides an insufficient basis for substantive moral reflection. We will first look at the objection that it is too thick and relies on too many restrictive requirements before briefly considering the objection that it is too thin and should include a richer description of the person. The first charge is the more serious, since it is alleged that the model of the person makes the theory too exclusive. Individuals who do not meet the requirements are left out and are not provided with an account of the principles of justice that they could accept from within their own comprehensive doctrine.

Given the understanding of the basic structure that we have assumed, it is hard to see how one might think we could get by without postulating the first moral power, a sense of justice. As we have seen, the basic structure of society is not an object that is independent of the actions and attitudes of the individuals living in society. Nor can we expect a just society to continue to exist "from one generation to the next" unless it has the active support of the individuals living in it. A just basic structure must draw its support from its citizens. Furthermore, we cannot expect this support to come from the purely instrumental calculations of individuals concerned solely with pursuing their own conception of the good.

Justice as fairness rejects the model of justice as mutual advantage. The stability of a just basic structure depends on the willingness of individuals and groups to support those institutions for moral reasons. Furthermore, it requires that, at least in normal circumstances, citizens be willing to sacrifice the pursuit of their own conceptions of the good to follow the requirements of justice. Even when they could get away with violating the requirements of the basic structure, individuals are (generally) unwilling to take advantage of these opportunities. As Rawls puts it, in a well-ordered society, "the general desire for justice limits the pursuit of other ends." (*TJ*, 5 [5])

Thus, while the two moral powers are "distinct in that there is no thought of deriving one from the other," (*PL*, 51) we must grant the sense of justice normative priority over the conception of the good when they come into conflict (again, at least in normal circumstances). Without this priority, a well-ordered society would not be stably just. Thus: "In justice as fairness the priority of right means that the principles of political justice impose limits on permissible ways of life; and hence the claims citizens make to pursue ends that transgress those limits have no weight." (*PL*, 174)[104] It is worth anticipating that the conception of justice that we will ultimately endorse will attempt to be compatible with as wide a range of reasonable comprehensive doctrines as possible. This means that, at least relative to alternative conceptions of justice, the occasions on which its principles will be incompatible with a reasonable conception of the good are likely to be less frequent.

Now consider the second moral power. Rawls insists that it includes three capacities: "to form, to revise, and rationally to pursue a conception of one's rational advantage."[105] Unfortunately, he has not adequately explained the grounds for his assertion, and he has been roundly criticized on this point even by those who are generally sympathetic to his approach. Most critics would agree, I take it, that we must assume that each individual has a conception of the good—a system of ends he or she believes to be worth pursuing. The question is: Why must we assume, in addition, these three capacities? Moon, for example, claims that such an assumption works to exclude from consideration people "for whom the capacity for agency may be overridden by their particular moral beliefs or religious views."[106] The thought seems to be that Rawls is insisting

---

104. We will return to discuss the priority of right in chapter 4.

105. In *A Theory of Justice*, Rawls only assumes that moral persons "are capable of having (and are assumed to have) a conception of their good." (*TJ*, 505 [442]) and did not specify the capacities to form, to revise, and rationally to pursue it. This changed in his "Reply to Alexander and Musgrave," *Quarterly Journal of Economics* 88 (1974), 641. Compare the revised edition of *TJ* [131-132, 475]. See also the discussion in Allen Buchanan, "Revisability and Rational Choice," *The Canadian Journal of Philosophy* 5, no. 3 (Nov. 1975).

106. Moon, *Constructing Community*, 57. See also Will Kymlicka, "Two Models of Pluralism and Tolerance," in *Toleration: An Elusive Virtue*, David Heyd, ed. (Princeton:

that one must live a life the values of which are one's own creation, the result of one's deliberate choices. The normative authority of our values is supposed to derive from an act of choice rather than from their content. The problem is that this view would be rejected by those who view themselves as part of a tradition, such as a religion, that is not of their own creation. Rawls certainly would want to include these people and has given no grounds for excluding them. Although it may turn out that some ways of life are incompatible with principles of justice, we surely do not yet have adequate grounds in this type of case.

Here we must be very careful in order to distinguish justice as fairness from traditional (comprehensive) forms of liberalism. Consider a common reading of one strand of argument in John Stuart Mill's *On Liberty*. Mill argues in favor of "individuality" in one's "mode of life": "Where not the person's own character but the traditions or customs of other people are the rule of conduct, there is wanting one of the principal ingredients of human happiness, and quite the chief ingredient of individual and social progress."[107] Ignore the second argument, that relying on one's character leads to "individual and social progress," and consider the claim that taking your rule of conduct from custom or other people deprives you of "one of the principal ingredients of human happiness." If we identify human happiness with our good, as Mill does, we get a strong argument for the importance of exercising choice in determining our mode of life. Not only must we have the capacity to make such choices, but in addition, if we fail to exercise this power to choose our mode of life for ourselves, we will necessarily fail to achieve our good. As John Gray reconstructs the argument, Mill believes that "the idea of autonomous choice . . . is a necessary ingredient of any higher pleasure and of any form of life or activity expressive of individuality."[108] For Mill, of course, the higher pleasures are important ingredients in every good human life. Thus, a life in which tradition is passively accepted is less good than one of active choice.

Justice as fairness does not make this argument. Although critics often falsely attribute this view to Rawls, justice as fairness does not assume that one's conception of the good carries normative force only if it has been the product of self-conscious, deliberate choice. Justice as fairness requires far less. In fact, it assumes just what it says: persons have the capacity to form, to revise, and rationally to pursue a conception of their good. Rawls makes the point clearly enough: "Of course, many persons may not examine their acquired

---

Princeton University Press, 1996); and my discussion in chapter 4.

107. J. S. Mill, *On Liberty*, Elizabeth Rapaport, ed. (Indianapolis: Hackett, 1978), 54.

108. John Gray, *Mill on Liberty: A Defense*, second edition (New York: Routledge, 1996, first edition, 1983), 70. According to Gray, although necessary, autonomous choice is not a sufficient condition: "Mill's view is not, indeed, that highly autonomous men are bound to be happy, but rather that autonomous thought and action is a necessary feature of the life of a man who enjoys the higher pleasures." (72)

beliefs and ends but take them on faith, or be satisfied that they are matters of custom and tradition. They are not to be criticized for this." (*PL*, 314)

Part of the confusion on this point may be explained by the following observations. In the next chapter, we will see that for certain special purposes, Rawls requires that we look only at the model-conception of the person, without taking notice of the determinate conception of the good that an individual may be attempting to advance. When we take such a restricted view, there will naturally be an emphasis on the two moral powers. Furthermore, as we will see, we can understand these moral powers as giving rise to two "'higher-order interests' in developing and exercising [each of] these powers." (*PL*, 74) Some have thought that Rawls places too much emphasis on these higher-order interests and that he assumes choice is always more important than what is chosen. We will see in detail that this is mistaken, but for now notice that Rawls only insists that citizens have a higher-order interest in maintaining their second moral power (their capacity for a conception of the good) at a level above a certain minimal threshold. Without the capacities associated with this second moral power, Rawls claims, a citizen "cannot be a normal and fully cooperating member of society over a complete life." (*PL*, 74; cf. 18, 300-301) Our question now is: Why is this power necessary for participation in a scheme of social cooperation?

Recall that the second moral power involves the capacities to form, to revise and rationally to pursue a conception of the good. The capacity to form a conception of the good should be uncontroversial, since without this capacity individuals would never come to have a conception of the good in the first place. Still, some might think that justice as fairness requires that we be able to choose a conception of the good instantly, by a pure act of will, without relying on any presuppositions. This, too, is wrong, and it is hard to know why such a view is so often attributed to Rawls. Rawls associates a conception of the good with a "rational plan of life." (*TJ*, 92-93 [79-80]) This could give the impression that Rawls requires us to once and for all choose a complete plan for our entire life, but Rawls denies this: "We must not imagine that a rational plan is a detailed blueprint for action stretching over the whole course of a life. It consists of a hierarchy of plans, the more specific subplans being filled in at the appropriate time." (*TJ*, 410 [360]) Typically, as we work out the details of a plan, and hence the details of a conception of the good, we are relying on higher-order elements. As we live our lives, we form and pursue our plan against a background of other values already in place.

Similarly, it would also be hard to see any objection to the capacity to pursue one's conception of the good in a rational manner. Unless one's conception of the good is rationally action-guiding, it is doing no work at all. We should not underestimate what is involved in being able to apply a conception of the good. At least instrumental reasoning is necessary. We must be able to identify the means with which we can accomplish our ends (at least to a certain extent). Given an end, we assume that we have the capacity to identify the causal means with which we can bring about our goal—which levers to push, so to speak. Of course, we are not infallible in our abilities, but unless we have this capacity to a minimal degree, our conception of the good would not be action-guiding in any recognizable sense. As we will see below, however, more than instrumental reasoning is required.

Clearly, the capacity to revise one's conception of the good is the most controversial element of the second moral power. Critics have charged that by insisting on the capacity to revise our conception of the good, Rawls is improperly ruling out certain comprehensive doctrines. As noted above, some critics charge that a conception of the good based on religious faith may be incompatible with the assumption that it is rationally revisable. Part of the content of this conception of the good, one might say, is precisely that it is not amenable to rational reconstruction and revision. Perhaps this system of ends is thought to be a gift from God. Such an example, however, is not incompatible with Rawls's model. In order to conflict with the model, we need an example in which the content of the conception of the good is incompatible with the *capacity* to choose an alternative conception, not only with the *desirability* of doing so. As we have seen, as long as the conception of the good is compatible with the principles of justice there is no requirement (from the point of view of justice) that people engage in any particular degree of critical reflection. Unlike some forms of liberalism, justice as fairness does not require that individuals constantly choose original conceptions of the good. The assumption that people have the capacity to revise their conception of the good requires far less than is commonly thought and is compatible with most forms of faith.

Consider what happens when the most effective (or only available) means with which to realize one's conception of the good come into conflict with the requirements of justice. Recall that we are attempting to generate a model of the person based on what is required in order to be a fully cooperating member of a well-ordered society, conceived of as a fair system of cooperation. As we have seen, the stability of such a system depends on citizens' effective sense of justice, which normally overrides their conception of the good when they conflict. Citizens must "conform their conceptions of their good to what the principles of justice require, or at least not to press claims which directly violate them." (*TJ*, 31 [27]) If there is a chance that citizens' conceptions of the good might conflict with the requirements of justice, the stability of a well-ordered society will require that citizens be able to revise their conceptions of the good.

I mentioned above that the ability to identify the causal means to a given end is a requirement of being able to pursue one's conception of the good in a rational manner. In addition, however, given a general specification of an end, we need to be able to determine what accomplishing that end would consist of, given specific circumstances and context.[109] The fact that we must apply abstract formulations to concrete circumstances in order to determine what specifically they require in some particular context reminds us that we have ends at many levels of generality and abstraction. This introduces an unavoidable complexity into any reasonable system of ends. Any conception of the good is composed of general long-term goals, more immediate instrumental means to those ends, as well as many levels in between. We can only work out the details of a long-range plan as we come to know the specific circumstances in which we find ourselves and judge how to pursue our goals from where we are. As Elijah Millgram has recently argued, we must recognize that "Genuine novelty is an inescapable feature of our world."[110] There is simply no way to tell ahead of time when we might find ourselves in circumstances in which the pursuit of our conception of the good may conflict with the demands of justice. Given the requirements of participation in a fair system of cooperation, this means that we must have the capacity to revise our conception of the good.

In fact, this point holds even in the absence of conflict between one's conception of the good and the requirements of justice: it is always possible that as we work out our conception of the good in particular circumstances, there may emerge internal conflicts.[111] As Millgram observes: "We live in a world in which ends or goals or desires conflict, that is, in which desires that one has cannot be jointly satisfied. Such conflicts are pervasive; it is *normally* true that, for any desire one has, one has a conflicting desire."[112]

Consider a typical case. Jane holds a conception of the good according to which she values her family life, her career, and her participation in the civic life of her community. If she were concerned only with one of these, she could easily devote much more of her time and energy to it. Sooner or later, circumstances will arise when these goals come into conflict with one another. Her child will be sick on the night of a school board meeting, or her work will keep her late the night of the school play, or her husband can only get work in

---

109. Some authors think of these as both aspects of instrumental reasoning. See Bernard Williams, "Internal and External Reasons," in *Moral Luck* (New York: Cambridge University Press, 1981). Christine Korsgaard argues against this in "The Normativity of Instrumental Reason," in *Ethics and Practical Reason*, Garrett Cullity and Berys Gaut, eds. (New York: Oxford University Press, 1997), 216.

110. Elijah Millgram, *Practical Induction* (Cambridge: Harvard University Press, 1997), 6. On the impossibility of an abstract statement of a conception of the good that could be specific in all possible circumstances, see his chapters 4 and 5.

111. It is (in part) for this reason that Amy Gutmann is correct when she observes that "The skills of political reflection cannot be neatly differentiated from the skills involved in evaluating one's own way of life." ("Civic Education and Social Diversity," *Ethics* 105, no. 3 [April 1995], 578)

112. Elijah Millgram, "Incommensurability and Practical Reason," in *Incommensurability, Incomparability, and Practical Reason*, Ruth Chang, ed. (Cambridge: Harvard University Press, 1997), 153.

another town. She cannot pursue all of her ends fully. If these conflicts are rare, she might try to balance these commitments as best she can without making any fundamental shifts. She will simply make modifications in her plans as circumstances dictate. Although she may have rules of thumb to help with making such decisions, there is no way to anticipate all of the situations in which she will have to make such choices. If she retains a commitment to these three ends, she must be able to reflect on and revise intermediate-level plans when necessary. Although her final ends may not change, the intermediate levels are frequently in flux, dictated by choices made in light of the specific circumstances. This means that her interpretation and understanding of each of these ends changes. She thought that being an active community member required going to all of the school board meetings, but when her child becomes sick, she realizes that this is not actually necessary. On the other hand, if these conflicts are frequent and fundamental enough and she feels that she cannot adequately meet her responsibilities in one of the areas, she might seek to make a major change in her responsibilities—quit her job, resign from the school board, or move to be with her husband. In either case, whether the revisions are at intermediate levels or at fundamental levels, she must have the capacity to reinterpret and revise her conception of the good.

Perhaps it will be said that this example is misleading since it relies on a plurality of fundamental values that may come into conflict. So let us consider another example. Jim's conception of the good is based on a single authoritative source: the Bible. Once again, however, it is clear that to serve as a guide, the Bible must be interpreted in light of the specific decisions an individual faces in a particular context. Not only are there different interpretations of the Bible, but different parts of the Bible may very well suggest different courses of action in a particular situation. Again, there is no way to anticipate ahead of time the full details of a particular situation in which abstract principles may come into conflict. When this happens, we must have some way of revising our interpretations or specifications of those principles. Once again, even without revising a fundamental commitment to follow the teachings of the Bible, a follower must have the ability to reflect on and revise his more specific goals in light of interpretations and applications and cannot be fully anticipated.

The arguments I made in the cases of Jane and Jim both rely on the complexity of ends and the need to make choices among them in particular circumstances. Consider a third example, which might be thought to avoid this problem: the classical hedonist who is concerned only to maximize her own total utility as determined by the satisfaction of her preferences. Even in this case, however, there is the potential for conflicts that must somehow be resolved. All of us have, at any given moment, a wide variety of preferences and plans that are in the process of being carried out. Some require delayed gratification, while others result in immediate pleasure. Even the egoist will have to make decisions concerning how to balance these, and this requires critical reflection on her preferences. Sometimes she will have to revise her plans in light of unanticipated circumstances and she will have to decide how to resolve conflicts among her various preferences and plans. Rawls's second moral power is not incompatible with such fanatical devotion to a single end (although requirement of a sense of justice certainly is). What Rawls does rule out with the second moral power is someone who is only capable of acting on her immediate inclinations. This is not much of a loss, since such an individual would hardly be recognizable as a person at all.[113]

Now it might be objected that in these examples the individuals are not really changing their conception of the good because they are always making revisions on the basis of other values they hold and do not revise. They are only adjusting elements in their conception of the good. Once again, this objection misunderstands what Rawls's model requires. The second moral power does not require that one's conception of the good be made from a detached point of view, removed from all values and contingent influences. As we have seen, Rawls agrees that the environment in which we are socialized shapes our values and ends. Even when we do make deliberate choices, we do so from within a particular social context. Justice as fairness disputes none of these obvious points. It does insist, however, that for the purpose of constructing principles of justice, none of these values or ends be placed permanently beyond reflection and reconsideration. As Will Kymlicka puts the point:

> What is central to the liberal view is . . . that we understand ourselves to be prior to our ends, *in the sense that no end or goal is exempt from possible re-examination.* . . . There must always be some ends given with the self when we engage in such reasoning, but it doesn't follow that any *particular* ends must always be taken as given with the self.[114]

The capacity to revise our conception of the good does not require that we be able to transform our conception of the good in an arbitrary and baseless way from some transhistorical perspective. Nor, for that matter, does Rawls assume that the revision of one's ends can come easily or instantaneously as a simple act of will. On the contrary, he writes: "I shall assume that human actions spring from existing desires and that these can be changed only gradually. We cannot just decide at a given moment to alter our system of ends." (*TJ*, 568 [498]; cf. 415 [364-365])

---

113. For accounts of such a creature, see Stephen Darwall, *Impartial Reason* (Ithaca, N.Y.: Cornell University Press, 1983), chapter 9; and Jean Hampton "Rethinking Reason," *American Philosophical Quarterly* 29, no. 3 (July 1992).

114. Will Kymlicka, "Liberalism and Communitarianism," *The Canadian Journal of Philosophy* 18, no. 2 (June 1988), 190. See also his *Liberalism, Community, and Culture* (New York: Oxford University Press, 1989). It seems to be this point which Rawls endorses at *PL*, 27n29.

There is one further point to make before moving on to consider the opposite objection—that this model of the person is too thin. Since the basic structure "provides the framework for a self-sufficient scheme of cooperation for all the essential purposes of human life, which purposes are served by the variety of associations and groups within this framework," it is appropriate to idealize our discussion in the following way: we assume that persons are "capable of being normal and fully cooperating members of society over a complete life." (*PL*, 301) This means, on the one hand, that we are excluding cases of extreme incapacity that prevent an individual from understanding or functioning according to the norms of society. This assumption is not because justice has nothing to say about such cases; it is merely a simplifying idealization. Although a full account certainly will have to include a discussion of such cases, they are not the norm, and it seems that abstracting away from them is a reasonable first step in identifying the requirements of basic social justice. On the other hand, there are several important elements that get included in this model that are commonly believed to be excluded from social contract approaches. For example, the normal course of "a complete life" begins with a period of years in which the individual is completely dependent on the care of others for survival and development. This is followed by a period of social development into maturity. Over the course of one's life, it is very likely that the individual will suffer various periods of illness and heightened need that typically become more frequent as he or she ages. All of this is to be expected and must be taken into account if our model is to reflect important facts about human lives. The frequent claim that Rawls assumes we are "disembodied" is simply mistaken.[115]

This concludes my explanation of the features that justice as fairness includes in the model of the person. We now must briefly consider the objection that with only these features our account of the person is too thin. After all, each of our lives, when considered in all its fullness and specificity is infinitely richer than this bare account suggests. It is important to realize that this model of the person includes only what is absolutely necessary in order to view society as a fair system of cooperation from one generation to the next. This is a normative model, derived from the requirements of a just basic structure that embodies stable reciprocity. It is designed to help us identify the principles to be used in making such an assessment. (See *PL*, 18n20.) Justice as fairness does not deny that individuals conceive of themselves as much richer and more fully articulated than this model suggests, nor does it discourage them from doing so. As Moon points out:

---

115. Similarly, it is a mistake to suppose that Rawls assumes people are not dependent on one another. See Eva Feder Kittay, "Human Dependency and Rawlsian Equality," in *Feminists Rethink the Self,* Diana Meyers, ed. (Boulder, Colo.: Westview, 1997). Compare Rawls's remarks on the family in "The Idea of Public Reason Revisited," 787-794.

Liberal constructions of the self should, in the first instance, be thought of as models designed to capture the relationships that are possible under such conditions [of pluralism] and to indicate the forms of political association that will enable people to enjoy diverse and rich ways of life. Because these images of the self are partial, they are thin. But their very thinness is what, in a sense, makes rich lives possible.[116]

Relying on a thin model of the person is what makes a diversity of thick, full lives possible. For if we assumed further moral commitments, for example, we would be excluding the possibility that some individuals might reasonably reject those values. Justice as fairness tries to keep such assumptions to a minimum precisely so that it is as inclusive as possible. The two moral powers are normative requirements, to be sure, but they are the minimum requirements that individuals must meet if society is to be a fair system of cooperation from one generation to the next. As Rawls puts the point: "In order to fulfill their political role, citizens are viewed as having the intellectual and moral powers appropriate to that role, such as a capacity for a sense of political justice given by a liberal conception and a capacity to form, follow, and revise their individual doctrines of the good, and capable also of the political virtues necessary for them to cooperate in maintaining a just political society. (Their capacity for the other virtues and moral motives beyond this is not of course denied.)" (*PL*, xlvi-xlvii)

We can now tease out the normative commitments implicit in this model of the person. In very specific senses, for very specific purposes, we can now say that individuals are considered free and equal citizens: "The basic idea is that in virtue of their two moral powers (a capacity for a sense of justice and for a conception of the good) and the powers of reason (of judgment, thought, and inference connected with these powers), persons are free. Their having these powers to the requisite minimum degree to be fully cooperating members of society makes persons equal." (*PL*, 19; cf. *TJ*, sec.77) Liberal doctrines are often criticized for perpetrating a blatant falsehood: that all people are created equal. However, to repeat, there are specific senses in which justice as fairness does say individuals are to be treated as free and equal. It is not committed to any particular metaphysical doctrine concerning freedom, nor does it assert that "the activities and accomplishments [of various individuals] are of equal excellence." (*TJ*, 329 [289]) From within a comprehensive doctrine, for purposes other than assessing basic social justice we may judge different individuals (or their activities) to be of different worth, but for the purpose of making assessments of the justice of the basic structure, there are specific senses in which individuals are to be considered free and equal.

Consider three senses related to the second moral power in which justice as fairness views citizens as free. First, in virtue of their second moral power, they are free since they are not inevitably tied to the conception of the good that they hold at any given moment. "Rather, as citizens, they are seen as capable of

116. Moon, *Constructing Community*, 45.

revising and changing this conception on reasonable and rational grounds, and they may do this if they so desire. As free persons, citizens claim the right to view their persons as independent from and not identified with any particular such conception with its scheme of final ends." (*PL*, 30) Rawls acknowledges that there is a sense in which a radical change in ends, either gradually over time or suddenly in conversion, may lead us to say that one is a different person than one was before the change. (See *PL*, 31.) For some purposes, certain commitments may appropriately be viewed as constitutive of who we are, and therefore a change in these constitutive commitments may be described as a shift in identity. It is not difficult to imagine a case in which, say, you are reacquainted with a former colleague whom you remember as exceptionally devout, and finding that he has lost his faith completely, you are moved to utter the cliché, "I don't know who you are anymore!" He might even agree that he is a "new man." Yet, from the point of view of the justice of the basic structure, such a change in identity is simply not relevant (as long as both conceptions of the good are permissible). From the point of view of the design of the basic structure, this conversion involves no change in our "public or institutional identity." The claims that citizens are justly entitled to make on the basic structure do not depend on affirming any particular conception of the good. Of course, a change like the one described above may mean that your colleague is excommunicated from his church, but it cannot have an analogous consequence with respect to the basic structure. Notice one further point. I have assumed that both constitutive commitments are permissible, but what if one is not? Often constitutive attachments are treated as a kind of conversation stopper—once you say "but that's who I am," further evaluation and argument ends. Justice as fairness rejects this move. If, in fact, a constitutive attachment commits you to an impermissible conception of the good, then justice requires that you revise that conception of the good and, if need be, become a "new person"—a *just* one.

A second sense in which justice as fairness views citizens as free is in its recognition that they may claim a fair share of resources for pursuit of their permissible ends. There is no requirement that they provide public justification for the affirmation of their (permissible) conception of the good. It is not necessary to publicly affirm a particular faith or a commitment to using the resources for popular ends, for example, in order to validate the legitimacy of an individual's legitimate entitlements to social resources. Citizens are free to press claims for social resources based on their own authority. As Rawls writes: "A second respect in which citizens view themselves as free is that they regard themselves as self-authenticating sources of valid claims. That is, they regard themselves as being entitled to make claims on their institutions so as to advance their conception of the good (provided these conceptions fall within the range permitted by the public conception of justice)." (*PL*, 32)[117]

---

117. In his "Dewey Lectures," Rawls refers to "self-originating source of valid claims." ("Kantian Constructivism in Moral Theory," 543) This could be read

Finally, a third respect in which justice as fairness views citizens as free is that "they are viewed as capable of taking responsibility for their ends and this affects how their various claims are assessed." (*PL*, 33) This follows from the second moral power, according to which individuals are assumed to have the ability to assess and revise their conceptions of the good. From the point of view of the basic structure, our conceptions of the good are not simply given to us. It is important to note, once again, that justice as fairness insists on responsibility for one's conception of the good only for the limited purpose of constructing principles of basic social justice. For other purposes, we may think of a conception of the good in other ways. As we have seen, some may think of their religious faith as a kind of calling. In *A Theory of Justice*, Rawls sometimes speaks of the "choice" of a conception of the good. (See, e.g., *TJ*, sections 63-64.) This may have misled some to think that he assumes that there must be a moment of deliberate choice. As we have seen, this is not the case. Having grown up in a certain community, we may find ourselves with certain values without ever having made a deliberate decision to select them. Also as we have seen, justice as fairness does not say that conceptions of the good are only valuable if actually chosen through an act of will with deliberative rationality. Nonetheless, for purposes of assessing basic social justice, justice as fairness views citizens as responsible for the conception of the good which they affirm because of their second moral power: the capacity for deliberation and revision of one's conception of the good. Thus, Rawls writes:

> Whatever comprehensive religious, philosophical, or moral views we hold are also freely accepted, politically speaking; for given liberty of conscience and freedom of thought, we impose any such doctrine on ourselves. By this I do not mean that we do this by an act of free choice, as it were, apart from all prior loyalties and commitments, attachments, and affections. I mean that, as free and equal citizens, whether we affirm these views is regarded as within our political competence specified by the basic constitutional rights and liberties. (*PL*, 221-222; cf. 185-186)

To conclude this section, consider the ways in which, from the point of view of justice as fairness, the model-conception of the person generates a sense in which citizens are equal. The basis of equality is founded on the assumption that individuals manifest the two moral powers to at least the minimal degree necessary for them to be full participants in the institutional scheme defined by the basic structure. (See *TJ*, 504ff. [441ff.]) Above this threshold, as long as their conception of the good is permissible, there is no further qualification that individuals must meet in order to have their claims on the basic structure treated with respect. In particular, there is no further evaluation of the worth or value of their conception of their good from the point of view of social justice.

(mistakenly) to suggest a kind of voluntarism in which individuals are only under obligations that originate in their choices. See Rawls's clarification at *PL*, 32.

"Moreover, all conceptions of the good (consistent with justice) are regarded as equally worthy, not in the sense that there is an agreed public measure of intrinsic value or satisfaction with respect to which all these conceptions come out equal, but in the sense that they are not evaluated at all from a social standpoint."[118] The model-conceptions we have just been discussing simply do not have the resources to make such evaluations. Of course, most comprehensive doctrines will have internal standards with which to make these assessments. For purposes other than judging the justice of the basic structure, it may be entirely appropriate to rely on one's full comprehensive doctrine. Justice as fairness, however, insists that in evaluating basic social justice in circumstances of reasonable diversity, we must avoid such assessments. To see why, we must consider the ideas of a political conception of justice and public reason.

Public Reason

Having explored the model of the person, let us now return to consider further the idea that a just basic structure realizes "fair terms of cooperation." Recall that fair terms of cooperation, according to Rawls, "are terms that each participant may reasonably accept." (*PL*, 16) The thought that social institutions and collective political decisions should be justified in terms that can reasonably be accepted by the people who are bound to them is frequently invoked by liberal political philosophers.[119] Rawls's version of this idea is his "liberal principle of legitimacy," which he states as follows: "our exercise of political power is proper and hence justifiable only when it is exercised in accordance with a constitution the essentials of which all citizens may reasonably be expected to endorse in the light of principles and ideals acceptable to them as reasonable and rational." (*PL*, 217)[120] While some theories attempt to use a similar liberal principle of legitimacy to generate a comprehensive moral doctrine, Rawls's discussion is limited to the constitution and matters of basic social justice, including the design of the institutions of the basic structure of

---

118. Rawls, "Social Unity and Primary Goods," 172; cf. *TJ*, 19 [17], 328-329 [288-289].

119. Compare, for example, three statements of similar (although not identical) principles: T. M. Scanlon, "Contractualism and Utilitarianism," in *Utilitarianism and Beyond*, Amartya Sen and Bernard Williams, eds. (New York: Cambridge University Press, 1982), 110; Jeremy Waldron, "Theoretical Foundations of Liberalism," in *Liberal Rights* (New York: Cambridge University Press, 1993), 61; Charles Larmore, *The Morals of Modernity*, 12-13.

120. Compare the statements of this principle on 137 and xlvi. The statement on 137 refers explicitly to citizens as "free and equal." See the previous section for the senses in which justice as fairness understands citizens as free and equal. As I will explain below, Rawls treats these ideas as implicit in the notion of the reasonable.

society.[121] This principle of legitimacy has an important implication concerning the arguments that it is appropriate for citizens to offer one another when discussing matters of basic social justice. This is what Rawls calls "the duty of civility." Citizens must "be able to explain to one another on those fundamental questions how the principles and policies they advocate and vote for can be supported by the political values of public reason. This duty also involves a willingness to listen to others and a fairmindedness in deciding when accommodations to their views should reasonably be made." (PL, 217) This moral (as opposed to legal) duty regulates which justifications are to carry moral weight when the justice of the basic structure is at issue.

The introduction of the liberal principle of legitimacy and the duty of civility are crucial moves for Rawls. Recognition of this pair means that the moral judgments of others, even those whose (reasonable) comprehensive doctrines we reject, must be incorporated into our own moral reflection. As Nagel writes, we must find a way "to take into account values that we do not share but whose force, for others we must acknowledge."[122] Given this commitment, our effort to reach reflective equilibrium must cope not only with our own diverse moral commitments and ideals but also with the frequently conflicting judgments of others. Rawls now calls this intersubjective goal "full" reflective equilibrium. (PL, 384n16) This may seem to be an impossible goal, but two limitations are crucial.

The first limitation on the project is that we are only attempting to generate principles of justice for the basic structure. Our goal is not the complete reconciliation of all reasonable comprehensive moral doctrines. It is possible— indeed, justice as fairness is predicated on this possibility—that comprehensive doctrines that disagree on many fundamental matters may still agree on a specific issue. Surely it's possible for two people to strike a similar balance between, say, money-making and family concerns in their conceptions of the good, but to ground them in very different comprehensive doctrines, say, one religious and one secular. Similarly, different individuals may come to endorse shared principles of justice on the basis of different comprehensive doctrines.

Indeed, we may be hopeful that there is a greater likelihood of generating an overlapping consensus among diverse comprehensive doctrines concerning matters of basic social justice than of identifying the most favored conception of

---

121. Unfortunately, in the statement quoted above Rawls may appear to limit its application to the Constitution alone. This is incorrect, and in the earlier statement of the principle he explicitly extends its use beyond the Constitution to cover "all questions arising in the legislature that concern or border on constitutional essentials, or basic questions of justice." (PL, 137) Note also that the duty of civility, which Rawls introduces immediately after the quote from 217, applies not only to legislators but to citizens generally when they consider "fundamental questions."

122. Thomas Nagel, The View from Nowhere (New York: Oxford University Press, 1986), 188.

the good. Following Weber, Rawls reminds us that "political power is always coercive power backed by the government's use of sanctions." (*PL*, 136; cf. *TJ*, 235-236 [207]) Even as they disagree about other matters, many comprehensive doctrines will recognize that coercion with regard to something as fundamental and important as the basic structure of society requires a special form of justification. In particular, many will recognize the need for a justification that in some way appeals to the reasonableness of the very persons subjected to the coercive requirements of the structures. Of course, they may justify this requirement in different ways. We should note here the structural similarity to the affirmation of free faith by various religions. While each has its own view of religious truth, each also recognizes that the coercive imposition of this dogma would itself be wrong. This affirmation depends on each group's valuing the absence of coercion in matters of faith more highly than the correct external practice. Each may make such a judgment, however, for different reasons.[123]

Many comprehensive doctrines will recognize the liberal principle of legitimacy (or some variant), but not all will, and this leads to the second limitation. Because it accepts the liberal principle of legitimacy, justice as fairness aspires to present a justification of a conception of justice that all people can *reasonably* accept. Alternatively, we may say that justice as fairness seeks to justify its principles to all reasonable people. Assuming that an individual's acceptance or rejection of principles of justice is based, in part, on her comprehensive doctrine, we may also speak of reasonable comprehensive doctrines. The point is that justice as fairness does not aspire to present justifications that are necessarily acceptable to people who hold unreasonable comprehensive doctrines or who are themselves unreasonable. Indeed, some comprehensive doctrines may be so unreasonable or so intrinsically unjust that far from attempting to accommodate them within an overlapping consensus, our task must be "to contain them so that they do not undermine the unity and justice of society." (*PL*, xix; cf. 64n19)[124]

---

123. In many cases such a judgment is based in the belief that without free affirmation, the practice is less valuable. See the discussion in Harlan Beckley, "A Christian Affirmation of Rawls's Idea of Justice as Fairness—Part I," *Journal of Religious Ethics* 13 (1985). In 1965, the Catholic Church's Declaration on Religious Freedom during the Second Vatican rejected the principle that the ideal state should suppress religious error. For discussion, see John Langan, "Catholicism and Liberalism" in *Liberalism and the Good*, R. Bruce Douglass, Gerald Mara, and Henry Richardson, eds. (New York: Routledge, 1990); R. Bruce Douglass and David Hollenbach, eds. *Catholicism and Liberalism* (New York: Cambridge University Press, 1994); and Kenneth Grasso, Gerard Bradley, and Robert Hunt, eds., *Catholicism, Liberalism, and Communitarianism* (Lanham, Md.: Rowman and Littlefield, 1995).

124. On the issue of the toleration of unreasonable comprehensive doctrines, see my "The Reasonable in Justice As Fairness," especially section 5. The following discussion draws on this work.

The different uses of the term *reasonable*—in modifying *people*, in modifying *comprehensive doctrines*, and in the phrase *the reasonable*—are obviously related. It may be unclear, however, exactly what the criteria of reasonableness should be in each of these contexts. In fact, Rawls seems somewhat torn on this issue. Sometimes, for example when discussing what makes a comprehensive doctrine reasonable, he presents the requirements of reasonableness as minimal, even formal. Officially, a comprehensive doctrine is reasonable if it satisfies three conditions:

> One is that a reasonable doctrine is an exercise of theoretical reason: it covers the major religious, philosophical, and moral aspects of human life in a more or less consistent and coherent manner. It organizes and characterizes recognized values so that they are compatible with one another and express an intelligible view of the world.... In singling out which values to count as especially significant and how to balance them when they conflict, a reasonable comprehensive doctrine is also an exercise of practical reason. . . . Finally, a third feature is that while a reasonable comprehensive view is not necessarily fixed and unchanging, it normally belongs to, or draws upon, a tradition of thought and doctrine. (*PL*, 59)

Notice that these conditions put no restrictions on how a comprehensive doctrine is to balance the various values when they conflict. Joshua Cohen suggests that a further condition is necessary in order for a comprehensive doctrine to be reasonable: "An understanding of value is fully reasonable just in case its adherents are stably disposed to affirm it as they acquire new information and subject it to critical reflection."[125] Even this further stipulation remains rather formal, however. The most heinous fascist doctrine, if comprehensive, consistent, and part of a tradition would count as reasonable according to Rawls's official definition. Moreover, depending on what "new information" and what kind of "critical reflection" it was subjected to, it certainly might be stable for those who accept it. In sharp contrast, however, sometimes Rawls assumes that "a reasonable comprehensive doctrine does not reject the essentials of a democratic regime." (*PL*, xviii)[126]

Despite the formal account of the reasonableness of comprehensive doctrines, recall that for Rawls, *the reasonable* itself has significant moral content. It was introduced in connection with the first moral power in the model-conception of the person and requires that individuals be motivated to uphold the ideal of reciprocity (in a scheme of social cooperation). Rawls has a similarly demanding characterization of the reasonableness of persons. As we should expect, the key element in this context is the first moral power, a sense of justice:

---

125. Joshua Cohen, "Moral Pluralism and Political Consensus," in *The Idea of Democracy*, David Copp, Jean Hampton, and John Roemer, eds. (New York: Cambridge University Press, 1993), 281-282.

126. This is reiterated in Rawls, "The Idea of Public Reason Revisited," 801, 805.

When attributed to persons, the two basic elements of the conception of the
reasonable are, first, a willingness to propose fair terms of social cooperation that
others as free and equal also might endorse, and to act on these terms, provided
others do, even contrary to one's own interest; and, second, a recognition of the
burdens of judgment (*PL* II:2-3) and accepting their consequences for one's attitude
(including toleration) toward other comprehensive doctrines. (*PL*, 375; cf. 49-54;
394-395)

Now obviously this account is much more demanding than the formal
criteria that Rawls proposes in order for a comprehensive doctrine to be
reasonable. If not exactly an inconsistency, this certainly may be confusing,
especially when we consider the close relationship between the reasonableness
of a person and her comprehensive doctrine. After all, it is primarily on the basis
of a comprehensive doctrine that a person is going to accept or reject the model-
conceptions of society and of the person and the duty of civility. If, as we have
seen, a fascist doctrine might satisfy the formal conditions of reasonableness, a
person who endorsed such a doctrine would not be reasonable. Such a person
would not accept the idea of society as a fair system of cooperation and the
associated model of free and equal moral persons, and therefore could not be
said to be reasonable. Her unreasonableness would be a direct consequence of
her comprehensive doctrine.

We would do better to rely consistently on the stronger criteria for
reasonableness. In matters of basic social justice, reasonable comprehensive
doctrines must treat society as a fair system of cooperation among free and equal
moral persons and recognize the burdens of judgment. With this adjustment, it
still would be possible for a person to be unreasonable despite endorsing a
reasonable comprehensive doctrine, but it would no longer be possible for her to
be unreasonable because she holds a reasonable comprehensive doctrine. It is a
plausible conjecture (to be made good by the argument from the original
position and the principles of justice chosen there) that reasonable
comprehensive doctrines in this strong sense, and of course the reasonable
citizens who hold them, will not reject the essentials of a democratic regime.

Rawls chooses not to invoke this stronger understanding of reasonable
comprehensive doctrines apparently because he worries that this would be too
exclusive: "We avoid excluding doctrines as unreasonable without strong
grounds based on clear aspects of the reasonable itself. Otherwise our account
runs the danger of being arbitrary and exclusive." (*PL*, 59) But if a
comprehensive doctrine thoroughly rejects the criterion of reciprocity and the
need to justify principles of justice to the citizens living under them (and thus
fails to treat society as a fair system of cooperation) or if it rejects the burdens of
judgment (and thus the diversity of reasonable comprehensive doctrines), it
is rejecting a clear aspect of the reasonable itself. It is hard to see how we could,
or why we should, accommodate into our conception of justice the views of
someone who rejects the basic conceptual requirements of justice itself.

Note that this account does not imply that those who hold an unreasonable comprehensive doctrine somehow escape the requirements of justice. As Rawls observes: "There is not one account of toleration for reasonable doctrines and another for unreasonable ones. Both cases are settled by the appropriate political principles of justice and the conduct those principles permit."[127] Although a person holding an unreasonable comprehensive doctrine is still subject to the principles of justice, she very well might not accept their legitimacy. This, however, is her failing—her unreasonableness—not a violation of the liberal principle of legitimacy or the duty of civility. Nor is calling a comprehensive doctrine or a person that rejects the duty of civility and the burdens of judgment unreasonable simply an illiberal, *ad hominem* attack.[128] In this context, *reasonable* has been given a clear and precise technical use. To deny that a comprehensive doctrine or person is reasonable is to point out that certain grounds are no longer available for reasoned agreement based on certain shared moral premises. It remains possible, of course, that other grounds for constructive dialogue might be found.[129]

The point, to repeat once again, is that the liberal principle of legitimacy does not require that we provide justifications that literally everyone can accept. Presumably that would be impossible since there are no points on which all possible comprehensive doctrines agree or could be brought to agree. Respecting the liberal principle of legitimacy and the duty of civility requires that we be able to present justifications of our conception of justice that can be accepted by all reasonable people who hold reasonable comprehensive doctrines. We will return to this point but for now I want to emphasize that the determination of which comprehensive doctrines are reasonable is based on moral considerations (and the idea of the reasonable itself), not from a survey of which comprehensive doctrines happen to be widely accepted in a given society.

Many different comprehensive doctrines may be reasonable (in the technical sense just discussed) because there are many possible grounds on which one might endorse the importance of social justice, view society as a fair system of cooperation, treat fellow citizens as free and equal, and recognize the burdens of judgment. These include comprehensive doctrines that ground the value of social justice in various understandings of "autonomy, or self-realization, or human happiness properly understood, or the appropriate response to life's challenges, or to the value of individuality, or the equality of human beings as God's creatures,"[130] among many other possibilities. One

---

127. Rawls, "The Idea of Public Reason Revisited," 806.

128. Essentially this charge is made by Jean Hampton in "The Common Faith of Liberalism," *Pacific Philosophical Quarterly* 75, no. 3&4 (Sept./Dec. 1994), 208-211.

129. For an example of what such grounds might look like, see S. A. Lloyd, "Relativizing Rawls," *Chicago-Kent Law Review* 69, no. 3, (1994), 716-718.

130. This list is from Joshua Cohen, "A More Democratic Liberalism," 1505, who cites a plausible candidate for each of these views.

individual cannot believe that all of these comprehensive doctrines are correct, however, since they contradict one another on many points. In circumstances of diversity, the duty of civility requires that we consider the points of view of people who hold comprehensive doctrines that, while we do not accept, we recognize as reasonable. In the absence of the duty of civility (or some closely related principle) we could simply ignore the reasonable moral, philosophical and religious attitudes of others with whom we disagree and rely on our own (full or partial) comprehensive doctrine.

If we follow Rawls and share a strong commitment to presenting evaluations of the justice of the basic structure that all reasonable people living under it can share, this means that we cannot rely on our full comprehensive doctrines because each will include elements that some reasonable people will reject. In certain conditions, we must be willing to bracket our commitments that go beyond what all reasonable people share. To repeat: what is shared by reasonable persons (for purposes of assessing the justice of the basic structure) includes the model-conceptions of society and of the person, the duty of civility, and the burdens of judgment. It is crucial to recognize that this limitation on the resources of justification is not imposed by any external constraint or metaphysical commitment, as some have supposed. Nor is it the result of giving priority to the practical goal of reaching consensus, as many more have assumed, since it makes no effort to incorporate the views of those that are not reasonable. Rather, the restriction follows from our attempt to reach full reflective equilibrium concerning principles of basic social justice when we recognize that there is a diversity of reasonable comprehensive doctrines and accept the liberal principle of legitimacy and the duty of civility.

Notice that the discussion is not (yet) over the specific content of the most favored conception of justice, but rather it concerns the framework within which matters of basic social justice are to be discussed. The name that Rawls gives this framework within which we address matters of basic social justice while respecting the duty of civility is *public reason*. It is the framework of moral reasoning that citizens use when, "as a collective body," they address "'constitutional essentials' and matters of basic social justice." (*PL*, 214) Note that it includes, therefore, arguments concerning the content of the fundamental principles of justice as well as their application to the basic structure. Recognizing the duty of civility, public reason requires that we bracket those elements of our full comprehensive doctrine that not all reasonable people share, and to the extent possible, take our normative premises only from the idea of the reasonable itself.

Perhaps the phrase *public reason* has suggested to some that Rawls is advocating a restriction on what can be said in public. This is mistaken in two ways. First, the point has nothing to do with the legal issue of what people are permitted to say in any context. The point, rather, is to help distinguish good arguments from bad. Rawls is claiming that an argument that violates the requirements of public reason violates an important norm that reasonable citizens recognize: the duty of civility. Rawls no more advocates enforcing legal restrictions against violations of public reason than he advocates enforcing them against affirming the consequent. It is simply a matter of what we should count as a morally weighty argument and what not. The exemplar of public reason that Rawls has in mind is an ideal Supreme Court when it considers matters of basic social justice and addresses its verdicts to a general public. Thus, Rawls suggests: "To check whether we are following public reason we might ask: how would our argument strike us presented in the form of a supreme court opinion? Reasonable? Outrageous?" (*PL*, 254)

Second, it is also important to recognize that Rawls is not claiming that every argument that relies on a specific comprehensive doctrine and is made in public violates this duty. Context is crucial. The limits of public reason are only violated when all four of the following conditions are met: 1. constitutional essentials or matters of basic justice are at stake; 2. the argument is addressed to a general public which cannot be assumed to share a specific comprehensive doctrine; 3. the argument relies on premises that not all reasonable comprehensive doctrines share; 4. there is no commitment that "in due course public reasons, given by a reasonable political conception, are presented sufficient to support whatever the comprehensive doctrines are introduced to support." (*PL*, li-lii) Rawls calls this last condition "the proviso" and it is distinctive of the *wide* public reason he now defends.[131] The proviso allows temporary violations, as it were, of a more narrow conception of public reason to be redeemed at a later date: citizens may cite any element of their comprehensive doctrine, provided that "in due course" these claims are defended on the basis of reasons that all reasonable comprehensive doctrines can share. As Rawls notes, this statement of the proviso leaves several questions unanswered, including "when does it need to be satisfied, on the same day or some later day? Also, on whom does the obligation to honor it fall?" (*PL*, lii n26) But the basic idea is clear: temporary violations of the restrictions of public reason can be redeemed later without violating the spirit of public reason and the duty of civility. Certainly Rawls is right when he observes that "the details about how to satisfy the proviso must be worked out in practice and cannot feasibly be governed by a clear family of rules given in advance. How they work out is determined by the nature of the public political culture and calls for good sense and understanding."[132] Rawls cites abolitionist dissent and the Civil Rights movement as examples of social movements that drew on religious arguments allowed by the proviso.[133]

---

131. See *PL*, li-lii, and Rawls, "The Idea of Public Reason Revisited," 783-784.

132. Rawls, "The Idea of Public Reason Revisited," 784.

133. Rawls, "The Idea of Public Reason Revisited," 802. See also David Richards, "Public Reason and Abolitionist Dissent," *Chicago-Kent Law Review* 69, no. 3 (1994).

Consider some of the implications of this idea of public reason. Contrary to what some seem to believe, there is no violation of the requirements of public reason in, say, proselytizing to a public audience for a specific comprehensive religious, philosophical, or moral doctrine or conception of the good. Furthermore, there are many questions that cannot adequately be resolved within the limits of public reason, including, but not limited to: the existence and nature of God or gods; the metaphysical conditions that underlie moral or non-moral truths; the most favored conception of the good for a particular individual or for all. Although certain extreme answers to these questions may be incompatible with public reason and therefore may be unreasonable, public reason does not have the resources within itself to determine definitive answers to these and many other questions. This does not mean that they have no answer or that individuals are not permitted to pursue answers to them in public. What it does mean is that the answers to these questions will have to draw on assumptions that not all reasonable comprehensive doctrines will accept. Neither public reason nor the duty of civility prevents us from addressing these issues with whatever intellectual resources we believe appropriate. On the other hand, precisely because the answers to these questions go beyond the limits of public reason, they form an inappropriate basis on which to argue for principles of basic social justice (unless the proviso can be met and a basis within public reason established).

There is also no violation of the requirements of public reason in arguing from a particular comprehensive doctrine when engaged in public advocacy for a particular public policy that does not concern matters of basic social justice. Rawls gives the following examples of day-to-day political decisions that do not involve matters of basic social justice and therefore may be based on more than what public reason allows: "much tax legislation and many laws regulating property; statutes protecting the environment and controlling pollution; establishing national parks and preserving wilderness areas and animal and plant species; and laying aside funds for museums and the arts." (*PL*, 214) To the extent that these are not matters of basic social justice, we may go beyond the limits of public reason in making and enforcing decisions concerning them. We will discuss neutrality in the next chapter, but for now note that in taking this position, Rawls differs from some influential statements of liberal neutrality.[134]

Note finally that there is no violation of the requirements of public reason in relying on a particular comprehensive doctrine in order to show that it is reasonable. This kind of dialogue will typically occur among those who share a comprehensive doctrine when they examine and explain the grounds on which they can understand society as a fair system of cooperation among free and

---

134. Compare, for example, Ronald Dworkin, "Liberalism," in *Public and Private Morality*, Stuart Hampshire, ed. (New York: Cambridge University Press, 1978). For discussions see Peter de Marneffe, "Liberalism, Liberty, and Neutrality," *Philosophy and Public Affairs* 19, no. 3 (summer 1990), and my "Having It Both Ways," 313-314.

equal citizens, recognize the burdens of judgment, and accept the requirements of public reason. Rawls now calls such a dialogue "full justification" in which a citizen "accepts a political conception [of justice] and fills out its justification by embedding it in some way into the citizen's comprehensive doctrine as either true or reasonable, depending on what that doctrine allows." (*PL*, 386) Full justification (which I repeat does not violate the restrictions of public reason) will reveal the deep foundations that shared principles of justice have in a particular reasonable comprehensive doctrine. It may be addressed either to a general public, in order to show that a certain comprehensive doctrine is reasonable, or to those who already share the comprehensive doctrine in an effort to establish the link between a matter of basic social justice and its ultimate foundation. This may be especially important when different social factions come to question each others' motives. By presenting their full justifications, each group may publicly display that they are, in fact, deeply committed to reciprocity and reasonableness. This may help to relieve suspicion and help to "foster the kind of society that [the] ideal [of public reason] exemplifies."[135]

Some have argued recently against an ideal of public reason that imposes any restrictions at all. Typically, these critics focus on the example of religion which, they argue, should not be excluded from "the public square." Jean Bethke Elshtain, for example, has argued against those who believe that "religion necessarily narrows rather than expands the horizon of civic possibility."[136] Elshtain invokes the late Cardinal Bernardin as an exemplar of how religious faith can enrich political dialogue. In a speech at Georgetown University shortly before his death Bernardin argued that there are broad areas of civil society in which religion can contribute to the richness and value of life for those of faith. Furthermore, religious organizations can contribute "through the ministry and work of religious institutions of education, health care, family service and direct outreach to the poorest parts of our society." Justice as fairness welcomes these roles for religion in civil society. But justice as fairness also recognizes the duty of civility when it comes to the coercive use of state power in matters concerning the basic structure and the constraints this puts on acceptable justifications addressed to the society as a whole.

Remarkably (and apparently unnoticed by Elshtain), Bernardin seems to agree. Persons of faith, he insists, must be sensitive to different contexts of

---

135. Rawls, "The Idea of Public Reason Revisited," 785.

136. Jean Bethke Elshtain, "Cardinal Virtue," *The New Republic*, 9 Dec. 1996, 25. Quotations from Cardinal Bernardin's Georgetown speech are from this article. In private correspondence, Elshtain confirms that she was thinking of Rawls, among others, when she wrote this. See also Michael Sandel, *Democracy's Discontent* (Cambridge: Harvard University Press, 1996); Stephen Carter, *The Culture of Disbelief* (New York: Basic Books, 1993); and the discussion in Richard Rorty, "Religion as a Conversation-Stopper," *Common Knowledge* 3, no. 1 (spring 1994).

argument. Within the Church, "the full range of biblical, theological themes that structure our belief should be used. Within civil society, explicit appeal to religious warrants and imperatives is both legitimate and needed if we are to address some of the profoundly human themes that are at the heart of our policy debates. But when we address the state . . . we should be ascetic, that is, sparing, in our use of explicit religious appeals." This is because "we accept the responsibility of making our religiously grounded convictions intelligible to those who do not share the faith that yields these convictions." We could hardly ask for a clearer statement of the grounds of the duty of civility and the idea of public reason that it generates.

We can now introduce a term that Rawls uses to characterize this approach to matters of basic social justice. Justice as fairness, with its defense of specific principles of justice, is just one example of a *political* conception of justice, in the technical sense. Three features suffice to characterize a conception of justice as political. (See *PL*, 11-15.) First, it is designed to apply to a specific subject: the basic structure of society. Although one might attempt to use certain elements in the conception to address further issues, or even to generate a partially or fully comprehensive doctrine, these further possibilities are not considered in working out the principles for this special subject. While not itself a comprehensive doctrine, Rawls reminds us that "such a conception is, of course, a moral conception." (*PL*, 11) It is not simply a prediction, say, of the future course of various social reforms or of which proposals might receive widespread support based on the balance of existing political pressures. As I have stressed from the beginning, a political conception of justice is a proposal concerning which principles are right and correct for the evaluation of the basic structure of society.

The second feature of a political conception refers to what we have just been discussing: the principles are not justified by appealing to any particular comprehensive doctrine. Of course, they can be imbedded in various comprehensive doctrines—indeed, hopefully in all reasonable comprehensive doctrines. Nevertheless, the conception of justice is defended only by appeal to ideas that all reasonable comprehensive doctrines share. It is presented as a freestanding doctrine and only explicitly embedded in particular comprehensive doctrines subject to the proviso (or for purposes other than the evaluation of the justice of the basic structure). How various comprehensive doctrines understand and justify the various elements of the reasonable and relate them to other values are further questions for each comprehensive doctrine to answer for itself; public reason and political conceptions by themselves do not answer them.

Third and finally, a political conception "is expressed in terms of certain fundamental ideas seen as implicit in the public political culture of a democratic society." (*PL*, 13) Specifically, the "fundamental ideas" with which justice as fairness begins is the model of society as a fair system of cooperation together with the idea of citizens as free and equal persons and the idea of a well-ordered society. (*PL*, 14) Some have read this statement (together with a misreading of the idea of an overlapping consensus discussed below) to suggest that a political conception of justice draws on whatever ideas happen to be present in a given society. This is a fundamental misreading of the idea of a political conception of justice. As the first criterion states, a political conception is a moral conception. Finding certain ideas present in the public political culture of a society is not a foundation in lieu of further moral reflection and justification. As we have seen, this further justification is found within specific reasonable comprehensive doctrines. Why, then, does Rawls insist on this third condition—that a political conception draw on ideas found in the public political culture of a society?

The answer is quite simple. Charles Larmore explains the point perfectly:

> Rawls often writes that the basis of his political liberalism is drawn from notions implicit in our political culture. That does not mean that it is important only that these notions are widely affirmed, and not that they express valid principles. The point is rather that valid principles, which are also alien to a culture, can be of no help in solving its problems of finding terms of political association amid reasonable disagreement about the good life.[137]

The requirement that the basic resources of a political conception be found in the public political culture is an additional requirement, putting yet another constraint on which forms of moral argument are acceptable. This point has been very widely misunderstood. I will conclude this chapter by attempting to diagnose this misunderstanding and argue against it.

One of the main goals of *Political Liberalism* is to develop the conceptual tools needed to present justice as fairness as a political conception of justice. I believe it is fair to say that Rawls's so-called *political turn* has been greeted with widespread disappointment. Kukathas and Pettit, for example, conclude their book on Rawls (published in 1990, before the full implications of the latest developments were clear) by remarking that Rawls's political turn "suggests despair as to the possibility of anything being accomplished in politics by philosophical inquiry."[138] In a paper originally published in 1994, Patrick Neal observes that "hardly anyone is happy about the direction Rawls' later work has taken."[139] Another critic writes that "A reasonable perception is that Rawlsianism has become a moving target running for cover in political

---

137. Larmore, *The Morals of Modernity*, 149-150. He continues in footnote 36: "I believe that Rawls has in mind another point as well: in moral argument, as in other domains, we do not reason from scratch, but rather build on beliefs that we already have and that we have (so far) no positive reason to doubt. I share this view of moral epistemology. . . . But since many still hold older, more foundationalist views, it is probably best to minimize its role within political liberalism."

138. Kukathas and Pettit, *Rawls: A Theory of Justice and Its Critics*, 151.

139. Patrick Neal, "Does He Mean What He Says? (Mis)Understanding Rawls' Practical Turn," in *Liberalism and Its Discontents* (New York: NYU Press, 1997), 98.

categories."[140] Even someone as sympathetic to justice as fairness as Norman Daniels reports, "Some people have reacted to the politicization of justice with a sense of philosophical loss," and he admits that "at least initially" he shared this view.[141] While *A Theory of Justice* concentrates on articulating and defending specific principles of justice as an alternative to utilitarianism, *Political Liberalism* attempts to show how it is possible for this conception of justice to be understood as political (in the technical sense just described). In an effort to do this, Rawls develops many of the conceptual resources we have discussed, and makes a few revisions in the defense of the specific principles.[142] However, by far the most attention in the secondary literature on *Political Liberalism* has been devoted to the idea of an overlapping consensus. This is simply the idea that different reasonable comprehensive doctrines may agree on a political conception of justice while disagreeing on much else, including the ultimate foundation of those shared principles.

The widespread sense of loss experienced by many concerning the political conception of justice is, I believe, due primarily to a misunderstanding of the role played by the idea of an overlapping consensus. It is widely believed that Rawls is no longer interested in providing a moral (or normative) defense of his principles of justice. Rather, it is thought, he is only interested in defending them as a possible focus of an overlapping consensus. This view may be encouraged when Rawls himself claims that "political liberalism, rather than referring to its political conception of justice as true, refers to it as reasonable instead." (*PL*, xxii; cf. 94, 129) It might seem that since he rejects the claim that his principles are true, Rawls is left with no grounds for accepting them beyond their fitness for establishing an overlapping consensus. Rawls is very widely read, therefore, as searching directly for a conception of justice that could serve as the focus of an overlapping consensus. Roberto Alejandro, for example, claims that "In his articles after [*A*] *Theory* [*of Justice*] . . . the parties of the original position have been replaced by citizens in search of an overlapping consensus."[143] Contrasting Judith Shklar's view with that of Rawls, Seyla Benhabib writes: "Unlike for John Rawls, the guiding concern for Judith Shklar is not to establish the conceptual conditions for an 'overlapping consensus.'"[144] And Timothy Jackson

---

140. Alejandro, *The Limits of Rawlsian Justice*, 115.

141. Norman Daniels, "Reflective Equilibrium and Justice As Political," in *Justice and Justification*, 151.

142. For example: *Political Liberalism* emphasizes the importance of the models of society and the person (although both were present in *TJ*); it provides a new defense of primary goods that we will discuss in the next chapter; and it resolves an ambiguity in the formulation of the first principle by speaking consistently of "the basic liberties" instead of "liberty" as such.

143. Alejandro, *The Limits of Rawlsian Justice*, 125.

144. Seyla Benhabib, "Judith Shklar's Dystopic Liberalism," in *Liberalism without Illusions*, Bernard Yack, ed. (Chicago: University of Chicago Press, 1996), 56.

rejects Rawls's approach, claiming, "In the end, consensus alone does not give him the requisite critical purchase for a moral theory."[145] One could easily provide many more examples.

From here, it is but a short step to the conclusion that Rawls has taken the radical edge out of his theory. Thus, Bernard Williams argues that the difference principle (concerned with economic inequality) "has come to play a distinctly secondary role" because "anything as obviously a matter of contested politics as redistributive taxation cannot expect the support of the overlapping consensus."[146] Likewise, Bruce Ackerman maintains that Rawls's argument for the egalitarian difference principle (to be considered in the next chapter) "does not survive the transition to *Political Liberalism*" because "There is no democratic society in the world that adopts" Rawls's method of justification.[147]

Critics draw these conclusions despite the fact that Rawls is explicit in *Political Liberalism*: "some have thought that my working out the ideas of political liberalism meant giving up the egalitarian conception of [*A*] *Theory* [*of Justice*]. I am not aware of any revisions that imply such a change and think the surmise has no basis." (*PL*, 7n6) For many critics, then, Rawls's former concern with identifying the objectively correct principles has been replaced with the more political, less philosophical goal of establishing a point of widespread agreement. As I noted above (see note 73), this interpretation makes justice as fairness "political in the wrong way." (*PL*, 40) Rawls continues to insist: "Perhaps some think that a political conception is not a matter of (moral) right and wrong. If so, that is a mistake and is simply false. Political conceptions of justice are themselves intrinsically moral ideas, as I have stressed from the outset. As such they are a kind of normative value."[148]

The belief that Rawls has abandoned normative justification turns on misunderstanding both the idea of an overlapping consensus in justice as fairness, as well as a political conception's agnosticism with respect to truth. Consider, first, the issue of truth.[149] It is a little noticed fact that in *A Theory of Justice* Rawls does not call his favored conception of justice "true." In fact, in retrospect, this term is rather conspicuous for its absence from several passages. In the final section of *A Theory of Justice*, for example, Rawls reflects on the nature of the justification that he has given for justice as fairness: "[Justification] presumes a clash of views between persons or within one person, and seeks to convince others, or ourselves, of the *reasonableness* of the principles upon

---

145. Timothy Jackson, "To Bedlam and Part Way Back: John Rawls and Christian Justice," *Faith and Philosophy* 8, no. 4 (Oct. 1991), 424.

146. Bernard Williams, "A Fair State," *London Review of Books*, 13 May 1993, 8.

147. Bruce Ackerman, "Political Liberalisms," *The Journal of Philosophy* 91, no. 7 (July 1994), 371, 374.

148. John Rawls, "The Idea of Public Reason Revisited," 802n91.

149. This discussion draws on section 3 of my "The Reasonable in Justice As Fairness" where the argument is presented in more detail.

which our claims and judgments are founded." (*TJ*, 580 [508], my emphasis) One might have thought that justification seeks to convince others or ourselves of the truth of these principles, but this is not what Rawls claims. In *Political Liberalism*, he continues to decline to apply the term *true* to his theory, but now he calls attention to this fact.

In contrast to what has rapidly become the received view, Rawls's agnosticism with respect to truth must not be confused with agnosticism with respect to endorsement. While declining to call his conception true, Rawls has no qualms about calling it "reasonable" or "the most reasonable." There can be no doubt that by calling it "reasonable" Rawls is claiming that those principles are the objectively correct ones: "Reasonableness is [political constructivism's] standard of correctness, and given its political aims, it need not go beyond that." (*PL*, 127)[150] Relying on the term *reasonable* as opposed to *true* has three important advantages. "First, it indicates the more limited point of view of the political conception as articulating political and not all values, while providing at the same time a public basis of justification. Second, it indicates that the principles and ideals of the political conception are based on principles of practical reason in union with conceptions of society and person, themselves conceptions of practical reason." (*PL*, xxii) Finally, and most importantly, it allows justice as fairness to avoid philosophical controversies concerning the nature of truth.

For some, calling a claim or statement "true" has the same content as making the statement and so the introduction of the truth predicate is innocuous. However for others, including the rational intuitionists that Rawls discusses, truth is conceived of "in a traditional way by viewing moral judgments as true when they are both about and accurate to the independent order of moral values. Otherwise they are false." (*PL*, 92) Now disputes about the correct theory of truth and the appropriateness of calling a moral claim "true" are exactly the kind that can only be resolved from within a comprehensive (philosophical) doctrine. Better for justice as fairness simply to avoid the term and the attendant metaphysical controversy. Compare the fact that some may believe that the principles of justice are implications of the word of God.[151] Justice as fairness does not dispute this, but equally it does not assert it, either; to do so would be to exclude those who do not share that comprehensive (religious) doctrine. The essential point is as Larmore puts it:

---

150. Note the following contrast: Rawls is not endorsing a comprehensive doctrine when he calls it "reasonable." However, when he identifies a conception of justice as reasonable, he is.

151. See, for example, Beckley, "A Christian Affirmation of Rawls's Idea of Justice As Fairness—Part I"; and "A Christian Affirmation of Rawls's Idea of Justice As Fairness—Part II," *The Journal of Religious Ethics*, 14 (1986).

When Rawls declines to call his theory of justice "true," his intention is not to withdraw the claim that it is correct, that it is one we ought rationally to accept whether or not we do in fact believe it. On the contrary, his point is that its rational acceptability is independent of the claim that it is true of "*an independent metaphysical and moral order*". . . . His aim is to have political liberalism suspend judgment in a continuing controversy about what the correctness of a moral conception consists in.[152]

Finally, we come to the role that the idea of an overlapping consensus plays in justice as fairness. To understand the importance of the idea of an overlapping consensus, recall that justice as fairness aspires to develop principles to regulate the basic structure of society in a way that would be not only just but would tend to be stably just. As we have seen, Rawls states that the argument for the two principles of justice proceeds through two stages. The first stage presents a preliminary case for the principles. In particular, it involves a comparison between the two principles of justice and justice as fairness's great rival, utilitarianism. It is only after this preliminary defense of the principles that we move on to consider whether (and the extent to which) a society well ordered by those principles would be stable. (See *PL*, 64-65.) If we come to believe that a society founded on the two principles would not be stable, this would give us good reason to reconsider the original choice. Alternatively, if the initial argument leaves us unable to choose from among closely related sets of principles, considerations of stability might be decisive. Of course, no principles of justice will be absolutely stable in the sense that it would be impossible for a society that initially embraced them to stray or abandon them. The issue always concerns a comparison of the degree to which different conceptions of justice will tend to generate their own support through developing and supporting a strong sense of justice among most citizens.

The stability of a society (in the relevant sense) has two dimensions. First, a society must develop a sense of justice in its citizens as they mature. Of course, this is done in part through the explicit instruction of children. Rawls also stresses the educative role of the basic structure itself. For example, citizens raised in a political structure in which the rule of law is secure will tend to develop a stronger sense of justice than those raised where decisions are made arbitrarily at the whim of a ruler. Sections 69-75 of *A Theory of Justice* provide an account of the psychological development of a sense of justice that stresses the central role of reciprocity. Rawls is quite aware that this account is far from complete, but he believes that it serves his limited purpose of providing a basis for the comparison of different conceptions of justice along this first dimension.

The second dimension of stability concerns not the initial psychological development of a sense of justice, but what Rawls calls the "congruence" between the principles of justice and the conceptions of the good held by

---

152. Larmore, *The Morals of Modernity*, 147.

citizens. When mature individuals reflect on their values, will they affirm their sense of justice as a valuable and integral part of their self-conceptions or will they view it as an external imposition without which they would be better off? In *A Theory of Justice*, Rawls attempts to establish this congruence by showing that individuals in a society well ordered by his principles would tend to hold a conception of the good which places a very high value on justice. Rawls writes, for example:

> It follows that the collective activity of justice is the preeminent form of human flourishing. For given favorable conditions, it is by maintaining these public arrangements that persons best express their nature and achieve the widest regulative excellences of which each is capable. At the same time just institutions allow for and encourage the diverse internal life of associations in which individuals realize their more particular aims. (*TJ*, 529 [463])

It is crucial, even in *A Theory of Justice*, that justice as fairness makes room for diverse conceptions of the good or, as he put it, individuals' "more particular aims." Nonetheless, the assertion that there is a "preeminent form of human flourishing" may suggest that stability can be achieved only by citizens' sharing a deeper moral commitment concerning the good.

It is this argument concerning the second dimension of stability that Rawls has come to believe to be inadequate. The reconsideration of the second dimension of stability came about because of Rawls's growing appreciation of the depth of diversity in modern societies. Recalling the distinction between the diversity of conceptions of the good and of comprehensive doctrines, we can see what Rawls thinks went wrong in considerations of stability in *A Theory of Justice*: "Although the distinction between a political conception of justice and a comprehensive philosophical doctrine is not discussed in [*A*] *Theory* [*of Justice*], once the question is raised, it is clear, I think, that the text regards justice as fairness and utilitarianism as comprehensive, or partially comprehensive, doctrines." (*PL*, xviii)

On the one hand, I think Rawls overestimates the degree to which *A Theory of Justice* presupposes a single comprehensive doctrine. After all, there is a close relationship between diversity of comprehensive doctrines and diversity of conceptions of the good, and there is no doubt that *A Theory of Justice* presupposes a diversity of conceptions of the good. Furthermore, there are many passages in *A Theory of Justice* which come surprisingly close to asserting that justice as fairness does not (or should not) rely on such a comprehensive view. For example:

> What is essential is that when persons with different convictions make conflicting demands on the basic structure as a matter of political principle, they are to judge these claims by the principles of justice. The principles that would be chosen in the original position are the kernel of political morality. They not only specify the terms of cooperation between persons but they define a pact of reconciliation between

diverse religions and moral beliefs, and the forms of culture to which they belong. (*TJ*, 221 [194]; cf. 447-448 [393])[153]

On the other hand, there certainly is some evidence (beyond Rawls's own later interpretation) that *A Theory of Justice* presupposed a single comprehensive moral doctrine. Rawls would not now develop principles of justice on the assumption that "the collective activity of justice is the preeminent form of human flourishing." This will not do if a reasonable comprehensive doctrine can reject the view that justice is the preeminent form of human flourishing. Similarly, Rawls would no longer claim that the principles of justice "express our *nature* as a free and equal rational being." (*TJ*, 574 [503], my emphasis) As we have seen, our status as free and equal moral beings is assumed for purposes of constructing a political conception of justice, not as part of our nature.

To understand how justice as fairness relies on the idea of an overlapping consensus to provide an account of the second dimension of stability, consider the contrast between an overlapping consensus and a modus vivendi. In a modus vivendi different comprehensive doctrines can come to an agreement with each other concerning the arrangement of the institutions of the basic structure. However, each side regards its commitment to this arrangement as a compromise necessitated by the current balance of power in the society. If one group were to attain the power to enforce its most-preferred arrangement, it would abandon the compromise position. Therefore, Rawls says, under a modus vivendi, "social unity is only apparent, as its stability is contingent on circumstances remaining such as not to upset the fortunate convergence of interests." (*PL*, 147) In contrast, with an overlapping consensus each comprehensive doctrine affirms the principles as morally correct. To be sure, each comprehensive doctrine affirms more than what is present in the overlapping consensus, but it takes the overlapping consensus to be (morally) correct as far as its goes, and not merely a compromise necessitated by circumstances. As Rawls puts it:

> [An overlapping consensus] is affirmed on moral grounds, that is, it includes conceptions of society and of citizens as persons, as well as principles of justice, and an account of the political virtues through which those principles are embodied in human character and expressed in public life. An overlapping consensus, therefore, is not merely a consensus on accepting certain authorities, or on complying with certain institutional arrangements, founded on a convergence of self- or group interests. All those who affirm the political conception start from within their own comprehensive view and draw on the religious, philosophical, and moral grounds it provides. (*PL*, 147)

---

153. Brian Barry emphasizes the continuity between *A Theory of Justice* and *Political Liberalism* in "John Rawls and the Search for Stability," *Ethics* 105, no. 4 (July 1995).

In order for a comprehensive doctrine to be part of a true overlapping consensus and not merely a modus vivendi, it must affirm the principles of justice as being (morally) correct and not merely as being a compromise called for in light of its inability to realize its true ideal.

As Rawls suggests in this passage above, comprehensive doctrines will only do this if they also share the conceptions of the person and society that we have discussed earlier. This reminds us that justice as fairness only hopes to generate an overlapping consensus of reasonable comprehensive doctrines. We are not interested in an overlapping consensus of whatever comprehensive doctrines happen to exist at a given time any more than we are interested in ensuring that whatever institutional arrangements currently exist are preserved. This means that justice as fairness does not pursue the idea of an overlapping consensus directly by surveying possible points of agreement among existing comprehensive doctrines. To repeat one more time, this would make political liberalism "political in the wrong way." (*PL*, 40) Instead, we are to develop a freestanding view, identifying principles of justice based only on the elements shared by all reasonable comprehensive doctrines: a recognition of the duty of civility and the burdens of judgment together with the models of society and the person. The idea of an overlapping consensus serves as a check on the reasonableness of the choice of principles of justice. Remember, all of this occurs within our effort to reach full reflective equilibrium, and thus to identify the correct principles of justice.

Note, finally, that justice as fairness itself does not argue that any particular comprehensive doctrine will affirm the political conception of justice and be part of the overlapping consensus. Justice as fairness simply introduces the idea of an overlapping consensus as an account of how it is possible for there to be a stably just arrangement in the face of diverse, yet reasonable, comprehensive doctrines. Thus, a political conception of justice relies on a division of labor. It is up to each reasonable comprehensive doctrine to go beyond the limits of public reason and show why, in its own terms, its adherents should accept the models of society and the person and the duty of civility. It is up to justice as fairness to provide an argument for a specific conception of justice that draws only on what all reasonable comprehensive doctrines share so that it can fit as a "module" (*PL* 12) into each reasonable comprehensive doctrine. The next chapter will show how this is done.

Chapter 3
Justice As Fairness II: Principles

Primary Goods and Neutrality

Now that we have the background framework in place, we can begin to consider which specific principles of justice would best realize the ideal of a fair system of cooperation in a society in which citizens hold a diversity of reasonable comprehensive doctrines. Judging the fairness of a system of social cooperation requires some basis on which to compare the advantages afforded to various social positions. There is a problem in finding such a basis, however, since individuals are assumed to have diverse conceptions of the good. If all citizens embraced a single system of ends, we could compare social positions in terms of the degree to which these positions contribute to or interfere with the achievement of those goals. In circumstances of diversity, however, such a shared system of ends is unavailable. It would be an obvious violation of the requirements of public reason (and thus of the duty of civility and of the liberal principle of legitimacy) if we were to compare social positions on the basis of a conception of the good that some citizens reasonably rejected. For example, it would be unacceptable to assess the fairness of the basic structure based on the assumption, say, that individuals are only interested in experiencing pleasurable sensations. Some individuals have a conception of the good focused on this, but many reasonably will not. We need to rely on some understanding of the good so that we can compare social positions, but our comparison cannot depend on any particular comprehensive doctrine and its associated full conception of the good. Rawls's solution to this problem is to develop a "thin" theory of the good, and specifically, to rely on the idea of "primary goods."[1]

Rawls's thin theory of the good is *thin* because it proceeds strictly within the limits of public reason. It is used to generate an account of primary goods, those goods that all reasonable citizens hold to be valuable. Recall that the model of the citizen on which justice as fairness relies involves the two moral powers (a sense of justice and a capacity for a conception of the good) as well as a determinate conception of the good.[2] The determinate conceptions of the good

---

1. On the idea of a "thin theory of the good," see *TJ*, section 60 and *PL*, 176-178.

2. I follow the account in Rawls, "Social Unity and Primary Goods," in *Utilitarianism and Beyond*, Amartya Sen and Bernard Williams, eds. (New York: Cambridge University Press, 1982), and *PL*, 178-190. It differs somewhat from that presented in *A Theory of*

that citizens affirm are *thick* and diverge from one another on many points, in contrast to the account of primary goods that they all can share. We can think of primary goods, Rawls suggests, as "citizens' needs—that is, of persons' needs as citizens—and this allows justice as fairness to hold that the fulfillment of claims appropriately related to these needs is to be publicly accepted as advantageous, and thus counted as improving the circumstances of citizens for the purposes of political justice." (*PL*, 179) In other words, primary goods are the needs of the concrete, human embodiments of the model-conception of the person. The distribution of some of these primary goods will be controlled largely by the arrangement of social institutions. We can call these the primary *social* goods, while those that are not controlled mainly by social institutions are primary *natural* goods. When justice as fairness refers to primary goods, we almost always mean primary social goods.

Rawls gives the following list of types of primary social goods:

> a. basic rights and liberties . . . ;
> b. freedom of movement and free choice of occupation against a background of diverse opportunities;
> c. powers and prerogatives of offices and positions of responsibility in the political and economic institutions of the basic structure;
> d. income and wealth; and finally,
> e. the social bases of self-respect. (*PL*, 181)

Rawls indicates some flexibility with the list, stating that "we may add should it prove necessary." (*PL*, 181) Figuring prominently in the secondary literature as possible additions are health care and leisure.[3] Furthermore, Rawls allows that the identification of the details of some of these abstract goods may be made in light of the specifics of the society in question.[4] Finally, it is worth recalling that

---

Justice, where Rawls presents primary goods as all-purpose means for all (or most) determinate conceptions of the good, rather than stressing the model conception of the person. See, for example, *TJ*, 92 [79].

3. On health care, see the literature cited below in note 114, and *PL*, 184. Rawls mentions leisure time as a possible addition. (*PL*, 181n9) Counting time away from work as a primary social good may be a way to recognize that those who choose not to work or to work less may be reaping important benefits despite having a low income. See the discussions in R. A. Musgrave, "Maximin, Uncertainty, and the Leisure Trade-Off," *The Quarterly Journal of Economics* 88 (Nov. 1974); Ronald Dworkin, "What Is Equality? Part I: Equality of Welfare," *Philosophy and Public and Affairs* 10, no. 3 (summer 1981); "Part II: Equality of Resources," *Philosophy and Public and Affairs* 10, no. 4 (fall 1981); Philippe Van Parijs, "Why Surfers Should Be Fed: The Liberal Case for an Unconditional Basic Income," *Philosophy and Public Affairs* 20, no. 2 (spring 1991); Thomas Pogge, *Realizing Rawls* (Ithaca, N.Y.: Cornell University Press), 198-199; and Walter Schaller, "Rawls, the Difference Principle, and Economic Inequality," *Pacific Philosophical Quarterly* 79, no. 4 (Dec. 1998).

4. They can be specified at the later stages of the four-stage sequence. See *PL*, 188,

at this point, we have not yet determined what standard of justice we should use when assessing the distribution of these primary social goods.

Perhaps surprisingly, Rawls does not offer an authoritative list of which rights and liberties are *basic*. Instead he notes that an initial list could either be drawn up through a survey of the constitutions of democratic states that have worked reasonably well or alternatively we may "consider which liberties are essential social conditions for the adequate development and full exercise of the two powers of moral personality over a complete life." (*PL*, 293) It seems preferable to adopt the latter method and to use the former as a check in reflective equilibrium. The initial list can be improved and specified as we identify the principles that are to govern the distribution of these rights and consider the conditions of the society to which they are to be applying. In any event, Rawls relies on an initial, rough and ready list of basic liberties that includes *basic political liberties*, such as the right to vote and to be eligible for public office, free (political) speech, and the right to organize and assemble to address public issues. It also includes *basic civil liberties*, such as liberty of conscience and freedom of thought, together with rights of free speech and assembly (not limited to their political function), and "freedom from arbitrary arrest and seizure as defined by the concept of the rule of law." (*TJ*, 61 [53]) Finally, Rawls includes "the right to hold and to have the exclusive use of personal property." (*PL*, 298)

Note that Rawls does not include private ownership of the means of production nor "certain rights of acquisition and bequest," as basic liberties. (*PL*, 298; cf. *TJ*, 278 [245]) Nor, at this point, does he include "the equal right to participate in the control of means of production and natural resources." (*PL*, 298) The reason is simple: "These wider conceptions are not used because they cannot, I think, be accounted for as necessary for the development and exercise of the moral powers. The merits of these and other conceptions of the right of property are decided at later stages when much more information about a society's circumstances and historical traditions is available." (*PL*, 298; cf. 7-8n7; 338) In other words, Rawls does not want to build into his conception of justice a requirement or prohibition on any particular level of social control of the means of production. Such judgments are to be made after we have a basic conception and are attempting to determine which institutional arrangement will best realize that ideal in particular circumstances. (See *TJ*, 258 [228], 274 [242].)[5]

298, 333; Rawls, "Social Unity and Primary Goods," 168n8; John Rawls, "Reply to Alexander and Musgrave," *The Quarterly Journal of Economics* 88 (Nov. 1974), 642; Norman Daniels, "Equality of What: Welfare, Resources, or Capabilities?" in *Justice and Justification* (New York: Cambridge University Press, 1996), 216. On the four-stage sequence, see my "Having It Both Ways: Justification and Application in Justice As Fairness," *Pacific Philosophical Quarterly* 75, no. 3&4 (Sept./Dec. 1994).

5. Note also that the right to personal property by itself does not dictate any particular

Let us briefly consider a few examples of how the primary goods can be defended based on the model-conception of the person (that is, within the limits of public reason). Rawls suggests that we think of the basic liberties as "the background institutional conditions necessary for the development and the full and informed exercise of the two moral powers. . . ; these liberties are also indispensable for the protection of a wide range of determinate conceptions of the good (within the limits of justice)." (*PL*, 308) For simplicity, we will only consider the grounds related to the second moral power, the capacity for a conception of the good. For purposes of assessing matters of basic justice, citizens view themselves and others as responsible for their conceptions of the good. This requires that they be free to examine their comprehensive doctrines, compare them with others, revise them if they believe it necessary to do so, and affirm their own conscientious convictions on whatever grounds they believe most appropriate. Liberty of conscience protects the exercise of these capacities. Without this liberty, citizens could be subject to a central authority dictating to them a particular comprehensive doctrine, say, a religion or specific conception of the good. The rights to free speech and assembly are also necessary for adequate reflection on one's comprehensive doctrine.

The formal guarantee of these liberties, however, is insufficient to ensure the adequate development and exercise of the two moral powers or the pursuit of one's determinate conception of the good. Citizens must also have adequate income and wealth, "understood broadly as all-purpose means (having an exchange value) . . . [which] are needed to achieve directly or indirectly a wide range of ends, whatever they happen to be." (*PL*, 308) Without the provision of resources, the formal guarantee of the basic liberties will have little worth to citizens. Income and wealth are maximally flexible resources that individuals and groups can use in the pursuit of a wide range of goals. Rawls has a very broad understanding of wealth, including wealth that is collectively held, as "in an associational socialist economy, [where] the workers in the firm control its capital and means of production."[6] Note that there is no supposition that wealth and income are the only ends that citizens have, nor even that they are valued for their own sakes (though, of course, they may be by some). Rather, in light of the wide diversity of goals that citizens are presumed to have, and the complexity of modern societies, some mechanism of exchange is necessary for the realization of a wide range of ends. Furthermore, although *wealth* is a primary good, *being wealthy*, understood as the relational property of having more wealth than average, is not.

Finally, note the inclusion of the social bases of self-respect. Indeed, Rawls identifies self-respect as "perhaps the most important primary good." (*TJ*, 440

---

scheme of property rights. Unlike the other basic liberties which will be controlled by the first principle of justice, the detailed property rights which an individual may legitimately claim will depend, in part, on the difference principle.

6. John Rawls, "Fairness to Goodness," *The Philosophical Review* 84 (1975), 541.

[386]) Rawls thinks of self-respect as the psychological attitude in which one views oneself as of equal moral worth to other citizens. When a person has adequate self-respect, she views herself as entitled to press fair claims for social resources in order to pursue her (reasonable) conception of the good. Now self-respect in this sense, as a psychological attitude, is not a primary social good. It is not directly controlled by the institutions of the basic structure. Yet, it certainly is affected indirectly by those institutions. Rawls, therefore, is concerned with the *social basis* of self-respect. But how, on the basis of the model-conception of the person, are we to justify the importance of self-respect? Rawls suggests we think of self-respect as "not so much a part of any rational plan of life as the sense that one's plan is worth carrying out." (*TJ*, 178 [155]) It is justified most clearly, therefore, by the instrumental contribution it makes to realizing any conception of the good: "Without it nothing may seem worth doing, or if some things have value for us, we lack the will to strive for them. All desire and activity becomes empty and vain, and we sink into apathy and cynicism." (*TJ*, 440 [386]) Lacking this primary good would often be even more detrimental to the pursuit of one's goals as the lack of material resources would be. Furthermore, a lack of self-respect may undermine the desire to be a fully cooperating member of society. (See *PL*, 318.)

For the most part, Rawls assumes that the provision of the social bases of self-respect will be dependent on the principles which govern the distribution of the other primary goods. (See *TJ*, 546 [478-479]; and *PL*, 181.) Other primary goods will be distributed in a way that tends either to support or to undermine the development of self-respect. It sometimes looks as though Rawls believes that the social bases of self-respect can be fully secured through the distribution of the basic liberties alone, as when he writes: "The basis for self-esteem[7] in a just society is not then one's income share but the publicly affirmed distribution of fundamental rights and liberties." (*TJ*, 544 [477]) In other places, however, he ties it to the distribution of the other primary social goods, as when he writes that the difference principle (concerned with institutions that regulate the distribution of wealth and income) "explicates the distinction between treating men as a means only and treating them also as ends in themselves," and thereby secures "each man's rational interest in his self-respect." (*TJ*, 180)[8] In either case, however, one might suspect that the emphasis on the social bases of self-respect will be superfluous since they are tied to the distribution of other primary goods. This is mistaken; even though they do not have their own

---

7. In *A Theory of Justice*, Rawls does not distinguish self-esteem and self-respect. See *TJ*, 440 [386]. David Sachs discusses their relationship in "How to Distinguish Self-Respect from Self-Esteem," *Philosophy and Public Affairs* 10, no. 4 (fall 1981).

8. In the revised edition of *TJ*, Rawls substitutes the term "interprets" for "explicates" [157]. See also the discussion in Joshua Cohen, "Democratic Equality," *Ethics* 99, no. 4 (July 1989), 738n29; and Rex Martin, *Rawls and Rights* (Lawrence: University Press of Kansas, 1985), 191-195.

principle of justice tied directly and exclusively to their distribution, the social bases of self-respect play an important role in the selection of the principles of justice, as we shall see.

Now the inclusion of multiple primary social goods creates a possible difficulty in comparing social positions. The different dimensions that measure shares of the various primary social goods must be combined into a single index in order to compare social positions on a single scale. For example, of two social positions, one may have a greater share of one primary good, say, wealth, while the other has a greater share of a different good, say, social authority. Which is more advantaged, and, more generally, how are different primary goods to be balanced against one another in making such an assessment? To solve this problem, we need to create an index of the primary goods. (See *TJ*, 93-94 [80].) Rawls himself does not specify such an index, and often he relies on the simplifying assumption that an advantage with respect to one primary good usually comes with advantages concerning the others. (See *TJ*, 94 [80].) This may often be true—for example, positions of authority do frequently command higher income—but not always. I will not offer a specific index either, but I will suggest that the theoretical difficulties are not as great as might be supposed.

First, note that we do not have to solve the problem in its most general form. There is no reason to force ourselves to make choices concerning all possible combinations of primary goods. It suffices to confine ourselves to socially feasible social arrangements. Furthermore, this can be done when we have knowledge available concerning the specific circumstances of the society in question and when the relevant primary social goods can themselves be specified in more detail. Second, as we will see below, it turns out that Rawls defends two principles of justice that give priority to the equal basic liberties over the remaining primary social goods (which I will from now on call *social resources* or simply *resources*). This means that the principles of justice themselves resolve the indexing problem between the basic liberties and the social resources. The problem remains therefore to construct two simpler indices: one for the basic liberties and the other for social resources. Fortunately, Rawls has indicated how to do this for the basic liberties, and although I will not pursue it here, one could follow an analogous process for the social resources.[9]

Rawls's basic strategy for commensurating the various basic liberties into a single measure draws, once again, on the model-conception of the person.[10] The

---

9. For worries about the possibility of constructing such an index see Richard Arneson, "Primary Goods Reconsidered," *Nous* 24, no. 3 (June 1990), especially 445-446. See also John Roemer, *Theories of Distributive Justice* (Cambridge: Harvard University Press, 1996), 165-172.

10. *A Theory of Justice* seems to suggest that the basic liberties are to be reconciled by *maximizing* the extent of liberty. (See, for example, 60. Rawls changes this passage in the revised edition; compare [53].) As Hart pointed out, however, this produces a clear result only in the simplest cases, such as debating rules, without giving clear guidance in more

idea is to generate a notion of the *significance* of a liberty based on the degree to which it is "essentially involved in . . . the full and informed and effective exercise of the moral powers. . . . Thus, [for example] the weight of particular claims to freedom of speech, press, and discussion are to be judged by this criterion." (*PL*, 335-336) Notice that the idea of significance becomes relevant when we have a situation in which particular claims that appeal to different basic liberties conflict with one another. The assessment of significance is to be made with full knowledge of the details of the particular situation. On the other hand, significance is not to be judged on the basis of any particular comprehensive doctrine or conception of the good. Instead, our assessment of significance moves within the limits of public reason and is based on what all reasonable comprehensive doctrines share: a commitment to the model-conception of the person with its two moral powers necessary for full participation in a fair system of cooperation. Thus, the significance of a particular liberty is based on its importance in developing or exercising one's sense of justice or capacity for a conception of the good. Rawls illustrates this by discussing in considerable detail the significance of different claims to free speech. (See *PL*, 340-368.) Analogously, we could compare, say, the significance of a marginal increase in income to the significance of a marginal increase in the range of employment options. Surely such a comparison will depend on many details of the specific social circumstances in question. The point, however, is that when confronted with such a choice, we are to decide with reference to the higher-order interests of the model-conception of the person, rather than to any particular conception of the good.

Now while it is true that the justification of the primary social goods is based on the model-conception of the person rather than on any particular conception of the good, and thus it is based on what is shared by all reasonable comprehensive doctrines, it is not obvious that the primary goods are of equal value to all reasonable comprehensive doctrines. In fact, it is fairly clear that the primary goods are not of equal value to all reasonable comprehensive doctrines. There is no assumption that all reasonable comprehensive doctrines value the primary goods intrinsically nor put them to the same use. Many authors have challenged the use of primary goods on these grounds, claiming that relying on them reveals a fatal bias at the heart of justice as fairness. We can initially distinguish two reasons that explain why the same share of primary goods may predictably lead different individuals to achieve different levels of success in pursuit of their ends. First, the ends themselves may be more or less difficult to achieve with a given share of primary goods. Second, individuals have different talents and abilities, so even if they had the same ends and an equal share of

---

difficult cases. (See H. L. A. Hart, "Rawls on Liberty and Its Priority," in *Reading Rawls*, Norman Daniels, ed. [New York: Basic Books; reprint, Stanford: Stanford University Press, 1989], 240-242.) Rawls now accepts this criticism and now rejects the idea that there is anything to be maximized. (See *PL*, 332-333.)

social resources, they would not necessarily be equally successful in achieving their ends. There are, therefore, two corresponding criticisms of primary goods: that they are biased against certain conceptions of the good (those that are more difficult to achieve), and that they are biased against certain individuals (those who need a greater share of resources to achieve an equal level of success).

In an article published in 1973, Adina Schwartz presses the first criticism.[11] Although Schwartz concedes that "all rational individuals want a certain amount of wealth" and "the liberty to pursue a plan of life," still, some "rational individuals without a preference for more rather than less of Rawls's primary goods can claim that they would be harmed by the furtherance of this preference, at least to the extent that they would be better off in a society that did not further it." (301-302) For example, she claims, a person "somewhat in the lines of the early Marx" would believe:

> that a good life must rest on self-realization through labor, that the political structure of a society is determined by its economic structure, and that a person is morally harmed by the possession of more than a certain minimal amount of wealth. This individual's plan of life involves a preference for goods which can be generally characterized as wealth and liberty. However, he does not have a preference for the goods of wealth and liberty described in Rawls's specification of the primary goods. (302)

The problem with Rawls's understanding of liberty, according to Schwartz, is that it does not explicitly include "the freedom to realize his nature as a laboring being." (303) And the problem with wealth is that the socialist's good is only furthered by "just enough wealth so that he is decently fed, housed, and clothed." Schwartz does not claim that he would actually be harmed by having a claim to greater wealth, but she does claim that "he would be harmed by living in a society based on a preference for a greater rather than a lesser amount of wealth." (304) Thus, Schwartz's work exemplifies the first criticism—that in his selection of primary goods, specifically the basic liberties and wealth, Rawls reveals a bias toward individualistic conceptions of the good that infects the rest of the theory.

---

11. Adina Schwartz, "Moral Neutrality and Primary Goods," *Ethics* 83 (1973). Parenthetical references in this paragraph will be to this work. Other early criticisms along these lines can be found in Michael Teitelman, "The Limits of Individualism," *The Journal of Philosophy* 69, no. 18 (Oct. 1972), especially 551; and Thomas Nagel, "Rawls on Justice," in *Reading Rawls*, Daniels, ed., especially 9. Most of the arguments in the secondary literature against the reliance on primary goods are best understood as complaints with principles of justice that require *an egalitarian distribution* of primary goods. Until we see the reasons for selecting particular principles of justice, there is a sense in which complaints against the reliance on primary goods are premature. We will consider the second criticism when we return to this issue below.

Schwartz's criticisms of the basic liberties and of wealth miss the mark. She does not provide any reason to believe that the protection of the basic liberties as Rawls understands them would prevent her socialist from realizing his nature as a laboring being. Recall that Rawls does not include the right to private ownership of the means of production among the basic liberties. There is simply no reason to believe that the protection of the basic political liberties—liberty of conscience, the rule of law and freedoms of speech and association—are less important to the socialist than to a person who "realizes his nature" in activities other than labor. Perhaps, then, her complaint is not with what Rawls does include, but that he does not protect all of the liberties that would be beneficial to the socialist. Rawls never claims, however, that the primary goods include all goods that would be valuable to every (reasonable) conception of the good. Schwartz would have to show that all reasonable conceptions of the good share the socialist's priority concern with labor and therefore that if a comprehensive doctrine rejects such an understanding of human nature it is unreasonable (not only false or misguided). I know of no attempts to make such an argument.

With regard to wealth, Schwartz's objection is doubly mistaken. Her claim seems to be that the socialist is improperly harmed by the (reasonable) conception of the good of others. From her description of the case, it seems as though her socialist is unable to realize his conception of the good unless everyone in the society shares his view that human nature is fulfilled in a certain kind of laboring activity. But this is simply a demand that all citizens share her comprehensive doctrine and conception of the good. It is no more acceptable in its denial of reasonable pluralism than a true believer's insistence that his good is unjustly undermined by the mere presence of atheists. Furthermore, Schwartz seems to assume that Rawls is committed to a model of individuals as "possessive individualists,"[12] interested in accumulating unlimited amounts of wealth for its own sake. As we have seen, however, different individuals will value primary goods for different reasons. As Will Kymlicka observes:

> The socialist needs resources in order to pursue a life of self-realizing labor—she needs access to land or other raw materials and to the technology which enables work to be creative and variable rather than merely onerous and repetitive. . . . It is entirely wrong to suppose that the less materialistic someone is, the less of an interest she has in Rawls's primary goods.[13]

In fact, consistent with Schwartz's socialist who, once "decently fed, housed, and clothed" has little need for additional wealth, Rawls acknowledges the possibility, indeed, the likelihood, of the marginal utility of wealth and income

---

12. The phrase is from C. B. Macpherson, *The Political Theory of Possessive Individualism* (New York: Oxford University Press, 1962).

13. Will Kymlicka, "Liberal Individualism and Liberal Neutrality," *Ethics* 99, no. 4 (July 1989), 888.

sharply decreasing: "It is a mistake to believe that a just and good society must wait upon a high material standard of life. What men want is meaningful work in free association with others, these associations regulating their relations to one another within a framework of just basic institutions." (*TJ*, 290 [257])[14] Remember, shares of primary goods provide the basis for comparing social positions in the society for purposes of assessing basic social justice. They are not necessarily assumed to be valued by citizens for their own sake.

If poverty and the distribution of wealth in society are relevant to our assessment of the justice of a society, income and wealth (or some proxy for them) must be included as primary goods. It is very peculiar, then, that the left frequently criticizes Rawls's inclusion of wealth in his list of primary goods, arguing that this shows him to be objectionably individualistic. The complaint that primary goods are biased toward individualistic conceptions of the good has become a staple criticism of Rawls, repeated endlessly but rarely defended. One critic (not of the left) actually claims that "Rawls says that money is one of the most important, if not the most important, of such [primary] goods."[15] It is not surprising that he does not tell us where Rawls is supposed to say this. Seyla Benhabib is representative of the left on this point, writing: "Rawls' definition of 'primary goods' is not a neutral or even minimal definition, but one reflecting the biases of a way of life that is based on the private happiness of consumers."[16] Consumption certainly is one of the purposes to which citizens may devote their share of social resources—indeed, presumably, they must consume to a certain extent. In a free society, a reduction in poverty means that citizens will have greater wealth with which to pursue whatever permissible ends they endorse. However, there is nothing Rawls says that indicates these ends will be (or should be) exclusively focused on consumption.

Perhaps one source of the frequent charge that justice as fairness is objectionably individualistic is a misunderstanding of its commitment to pluralism. As we have seen, Rawls takes it to be a fundamental fact about modern societies that they are characterized by a plurality of reasonable conceptions of the good and comprehensive doctrines. Typically, these are not held lightly. Citizens are genuinely committed to these diverse ways of life. Treating citizens as free and equal requires allowing them to affirm any of a wide variety of permissible comprehensive doctrines based on their own

---

14. If read in a strong sense, this claim clearly violates the limits of a political conception of justice by introducing claims that not all reasonable comprehensive doctrines will endorse. However, it is made in a context discussing the matter of justice between generations. The point that justice does not require unlimited accumulation of wealth still stands within a political conception.

15. Allan Bloom, *Giants and Dwarfs* (New York: Simon and Schuster, 1990), 301.

16. Seyla Benhabib, *Critique, Norm, and Utopia* (New York: Columbia University Press, 1986), 313-314.

conscience and critical reflection.[17] Thus, Rawls concedes that justice as fairness "is individualistic in the minimal sense of stipulating that society is composed of a plurality of human persons for whom an equal liberty and the right of dissent is to be maintained."[18] This minimal individualism is a response to the fact of reasonable pluralism and must not be confused with an individualism in the content of reasonable comprehensive doctrines. That is, while justice as fairness recognizes that each citizen may affirm his or her own conception of the good, there is no supposition that these are individualistic in content. They may or may not be. (See *TJ*, 127-129 [110-111].)

In fact, far from assuming that citizens' conceptions of the good are individualistic, Rawls presents a compelling case that his principles represent the realization of a deep sense of community and human sociability. Rawls begins by describing the model of a "private society" as follows: first, the individuals that comprise it "have their own private ends which are either competing or independent, but not in any case complementary. And second, institutions are not thought to have any value in themselves, the activity of engaging in them not being counted as a good but if anything as a burden. Thus each person assesses social arrangements solely as a means to his private aims." (*TJ*, 521 [457]) It seems that many of his critics believe that Rawls endorses this model, but he does not.

Instead, he adopts Wilhelm von Humboldt's idea of a *social union*. A brief summary of this important idea will have to suffice here. It is a deep fact about human beings that "no one person can do everything that he might do; nor a fortiori can he do everything that any other person can do. The potentialities of each individual are greater than those he can hope to realize; and they fall far short of the powers among men generally." (*TJ*, 523 [458-459]) We form a social union with others when we participate in projects and activities that we judge to be valuable for their own sakes, and in which our realized abilities complement those of others. Examples include an orchestra (*PL*, 321), various sports and games, as well as, more broadly, the collective activities of "art and science . . . religion and culture of all kinds." (*TJ*, 526 [461]) "A well-ordered society," Rawls observes, "and indeed, most societies, will presumably contain countless social unions of many different kinds." (*TJ*, 527 [462]) Justice as fairness, however, allows us to see society itself as a social union. "Indeed, it is a social union of social unions." (*TJ*, 527 [462]) This implies first, that there is a shared goal corresponding to the larger social union. This is the goal of justice

---

17. As we saw in the previous chapter, there is no requirement that citizens constantly reexamine their comprehensive doctrine nor that it be the product of some sort of radically decontextualized choice. Nonetheless, for purposes of assessing basic social justice, individuals are assumed to be responsible for their own comprehensive doctrines and conceptions of the good.

18. John Rawls, "Reply to Lyons and Teitelman," *The Journal of Philosophy* 69, no. 18 (Oct. 1972), 557. See also *PL*, 286.

itself. This higher goal, however, does not imply that all other goods are valuable merely as means to this higher end. Justice as fairness presupposes the existence of a diversity of reasonable conceptions of the good that citizens view as valuable for their own sakes. Second, the idea of a social union of social unions also implies that citizens view (at least some of) their conceptions of the good as complementing one another. They are thereby able to realize goals collectively that they could not realize individually. There is, of course, no requirement that citizens view their conceptions of the good in this way. But unlike many rival theories, and unlike the model of a private society, justice as fairness makes it possible for them to realize collective, higher-order ends that themselves depend on the existence of complementary conceptions of the good.

Returning to Schwartz's criticism, even if she is incorrect that the primary goods are biased against socialist conceptions of the good, she is correct that an equal share of primary goods will not translate into the same degree of success for all reasonable conceptions of the good. Although we have not yet discussed the principles of justice in any detail, we can take this opportunity to consider the broader question of whether justice as fairness is neutral among conceptions of the good or whether it favors some at the expense of others. In *A Theory of Justice*, Rawls studiously avoids characterizing the use of primary goods or his conception of justice generally, as neutral. In fact, in a 1975 article he explicitly rejected this characterization.[19] Nonetheless, critics have attributed to justice as fairness an aspiration to neutrality and then subjected it to the charge that it fails to achieve this goal.[20] These critics have forced Rawls's hand, and in an article published in 1988, he does use what he calls the "unfortunate" term *neutrality*. The problem, he claims, is that "some of its connotations are highly misleading, others suggest altogether impracticable principles."[21]

There are several ways in which *neutrality* can be understood. William Galston, for example, attributes to justice as fairness the aspiration to be neutral, understood as relying on no ideas of the good except those which are purely instrumental.[22] A second conception understands neutrality to require procedures which can be justified without appealing to any moral values at all. Justice as fairness is obviously not neutral in either of these senses. (See *PL*, 191-192.)

---

19. See Rawls, "Fairness to Goodness," 539.

20. For a discussion of these charges concerning liberalism generally, see Stephen Holmes, *The Anatomy of Antiliberalism* (Cambridge: Harvard University Press, 1993), especially 240-244. Holmes also expresses hesitancy with the word *neutral*: "Perhaps the concept of 'neutrality' should be reserved for foreign affairs." (241)

21. John Rawls, "The Priority of Right and Ideas of the Good," *Philosophy and Public Affairs* 17, no. 4 (fall 1988), 260; cf. *PL*, 191.

22. William Galston, "Defending Liberalism," *American Political Science Review* 72 (Sept. 1982). He then argues, unsurprisingly, that justice as fairness fails to be neutral in this sense.

Consider, then, three further senses of neutrality which may characterize, as Rawls puts it, "the aims of basic institutions and public policy":

a. that the state is to ensure for all citizens equal opportunity to advance any conception of the good they freely affirm;

b. that the state is not to do anything intended to favor or promote any particular comprehensive doctrine rather than another, or to give greater assistance to those who pursue it;

c. that the state is not to do anything that makes it more likely that individuals accept any particular conception rather than another unless steps are taken to cancel, or to compensate for, the effects of policies that do this. (*PL*, 192-193)

Justice as fairness is not neutral in the first of these senses, for not all conceptions of the good are permissible. Some directly conflict with the demands of justice and therefore, according to justice as fairness, carry no weight in the design of institutions and policies. Rawls does, however, believe that justice as fairness is neutral in the second sense: "its institutions are not intended to favor any comprehensive doctrine." (*PL*, 193)

However, intent is not the same as effect, and justice as fairness is not neutral in the third sense. Indeed, Rawls claims, "it is surely impossible for the basic structure of a just constitutional regime not to have important effects and influences as to which comprehensive doctrines endure and gain adherents over time; and it is futile to try to counteract these effects and influences, or even to ascertain for political purposes how deep and pervasive they are." (*PL*, 193) As Kymlicka points out, "respect for civil liberties will necessarily have nonneutral consequences" because some comprehensive doctrines will be better able to attract followers than others.[23] Furthermore, these nonneutral consequences will often be unpredictable. As J. Donald Moon has argued:

Providing social space for individuals to make important choices in certain areas of their lives in accordance with their own judgments, without being answerable to others for what they decide, is a major source of opacity in society. To the extent that individuals are free to make such choices and to act on them, significant areas of social life will exhibit an unplanned and uncontrolled process of development.[24]

Moon goes on to point out that "cultural life" is such an unpredictable area in a free society. The point more generally applies to comprehensive doctrines.

Justice as fairness's rejection of the first and third of these conceptions of neutrality (i.e., the fact that it does not embrace all conceptions of the good nor does it have equal effects on all permissible conceptions of the good) suggests two ways in which a comprehensive doctrine may be discouraged: "their

---

23. Will Kymlicka, "Liberal Individualism and Liberal Neutrality," 884.

24. J. Donald Moon, *Constructing Community* (Princeton: Princeton University Press, 1993), 199.

associated ways of life may be in direct conflict with the principles of justice; or else they may be admissible but fail to gain adherents under the political and social conditions of a just constitutional regime." (*PL*, 196) This, however, will be true in all societies and for any conception of justice. Rawls puts the point dramatically, following Isaiah Berlin:

> No society can include within itself all forms of life. We may indeed lament the limited space, as it were, of social worlds, and of ours in particular; and we may regret some of the inevitable effects of our culture and social structure. As Berlin has long maintained (it is one of his fundamental themes), there is no social world without loss: that is, no social world that does not exclude some ways of life that realize in special ways certain fundamental values. (*PL*, 197)

If some such exclusions are necessary in any society, the question remains whether the particular exclusions engendered by justice as fairness are arbitrarily biased and unjust. To sustain the charge of bias, it is insufficient to show that justice as fairness, and its reliance on primary goods, is likely to encourage some and discourage other conceptions of the good. That much is conceded since every society and every conception of justice will do that. The question is whether justice as fairness does this in an unfair way. (See *PL*, 199.) What distinguishes a just basic structure is not that it has an equal impact on all permissible comprehensive doctrines but that it treats all citizens fairly. As Rawls puts it: "We should not speak of fairness to conceptions of the good, but of fairness to moral persons with a capacity for adopting these conceptions and caring about the conditions under which they are formed."[25] Fair treatment of citizens may result, unintentionally yet predictably, in the unequal success of different reasonable comprehensive doctrines.

To conclude this section, let us distinguish two ways in which permissible comprehensive doctrines may be encouraged or discouraged by a just basic structure. Consider first what we may call a *passive influence*. Imagine a society in which literacy is at a low level and the majority of individuals hold a certain comprehensive view. As the society devotes greater resources to increasing literacy in accordance with the principles of justice, many citizens come to view this doctrine as an outmoded superstition, and they abandon it for what they take to be more enlightened views. This is not because the society aims at preventing individuals from accepting the old view. It is simply that in these new circumstances, the freedoms which citizens enjoy result in changes in their views. The institutions have a passive influence because although they do not aim at creating any particular kind of citizen, they nonetheless affect the comprehensive doctrines that citizens tend to endorse.

To understand how a just basic structure may permissibly have an *active influence* on which reasonable comprehensive doctrines citizens tend to endorse,

---

25. Rawls, "Fairness to Goodness," 554. See also *PL*, 40, 184-185.

recall that justice as fairness is concerned with the stability of a just basic structure. As we have seen, one of the components of stability is that as they mature, citizens must acquire a sense of justice. A just basic structure, therefore, may actively encourage the development of an adequate sense of justice and of the virtues that are necessary for the stability of a just basic structure. Contrary to critics who insist that liberalism cannot take an active interest in the virtue of its citizens, justice as fairness is very much concerned with the "formative project" of developing good citizens (i.e., those who fully can take part in a fair scheme of cooperation).[26] Institutions charged with nurturing and educating children are crucially part of a just basic structure. As Rawls writes, "reproductive labor is socially necessary labor," since citizens "must have a sense of justice and [of] the political virtues that support political and social institutions."[27]

Now it is important that the virtues that a just basic structure may actively encourage are limited to *political* virtues, that is, those necessary for the stability of a just basic structure. Citizens are to be encouraged, when assessing the basic structure, to treat fellow citizens as free and equal moral persons in the senses discussed in the previous chapter. (See the examples of political virtues that Rawls gives at *PL*, 122, 163, 194.) All reasonable comprehensive doctrines will recognize these virtues, but each comprehensive doctrine will go beyond them, endorsing additional virtues and condemning vices that are not political in this sense. Although parents, on the basis of their reasonable comprehensive doctrine, may aim at encouraging certain nonpolitical virtues in their children, a just basic structure will not do so. Public schools, for example, will not aim at developing (what is from the point of view of some comprehensive doctrine) a complete set of virtues. Rather, they will only aim at developing those virtues that all reasonable comprehensive doctrines share in their commitment to basic social justice, that is, the political virtues.

Nonetheless, it seems quite likely that by encouraging these political virtues there will be some "spill-over," and that attitudes not limited to the political will be affected.[28] Imagine a comprehensive doctrine that treats all individuals as free

---

26. Michael Sandel, for example, insists in *Democracy's Discontent* (Cambridge: Harvard University Press, 1996), that liberalism, unlike his republicanism, is not concerned with the "formative project" of developing virtuous citizens. See, for example, 6, and my discussion in chapter 4.

27. Rawls, "The Idea of Public Reason Revisited," 788. Rawls assumes that the family, in whatever form, will be an important part of the institutional arrangements that provide this form of social reproduction.

28. On the relationship between civic education and liberal toleration see, for example, Amy Gutmann, "Civic Education and Social Diversity," *Ethics* 105, no. 3 (April 1995); Stephen Macedo, "Liberal Civic Education and Religious Fundamentalism: The Case of God v. John Rawls?" *Ethics* 105, no. 3 (April 1995); Nomi Maya Stolzenberg, "'He Drew a Circle That Shut Me Out': Assimilation, Indoctrination, and the Paradox of Liberal Education," *Harvard Law Review* 106 (1993); Joe Coleman, "Civic Pedagogies

and equal in matters of basic social justice and yet in other contexts—say, in religious practices—insists that women, for example, are intrinsically unsuited for certain positions of authority. By encouraging the political virtues in citizens, a just basic structure may make it more difficult for such a comprehensive doctrine to attract adherents. Some might conclude that justice as fairness is covertly relying on a particular comprehensive doctrine. This is mistaken. Justice as fairness does not specify an ideal of the good life and then identify just institutions as those which encourage that type. Rather, it identifies certain political virtues as those that are necessary for the stability of a just society. If encouraging the development of those virtues makes certain reasonable comprehensive doctrines less attractive, this is not due to bias on the part of justice as fairness. It is due to the requirements of a stable and just society.

The Original Position and the First Principle of Justice

A political conception of justice, recall, is a moral conception worked out for the basic structure of society and presented in terms that respect the limits of public reason. As I remarked in the previous chapter, this definition does not itself specify particular principles of justice. We now turn to what distinguishes justice as fairness from other political conceptions. Up to this point we have not discussed the idea for which Rawls is most famous: the presentation of specific principles of justice as the result of the choice made by parties in the original position. Rawls sees justice as fairness as an attempt to "generalize and carry to a higher order of abstraction the traditional theory of the social contract as represented by Locke, Rousseau, and Kant." (*TJ*, viii [xviii]) The basic idea is that the principles of justice are the result of a social contract made from a fair initial situation. (See *TJ*, 118 [102].) We can of course imagine many different choice situations. Rawls argues that the original position "best expresses the conditions that are widely thought reasonable to impose on the choice of principles yet which, at the same time, leads to a conception that characterizes our considered judgments in reflective equilibrium." (*TJ*, 121 [105])

Before elaborating the features of the original position and discussing the choice that would be made there, it is crucial that we understand how this construction fits into the broader framework that we have surveyed. Many of the misunderstandings of justice as fairness derive from a failure to appreciate how the original position is embedded in this background. Most importantly, we must keep in mind that the original position is not an alternative to reflective equilibrium.[29] Rather, it is a device to help us to achieve reflective equilibrium:

---

and Liberal-Democratic Curricula," *Ethics* 108, no. 4 (July 1998); Harry Brighouse, "Civic Education and Liberal Legitimacy," *Ethics* 108, no. 4 (July 1998).

29. The following draws on my "The Reasonable in Justice As Fairness," *The Canadian Journal of Philosophy* 29, no. 1 (March 1999).

As a device of representation the idea of the original position serves as a means of public reflection and self-clarification. . . . The original position serves as a mediating idea by which all our considered convictions, whatever their level of generality—whether they concern fair conditions for situating the parties or reasonable constraints on reasons, or first principles and precepts, or judgments about particular institutions and actions—can be brought to bear on one another. This enables us to establish greater coherence among all our judgments; and with this deeper self-understanding we can attain wider agreement among one another. (*PL*, 26)[30]

Perhaps by looking to a hypothetical choice procedure we can establish more clearly for ourselves the relationships among our various commitments concerning justice. As Joshua Cohen emphasizes, the original position helps provide a unified defense of many of our most important considered convictions (such as our views concerning religious toleration, rights of political participation, and racial and sexual discrimination), together with distributive principles about which "we have much less assurance" and are often in need of guidance.[31] Furthermore, as Cohen emphasizes, although we may have certain provisional fixed points, presumably there is no conception of justice that fully accommodates all of our judgments and precepts as they currently stand.[32]

Rawls notes that the device of the original position allows justice as fairness to rely on pure procedural justice "from the beginning." (*TJ*, 120 [104]) The idea of pure procedural justice holds when "there is a correct or fair procedure such that the outcome is likewise correct or fair, whatever it is, provided that the procedure has been properly followed" and there is no criterion for the correct outcome independent of the procedure itself. (*TJ*, 86 [75]; cf. *PL*, 72-73) Thus, precisely because we do not (yet) have a conception of justice with which we can reach reflective equilibrium, we rely on a procedure to help identify such an outcome. Rawls thinks of the choice from the original position as an instance of pure procedural justice because the parties "recognize no standpoint external to their own point of view as rational representatives from which they are constrained by prior and independent principles of justice." (*PL*, 73) Furthermore, it will become important later that the parties are to think of their selection of principles as binding and as being "final and made in perpetuity, there is no second chance. . . . A person is choosing once and for all the standards which are to govern his life prospects." (*TJ*, 176 [153]) The parties are to make their choice with the assumption that the principles they select will structure their well-ordered society and that they will not have an opportunity to revisit their choice.

It is important to emphasize, however, that this entire construction takes place within *our* goal of attempting to reach reflective equilibrium. We—the real

---

30. See also *TJ*, 18 [16], 21 [19]; Rawls, "Fairness to Goodness," 538-539.
31. See the discussion in Cohen, "Democratic Equality," especially 728-729.
32. See Cohen, "Democratic Equality," 730-731.

people interested in achieving reflective equilibrium—are free to accept or reject the principles chosen from the original position (or from any other choice situation, for that matter) in our effort to reach reflective equilibrium. Although *the parties* view their choice as being irrevocable, *we* are free to reconsider the selection of principles from the original position whenever we want. We can "*at any time* enter this position, or perhaps, better, simulate the deliberations of this hypothetical situation, simply by reasoning in accordance with the appropriate restrictions." (*TJ*, 138 [119], my emphasis; cf. 139 [120]) Similarly, while the parties do not view themselves as constrained by any prior and independent commitments concerning justice, we are free to accept or reject any conception on the basis of the best arguments available with the full knowledge to which we have access. If, therefore, the choice procedure from the original position generates a conception of justice clearly inconsistent with strongly held commitments of our moral sense, it is open to us to reject the procedure and consider a new choice situation: "the outcome of the original position yields, *we conjecture*, the appropriate principles of justice for free and equal citizens." (*PL*, 72, my emphasis) It seems, therefore, that the choice from the original position is an example of pure procedural justice only if the outcome falls within an acceptable range of possible outcomes.

At two points in *A Theory of Justice*, Rawls calls such a case an instance of "quasi-pure procedural justice." (*TJ*, 201 [176], 362 [318]) There is no scandal, therefore, in Rawls's admission that "We want to define the original position so that we get the desired solution." (*TJ*, 141 [122])[33] Clearly in this context the point is not that we want it to generate a particular conception of justice that we have already chosen in some other way. This is exactly what we lack prior to reaching reflective equilibrium. What we want is a device to help us reach a reflective equilibrium between a specific conception and our more firmly held fixed points.

The original position is, of course, hypothetical. As such, it remains up to us to determine, as best we can, what the parties there would choose. If we simply imagined the parties to be considering which principles of justice matched their (or our) considered convictions about justice, the original position would be unable to serve its clarifying role. This is for the simple reason that in our attempt to determine what the parties would choose, we would be forced to reconsider the question we started with: Which principles of justice are best supported by our considered convictions?[34] The original position would not help because the problem with which we started would simply be reiterated within the original position. On the other hand, if we could specify a procedure in

---

33. Many have taken this claim to be an admission that the entire construction of the original position is a sham. See, for example, R. M. Hare, "Rawls' Theory of Justice," in *Reading Rawls*, Daniels, ed., 84.

34. See the discussion in my "Having It Both Ways," *Pacific Philosophical Quarterly* 75, no. 3&4 (Sept./Dec. 1994).

which the parties consider a different question than the one that we ourselves are considering, and if we had reason to believe that the answer to that question would be the same as the answer to our question, perhaps the problem would be more tractable. This is exactly what the original position attempts to do.

In general, a choice situation is defined by specifying the motivation of the parties and the epistemic condition in which they are making their choice. As Rawls puts it following Pareto, we must specify their "tastes and obstacles." (*TJ*, 119 [103]) Again, only if the tastes and obstacles of the parties are different from ours, and yet we have reason to believe that their choice will help us reach reflective equilibrium, will the original position serve a useful role. Therefore, we must find a way to design the choice situation so that it generates principles appropriate for the regulation of the basic structure of society, conceived of as a fair system of cooperation among free and equal moral persons. Justice as fairness does this by modeling the reasonable and the rational in different ways in the original position. The idea is to model the reasonable with the structure of the choice situation, while we model the rational with the motivation of the parties.

Most importantly, and most famously, the parties are situated symmetrically behind a (thick) veil of ignorance. Specifically, the parties do not know any of the details of the situation of those they represent.[35] "First of all, no one knows his place in society, his class position or social status; nor does he know his fortune in the distribution of natural assets and abilities, his intelligence and strength, and the like. Nor, again, does anyone know his conception of the good, the particulars of his rational plan of life, or even the special features of his psychology such as his aversion to risk or liability to optimism or pessimism." (*TJ*, 137 [118]) Although they do not know which specific conception of the good will be held by those they represent, they do know that it will be based on a reasonable comprehensive doctrine. "This requirement is fair because in establishing the fair terms of social cooperation (in the case of the basic structure) the only relevant feature of persons is their possessing the moral powers (to the sufficient minimum degree) and having the normal capacities to be a cooperating member of society over a complete life." (*PL*, 79)[36] The original position, "we conjecture, embodies all the relevant requirements of practical reason and shows how the principles of justice follow from the principles of practical reason in union with conceptions of society and person,

---

35. Sometimes Rawls speaks of the parties not knowing *their own* interests (as in the next quotation). Especially in his more recent work however, Rawls describes the parties as acting as trustees for and representing citizens. This difference does not affect their motivation or the principles they would choose. Having the parties choose for themselves may have expository advantages, but it risks suggesting the voluntaristic model that I discuss below.

36. The passage continues by emphasizing that this is only appropriate for the choice of first principles of justice concerned with the basic structure of society.

themselves ideas of practical reason." (*PL*, 90) In specifying the choice conditions in the original position, we draw on the model-conceptions of the person and of society and the ideas of the reasonable and the rational.

From their position of ignorance, the parties are motivated by, and reason as best they can toward, the (unknown) rational good of those they represent. The parties "decide solely on the basis of what seems best calculated to further their interests so far as they can ascertain them." (*TJ*, 584 [512]) They have what Rawls calls *rational autonomy*, as opposed to *full autonomy*. (See *PL*, 72-81.) The parties in the original position are not themselves motivated by a sense of justice. Thus, their practical reasoning is importantly different from that of citizens in a well-ordered society, who constrain their pursuit of their good, when necessary, by their sense of justice. Contrary to persistent misinterpretation in the secondary literature, Rawls's characterization of the motivation of the parties does not imply that they are selfish, however. Whether one is selfish or not depends on the content of one's conception of the good and how one pursues one's goals. Since the parties in the original position do not know the content of the conceptions of the good of those they represent, they cannot assume them to be either selfish or altruistic. Still, "although the interests advanced by these plans are not assumed to be interests in the self, they are the interests of a self that regards its conception of the good as worthy of recognition and that advances claims in its behalf as deserving satisfaction." (*TJ*, 127 [110]) So, we assume that the parties are motivated strictly by their goal of choosing principles that will best enable the pursuit of an unknown conception of the good. By considering the principles chosen from the original position, we transform our inchoate attempt to reach reflective equilibrium into a problem of "rational prudential choice." (*TJ*, 584 [512])[37]

We have already established that in addition to their determinate conception of the good, citizens have two higher-order interests in developing and maintaining their two moral powers above the threshold necessary to be fully cooperating members of the scheme of social institutions. We have also seen how the primary goods can be defended on the basis of the model-conception of the person. This is from the point of view of citizens, however, and we have not yet seen how this affects the parties in the original position. One might think that we simply stipulate that the parties are to secure these higher-order interests in addition to the resources necessary for the pursuit of the (unknown) conception of the good of those they represent. Rawls rejects such a stipulation, however. If the parties are interested in securing the higher-order interests of those they represent, this must be because they believe that doing so would contribute to the realization of reasonable conceptions of the good. (See *PL*, 315.) This is exactly what Rawls argues.

---

37. See also *TJ*, 44 [39]; and Rawls, "Fairness to Goodness," 543.

Before explaining this argument, however, let me say a word about why Rawls relies on this complicated argument concerning the preference of the parties for primary goods. One might think that Rawls could drop the reference to the higher-order interests and argue directly that primary goods are necessary means with which to pursue any (reasonable) conception of the good. This is the kind of argument that he attempted to make in *A Theory of Justice*: primary goods are "things that every rational man is presumed to want. These goods normally have a use whatever a person's rational plan of life." (*TJ*, 62 [54]) The problem with such an argument, Rawls has come to believe, is that it provides an insufficient defense of the basic liberties and their importance relative to the other primary goods. This is because according to the account in *A Theory of Justice*, the relative importance of different primary goods depends on the content of the particular conception of the good that an individual happens to hold. (See *TJ*, 542. Rawls changes this account in the revised edition of *TJ*.) The parties, therefore, would have insufficient grounds on which to rank the importance of different primary goods. His more recent strategy is to show that the basic liberties are necessary for the development and maintenance of the two moral powers, and that the parties in the original position would give a high priority to these higher-order interests.

In order to show that the parties in the original position would place a high priority on the two higher-order interests of citizens, we must establish that they have reason to believe that the moral powers contribute significantly to the realization of citizens' reasonable conceptions of the good. In light of the discussion in the previous chapter, it is fairly clear why the parties would take such a view of the second moral power, the capacity for a conception of the good. Since the parties are motivated by the pursuit of an unknown but determinate conception of the good, they will attach a very high priority to securing the capacities to form, to revise, and rationally to pursue such a good. For reasons we saw in the previous chapter, there is little hope that citizens will achieve their good without these abilities. The case here is analogous to the argument for the importance of self-respect: without it, the vigorous pursuit and successful achievement of one's good becomes very unlikely. Furthermore, the parties cannot discount the possibility that if the citizens they represent were to reflect on their conception of the good, they might come to view it as inadequate. The parties would want to secure at least the capacity to engage in such reflection, for they would not want to trap those they represent in the pursuit of a conception of the good that, on reflection, citizens would view as inadequate. (See *PL*, 313.) Finally, for some reasonable citizens, such critical reflection will itself be an important component of their conception of the good. It bears repeating a point from the previous chapter, however: there is no requirement that citizens actually engage in a certain amount of critical reflection on their (permissible) conceptions of the good. The point here is that the parties would be motivated to secure the grounds for that capacity.

The case for the first moral power—the sense of justice—is more subtle, but we will only be able to touch on three considerations. First, recall that the parties are choosing principles that will be publicly affirmed by citizens in a well-ordered society. As Rawls observes: "Clearly, the public knowledge that everyone has an effective sense of justice and can be relied upon as a fully cooperating member of society is a great advantage to everyone's conception of the good." (*PL*, 316) Therefore, the parties will want to select principles that make it more likely that a strong sense of justice will be secured in all citizens. This is obviously related to the issue of stability. It seems clear that the parties would want to select principles that would make the basic social institutions stable. Rawls introduces two additional grounds that account for why the parties would be motivated to secure the first moral power. Although as we have seen self-respect is the product of many elements, the ability to participate in a fair system of cooperation as a free and equal member is surely an important factor. Therefore, given the importance to the parties of securing the social bases of self-respect, they will give a high priority to the necessary conditions for such participation. Finally, Rawls mentions that the sense of justice allows different conceptions of the good to complement each other to allow the formation of "a social union of social unions."

Drawing these arguments together, we reach the following conclusions. In their effort to achieve the conditions necessary for the realization of the unknown conception of the good of those they represent, the parties in the original position will be moved to secure the functioning of the two moral powers. Given the connection between the primary goods and the two moral powers, the parties would be interested in securing primary goods for those they represent. Although it is true that other things equal, a greater share of resources would be likely to allow a more successful pursuit of one's conception of the good, the parties would be more concerned with ensuring that their higher-order interests are satisfied, at least to a certain extent. That is, there is a certain priority that they would establish with concerning the primary goods: those necessary for securing the two moral powers are more important than those which may allow for marginally more success once those conditions have been achieved. This does not mean, however, that they will seek to develop the moral capacities to an unlimited degree, at all costs. Rather, it means that they will put a high priority on securing the conditions necessary to allow those they represent to be fully cooperating members of a fair system of cooperation. Beyond that threshold, they will focus their attention on securing the resources with which citizens can pursue their specific ends, which, of course, are unknown to the parties.

Turning from the motivation of the parties in the original position to their knowledge, we assume that they know that they are choosing principles to regulate a well-ordered society characterized by reasonable pluralism. Furthermore, the parties have whatever general sociological and psychological information that might be relevant to their choice. This becomes especially important when we consider stability in the next section. The parties have information, for example, concerning which practices tend to generate a stronger sense of justice among children. Some critics have thought that including such information somehow commits Rawls to a positivist view of social science. They object that there is no uncontested social scientific knowledge and that it is always historically and socially specific.[38] The reply is that the parties should be aware of all these controversies. Critics get into difficulty when they forget that in the end we are the ones who must assess what a rational choice from the original position would be. If we think the rationality of the choice depends in important ways on psychological or sociological facts, we must do the best we can with the information available to us.

Since the time when Hobbes wrote that there is "no Obligation on any man, which ariseth not from some Act of his own,"[39] the idea of a social contract has often been associated with the attempt to ground moral obligations on some kind of voluntary undertaking along the model of a promise. This strategy aims to reduce more mysterious and unclear moral or political obligations to a more familiar sort.[40] However, this cannot be the idea of Rawls's contract because his contract is strictly hypothetical. Rawls rejects what many take to be the distinctive thesis of liberalism: that only individual consent can generate moral requirements.[41] The model of the original position does not contain any act of consent by the real, flesh-and-blood citizens who are supposed to be bound by the results. Ronald Dworkin presses this point with great clarity in an early review of *A Theory of Justice*: "A hypothetical contract is not simply a pale form of an actual contract; it is no contract at all."[42] Unlike many other versions of the social contract, Rawls's use of this model is not an attempt to introduce some kind of constraint on us through an act of consent. Instead, as we have seen, it is an attempt to help us reach reflective equilibrium and to clarify the content of our sense of justice.

Normally, when we make an agreement, we do so on the basis of its contribution to our conception of the good. In the original position, the details of these conceptions are denied to the parties, and so they are only able to base their choice on what they assume all reasonable conceptions of the good share:

---

38. See, for example, Robert Paul Wolff, *Understanding Rawls*, ch. 13; and Seyla Benhabib, "The Methodological Illusions of Modern Political Theory," *Neue Hefte für Philosophie* 21 (1982), 64-69.

39. Thomas Hobbes, *Leviathan*, C. B. Macpherson, ed. (New York: Penguin, 1968), 268.

40. Of course, it does not explain why the underlying promises are binding, as Hobbes's Foole was well aware. See *Leviathan*, 203-205 (chapter 15).

41. See his distinction between "obligations" and "natural duties," which "apply to us without regard to our voluntary acts." (*TJ*, 114 [98])

42. Ronald Dworkin, "The Original Position," in Daniels, *Reading Rawls*, 18.

the primary social goods. Furthermore, although normal contracts are subject to mistaken judgments concerning their contribution to our good, we stipulate that the parties in the original position make no such errors. Their choice is not based on any peculiar psychological propensities that may vary from individual to individual, but is determined strictly by considerations of instrumental rationality, applied in their unusual circumstance. Again, we simply stipulate this, as we can build in any conditions that we choose. Notice, then, that the motivation of all of the parties is the same, the information they have is the same, and they are all equally rational. Since they have the same motivation and the same information, "each is convinced by the same arguments." Oddly, therefore, "we can view the choice in the original position from the standpoint of one person [in the original position] selected at random. If anyone after due reflection prefers a conception of justice to another, then they all do, and a unanimous agreement can be reached." This means that "the parties have no basis for bargaining in the usual sense." (*TJ*, 139 [120]) The fact that Rawls's model of the social contract is so far from the features of normal contracts—in particular, that it can be modeled by a single deliberator—has led many commentators to deny that Rawls has a social contract theory at all.[43] This seems right only if we assume that the decisive feature of a contract is the generation of an obligation from an act of consent.

Rawls, however, insists on the importance of the contract model even though it differs from ordinary agreements and is not an attempt to reduce political obligations to a promise or an act of consent. Instead, this model conveys three important ideas that he wants to emphasize. First, relying on the image of a contract provides a useful reminder of the circumstances of justice. We are considering principles for people whose interests overlap to the point where cooperation is mutually advantageous, yet they are in conflict concerning how the benefits of cooperation are to be utilized. Second, consistent with the liberal principle of legitimacy and the duty of civility, the idea of a contract suggests that these principles must be publicly available and acceptable to the people living under them. Finally, it suggests that the choice of principles is binding. This final idea requires care in distinguishing the point of view of the parties in the original position and the point of view of "you and me," (*PL*, 28) who are attempting to reach reflective equilibrium. As we have seen, the parties are to choose principles to regulate the design of the basic structure on the assumption that they make this selection "once and for all." To repeat: we are not making any agreement at all, and so obviously there is nothing that is irrevocable for us. The fact that the parties view it as a permanent and binding agreement, however, is of great importance.

---

43. See, for example, Jean Hampton, "Contracts and Choices: Does Rawls Have a Social Contract Theory?" *The Journal of Philosophy* 77, no. 6 (June 1980); and Michael Sandel, *Liberalism and the Limits of Justice*, second edition (New York: Cambridge University Press, 1998), 122-124.

Consider an early objection to Rawls's theory made by Leonard Choptiany. He writes that while in the original position, the parties "will adopt a strategy they can agree on." Upon emerging from the original position, however, "each will have a second strategy for the practice itself, whose main feature will be the securing of the egoist's advantage."[44] Leaving aside the mistaken assumption that citizens' conceptions of the good will be egoistic, Choptiany raises the possibility of selecting principles with the intention of (possibly) betraying them once they are accepted by others. Such a strategy is exactly what Rawls's idea of a contract is intended to rule out.

In accordance with the idea of a contract, we stipulate that the parties may only agree to terms that they sincerely believe they will be able to accept, no matter what circumstances result from the choice. As Jeremy Waldron observes, "the issue facing those in the original position is not simply 'What principles would you choose?' but rather 'What principles would you be prepared to commit yourself to?'"[45] This is a significant difference, since as Rawls points out:

> In general, the class of things that can be agreed to is included within, and is smaller than, the class of things that can be rationally chosen. We can decide to take a chance and at the same time fully intend that, should things turn out badly, we shall do what we can to retrieve our situation. But if we make an agreement, we have to accept the outcome; and therefore to give an undertaking in good faith, we must not only intend to honor it but with reason believe that we can do so. Thus the contract condition is a significant further constraint.[46]

In particular, the parties are not "permitted to agree to a principle if they have reason to doubt that they will be able to honor the consequences of its consistent application."[47] If the parties are presented with a choice between two options, and if in "some possible circumstances, the first would permit, or require social positions that one could not accept, whereas the second results in arrangements that everyone can honor in all circumstances, then the second must be agreed to."[48] Of course, in judging the "strains of commitment" (*PL*, 17), that is, the limits of what they would be able to honor, the parties will have to rely on "a general knowledge of human psychology." (*TJ*, 176 [153])

We are almost ready to consider which principles would actually be chosen in the original position. To repeat the obvious one final time, because the parties in the original position are hypothetical constructs, it is up to us to determine

---

44. Leonard Choptiany, "A Critique of John Rawls's Principles of Justice," *Ethics* 83, no. 2 (Jan. 1973), 149.

45. Jeremy Waldron, "John Rawls and the Social Minimum," in *Liberal Rights* (New York: Cambridge University Press, 1993), 259-260.

46. Rawls, "Reply to Alexander and Musgrave," 651.

47. Rawls, "Reply to Alexander and Musgrave," 652.

48. Rawls, "Reply to Alexander and Musgrave," 652.

what choice would rationally be made from that position. Furthermore, it is clear that our judgment in this matter will depend, in part, on which conceptions of justice we consider. Rawls does not claim that the two principles of justice that he defends are superior to all others. His claim is more modest: that his principles would be chosen ahead of "the leading traditional theories." (*TJ*, 581 [509]) He has no general argument that his principles are the best,[49] but rather proceeds through a pair-wise comparison of alternatives. Although limited, this strategy does allow us to determine whether Rawls has accomplished his major objective: "to offer an alternative systematic account of justice that is superior . . . to the dominant utilitarianism of the tradition." (*TJ*, viii [xviii]) If the model of the original position fails to allow us to recognize the superiority of Rawls's two principles to utilitarianism, "all is lost."[50] It will turn out that the superiority of Rawls's conception depends primarily on the first principle, so we will have little to say about the second principle in this section. In the following two sections, we will go on to discuss the second principle of justice in detail and compare it to other alternatives (so-called *mixed conceptions*).

First, let us have a statement of Rawls's two principles:

> a. Each person has an equal claim to a fully adequate scheme of equal basic rights and liberties, which scheme is compatible with the same scheme for all; and in this scheme the equal political liberties, and only those liberties, are to be guaranteed their fair value.
> b. Social and economic inequalities are to satisfy two conditions: first, they are to be attached to positions and offices open to all under conditions of fair equality of opportunity; and second, they are to be to the greatest benefit of the least advantaged members of society. (*PL*, 6)[51]

Rawls assigns "lexical" priority to the first principle over the second, and within the second, to fair equality of opportunity over the second condition, the difference principle. This means that possible arrangements are to be ranked by the first principle alone. If there are institutional arrangements which equally satisfy the first principle, we assess them in terms of the second principle (first with respect to fair equality of opportunity and then, if necessary, with respect to the difference principle). This ordering means that where an equal scheme of basic liberties is possible, we cannot impose an unequal scheme in order better to satisfy the second principle (by, for example, generating greater economic resources).

---

49. Indeed: "I doubt, however, that the principles of justice (as I have defined them) will be the preferred conception on anything resembling a complete list." (*TJ*, 581 [509])

50. John Rawls, "Justice As Fairness: A Brief Restatement" (unpublished, 1989), 77.

51. In this formulation, Rawls omits the issue of just savings as well as the requirement that the political liberties be ensured "fair value." On just savings, see *PL*, 273-274; on the political liberties, see *PL*, 324-331, and the discussion below.

Rawls asserts this lexical priority of the first principle only "under reasonably favorable conditions." (*TJ*, 542)[52] In less favorable circumstances (but still, presumably, in the circumstances of justice) the parties in the original position might not want completely to subordinate their economic interests to the guarantee of equality of the basic liberties. In his more recent work, together with a new account of primary goods that emphasizes the model-conception of the person, Rawls has revised his defense of this priority. He clarifies the priority by explaining more fully the idea of "reasonably favorable conditions":

> [The] priority of liberty is not required under all conditions. For our purposes here, however I assume that it is required under what I shall call "reasonably favorable conditions," that is, under social circumstances which, provided the political will exists, permit the effective establishment and the full exercise of these liberties. These conditions are determined by a society's culture, its traditions and acquired skills in running institutions, and its level of economic advance (which need not be especially high), and no doubt by other things as well. I assume as sufficiently evident for our purposes, that in our country today reasonably favorable conditions do obtain, so that for us the priority of the basic liberties is required. Of course, whether the political will exists is a different question entirely. While this will exists by definition in a well-ordered society, in our society part of the political task is to help fashion it. (*PL*, 297)

As this passage explains, the standard for determining whether these reasonably favorable conditions obtain is whether the circumstances "permit the effective establishment and the full exercise" of the basic liberties. This, in turn, explains more clearly why if those circumstances do not obtain, the parties would be reluctant to give priority to the liberties: they recognize that they simply could not be effectively utilized in such circumstances. Instead, resources might better be used to attempt to create those conditions in which the basic liberties could be effectively established and exercised: "The denial of equal liberty can be defended only if it is necessary to raise the level of civilization so that in due course these freedoms can be enjoyed." (*TJ*, 152)[53]

The left has long criticized liberal political theories that naively assume that a formal guarantee of basic liberties will translate into equal value for all

---

52. The point is explained more fully in the revised edition of *TJ* [476].

53. In the revised edition, this passage reads as follows: "The denial of the equal liberties can be defended only when it is essential to change the conditions of civilization so that in due course these liberties can be enjoyed." [132] This priority follows from the account of the higher-order interests, discussed above. However, one might object that the basic liberties are not more important than resources when the satisfaction of one's basic needs are at stake. Rawls agrees and is willing to grant that "the first principle . . . may easily be preceded by a lexically prior principle requiring that citizens' basic needs be met, at least insofar as their being met is necessary for citizens to understand and to be able fruitfully to exercise those rights and liberties. Certainly any such principle must be assumed in applying the first principle." (*PL*, 7)

citizens. Rawls has not escaped this criticism, in part because he is indeed reluctant to say that "poverty and ignorance, and a lack of means generally" diminishes the guarantee of equal liberties. "Rather," he writes, "I shall think of these things as affecting the worth of liberty, the value to individuals of the rights that the first principle defines." (*TJ*, 204 [179]) This means that in order to understand the full implications of Rawls's conception of justice, we must view the two principles as working together. Once the formal guarantee of the basic liberties is established, the worth of those liberties is controlled by the share of resources that an individual may devote toward ends protected by those liberties. While the second principle may allow inequalities in resources, it will only do so when these inequalities maximize the share of the least advantaged. Therefore: "Taking the two principles together, the basic structure is to be arranged to maximize the worth [of liberty] to the least advantaged of the complete scheme of equal liberty shared by all. This defines the end of social justice." (*TJ*, 205 [179]) Far from relying on merely formal liberties and denigrating their worth, Rawls in fact suggests that the end of social justice is precisely to maximize the worth of the basic liberties to the least advantaged members.

Rawls is clearly assuming, therefore, that the worth of a liberty is not affected by one's position relative to others in the distribution of resources. The worth of my religious liberty, say, is affected by the resources that I may devote to my religious ends, not my position relative to others in the distribution. The worth of my religious liberty increases if I have a greater share of such resources, even if my share relative to others diminishes (because they gain even more). This is not true, however, when it comes to the political liberties. That is because of the competitive nature of the political process and its "limited space," so to speak. The greater influence of some necessarily means a lesser influence of others. The worth of the political liberties does not simply track the absolute share of social resources that an individual controls. Therefore, Rawls stipulates that the worth of the political liberties must be guaranteed "fair value," and not be controlled by the difference principle. (See *PL*, 324-331.)

Finally, we can now turn to the argument for this conception of justice. Even accepting Rawls's account of the value and appropriateness of the choice from the original position, few have been convinced by his argument that the two principles would be accepted there. Jon Elster speaks for many, no doubt, when he says that Rawls's account of the reasoning of the parties in the original position "is notoriously elliptical or worse."[54] As we have seen, Rawls is particularly interested in arguing that the two principles are superior to utilitarianism. Defenders of utilitarianism have vigorously replied that the parties in the original position would choose principles that require the maximization of average utility (or happiness, welfare, well-being, or preference satisfaction). John Harsanyi makes perhaps the most famous argument that

---

54. Jon Elster, *Local Justice* (New York: Russell Sage Foundation, 1992), 227.

utilitarianism would be chosen from the original position. He agrees that the construction of the original position is a "powerful analytic tool for clarifying the concept of justice," and in fact he himself introduced a similar idea in an article published in 1957.[55] Harsanyi argues that there are basically two choice strategies that the parties might adopt: the maximin principle (which, he grants, would lead to the two principles) or expected-utility maximization (which, he claims, would lead to utilitarianism). "Unfortunately, Rawls chooses the maximin principle as decision rule for the participants in the original position."[56]

The maximin principle is a decision rule that compares options strictly in terms of the worst possible outcome for each available selection and chooses the selection in which the worst outcome is least bad—that is, it *maximizes* the *minimorum*. Essentially, Harsanyi's argument consists in pointing out the counter-intuitive results of a general reliance on the maximin principle. It is, after all, an extremely conservative (i.e., risk-averse) principle for choices made under uncertainty. Harsanyi has no difficulty at all in showing that the general reliance on such a policy would lead to many unsatisfactory results. For example, he considers the choice between remaining in an inferior job in New York or taking a vastly superior job which requires a plane flight to Chicago. There is a slight chance that the flight will crash, and that would certainly be a worse outcome than remaining in the unappealing job in New York. Maximin reasoning, therefore, would select the New York job, scared off, so to speak, by the slight possibility of the crash. Harsanyi is surely right that as a general decision rule, maximin is far too conservative.

Rawls's initial reply was to stress that Harsanyi's examples tended to concentrate on micro-level decisions, while the choice from the original position involves the choice of principles to govern the basic structure of society.[57] Harsanyi expresses "astonishment" with such a "singularly inept defense."[58] No doubt, he is right that he would be able to construct examples for which the maximin rule would be similarly counter-intuitive even though they involve many individuals, and he asks rhetorically, "Does Rawls seriously think that there is a certain number *x*, such that a situation involving *more* than *x* people will come under moral principles basically different from a situation involving *fewer* than *x* people?"[59] The answer, of course, is that there is no such number, but, as we saw in the previous chapter, the basic structure is a special case.

---

55. John Harsanyi, "Cardinal Utility in Welfare Economics and the Theory of Risk-Taking," *The Journal of Political Economy* 61 (1953).

56. John Harsanyi, "Can the Maximin Principle Serve As a Basis for Morality? A Critique of John Rawls's Theory," in *Essays on Ethics, Social Behavior, and Scientific Explanation* (Boston: D. Reidel, 1976), 38.

57. John Rawls, "Some Reasons for the Maximin Criterion," *American Economic Review* 64 (May 1974), 141-142.

58. Harsanyi, "Can the Maximin Principle Serve As a Basis for Morality?" 59.

59. Harsanyi, "Can the Maximin Principle Serve As a Basis for Morality?" 60.

There is no reason to assume ahead of time that the principles appropriate for making an irrevocable contract under extreme uncertainty concerning the standards for the evaluation of the basic structure will be the same as the principles appropriate to use when selecting a career or travel plans.

More significantly, Harsanyi misunderstands the role of maximin reasoning in Rawls's argument. Harsanyi suggests (and I believe that this is the most common interpretation of Rawls's argument) that Rawls defends the general use of maximin reasoning and then applies it to the choice from the original position. This understanding unfortunately may be encouraged by Rawls's statement that "The theory of justice is a part, perhaps the most significant part, of the theory of rational choice." (*TJ*, 16 [15]) Some have taken this to imply that justice as fairness aspires to generate principles of justice from value-free theorems of rational choice theory. Rawls has retracted this statement, acknowledging that it is misleading: "What should have been said is that the account of the parties, and of their reasoning, uses the theory of rational decision, though only in an intuitive way." (*PL*, 53n7) A careful reading of *A Theory of Justice* reveals that Rawls identifies the maximin principle of choice as a "useful . . . heuristic device" and as he clarifies, "that the two principles of justice would be chosen if the parties were forced to protect themselves against such a contingency [namely, the worst outcome] explains the sense in which this conception is the maximin solution." (*TJ*, 152-153 [132-133]) In other words, Rawls does not start from a commitment to the maximin decision rule, which "Clearly . . . is not, in general, a suitable guide for choices under uncertainty." (*TJ*, 153 [133]) Rather, for reasons we will explore, Rawls claims that the parties wind up reasoning in an extremely risk-averse manner analogous to that prescribed by the maximin rule. It would be inappropriate simply to posit a peculiarly risk-averse psychology: "it is not an argument for the two principles of justice that they express a peculiarly conservative point of view about taking chances in the original position. What must be shown is that choosing as if one had such an aversion is rational given the unique features of that situation irrespective of any special attitudes toward risk." (*TJ*, 172)[60] Indeed, as Rawls writes in an unpublished work: "in arguing for the difference principle over other distributive principles . . . there is no appeal *at all* to the maximin rule for decision under uncertainty. The widespread idea that the argument for the difference principle depends on an extreme aversion to uncertainty is a mistake, although a mistake unhappily encouraged by the faults of exposition in *TJ*."[61]

---

60. In the revised edition of *TJ*, the second sentence is replaced with the following: "What must be shown is that given the unique features of this situation, agreeing to these principles rather than the principle of utility is rational for anyone whose aversion to uncertainty in regard to being able to secure their fundamental interests is within the normal range." [149]

61. Rawls, "Justice As Fairness: A Brief Restatement," 35n5; cf. 75.

Recall that since we represent the parties as making a contract, we stipulate that they only select principles that they sincerely believe they can comply with "under all relevant and foreseeable circumstances. . . . Otherwise we have not acted in good faith. Thus the parties must weigh with care whether they will be able to stick by their commitment in all circumstances." (*TJ*, 175-176 [153]) It is this requirement (together with the veil of ignorance, of course) that explains the unusually conservative attitude among the parties. If, in choosing between two conceptions, one has an outcome with which the parties doubt citizens will be able to comply and the other does not, they *must* select the second. The parties "cannot enter into agreements that may have consequences they cannot accept." (*TJ*, 176 [153])

In this regard, Rawls's two principles enjoy a considerable advantage over utilitarianism since only they guarantee an equal scheme of basic liberties to all. Consider, for example, liberty of conscience. The veil of ignorance prevents the parties from knowing whether those they represent affirm a particular religious faith, and if they do, which one and whether adherents to this faith constitute a majority or minority in society. On the other hand, they know, as a general social-psychological fact, that many people identify strongly with their faith and would view it as an unacceptable outcome if they were governed by principles that unnecessarily prevent them from practicing their religion. Thus, the parties must protect this liberty if it is at all possible. The parties in the original position "cannot take chances with their [religious] liberty by permitting the dominant religious or moral doctrine to persecute or to suppress others if it wishes. Even granting (what may be questioned) that it is more probable than not that one will turn out to belong to the majority (if a majority exists), to gamble in this way would show that one did not take one's religious or moral convictions seriously." (*TJ*, 207 [181]; cf. *PL*, 310-312)[62] Citizens living in a society that did not allow them to practice their deeply held and reasonable religious faith would have great difficulty in accepting this restriction as a requirement of justice, especially knowing that religious liberty would be a feasible alternative. Therefore, a failure to guarantee religious liberties would not be a choice made in good faith and is ruled out.

Take free speech as another example. Here, I follow Joshua Cohen's account.[63] Consider three fundamental interests that are shared across a wide variety of reasonable comprehensive doctrines. First, many comprehensive doctrines have an *expressive* interest "in articulating thoughts, attitudes, and feelings on matters of personal or broader human concern, and perhaps through

---

62. In effect, this means that these religious interests are incommensurably greater in value than many other considerations. See Rawls, "Some Reasons for the Maximin Criterion," 143.

63. Joshua Cohen, "Freedom of Expression," *Philosophy and Public Affairs* 22, no. 3 (summer 1993). Parenthetical references in this and the next two paragraphs will be to this work. See also *PL*, 340-368.

that articulation influencing the thought and conduct of others." (224) Among these expressive interests include "bearing witness" (which Cohen notes "is on a footing with liberty of conscience"), addressing issues of justice and morality, and expressing views concerning "human welfare and the quality of human life." (225) As with the case of religious liberties, many different comprehensive doctrines will reject unnecessary restrictions on the expressive function of speech. Although a discussion of precisely what is to count as a necessary restriction would take us too far afield, it seems clear that utilitarianism, which allows restrictions based on the balance of contingent preferences in the society, provides a rather insecure basis for these fundamental interests. The parties in the original position would be unwilling to risk compromising these fundamental values for other possible gains.

Next, Cohen observes the importance of the *deliberative* interest in free speech protections. Virtually every reasonable comprehensive doctrine presents itself as affirming not an arbitrary system of values, but one that is correct (or defensible, rational, reasonable, true, or affirmed on the basis of some other objective standard). Furthermore, most attempt to defend their values in some way. This is most obviously true, of course, for those who hold strictly rationalist doctrines, but is also true of those who affirm the value of faith or tradition. These individuals will often find it important to explain the limits of rationalism or individualism, for example. As Cohen points out, however, "reflection on matters of human concern typically cannot be pursued in isolation." (229) Most comprehensive doctrines, therefore, will find that their ability to provide an adequate defense of their values depends on a context in which freedom of speech is secure. Notice that this protection must extend beyond political questions to cover investigations and arguments regarding all of the areas covered by comprehensive doctrines.

A third and related ground for defending free speech concerns the interests universally shared in "securing reliable information about the conditions required for pursuing one's aims and aspirations." (229) Without such information, we would be at a loss as to how to pursue our aims. Effectively pursuing our more abstract aims requires both interpreting what would constitute their accomplishment in our particular circumstances, as well as identifying what means would be likely to achieve them. Both of these tasks are much more effectively pursued when we have access to the insights of others.[64] This interest depends on the second moral power. Analogous arguments could be made with respect to reflection on and application of one's sense of justice (the first moral power). Abstract principles of justice, like abstract conceptions of the good, require interpretation in specific circumstances and the identification of effective means. All of these arguments, then, appeal to a wide variety (if not all) reasonable comprehensive doctrines. Not all reasonable citizens will value their

---

64. See the discussion in Elijah Millgram, *Practical Induction* (Cambridge: Harvard University Press, 1997), chapter 8.

liberties for the same reasons or to the same degree—not all will require bearing witness, while only some will place a very high value on critical self-examination—but the parties in the original position will certainly want to provide secure grounding for them.

Notice how these arguments rely on three elements that Rawls finds in the idea of a contract—the diversity of ends, publicity, and its binding nature. Together with the veil, these elements force the parties to consider the worst possible outcome. It is not an arbitrary preference for risk-aversion, but rather the nature of the choice that forces the parties to focus on the least advantaged position:

> If the parties proceed in a cautious manner in organizing their deliberations by the maximin rule, or [if] it seems *as if* they are peculiarly averse to uncertainty, this is *not* because they *are* moved by some special psychology, or are peculiarly averse to uncertainty. Rather, it is because it is *rational* for them as trustees, and so as *responsible* for citizens' (unknown) determinate and complete good, to deliberate in this way, given the overriding importance of establishing a public conception of justice that guarantees the basic rights and liberties.[65]

The strains of commitment require the parties to rule out any choices that may have results which conflict with their fundamental interests and therefore would be difficult, if not impossible, to comply with. Soon after the publication of *A Theory of Justice*, Rawls reiterated: "I did not . . . simply postulate that the parties have some peculiar or special aversion to risk; that would indeed have been no argument at all. Rather, the features of the original position, when one considers their combined force, would lead reasonable people to choose as if they were highly risk-averse. Or put another way: a conservative decision is the only sensible one, given the list of alternatives available."[66]

Now a defender of utilitarianism might attempt to reply to this argument by claiming that on realistic empirical assumptions, utilitarian principles will lead to a defense of the same basic liberties.[67] After all, if religious commitments are often as strong as Rawls's argument suggests, they will weigh very heavily in the utilitarian calculus, and so utilitarianism will also protect the basic liberties. Furthermore, the utilitarian may continue, where utilitarianism diverges from the two principles, especially when compared to the second principle, it is superior. We will consider this second possibility below, but let us consider the first argument that grants the importance of the basic liberties and argues that utilitarianism would secure them as well as Rawls's first principle. It might be thought that if the utilitarian standard typically leads to securing the basic

---

65. Rawls, "Justice As Fairness: A Brief Restatement," 86.

66. Rawls, "Reply to Alexander and Musgrave," 169.

67. The classic defense of this thesis, of course, is J. S. Mill, *On Liberty*, Elizabeth Rapaport, ed. (Indianapolis: Hackett, 1978).

liberties, there would be no basis for the parties to choose between utilitarianism and the two principles.

The possibility of an overlap between utilitarianism and the first principle means that we must look for other grounds on which to make the choice, specifically those related to stability and to the fact that the idea of a contract carries with it the idea of publicity. Recall that the principles selected in the original position are to be the principles with which citizens debate and justify their choice of institutional arrangements for the basic structure. With this in mind, it seems that relying on utilitarian calculations would provide less secure ground for the basic liberties than the two principles. If they depended on utilitarian calculations, two important questions become subject to highly complex and controversial calculations: Who is to receive these basic liberties and how secure are they to be?

First of all, it is not as clear as utilitarians sometimes suggest that the utilitarian calculations will turn out "right" and that an unpopular religious minority, say, would have their religious liberties protected against the strong disapproval of the majority. Perhaps as important, however, is the fact that the publicity requirement implies that individuals would know that the security of their basic liberties depends on the outcome of such difficult calculations. Utilitarianism requires that we determine which groups are to receive the basic liberties on the basis of complicated and controversial calculations, themselves based on the shifting and uncertain fortunes of population and preferences. These calculations are much more difficult to assess and are more liable to controversy than the application of the two principles of justice. As Rawls observes in unpublished work: "The information these complex arguments presuppose is often hard if not impossible to obtain, and frequently there are grave problems in reaching an objective and agreed assessment. Moreover, even though we think *our* arguments sincere and not self-serving when *we* present them, we must consider what it is reasonable to expect others to think who stand to lose should our reasoning prevail."[68] It is crucial to remember that we are selecting the standards that citizens will use when publicly assessing the justice of their basic structure. We must attempt to anticipate the likely results, including indirect consequences of actually relying on various conceptions.

Consider the likely effects of someone raising the issue of "which faiths are to have liberty of conscience, or groups are to have the right to vote."[69] Surely even raising these questions in a context in which their security is in question is likely to increase distrust and suspicion among the relevant groups. Individuals and groups may be tempted to misrepresent the structure of their preferences or suspect others of doing the same. Especially when such fundamental matters are at stake, the tendency to suspect that others have misrepresented their interests may be quite strong. Far better, Rawls claims, to guarantee these basic liberties

---

68. Rawls, "Justice As Fairness: A Brief Restatement," 93.
69. Rawls, "Justice As Fairness: A Brief Restatement," 92-93.

by taking them "off the political agenda" so that they are no longer subject to "the calculus of social interests."[70] Doing so will provide the basic liberties with much greater security as well as provide a clearer standard for determining when justice is done. This, in turn, will tend to increase the reciprocal sense of justice among citizens. When it is manifest that society conforms to the demands of justice and that other citizens are acting on the principles, citizens will tend to have their own sense of justice strengthened. As I have pointed out, no conception of justice can be guaranteed always to generate its own support and to be fully stable. The issue, however, is not complete stability but relative stability, and it seems that a direct statement of the two principles would lead to a significantly more stable society than would utilitarianism.[71]

We saw above that the parties would be motivated by considerations of stability because, as Rawls puts it: "Clearly, the public knowledge that everyone has an effective sense of justice and can be relied upon as a fully cooperating member of society is a great advantage to everyone's conception of the good." (*PL*, 316) The parties, therefore, view the stability of a conception of justice as instrumentally valuable (although we, of course, view it as more than just that). Other things equal, they would greatly prefer a conception of justice that was likely to engender its own support. Recall that stability involves two elements: the initial acquisition of a sense of justice and the continued affirmation of one's sense of justice in light of one's comprehensive doctrine and conception of the good. In fact, both elements of stability will be important to the parties. It will be of great importance to them that citizens generally come to acquire a strong sense of justice. Since the parties do not know the location in the history of a society in which those they represent will live their lives, it will be crucial to them that a just society continue from generation to generation.[72] This obviously depends on each generation's acquiring a sense of justice as its members mature. In addition, the parties will be interested in whether a conception of justice can serve as the focus of an overlapping consensus (of reasonable comprehensive doctrines). This is because the ability to serve as such a focus is an important check on the acceptability of a conception from the point of view of all reasonable comprehensive doctrines. The parties, knowing that those they

---

70. Rawls, "Justice As Fairness: A Brief Restatement," 92. See also *PL*, 151n16; and *TJ*, 4 [3-4]. Of course, this does not mean that citizens cannot discuss the reasons for securely establishing these liberties, as some have thought. The publicity requirement allows them to do so whenever they choose.

71. Rawls also argues that the second element of stability would tend to support his two principles over utilitarianism. He claims that utilitarianism is less congruent with the empirical laws of developmental psychology than are principles that are based on reciprocity. See *TJ*, 499-501 [437-439].

72. I abandon the "present time entry" interpretation of the original position. See *TJ*, 292 and the changes he makes in the revised edition [257-258]. Compare *PL*, 274, and see also Jane English, "Justice between Generations," *Philosophical Studies* 31 (1977).

represent hold some reasonable comprehensive doctrine, will want to ensure the acceptability of the conception of justice from the point of view of all reasonable comprehensive doctrines.

I conclude therefore, that if utilitarianism does not secure the basic liberties, the two principles of justice are superior on the grounds that the parties in the original position would want to protect their basic liberties if at all possible. The strains of commitment involved in sacrificing one's basic liberties when it would have been possible to secure them makes such an option intolerable to the parties in the original position. On the other hand, if utilitarianism does secure the basic liberties, it does so in a way that is less stable than doing so directly. Here, the two principles seem to enjoy a marked advantage. Finally, notice that this first comparison between the two principles and utilitarianism turns exclusively on arguments concerning the first principle (provided there is some kind of assurance that resources will be distributed in such a way as to render the liberties valuable). We will now move on to consider the second principle and possible alternatives.

The Second Principle of Justice

The choice between the two principles of justice and utilitarianism turns decisively on the first principle of justice. This suggests the possibility of a mixed conception of justice which shares Rawls's first principle, but substitutes a different second principle. In the next section, we will compare Rawls's two principles of justice to four different mixed conceptions.[73] First, however, we must be clear about how the two parts of the second principle work together. Recall that the principles of justice are designed to evaluate institutional schemes, each of which is characterized by various social positions and their relations. The difference principle (the second part of the second principle) governs which inequalities among these positions are permissible. It states that these structural inequalities are only just when they work to everyone's advantage, or more specifically, when they "are to the greatest benefit of the least advantaged members of society." Fair equality of opportunity (the first part of the second principle) governs how these positions are to be filled. It says that those positions are "open to all under fair equality of opportunity." Remember that we are to evaluate possible schemes first in terms of their provision of an equal scheme of basic liberties, second in terms of fair equality of opportunity, and finally in terms of the difference principle.

Although Rawls's formulation of the difference principle may make it seem straightforward, I believe that it has been very widely misinterpreted. Critics and

---

73. Only one of the mixed conceptions I discuss here is included among the three that Rawls and Cohen discuss. See Rawls, "Reply to Alexander and Musgrave"; "Justice As Fairness: A Brief Restatement"; and Cohen, "Democratic Equality."

defenders alike get the abstract statement right—the difference principle requires that we arrange inequalities to work to the advantage of the least advantaged—but when it comes to discussing what this means, there are frequent misunderstandings and confusion. For example, critics often pay insufficient attention to the issue of how the least advantaged is to be identified. The representative individual[74] who receives the smallest share of primary social goods is not necessarily the one with the lowest level of utility. The difference principle does not refer to utility (or welfare or satisfaction) at all; it identifies the least advantaged strictly in terms of expected shares of primary social goods over a complete life.

To understand more clearly what is at issue here, let us define *talent* as the ability to generate a net increase in social resources. Simply turning social resources into one's own satisfaction through consumption, for example, is not a talent on this definition. Rather, talent involves productive activity of whatever kind as measured by the balance of investment and production of social resources. Note, therefore, that there is no necessary connection between being talented in this sense and achieving a high level of personal satisfaction. As a matter of psychological fact, they may or may not tend to be related. Now if, as I claim, the difference principle only aims to maximize the share of social resources of whichever social position receives the smallest share, that means it does not aim to achieve equality in the levels of satisfaction of different individuals nor does it seek to compensate individuals for inequalities in talent. Both of these points, although especially the latter, have been widely misunderstood.

Rawls himself must share some of the blame for the persistent misinterpretation of his theory on this point. There are two places in *A Theory of Justice* where he has been taken to suggest that the difference principle serves to compensate for inequalities in natural talent. In chapter 2 of *A Theory of Justice*, Rawls presents and interprets his principles of justice before arguing in chapter 3 that they would be chosen from the original position. He does this in order to "prepare the way for the favored interpretation of the two principles so that these criteria, especially the second one, will not strike the reader as too eccentric or bizarre." (*TJ*, 75)[75] By way of preparing the reader, Rawls points out that an initial formulation of the second principle of justice has an ambiguous phrase in each of its two parts. The preliminary statement reads: "social and economic inequalities are to be arranged so that they are both (a) reasonably expected to be to everyone's advantage, and (b) attached to positions and offices open to all." (*TJ*, 60 [53]) The ambiguities concern the phrases "everyone's advantage" and "open to all." Each of these phrases is open to two interpretations, jointly

---

74. Recall that we are concerned with social positions generated by the institutions of the basic structure.

75. In the revised edition of *TJ*, Rawls substitutes the word "extreme" for "too eccentric or bizarre." [65]

yielding four possible interpretations of the principle. (See the chart in *TJ*, 65 [57].)

The first phrase, "open to all," could be interpreted to mean either that there is merely "*formal* equality of opportunity in that all have at least the same legal rights of access to all advantaged social positions," (*TJ*, 72 [62], my emphasis) or it may be understood to require "*fair* equality of opportunity." (*TJ*, 73 [63], my emphasis) Rawls calls the former interpretation "careers open to talent." Although this is a standard label for such a libertarian conception, it is potentially misleading because it allows "careers" (and therefore the distribution of social resources) to be affected not only by natural talent but also by initial social position. Fair equality of opportunity, in contrast, requires that "those who are at the same level of talent and ability, and have the same willingness to use them, should have the same prospects of success regardless of their initial place in the social system, that is, irrespective of the income class into which they are born." (*TJ*, 73)[76]

"Fair equality of opportunity" is superior to "careers open to talent" (in this initial presentation) because it does not allow social inequalities to perpetuate from one generation to the next simply in virtue of the social class into which one is born. Notice, however, that it does allow inequalities based on differences in talent (and motivation). Indeed, by screening off inequalities in social background, "fair equality of opportunity" ties distributive shares to talent even more strongly than does "careers open to talents," which allows one's prospects to be influenced by one's initial social class as long as there is no explicit or formal exclusion. Again: fair equality of opportunity requires, in addition to mere formal equality of opportunity, that "Chances to acquire cultural knowledge and skills should not depend upon one's class position, and so the school system, whether public or private, should be designed to even out class barriers." (*TJ*, 73 [63])

The second phrase, "everyone's advantage," also is open to two interpretations. It can direct our attention either to the collective advantage (maximizing the total supply of resources) or to the least advantaged (maximizing the share of resources of those with the least). The former Rawls calls "the principle of efficiency" while the latter, of course, is the difference principle. Once again, the choice of names is unfortunate because it suggests that the difference principle is somehow inefficient. If efficiency is understood in the sense of Pareto, and certain assumptions hold, both interpretations are efficient.[77] Indeed, the difference principle can be understood as the most

---

76. In the revised edition of *TJ*, Rawls shortens this sentence by dropping the clause following "social system." [63]

77. Pareto efficiency is satisfied when no resources are wasted in the following sense: there are no possible transfers of resources in which (at least) someone would improve gain while no one would lose. This is much weaker than the (quasi-) utilitarian requirement that resources be devoted to maximize productivity (or satisfaction). The two

egalitarian efficient point. (See *TJ*, 79 [69].)[78] The principle of efficiency, like utilitarianism, doesn't itself require any particular distribution of resources and is compatible with a very unequal distribution. Rawls opts for the difference principle rather than the principle of efficiency, but in explaining this choice, he muddies the waters considerably. (Recall that this is only a preliminary explanation of the content of the principle and not yet the official defense.)[79] He suggests that just as the resolution of the first ambiguity (between formal or fair equality of opportunity) depends on "eliminating the influence of social contingencies," so the resolution of this second ambiguity depends on eliminating the influence of "the natural distribution of abilities and talents." (*TJ*, 73-74 [64]) This is doubly misleading.

First, Rawls must be assuming, although he does not say so, that those who lose out in the natural distribution of talents and abilities will be the ones who are least advantaged in terms of the primary social goods. Without this assumption there would be no reason to think that either interpretation has any particular implications for those with more or less talents since neither the difference principle nor the principle of efficiency refers to the natural distribution of talents and abilities. Second, Rawls argues that the outcome of the "natural lottery" of talents and abilities "is arbitrary from a moral perspective. There is no more reason to permit the distribution of income and wealth to be settled by the distribution of natural assets than by historical and social fortune." (*TJ*, 74 [64])

Contrary to Rawls's suggestion, both the principle of efficiency and the difference principle allow (under certain conditions) the distribution of resources to be influenced by the distribution of natural talents and abilities. The principle of efficiency allows an inequality in social resources when it results in an increase in the total supply of resources, while the difference principle allows it when it works to the advantage of those receiving the smallest share. Both principles, then, allow the distribution of social resources to be tied to (socially productive) talent. What distinguishes the principle of efficiency and the difference principle is not that one of them compensates for the inequalities of the natural lottery. What distinguishes them is the conditions under which they

---

conditions are *chain connection* and *close-knittedness*. See *TJ*, 79-83 [69-73]; and the discussion in Martin, *Rawls and Rights*, especially the appendix. For a discussion of the difficulties when chain-connection fails, see Andrew Williams, "The Revisionist Difference Principle," *Canadian Journal of Philosophy* 25, no. 2 (June 1995).

78. Elsewhere, Rawls observes that the difference principle "is efficient while strict equality is not." See John Rawls, "Some Reasons for the Maximin Criterion," *American Economic Review* 64, no. 2 (May 1974), 144. Compare Edward McClennen, "Justice and the Problem of Stability," *Philosophy and Public Affairs* 18, no. 1 (winter 1989), 20.

79. As he reminds us at the end of the section: "none of the preceding remarks are an argument for this conception, since in a contract theory all arguments, strictly speaking, are to be made in terms of what it would be rational to choose in the original position." (*TJ*, 75 [65])

allow unequal shares of social resources to be based on differences in talent. Now in fairness to Rawls, it is true that the difference principle will allow fewer inequalities based on talent than the principle of efficiency will. Every inequality permitted by the difference principle will be permitted by the principle of efficiency; not every inequality permitted by the principles of efficiency will be permitted by the difference principle. Thus, Rawls is correct that when compared to the principle of efficiency, the difference principle *"mitigates* the arbitrary effects of the natural lottery itself." (*TJ*, 74 [64], my emphasis) This is not in order to compensate the less-talented for their unfortunate position in the natural lottery, however, but to raise the share of those receiving the minimum share whether they are the less-talented or not. Rawls's suggestion that inequalities in natural endowment are to be treated analogously to inequalities in one's initial social position has sent a generation of commentators down a path irrelevant to the main contentions of justice as fairness.

The reference to the arbitrariness of the natural lottery is related to the second passage that has contributed to the misinterpretation. At the end of chapter 2, still before the presentation of the choice from the original position, Rawls compares the difference principle to the principle of redress. The principle of redress says that

> undeserved inequalities call for redress; and since inequalities of birth and natural endowment are undeserved, these inequalities are to be somehow compensated for. Thus the principle holds that in order to treat all persons equally, to provide genuine equality of opportunity, society must give more attention to those with fewer native assets and to those born into the less favorable social positions. The idea is to redress the bias of contingencies in the direction of equality. (*TJ*, 100-101 [86])

As before, Rawls is concerned with two kinds of undeserved contingencies: one's natural endowments and the social position into which one is born. These are undeserved, for Rawls, because they do not reflect one's moral merit.[80] Because both are undeserved, the principle of redress requires that we attempt to eliminate both types of inequalities.

Contrary to widespread misinterpretation, Rawls is explicit: "the difference principle is not of course the principle of redress. It does not require society to try to even out handicaps as if all were expected to compete on a fair basis in the same race." (*TJ*, 101 [86]) Still, there is an element of the principle of redress which may be appealing, especially in comparison with the principle of efficiency. While the principle of efficiency requires an impersonal maximization of the total social product without concern for its distribution, the principle of redress requires that we be concerned with the effects of that social

---

80. This does not mean that individuals are not *entitled* to them. Rawls reserves the term *desert* for cases of entitlement based on moral virtue. See my "Justice, Desert, and Ideal Theory"; and Pogge, *Realizing Rawls*, 73-86.

product on each individual. This intuitively appealing element is shared by the principle of redress as well as the difference principle:

> Thus although the difference principle is not the same as that of redress, it does achieve some of the intent of the latter principle. It transforms the aims of the basic structure so that the total scheme of institutions no longer emphasizes social efficiency and technocratic values. (*TJ*, 101 [87])

Notice, however, that while both the principle of redress and the difference principle turn the aims of the basic structure away from global maximization, they do not turn them to the same end—if they did, they would be the same principle, and as we have seen, Rawls is clear that they are not. The principle of redress aims to even out all undeserved contingencies, while the difference principle aims to maximize the minimum share of social resources.

Immediately after pointing out that the principle of redress and the difference principle both reject the principle of efficiency, Rawls introduces a metaphor that has been widely misread as supporting the principle of redress. Rawls writes:

> We see then that the difference principle represents, in effect, an agreement to regard the distribution of natural talents as a common asset and to share in the benefits of this distribution whatever it turns out to be. Those who have been favored by nature, whoever they are, may gain from their good fortune only on terms that improve the situation of those who have lost out. (*TJ*, 101)[81]

The passage appears to be ambiguous. The phrase "the distribution of natural talents" could suggest that the natural talents themselves are to be viewed as a common asset, or it could be read as stating that the array or range or variety of talents is to be regarded that way. It is usually read the first way, as when Anthony Kronman glosses the passage as follows: "Rawls views the [difference] principle as expressing a commitment to the idea that individual talents and capacities should be treated as part of a common fund or pool from which each has the right to draw an equal share, regardless of what his own endowment happens to be. . . ."[82] The thought here is that justice as fairness holds that since the talents themselves are arbitrary from a moral point of view they are to be viewed as collective assets, and justice requires that we take compensating steps

---

81. In the revised edition of *TJ*, the first sentence reads: "The difference principle represents, in effect, an agreement to regard the distribution of natural talents as in some respects a common asset and to share in the greater social and economic benefits made possible by the complementarities of this distribution." [87] This strongly supports the interpretation I defend below.

82. Anthony Kronman, "Talent Pooling," in *Human Rights (NOMOS XXIII)*, J. Roland Pennock and John Chapman, eds. (New York: NYU Press, 1981), 58.

to equalize any inequality that is arbitrary from a moral point of view.[83] This view is easy fodder for many critics such as Robert Nozick, who writes that "Rawls' view seems to be that everyone has some entitlement or claim on the totality of natural assets (viewed as a pool), with no one having differential claims."[84] Nozick claims that if the pool of natural assets is a collective resource and we are to maximize the share of the least advantaged (as identified by their share of those collective assets), there would seem to be no obstacle to "forcible redistribution of bodily parts . . . or killing some people early to use their bodies in order to provide material necessary to save the lives of those who otherwise would die young."[85] Such policies are morally outrageous, he asserts, because they involve using people as means only. Specifically, they violate the property right that individuals have in themselves.[86]

Rather than claiming that individual talents themselves are collective assets, Rawls's "collective asset" passage should be read as referring to the fact that there is a particular distribution of natural talents throughout society (due, in part, to the natural lottery) and suggesting that the difference principle regards this fact as a common asset. On this interpretation, Rawls is not claiming that society may claim the talents themselves as collective assets, but rather that it may use its knowledge of the pattern of distribution of talents as a social resource. The key to interpreting the passage is to observe that it says that the difference principle can be understood as an agreement "to share in the *benefits* of this distribution" (my emphasis). This suggests that the issue is not the talents themselves, but rather the consequences of the array of talents in society. This is confirmed in the second quoted sentence, which refers to the conditions under which individuals "may *gain* from their good fortune" as well as at the end of

---

83. To take an almost random example, see John Roemer's remark that "because people are in large part not responsible for their inborn talents and characteristics . . . the highly talented should be taxed to compensate those with low talent" and the footnote that reads: "This point is fully articulated by Rawls (1971) [*TJ*], who states that the distribution of talents is 'morally arbitrary.'" (*Egalitarian Perspectives* [New York: Cambridge University Press, 1996], 4)

84. Robert Nozick, *Anarchy, State, and Utopia* (New York: Basic Books, 1974), 228.

85. Nozick, *Anarchy, State, and Utopia*, 206. John Kekes makes a similar argument in "A Question for Egalitarians," *Ethics* 107, no. 4 (July 1997).

86. At least this seems to be what he has in mind when he refers to "a line (or hyperplane) [which] circumscribes an area in moral space around an individual." (*Anarchy, State, and Utopia*, 57) See also his claim that individuals may sell themselves into slavery on 331. G. A. Cohen claims that "the primary commitment of [Nozick's] philosophy is not to liberty but to the thesis of self-ownership, which says that each person is the morally rightful owner of his own person and powers, and *consequently*, that he is free (morally speaking) to use those powers as he wishes, provided that he does not deploy them aggressively against others." ("Self-Ownership, World-Ownership, and Equality," in *Self-Ownership, Freedom, and Equality* [New York: Cambridge University Press, 1995], 67)

the paragraph, where Rawls writes that according to the difference principle, "no one *gains or loses* from his arbitrary place in the distribution of natural assets or his initial position in society without giving or receiving compensating advantages in return." (*TJ*, 102 [87], my emphasis) In a 1974 article, Rawls clarified the point: "Greater natural talents are not a collective asset in the sense that society should compel those who have them to put them to work for the less favored."[87] Even if we agree that it is not the talents themselves which may be regarded as a common asset, it still may be unclear how knowledge of the distribution of these talents could possibly be an asset.

Consider the analogy provided by Thomas Pogge:

> A travel company operating with run-down accommodations, unsafe flights, hidden charges, and the like may be said to use the needs and desires of its customers as means for its own enrichment. . . . By contrast, consider a travel company that charges different prices for identical services provided at different times of the year (off-peak, high season, etc.), so as to equalize demand. In this case it is the distribution of customer interests and desires, the fact that customers are different in various relevant respects, that is used as a means.[88]

Knowledge of the distribution of talents allows society to allocate resources in such a way to encourage the development and employment of socially valuable but scarce talents. Talents, of course, come in different kinds as well as amounts. As Rex Martin writes: "the differences among persons—the sheer variety of talents and the differences in level of achievement for a given talent—should constitute common good fortune, to be used to mutual advantage."[89] The diversity of talents allows us to share in the complementary achievements of our fellow citizens, as the model of a social union of social unions suggests.[90] As Rawls clarifies:

> natural variations are recognized as an opportunity for mutual advantage, especially as they are generally complementary and form a basis for social ties. Institutions may make use of the full range of abilities provided that the inequalities are no greater than is necessary to yield corresponding advantages for the less fortunate, and the scheme of equal democratic liberties is not adversely affected.[91]

Let us take stock before moving on. Fair equality of opportunity requires that the shares of social resources to which an individual has access should not

---

87. Rawls, "Some Reasons for the Maximin Criterion," 145. Compare John Rawls, "A Well-Ordered Society" in *Philosophy, Politics and Society*, fifth series, Peter Laslett and James Fishkin, eds. (New Haven: Yale University Press, 1979), 16. Finally, see the explicit confirmation of this reading in "Justice As Fairness: A Brief Restatement," 60.

88. Pogge, *Realizing Rawls*, 74.

89. Martin, *Rawls and Rights*, 77.

90. See *TJ*, sec.79. I discuss this in chapter 4.

91. Rawls, "Reply to Alexander and Musgrave," 647.

be affected by his or her initial social position. The difference principle allows inequalities in shares of social resources when they result in a greater share for whomever receives the smallest share in each of the possible arrangements. This implies that society may allow shares of social resources to be affected by levels of natural talent when doing so works to maximize the minimum share. Rawls's discussion of the second principle is misleading insofar as it suggests analogous treatment of initial social inequalities and differences in natural talents. But social positions and natural talents are very different kinds of things even if they are both arbitrary from a moral point of view (i.e., neither corresponds to moral virtue). Remember, "The social system is not an unchangeable order beyond human control but a pattern of human action." (*TJ*, 102 [88]) The whole point of our investigation is to try to determine when a social scheme is just and which feasible alternatives might be superior. In contrast, "The natural distribution is neither just nor unjust; nor is it unjust that persons are born into society at some particular position. These are simply natural facts. What is just and unjust is the way that institutions deal with these facts." (*TJ*, 102 [87]) The distribution of natural talents, in other words, does not in itself call for redress even though it is arbitrary. On the other hand, society should use its knowledge of the array of talents as a collective asset in a way that works to everyone's advantage.

I have just argued that, contrary to what Rawls seems to suggest at one point, the difference principle treats natural talents and initial social positions differently, even though both are arbitrary from a moral point of view. In contrast, the original position itself (as opposed to the principles chosen there) does treat the arbitrary contingencies of social position and natural talent in an analogous manner. The veil of ignorance "nullif[ies] the effects of specific contingencies" (*TJ*, 136 [118]) such as initial social position and natural talents, which are "arbitrary from a moral point of view." The point, in Pogge's words, is that "the better endowed have no special claims upon the construction of the criterion of social justice."[92] So, while the construction of the original position itself nullifies the influence of what is arbitrary from a moral point of view, Rawls claims that the parties in the original position would not choose principles that would redress all morally arbitrary inequalities.[93] Rawls never explains this contrast explicitly and it is possible that he may not have seen it clearly himself.

---

92. Pogge, *Realizing Rawls*, 73. Compare David Gauthier's theory, which gives the better endowed a greater weight in the construction of the criterion of social justice through their superior threat advantage in the bargaining over principles of justice. See *Morals by Agreement* (New York: Oxford University Press, 1986).

93. There is one passage that might be taken to suggest (misleadingly) that the principles of justice themselves, rather than the original position, nullify contingencies of social position and natural endowments. This passage occurs early in *A Theory of Justice*, when Rawls is providing an overview of the theory. He writes: "Once we decide to look for a conception of justice that nullifies the accidents of natural endowment and the contingencies of social circumstance as counters in quest for political and economic

To conclude this section, consider briefly the Americans with Disabilities Act of 1990.[94] The act states that no employers with at least fifteen employees "shall discriminate against a qualified individual with a disability because of the disability of such individual in regard to job application procedures, the hiring, advancement, or discharge of employees, employee compensation, job training, and other terms, conditions, and privileges of employment." It defines "a disability" as "a physical or mental impairment that substantially limits one or more of the major life activities of such individual." Now distinguish three possible aims of such a law. First, most plausibly, it is to ensure fair equality of opportunity. Providing "equality of opportunity" and "full participation" are among the law's explicit goals. Those who have equal talents and motivation should have equal access to positions which rely on those talents. Handicaps or disabilities not relevant to the positions should not be allowed to be obstacles to competition for those positions. The law applies to "a *qualified* individual with a disability" (my emphasis), which it defines as "an individual with a disability who, with or without reasonable accommodation, can perform the essential functions of the employment position that such individual holds or desires." Thus, employers must make "reasonable accommodation" for such employees. On the other hand, employers are not required to endure "undue hardship." This defense, based on fair equality of opportunity, is fully in keeping with justice as fairness. As a second interpretation, consider that, as a matter of empirical fact, it may turn out that people with certain disabilities may be the ones who receive the smallest share of social resources. The act may be seen as an effort to increase their share in accordance with the difference principle. This, too, would be in keeping with justice as fairness, although it may or may not be a particularly effective way of achieving this goal. Finally, the act might be defended as a way of compensating individuals with disabilities for those handicaps. One might think that their handicaps mean that those individuals will be less able to utilize their share of social resources to live fulfilling lives and therefore should be entitled to a greater share of resources in an effort to raise their levels of satisfaction. Notice that this could potentially come at the expense of people who achieve a higher level of satisfaction with a smaller share of resources. Justice as fairness rejects this possible justification. Justice as fairness

---

advantage, we are led to these principles." But in the next sentence he suggests that the "nullification" occurs in the process of searching for the principles rather than in the principles themselves: "They express the result of leaving aside those aspects of the social world that seem arbitrary from a moral point of view." (*TJ*, 15) Furthermore, in the revised edition, Rawls replaced the sentence with the following: "Once we decide to look for a conception of justice that prevents the use of the accidents of natural endowment and the contingencies of social circumstance as counters in a quest for political and economic advantage, we are led to these principles." [14]

94. The relevant portions can be found at <http://www.eeoc.gov/laws/ada.html>.

does not attempt to redress all inequalities, not even all inequalities that are arbitrary from a moral point of view.

Comparison with Mixed Conceptions

With this understanding of the second principle, we can now return to the original position and compare Rawls's principles to various mixed conceptions. All four of the mixed conceptions that we will consider share the first principle's guarantee of an equal scheme of basic liberties for all. The first mixed conception substitutes utilitarianism for fair equality of opportunity and the difference principle. This will allow us to isolate and consider the grounds for fair equality of opportunity. Next, we will examine the mixed conception which affirms both the first principle and fair equality of opportunity, but which substitutes utilitarianism, subject to a guaranteed minimum, for the difference principle. This allows us to consider the grounds for the difference principle by comparing it to a constrained form of utilitarianism. The third mixed conception grants fair equality of opportunity but substitutes for the difference principle a standard that maximizes the level of utility of the least advantaged. It requires an equalization of levels of utility except when an inequality works to the advantage of the least well off (as identified by levels of utility, rather than by shares of primary social goods). There are problems with this conception that will lead us to consider the fourth mixed conception as a superior variant on this same basic idea. The fourth mixed conception is similar to the third except that it substitutes for the difference principle a principle of equality of opportunity for welfare. Defenders of this conception present it as an extension of the idea of fair equality of opportunity. The final two mixed conceptions will allow us to reconsider the reliance on primary goods and clarify the sense in which justice as fairness is an egalitarian conception.

The first mixed conception recognizes Rawls's first principle of justice (as all of the mixed conceptions do) but substitutes utilitarianism for the entire second principle. Our focus will be on fair equality of opportunity.[95] As we have seen, fair equality of opportunity requires that the distribution of social resources not be affected by the social class into which an individual is born. Everyone with the same natural talents and level of motivation should have an equal chance to attain positions of higher authority and reward. Such a provision may very well contribute to the overall efficiency of the system. After all, without such a provision the pool of potentially qualified candidates for positions

---

95. This has received very little discussion in the literature on Rawls, and most of that has been decidedly hostile. See James Fishkin, *Justice, Equal Opportunity, and the Family* (New Haven: Yale University Press, 1983); Larry Alexander, "Fair Equality of Opportunity: John Rawls' (Best) Forgotten Principle," *Philosophy Research Archives* 11 (March 1986); and Richard Arneson, "Against Rawlsian Equality of Opportunity," *Philosophical Studies* 93, no. 1 (Jan. 1999).

requiring relatively rare talents and skills will be smaller, since some may be excluded on the basis of their initial social position. If this is the case, we have a situation that is similar to that discussed earlier with respect to the basic liberties and utilitarianism: two different conceptions that (it is claimed) would support the same institutional arrangements. As in that discussion, I will argue that the parties would have good reasons to place fair equality of opportunity on a more secure foundation than utilitarianism can provide.

Suppose first, however, that the two diverge. Assume that a greater total product, and thus a greater average share, could be generated by restricting access to positions of higher authority and reward to members of a certain social class.[96] The claim is that the parties in the original position would forgo such possible advantages. Consider the effects of such a system on what Rawls calls "perhaps the most important primary good," self-respect. As we have seen, the parties in the original position realize that there is little hope of achieving one's ends if one becomes disillusioned with oneself and drifts into apathetic indifference. Such an attitude will often be a far greater handicap than a loss of resources. As we have seen, although no arrangement of the basic structure can guarantee the development and preservation of self-respect, the parties would still be concerned to secure the social bases of self-respect. An arrangement of the basic structure that prevents individuals from achieving positions of greater authority and command of resources because of the social position of their birth almost certainly would tend to have a significant impact on their self-respect. They are being told, in effect, that whatever potential they might have, they will not be given a fair opportunity to assume certain positions of authority and possibly claim a larger share of resources. Their opportunities to attain such positions must be sacrificed for a greater social product that itself will provide increased benefits for those born into a superior class. It is easy to imagine that they would understand this to be a judgment that they are worth less than others. This would tend to undermine the value they place in themselves and in their own projects. The parties would be willing to sacrifice a greater average share of social resources to prevent this result.

On the other hand, as I mentioned above, one might argue that fair equality of opportunity would tend to maximize the total social product. Like the case of the basic liberties, the parties would want to provide greater security for fair equality of opportunity than utilitarianism can provide. To rely on a utilitarian basis for the basic liberties or fair equality of opportunity would be to subject them to uncertain and variable calculations. Publicity would require that the

---

96. In the discussion of this and the second mixed conception, I assume that the highest level of utility would be achieved by maximizing the total social product. This is not necessarily true of course, but this assumption will not affect the discussion, since the relevant issue concerns provision of fair equality of opportunity as opposed to any maximizing conception. We will examine the choice between resource egalitarianism and utility egalitarianism when we discuss the final two mixed conceptions.

public debate over the basic structure be conducted in utilitarian terms. The public knowledge that society would be willing to sacrifice the resources of the lower classes for the greater gains of the upper would itself tend to undermine the self-respect of those in the lower classes. If this argument is correct, the parties would want to provide a more secure ground for fair equality of opportunity by requiring it directly rather than subjecting it to the uncertain calculations offered by utilitarianism.

Finally, note that utilitarianism provides no floor to the share of resources received by the least advantaged. The strains of commitment will prevent the parties from choosing a conception if there is a chance that it will result in a social position that receives an inadequate share of resources to allow an individual to be "a normal and fully cooperating member of society over a complete life." (*PL*, 74) On the assumption of decreasing marginal utilities, utilitarianism may seem unlikely to generate such positions, but, once again, the parties would be unwilling to risk this possibility. These criticisms suggest the next mixed conception, which is designed to avoid them by providing fair equality of opportunity and a guaranteed minimum share of resources.

The second mixed conception grants fair equality of opportunity, but substitutes for the difference principle a utilitarian standard constrained by a guaranteed social minimum. The first thing to note is that this standard seems likely to endorse institutional designs very close to those endorsed by the two principles themselves. Although this mixed conception incorporates a utilitarian element, it is far from utilitarianism since the maximizing component is constrained by three prior requirements: an equal scheme of basic liberties; fair equality of opportunity; and a guaranteed social minimum. As we saw in previous discussions, to the extent that principles generate similar or identical institutions, we will have to rely on secondary considerations in order to find grounds to choose between them. Since this mixed conception has a guaranteed social minimum, the strains of commitment are greatly reduced and so we need to concentrate on other grounds.

In this discussion I will emphasize the relative stability of the two conceptions. Just as one's sense of self-respect is not determined solely by the social structure, so too the acquisition of a sense of justice is dependent on far more than the arrangement of the basic institutions. Certainly no basic structure can ensure a sufficiently strong sense of justice to prevent defections in all circumstances. Yet to repeat one final time, we are only interested here in comparing the relative strengths of the sense of justice likely to be generated under each of these two conceptions (other things equal). Consider, first, who would find the temptation to defect—whose sense of justice would tend to be under the greatest strain—in the well-ordered society of each of these two conceptions. Under justice as fairness, those in the least advantaged position know that under no other possible arrangements would they (or whoever is in the least advantaged position) do any better. It seems then that the most advantaged would have grounds for complaint, if anyone does.

In fact, Robert Nozick has urged exactly this criticism of the difference principle:

> No doubt, the difference principle presents terms on the basis of which those less well endowed would be willing to cooperate. (What *better* terms could they propose for themselves?) But is this a fair agreement on the basis of which those *worse* endowed could expect the *willing* cooperation of others? . . . With regard to the existence of gains from social cooperation, the situation is symmetrical. . . . Yet the difference principle is not neutral between the better and worse endowed.[97]

He continues by imagining negotiations between the better endowed and the worse endowed:

> Rawls would have us imagine the worse-endowed persons say something like the following: "Look, better endowed: you gain by cooperating with us. If you want our cooperation you'll have to accept reasonable terms. We suggest these terms: We'll cooperate with you only if we get *as much as possible*. That is, the terms of our cooperation should give us that maximal share such that, if it was tried to give us more, we'd end up with less." How generous these proposed terms are might be seen by imagining that the better endowed make the almost symmetrical opposite proposal: "Look, worse endowed: you gain by cooperating with *us*. If you want our cooperation you'll have to accept reasonable terms. We propose these terms: We'll cooperate with you so long as *we* get as much as possible. That is, the terms of our cooperation should give us the maximal share such that, if it was tried to give us more, we'd end up with less." If these terms seem outrageous, as they are, why don't the terms proposed by those worse endowed seem the same?[98]

To see what is really at issue here, we need to put aside two misunderstandings. As we have seen, the difference principle requires that we maximize the share of the least advantaged (as identified by shares of resources), not necessarily the "worse endowed," as Nozick assumes. Furthermore, contrary to Nozick's suggestion, particular individuals are not claiming that they receive the greatest share possible. From behind the veil of ignorance, these identities are not known. The point, however, is that on Nozick's interpretation, the difference principle requires the advantaged to sacrifice for the less advantaged. This reading is very widely shared. To choose three typical examples: Nagel speaks of the "sacrifices" that the difference principle "requires of those at the top of the social order";[99] Hare questions how just it could be "to impose any loss, however great, upon a better-off group in order to bring a gain, however small,

---

97. Nozick, *Anarchy, State, and Utopia*, 192.
98. Nozick, *Anarchy, State, and Utopia*, 195.
99. Nagel, "Rawls on Justice," 13.

to the least advantaged group, however affluent the latter's starting point";[100] and Arrow observes that "A maximin principle certainly seems to imply that the better off should sacrifice for the less well off, if that will in fact help."[101]

Rawls rejects this interpretation. For him, the difference principle "is a principle of mutual benefit" in which people "do not gain at one another's expense since only reciprocal advantages are allowed." (*TJ*, 102 [88], 104 [89]) Clearly there is a misunderstanding somewhere: the difference principle cannot both require "loss, however great" from the most-advantaged and be a principle of mutual advantage. This is not merely a rhetorical difference, either. Rawls argues—plausibly, I believe—that principles that manifest reciprocity will tend to be more stable than principles that depend strictly on unconditional sympathy alone. (See *TJ*, section 76, especially 498-501 [436-439].) Everyone agrees that a standard that relies on utilitarianism depends very heavily on sympathy, because it may require that one individual forgo advantages in order to provide a larger gain for another. (See *TJ*, 177-178 [154].) On the common reading of the difference principle, justice as fairness also depends heavily on the sympathy of the most advantaged, for they must sacrifice for the least advantaged. Rawls's argument that the difference principle would tend to be more stable than utilitarianism (even in a constrained form) depends on understanding the difference principle as a principle of reciprocity rather than one of strong and unconditional sympathy.

The disagreement between Rawls's interpretation and the more common one held by Nozick turns on which baseline is most appropriate for assessing advantages and losses. One obvious baseline is the status quo, whatever it happens to be. It might be thought that Rawls's claim of mutual benefit means that in the transition from the status quo to a just distribution of resources, nobody will lose relative to their status quo ante position. This would be an extremely implausible claim. Whether such a transition would require sacrifices for some depends in large measure on the nature and extent of injustices that are to be corrected. Surely we must recognize at least the possibility that those who gained most from an unjust system would not do as well when just institutions were implemented. That Rawls is not thinking of the status quo as the baseline for measuring mutual advantage is clear from the following passage: "The beneficiaries of clearly unjust institutions (those founded on principles which have no claim to acceptance) may find it hard to reconcile themselves to the changes that will have to be made." (*TJ*, 176 [154])[102]

---

100. Hare, "Rawls' Theory of Justice," 107.

101. Kenneth Arrow, "Some Ordinalist-Utilitarian Notes on Rawls's Theory of Justice," *The Journal of Philosophy* 70, no. 9 (May 1973), 257.

102. Rawls continues: "But in this case they will know that they could not have maintained their position anyway." Clearly, this is overly optimistic. Unjust arrangements can be quite difficult to change, as Rawls recognizes when he takes back this statement in his "Reply to Alexander and Musgrave," 653n13.

Another possible baseline is the hypothetical distribution of resources that would result from self-interested bargaining between the better endowed and the less endowed. This is suggested by Nozick's formulation. A third alternative is to take the principle of efficiency (the maximization of total social resources) to be the baseline. This seems to be what Hare and Arrow have in mind. The difference principle is likely to allow smaller inequalities than either of these. If either of these is taken as a baseline, movement to the difference principle will likely involve sacrifice on the part of the most advantaged.

In contrast, what Rawls has in mind is a baseline of equality of social resources.[103] This baseline seems appropriate for our assessment here because it involves a commitment to reciprocity in a way that the status quo, self-interested bargaining, and overall maximization do not. From equality as a baseline, the difference principle allows inequalities only when they work to everyone's advantage.[104] Up to the point at which the share of the least advantaged is maximized there are some inequalities that would be mutually advantageous. Beyond the point at which the difference principle is fully satisfied, however, an increase in the share of the better off will only come at the cost of the least advantaged. When this happens, the self-interests of different groups comes into direct conflict with one another and "a harmony of interests no longer exists. As the more favored gain the less advantaged lose, and vice versa." (*TJ*, 105 [90]) For this reason Rawls writes that society "should try to avoid the region where the marginal contributions of those better off [to those less well off] are negative, since, other things equal, this seems a greater fault than falling short of the best scheme when these contributions are positive." (*TJ*, 79 [68]) The difference principle embodies reciprocity then, since it assumes a baseline of an equal distribution of social resources and allows inequalities when they are mutually advantageous.

We can now return to examine the relative stability of Rawls's principles compared to the second mixed conception. If, as Rawls argues, principles that manifest reciprocity will tend to be more stable than those that rely on extended sympathy, then the difference principle has an advantage over utilitarianism (even when constrained by a guaranteed minimum). When they endorse the difference principle, citizens can see that people at every social position can gain relative to an equal distribution of resources, and in that sense they "agree to share one another's fate." (*TJ*, 102)[105] Utilitarianism, even when constrained by a guaranteed minimum, does not exhibit reciprocity in the same way. It may allow inequalities beyond the point at which there is mutual advantage, and

---

103. It is worth emphasizing again that we are talking about possible inequalities in the array of positions of the basic structure. We are not talking about the allocation of particular shares of goods to specific individuals, which Rawls treats as a matter of pure procedural justice. See my discussion in the first section of chapter 2.

104. This assumes that chain connection and close-knittedness hold. See note 77.

105. In the revised edition of *TJ*, Rawls drops this phrase from the passage at [87].

therefore it puts people at odds with one another. To be sure, this may be countered by sufficiently strong feelings of sympathy among the least advantaged. But, given publicity, there is no way to hide the fact that their interests are in conflict with the interests of the more advantaged and that their interests are being sacrificed for the interests of those who already have more. This cannot help but to create a tendency to undermine their sense of justice as well as their self-respect.

It must be conceded, of course, that even in a society well ordered by Rawls's two principles of justice, there will be temptations to defect. The more-advantaged might find it in their self-interest to press for inequalities beyond those allowed by the difference principle based on their superior bargaining power. Indeed, in every society there will be groups that could do better under different arrangements. That is exactly why a well-ordered society needs to rely on the sense of justice of citizens. The question of stability concerns the relative strength of the sense of justice that would be generated in different arrangements. Since citizens can see that Rawls's principles involve reciprocity, he argues that they will tend to be more stable than others.

In addition, consider the relative complexity of each conception and what is involved in assessing which institutions would best satisfy each. The difference principle relies on the distribution of primary social goods and requires only that we compare the share among the least advantaged groups in each of the possible institutional schemes. Certainly there are likely to be policy disagreements concerning the likely effects of different institutional designs, but this must be expected. In contrast, the case is much more difficult with the mixed conception we are considering. First of all, we need to determine the level at which the social minimum is to be set. There is not an obvious way in which this is to be done. This is not to say it cannot be done in a principled way, but only that there is going to be reasonable disagreement about the matter.[106] Next, in comparing alternative social arrangements, we must assess the effect on the total level of utility. This is more difficult than the difference principle for two reasons. First, the difference principle relies on shares of primary social goods that are much easier to measure than utility levels. The reliance on utility introduces difficulties in interpersonal comparisons. Second, while the difference principle only requires the comparison of the least advantaged position in each of the possible institutional schemes, utilitarianism requires the assignment of a utility level to every social position in each of the possible institutional schemes. The point, again, is not that such measurements or comparisons are impossible, but rather that they are considerably more difficult than the standard proposed by the difference principle.

---

106. See Waldron, "John Rawls and the Social Minimum"; and Cohen, "Democratic Equality."

All of this is relevant because stability is greatly enhanced when justice is not only done but is seen to be done.[107] When citizens are uncertain as to whether their society is just, and especially when they feel they are treated unjustly, there is a corresponding tendency for their sense of justice to weaken and erode. Other things equal, the parties will want to choose principles whose conditions of satisfaction are clear to all. I conclude, therefore, that in terms of stability, the difference principle is superior to the second mixed conception. As I indicated earlier, because these conceptions are likely to be so close in their institutional requirements, it is more difficult to judge which arguments would be most compelling to parties in the original position. To the extent that they do make similar evaluations, the parties would be forced to rely on considerations such as their relative stability when used as a public standard of justice.

We can now consider the third mixed conception, which grants fair equality of opportunity but requires that social institutions be designed to maximize the lowest level of utility, rather than the smallest share of primary social goods. We can think of this as the difference principle with respect to utility. In effect, this comparison forces us to reconsider the legitimacy (from the point of view of the original position) of the reliance on primary goods as a measure of advantage. One's level of utility is a product not only of one's share of social resources, but also the content of one's conception of the good, various social contingencies, one's natural talents, and, of course, sheer luck. Because of these many other variables, shares of primary goods are a very uncertain predictor of success in realizing one's conception of the good. If what we ultimately care about is the realization of our conception of the good, why wouldn't the parties seek to ensure a certain level of success in what is truly important to them?

One might attempt to reply to this question by stressing that social institutions do not have the same direct control over utility as they do over the primary social goods. We must remember, however, that in the original position the parties are not choosing social institutions directly. Instead, they are determining the standards to be used in public assessments of their institutions. The institutional arrangement which best realizes the difference principle, for example, may do so indirectly without explicitly relying on the difference principle itself. Similarly, the parties might choose principles that assess institutions according to the likely distribution of utility. The institutions that best satisfy this standard will still influence the allocation of primary social goods, but they will do so in a way that is aimed at maximizing the minimum level of utility.

Recently, there has been much discussion and criticism of Rawls under the heading of the question, "Equality of What?" This debate begins with the thought that egalitarians are more appropriately concerned with levels of well-being than with shares of primary goods. However, there are several

---

107. See Cohen, "Democratic Equality," 745.

complicating factors. The most obvious objection to an attempt to equalize utility is the problem of expensive tastes. Intuitively, the difficulty is that the effort to equalize levels of satisfaction will require the allocation of a larger share of resources to those with expensive tastes. Consider two people who are initially equally satisfied with cheap beer. One of them, however, successfully cultivates a taste for expensive champagne. At that point, an equal share of social resources will leave the champagne drinker at a lower level of satisfaction than the beer drinker. It seems, however, that her resulting fall in utility provides insufficient grounds for allocating more resources to the champagne drinker.[108]

The literature contains several ways to address this concern, but the most popular strategy involves some variation on distinguishing what was chosen by the individual and what is a result of factors beyond her control. "The right way for an erstwhile welfare egalitarian to respond" to the problem of expensive tastes, G. A. Cohen writes, is along these lines: "To the extent that people are indeed responsible for their tastes, the relevant welfare deficits do not command the attention of justice. We should therefore compensate only for those welfare deficits which are not in some way traceable to the individual's choices. We should replace equality of welfare by equality of opportunity for welfare."[109] Thus, we have a fourth mixed conception to consider. It substitutes for the difference principle (with respect to primary social goods) not equality of welfare but equality of opportunity for welfare.

Before discussing the problems with such a view, it will be worthwhile to distinguish it clearly from Rawls's approach, since its defenders often claim that Rawls himself holds such a view without fully appreciating its consequences. As we have seen, Rawls asserts that in light of the second moral power, the model-conception of the person assumes that (from a political perspective) citizens are responsible for their ends. Many of the defenders of equality of opportunity for welfare link this assertion with the misreading of natural endowments as collective assets that we discussed above. The thought, recall, was that society must strive to equalize everything that is arbitrary from a moral point of view. The things that are not arbitrary from a moral point of view are exactly the things for which one is responsible. Since we become responsible (on this view) only by choosing, society must strive to equalize everything that is not a result of choice, such as natural talents. One's tastes, on the other hand, are in part chosen, and therefore society need not equalize on the basis of those inequalities. We need not raise the champagne drinker's level of utility in the example above since she chose to cultivate that taste. Thus, it is thought, Rawls accepts (something like) the principle of redress because our talents are morally

---

108. See the discussion in Dworkin, "What Is Equality? Part 1: Equality of Welfare"; "What Is Equality? Part 2: Equality of Resources"; and Rawls, "Social Unity and Primary Goods."

109. G. A. Cohen, "On the Currency of Egalitarian Justice," *Ethics* 99, no. 4 (July 1989), 913-914.

arbitrary and therefore must be equalized, but he rejects equality of welfare because our ends are chosen by us and are therefore not to be equalized.

Having interpreted Rawls as asserting that everything that we have not chosen is arbitrary from a moral point of view and therefore to be equalized, these critics press for a refinement of the principles. While we exert some control over our preferences, surely everyone has preferences that are not the result of an act of deliberate choice. To carry through the project successfully, therefore, we must distinguish those preferences that have been chosen from those that have not. Justice, on this view, requires that unchosen preferences be satisfied to an equal degree; the individual is responsible for preferences that he chose. Consider now a second pair of individuals. Due to their upbringing (rather than to any deliberate choice) the first is satisfied with cheap beer while the other can only achieve a comparable level of satisfaction with expensive champagne. On the view we have just been examining, allocating to these individuals an equal share of resources would be unfair to the one with the champagne taste who, through no fault of her own, is unable to achieve as high a level of satisfaction as the beer drinker. According to this view, we must aim to give each person an equal opportunity to achieve well-being, and this means adjusting each person's share of resources to track the difficulty in satisfying unchosen preferences.

Before discussing equality of opportunity for welfare as an alternative to the difference principle, let us consider two things that are wrong with this view as an interpretation of justice as fairness. First, as we have seen, Rawls does not assert the general principle that everything that is unchosen or arbitrary from a moral point of view is to be equalized. Again: he rejects the principle of redress. Not everything that is arbitrary from a moral point of view is unjust. Some things, such as the distribution of natural talents, although arbitrary, are in themselves "neither just nor unjust." (*TJ*, 102 [87]) Nor, second, does Rawls assert a general principle to the effect that we are responsible only for what we have deliberately chosen. Choice is one common way to become responsible for something, but it is not the only way. From the point of view of a political conception of justice, since citizens are assumed to be responsible for their conception of the good, this responsibility holds whether or not acts of deliberation and choice form part of the etiology of a particular preference. As Rawls writes: "The use of primary goods, however, relies on a capacity *to assume responsibility* for our ends. This capacity is part of the moral power to form, to revise, and rationally to pursue a conception of the good."[110] As Daniels points out, "It is not actual choice that matters, but the underlying capacity for forming and revising one's ends that is at issue."[111]

One might think, however, that this tells against justice as fairness, rather than those who defend equality of opportunity for welfare. Some might believe

---

110. Rawls, "Social Unity and Primary Goods," 169, my emphasis; cf. *PL*, 186.
111. Daniels, "Equality of What: Welfare, Resources, or Capabilities?" 222.

that we should only hold people responsible for what they have chosen deliberately. Daniels argues, however, that our moral intuitions are better captured by abandoning this model of responsibility. He provides an example of an individual who, through no fault of his own "feels ill . . . at the very thought of eating fish." Because of this aversion, he is unable to pursue the career path that he most prizes (and that would bring him the most satisfaction) as a restaurant critic, and is therefore only able to achieve a relatively low level of welfare. Since this (relative) loss of utility is not due to any choices he made, if we were to attempt to equalize opportunity for welfare, society would owe him compensation. Daniels argues that this is mistaken: "unchosen preferences that make us worse off than others do not (generally) arouse egalitarian concerns unless they can be assimilated to the cases of psychological disability, that is, to a departure from normal functioning."[112] In other words, it is only if an individual's capacity to form, revise, and rationally to pursue a conception of the good falls below the threshold necessary to be a fully active member of society that we owe him the resources to help recover. We do not owe him resources to satisfy whatever conception of the good he happens to find himself with. Daniels elaborates the point with another example:

> If John was a compulsive or phobic personality, and the aversion to fish were symptomatic of a more generalized inability to accommodate to his preferences, or to reform and revise them over time, then I would be inclined to offer him some form of therapy for the underlying disorder. If, however, he then said that he really did not want the therapy, but preferred to "cash it in" for a week skiing in Vail, then I would refuse him the alternative. I am not interested in moving him to the point where his opportunity for welfare is equal to others; I am only interested in making sure that he has the mental capacity to form and revise his conception of the good in a normal fashion. Beyond that, I hold him responsible for his preferences.[113]

If we were interested in establishing equal opportunity for welfare, the particular form of compensation in principle would be irrelevant and therefore we should choose between therapy and the trip to Vail on the basis of efficiency alone.[114]

---

112. Daniels, "Equality of What: Welfare, Resources, or Capabilities?" 220.

113. Daniels, "Equality of What: Welfare, Resources, or Capabilities?" 221.

114. This perspective allows us to begin to answer the other main objection to primary goods: that it is insensitive to differences in needs, such as medical, among citizens. I cannot pursue the point here, but Daniels argues that fair equality of opportunity requires the preservation of "normal functioning" and that this may require an allocation of resources based on need. See "Equality of What: Welfare, Resources, or Capabilities?" "Health-Care Needs and Distributive Justice," and "The Prudential Lifespan Account of Justice across Generations," all in *Justice and Justification*; as well as *Just Health Care* (New York: Cambridge University Press, 1985). See also Rawls's remarks in *PL*, 184 and "Justice As Fairness: A Brief Restatement," 135-139; and the discussion in Pogge, *Realizing Rawls*, 183-194.

Now this argument is not made from within the original position, and so strictly speaking is not relevant here. The parties are not moved by considerations of (moral) responsibility, such as whether it is fair to hold someone responsible for something he did not chose. This is something that may or may not be important to us in achieving reflective equilibrium, but it is not a consideration that would move the parties, given our stipulations concerning their motivation. Nor are they moved by the thought that society has an obligation to equalize everything that is morally arbitrary. Such a moral principle, whatever its appeal to us, is not an independent source of motivation to the parties. Nonetheless, the considerations that Daniels raises may serve to support justice as fairness in reflective equilibrium.

Moving back to the perspective of the original position, it seems clear that the parties would reject the third mixed conception that requires the equalization of welfare. Knowing that the second moral power means that citizens will not simply be stuck with the conception of the good with which they find themselves but will view themselves and each other as responsible for their values, the parties will not be moved to allocate greater resources to satisfy expensive tastes. However, we still must consider the fourth mixed conception which substitutes equality of opportunity for welfare for the difference principle. I will concentrate on two reasons the parties would not select it, although I believe there are more.[115] Recall, once again, that the chosen principles are to serve as a public basis for justification with which citizens will debate possible reforms to their basic institutions. Any set of principles must provide workable criteria for assessment. Utilitarianism is often criticized for the excessive demands on information that it requires in order to make a determination, but the proposal we are considering requires far more. Not only must we assess total levels of utility for each of the various options confronting us, but we must do so against a background of the levels of utility of all of the past opportunities that we have had and may have over the course of a complete life.[116]

---

115. I will mention one additional consideration here. Suppose an individual has a low level of satisfaction because of his inability efficiently to convert resources into satisfaction. He is gloomy and a large supply of resources increases his satisfaction only slightly. The goal of equalizing levels of satisfaction may require that a virtually unlimited supply of resources be allocated to him, even though he is the least able to benefit from them. As Arneson points out: "Also, equal proportionate satisfaction requires that society continues to lavish resources on individuals who can derive but little benefit from them, so long as some tiny benefit accrues to those who are below average in satisfaction levels. The evident gross inefficiency of the norm counsels against adopting it." (Arneson, "Primary Goods Reconsidered," 435.) But the point holds almost as strongly against equalizing opportunity for welfare. Those who, through no fault of their own, have a low level of satisfaction and who do not efficiently convert resources into satisfaction will absorb potentially unlimited social resources for small marginal increases in their well-being. The focus on primary goods greatly mitigates this concern.

116. Any approach that aims to equalize opportunity for welfare will depend on a

Richard Arneson has developed the most philosophically sophisticated version of equality of opportunity for welfare. "For equal opportunity for welfare to obtain among a number of persons," he writes, "each must face an array of options that is equivalent to every other person's in terms of the prospects for preference satisfaction it offers."[117] Therefore, in order to judge whether people have equal opportunity for welfare, he proposes:

> We construct a decision tree that gives an individual's possible complete life-histories. We then add up the preference satisfaction expectation for each possible life history. In doing this we take into account the preferences that people have regarding being confronted with the particular range of options given at each decision point. Equal opportunity for welfare obtains among persons when all of them face equivalent decision trees—the expected value of each person's best (= most prudent) choice of options, second-best . . . nth-best is the same. The opportunities persons encounter are ranked by the prospects for welfare they afford.[118]

To begin to appreciate what is involved here, consider outlining all of the choices that you could have made over the course of your life that would have affected your level of utility over your lifetime. Next, consider all of the possible choices you could have made if you had made earlier decisions differently. (Don't forget how others would have responded differently if you made different choices and how this would have affected your available options, as well.) Now, determine the total level of utility for each of these possible life paths and order them from the highest to lowest. Finally, do this for everyone else and compare them all. I doubt that such a procedure is even coherent, but certainly it is hardly a process that realistically could be carried out.[119]

---

sharp contrast between the preferences that are chosen and those that are not. But most preferences are complicated mixes of the two. See the related comments of Christine Korsgaard, "Commentary [on Cohen and Sen]," in *The Quality of Life*, Martha Nussbaum and Amartya Sen, eds. (New York: Oxford University Press, 1993), especially 60-61.

117. Richard Arneson, "Equality and Equal Opportunity for Welfare," *Philosophical Studies* 56, no. 1 (May 1989), 85.

118. Arneson, "Equality and Equal Opportunity for Welfare," 85-86. I have excluded the footnote where he points out that there is a complication in determining the most prudent because choices will affect future preferences. In addition, Arneson goes on to observe that this is only an approximation since people may "differ in their awareness of these options, their ability to choose reasonably among them, and the strength of character that enables a person to persist in carrying out a chosen option." (86)

119. It's hard to understand why Arneson claims that it is more difficult to construct an index of primary goods than to undertake interpersonal comparisons of utility. There are roughly a half-dozen primary goods that must be commensurated, while in the United States there are over 250 million utility functions that must be commensurated. See Arneson, "Primary Goods Reconsidered," 446.

Furthermore, even if there were simplifications available for practical implementation,[120] any attempt to distinguish what is the result of a choice and what is due to factors beyond one's control will raise difficult issues of privacy and respect. G. A. Cohen memorably illustrates the objection that implementing a program of equality of welfare may "involve intolerably intrusive state surveillance. ('Hi! I'm from the Ministry of Equality. Are you, by any chance, unusually happy today?')"[121] A similar point holds in the case of implementing a program of equal opportunity for welfare. The question would be different, but it would be similarly objectionable: "So, is your genetically inherited below-average I.Q. still preventing you from contributing productively to society or are you sitting around just because you're lazy?" Jonathan Wolff has recently pointed out that if "fairness is understood in opportunity terms" and "the best opportunity conception of equality is equality of opportunity for resources," then we will inevitably have to confront the prospect of "shameful revelation."[122]

There is, however, an even more serious problem with all such welfare-based approaches from the point of view of justice as fairness: they exceed the limits of a political conception of justice. Whatever distinctions they make concerning responsibility and however they identify opportunities, they must rely on certain core assumptions regarding well-being (or welfare or utility). Specifically, they must understand well-being in such a way that it can be compared among individuals. This is the case even if they are going to equalize not welfare itself but the opportunity for welfare. There are two basic approaches familiar from utilitarian theory that we can rely on here. One approach is simply to stipulate which objective features well-being consists in. Sometimes this has been done by attempting to identify our ends with a certain feeling such as pleasure. The problem with what we might call egalitarian hedonism (or egalitarianism with respect to the opportunity for pleasure) is that not every reasonable comprehensive doctrine recognizes pleasure as an unqualified good, let alone the only good. The parties would not accept the design of the basic structure to be based on a hedonistic conception of the good that very well may be rejected by those they represent. Thus, they would not choose principles that would equalize pleasure, opportunities for pleasure, or any other psychological state.

---

120. See John Roemer, "A Pragmatic Theory of Responsibility for the Egalitarian Planner," in *Egalitarian Perspectives*.

121. G. A. Cohen, "On the Currency of Egalitarian Justice," 910.

122. Jonathan Wolff, "Fairness, Respect, and the Egalitarian Ethos," *Philosophy and Public Affairs* 27, no. 2 (spring 1998), 103. Elizabeth Anderson gives a similar example, imagining a letter from the "State Equality Board" in "What Is the Point of Equality?" *Ethics* 109, no. 2 (Jan. 1999), 305. She also points out that such a system would create incentives to individuals "*to deny personal responsibility for their problems*, and to represent their situation as one in which they were helpless before uncontrollable forces." (311) It would also encourage them to become helpless before uncontrollable forces.

The other common option is to rely on a measure of subjective preference satisfaction. There are several reasons one might be a subjectivist about values, but a measure of subjective preference satisfaction might be especially attractive here because such measures are often thought to be neutral in a way that hedonism is not. Within the limits to be set by the principles of justice themselves, subjectivism seems to put no limits on the content of one's preferences and conception of the good. As long as one's preferences satisfy certain axioms of rational choice theory, we can generate a utility function from them. An individual's preferences must be reconciled with one another, so to speak, but there seems to be no external imposition on their content.[123] Now there is a well-known difficulty in making interpersonal comparisons of utility when utility is understood as subjective preference satisfaction. How do we determine when different people's diverse preferences have been satisfied to an equal degree?[124] Although, I suspect it cannot be done with the precision needed to make the kinds of judgments required, I will leave aside this difficulty and assume that there is some principled way in which this can be done.[125] I claim, however, that this form of subjectivism is not neutral in the appropriate sense.

Remember, we are looking for a measure of advantage that can be publicly affirmed by all reasonable people for the purpose of evaluating social justice. If it is not acceptable to all reasonable people, the parties in the original position will not rely on it. Subjective preference satisfaction will not do the trick. The difficulty, quite simply, is that some people may reasonably believe that a person with a high level of subjective preference satisfaction is not always better off than a person with a low level of subjective preference satisfaction. That is, not everyone will agree that a person is better off whenever more of her

---

123. Gauthier presents an accessible account of subjective utility in chapter 2 of his *Morals by Agreement*. See, for example, 25, where he cites with approval Hume's dictum that it is "not contrary to reason to prefer the destruction of the whole world to the scratching of my finger."

124. See the discussion in Jon Elster and John Roemer, eds., *Interpersonal Comparisons of Well-Being* (New York: Cambridge University Press, 1991). The point I am about to make holds whether the utility functions are cardinal or ordinal. See Rawls's discussion of co-ordinal utilitarianism in "Social Unity and Primary Goods," 178-179.

125. Typically, the difficulty is addressed in the framework of rational choice theory in which it is assumed that we are comparing utility functions. But this assumes that the preferences satisfy the axioms of rational choice theory. In fact, this is not always the case. If a person holds that some goods are incommensurable, for example, she will not have a well-defined utility function. The difficulty this makes for interpersonal comparisons has not been adequately explored. See Joseph Raz, *The Morality of Freedom* (New York: Oxford University Press, 1986), chapter 13; Elizabeth Anderson, *Value in Ethics and Economics* (Cambridge: Harvard University Press, 1993), 55-64; Ruth Chang, ed., *Incommensurability, Incomparability, and Practical Reason* (Cambridge: Harvard University Press, 1998); and Larry Temkin, "A Continuum Argument for Intransitivity," *Philosophy and Public Affairs* 25, no. 3 (summer 1996).

preferences, whatever their content, are satisfied. Furthermore, we do not need unjust or impermissible preferences to make the point. Preferences that some people reasonably judge to be worthless or wasteful will do fine. Not everyone will agree that a person whose preferences are well satisfied by playing pushpin is better off than a person who is frustrated attempting to write poetry.

Consider a person—call her "Ambitious"—who judges another person's conception of the good—call him "Slacker"—to be worthless, although not unjust or morally permissible. If Ambitious is reasonable in the sense discussed in the previous chapter, her judgment that Slacker's conception of the good is worthless will not be grounds for coercing Slacker to change his conception of the good to a more ambitious one. Such a judgment may, of course, be grounds for attempting to convince him to change to (what Ambitious judges to be) an objectively superior system of values, but she certainly will not use the coercive apparatus of the state to enforce her assessment of an objectively superior system of values. The question we are examining is this: will Ambitious agree that subjective preference satisfaction is an appropriate public measure of well-being for the purposes of assessing basic social justice? The answer is no. She will reject any theory of justice that is predicated on the assumption that any two (permissible) conceptions of the good are equally valuable. Recall that justice as fairness "does not presuppose that the ends of different persons have the same intrinsic value." (*TJ*, 329 [289])

To make the point even more vivid, notice that there are in general two ways in which we can attempt to reach a higher degree of preference satisfaction: by raising our level of achievement or by adjusting our preferences. Consider a person who lowers her expectations by eliminating a religious commitment that is burdensome and difficult to satisfy. After doing so, her subjective level of satisfaction is higher. Not everyone will agree, however, that her level of well-being has increased. Specifically, those who believe that her previous faith was correct will think that she is less well-off for abandoning it. Indeed, contemplating this change, either prospectively or retrospectively, she might believe that her previous life was better, even though her previous desires were less fully satisfied. To take this a step further, consider the public policy implications that would be based on the adoption of this subjective standard. It might turn out that the most efficient way to achieve a high level of subjective satisfaction would be for the government to encourage low standards and preferences that are easily satisfied. This view would at least seem to require that we encourage a low level of hopes and expectations in our children as their preferences are being formed. In an attempt to equalize levels of (opportunity for) satisfaction, we may either direct shares of resources to those with low (opportunity for) satisfaction or encourage in them preferences that are more easily satisfied.[126]

---

126. It might be objected that there is a relevant difference here between satisfaction and opportunity for satisfaction. Encouraging the adoption of easily satisfied preferences

Brian Barry has denied the validity of this type of argument.[127] He argues that "attaching a value to want-satisfaction" does not "entail a rational obligation to modify one's desires so as to make them as easily satisfied as possible." (279) "The intuitively attractive proposition about want-satisfaction," he claims, "is that it is a good thing for the wants that I actually have to be satisfied." (279) But this intuitively attractive proposition is insufficient to underwrite an interpersonal comparison of subjective levels of well-being. To ground such comparisons, we would need the stronger thesis that it is a good thing for the wants that anyone has (not only those that I now have) to be satisfied. If we are committed to that stronger thesis, it does seem that the content of the preference and the agent whose preferences they are become irrelevant to the value of satisfaction as such. Barry concludes with the following example: "Thus, to be specific, we may feel that it is right to bring up our children with high standards, while recognizing that this will have the result of making them less easily satisfied than they might otherwise have been." (282) This is just the point. Most people do not think that preference-satisfaction, regardless of the content of the preferences, is an accurate measure of well-being. The individual with the demanding religious faith may recognize that she would have a higher level of subjective satisfaction without it, but she also may believe that subjective satisfaction is a false measure of her level of well-being.

All of this means what, in a sense, we knew already: there is not a single conception of the good that is affirmed by all reasonable citizens and can be used as a standard for assessing basic social justice. The parties in the original position will not agree to any publicly affirmed standard of overall well-being for assessment of the justice of the basic structure, including subjective levels of preference satisfaction. They will not select principles that attempt to equalize welfare or opportunity for welfare because there is no conception of welfare that all reasonable people share. They can only go as far as primary social goods. Shares of primary social goods are an appropriate basis for determining social advantage for the purpose of assessing the justice of the basic structure. As Rawls emphasizes, "fair shares of primary goods are clearly not intended as a measure of citizens' expected overall psychological well-being, or of their utility, as economists might say." (*PL*, 187-188) This is just as it should be, because reasonable comprehensive doctrines will disagree about the proper standard for assessing individual well-being, including whether such a standard

---

does not change the opportunity for welfare because one is responsible for what one has chosen. Recall, however, that nobody believes all of our preferences or changes in preferences are chosen. So, the social policy I just described should be directed toward changing our preferences without our making a deliberate choice, behind our backs, so to speak. If anything, this makes it even more objectionable.

127. Brian Barry, "Utilitarianism and Preference Change," *Utilitas* 1 (1989). Parenthetical references in this paragraph will be to this work.

should be objective or subjective. There is no single publicly acceptable measure of individual well-being for purposes of assessing basic social justice.

This completes my defense of the claim that the two principles would be chosen from the original position ahead of utilitarianism or of any of the mixed conceptions, and it also completes my overview of justice as fairness. Instead of retracing the argument of the last two chapters, let me conclude by emphasizing once again a point related to the issue of well-being. The conception of justice defended here is designed for a specific problem in particular circumstances. It is compatible with a wide variety (ideally, with all) reasonable comprehensive doctrines. Virtually all reasonable comprehensive doctrines will go beyond the limits of a political conception when addressing other issues, such as which conception of the good is best and how to assess the level of an individual's well-being. Furthermore, they will typically embed a concern with social justice within a broader system of values. Justice as fairness is silent on all of these further matters, as long as the comprehensive doctrines are reasonable. Thus, it does not deny a broader moral duty to redress natural inequalities, for example, or to equalize levels of well-being or opportunity for well-being. Such a view may certainly be part of a reasonable comprehensive doctrine, and citizens are free to pursue those goals. However, the duty of civility requires that when matters of basic social justice and the design of the basic structure is at stake, citizens rely not on their full comprehensive doctrines, but on principles that all reasonable people can share.

Chapter 4
Communitarianism and Conservatism

In this chapter we will begin by considering the communitarian critique of liberalism, focusing on their criticisms of justice as fairness. When we have a clear understanding of some of the main themes of communitarianism, we will be in a position to explore their many similarities to the arguments of traditional conservatives from Burke to Oakeshott and Scruton. Despite the large volume of work devoted to the so-called "liberal-communitarian debate," there is surprisingly little consensus concerning what exactly makes a doctrine communitarian. Indeed, the four philosophers most commonly identified as communitarians have all distanced themselves to a greater or lesser degree from that label.[1] Part of the difficulty is that communitarians largely define their positions in opposition to liberalism, or more specifically in opposition to liberal neutrality. In fact, with few exceptions, communitarian philosophers have generally been content to criticize perceived inadequacies in liberal theories rather than developing a detailed alternative of their own.[2]

What is clear at least is that communitarians stress the importance of community in some form or other and believe that liberalism neglects or undermines this important value. What is less clear—in fact, where communitarians do not agree with one another—is how community relates to other values, especially justice.[3] For some communitarians, the value of community competes with the value of justice. On this view, liberalism's preoccupation with justice leads it to neglect or denigrate rival values such as those found in certain forms of community. Attention to justice, some believe,

---

1. See Michael Sandel, *Liberalism and the Limits of Justice*, second edition (New York: Cambridge University Press, 1998), ix; Alasdair MacIntyre, "I'm Not a Communitarian, But . . . ," *The Responsive Community* 1 (1991); Charles Taylor, "Cross-Purposes: The Liberal-Communitarian Debate," in *Philosophical Arguments* (Cambridge: Harvard University Press, 1995); Michael Walzer, "The Communitarian Critique of Liberalism," *Political Theory* 18, no. 1 (Feb. 1990).

2. See Will Kymlicka, "Community," in *A Companion to Contemporary Political Philosophy*, Robert Goodin and Philip Pettit, eds. (New York: Blackwell, 1993), 375. Non-philosophers who identify themselves as communitarians have been more productive in addressing policy matters. See many of the contributions to the journal *The Responsive Community*, for example. It is often unclear, however, what unifies these more concrete discussions or how they differ from various forms of liberalism.

3. Kymlicka distinguishes different forms of communitarianism in "Community," 367.

undermines caring and nurturing relationships. For other communitarians, however, there is no necessary conflict between justice and community. In fact, for them a proper understanding of justice must incorporate the value of community. These communitarians believe that liberal theories of justice are excessively individualistic, but that a superior conception of justice will properly respect community values.

Most communitarians argue that liberalism's aspiration to fair treatment of citizens who hold a diversity of reasonable comprehensive doctrines is either undesirable, a sham, or both. Instead, they claim that a society should forthrightly acknowledge a particular comprehensive doctrine to be correct and arrange institutions to promote this good. This is the way Michael Sandel understands his own criticisms of justice as fairness (although I will raise questions about the adequacy of this characterization below): "What is at stake in the debate between Rawlsian liberalism and the view I advance in [*Liberalism and the Limits of Justice*] . . . is not whether individual or communal claims should carry greater weight but whether the principles of justice that govern the basic structure of society can be neutral with respect to the competing moral and religious convictions its citizens espouse."[4] If the principles of justice cannot be neutral, we are faced with the question of which of the competing moral and religious convictions should form the foundation of the basic structure of society. Oddly, there is a strange reluctance on the part of most communitarians to answer this question. Most fail to state in a forthright way which specific conception of the good they wish to place at the foundation of the social order. Nonetheless, we can distinguish two different approaches that can properly be labeled *communitarian*.

Some communitarians insist that each society must decide for itself which conception of the good will inform its basic structure. According to this approach, conceptions of justice should properly be based on the particular conception of the good that each society endorses. Some treat this relativism as necessary in order properly to respect the particular values of each community. They see it as ensuring a kind of democracy or anti-imperialism. Defenders of this view claim that liberalism fails to take seriously the fact that different communities affirm different values and instead callously imposes a purportedly universal conception of justice on all societies.

Notice that grounding a conception of justice in a community's conception of the good in this way does not imply that this conception of justice will give a prominent role to the value of community participation. It is possible for a society to affirm an individualistic conception of the good, and on this approach it would be proper for such a society to hold an individualistic conception of justice. Another society, which places great value on community participation, would appropriately hold a conception of justice that reserves a central place for

---

4. Sandel, *Liberalism and the Limits of Justice*, x.

the value of civic involvement. Thus, this first form of communitarianism does not necessarily rely on the importance of community participation, but rather relies on whatever values the community happens to affirm. Michael Walzer's theory of "complex equality" is arguably the most sophisticated version of this type of approach.

Other communitarians reject the dependence of principles of justice on the values and practices of particular communities. Sandel is explicit on this point: "The mere fact that certain practices are sanctioned by the traditions of a particular community is not enough to make them just."[5] Instead of resting a conception of justice on whatever conception of the good happens to be widely held in the society, these communitarians hold that society should be organized on the basis of the true (or best) comprehensive doctrine and conception of the good. The basic structure should aim to realize the most important human goods rather than what people, perhaps mistakenly, happen to affirm. Because this theory does not tie justice to the values that happen to be held in a particular community, Sandel claims that it is "not, strictly speaking, communitarian."[6]

Certainly this view is importantly different from the previous form of communitarianism. Like the previous form however, it is possible that this version will endorse an individualistic conception of justice. This would occur if one takes an individualistic conception of the good to be correct. More typically however, defenders of this view give a central role to community attachment and participation in the foundation of society. Therefore, it still seems appropriate to call this view a form of communitarianism. For Sandel, as we shall see, one of the most serious failures of liberalism is its inability to take seriously the importance of deep identifications between persons and their community. Thus, although the conception of the good that Sandel places at the foundation of the social order is not drawn from the community, its content gives a prominent role to community participation.

Both forms of communitarianism criticize liberalism for not taking community seriously enough in evaluating the basic structure of society—either the community should establish the goals that the basic structure should promote, or the value of community participation should be incorporated as an end of the basic structure. Sandel's criticisms of justice as fairness illustrate the latter possibility, and we will examine his view in the first section of this chapter. In the second section, we will consider the first form of communitarianism, exemplified by Walzer's complex equality. Finally, we will turn to an exploration of conservatism in order to bring out the important similarities between it and communitarianism.

---

5. Sandel, *Liberalism and the Limits of Justice*, xi.
6. Sandel, *Liberalism and the Limits of Justice*, xi; cf. 186.

Sandel and the Priority of Right

The author most commonly identified with communitarian criticisms of justice as fairness is Michael Sandel. The first edition of his *Liberalism and the Limits of Justice*, published in 1982, was a sustained critique of justice as fairness and is widely credited with being one of the defining statements in the liberal-communitarian debate. Sandel attacks various aspects of justice as fairness and, as one would expect, over the years defenders of liberalism have had various replies.[7] However, Charles Taylor believes that the liberal replies to Sandel largely miss the point of his critique. Taylor distinguishes "ontological questions," which are concerned with the fundamental terms of social explanation, from "advocacy issues," which concern "the moral stand or policy one adopts."[8] Taylor argues that while "the principal point" of *Liberalism and the Limits of Justice* is "ontological . . . the liberal response to it has generally been as a work of advocacy."[9] The main point of Sandel's critique, according to Taylor, was simply to identify a problem in the ontological foundations of liberalism rather than to advocate an alternative set of normative principles.

It is understandable why Taylor would think this. Much of Sandel's argument throughout *Liberalism and the Limits of Justice* is devoted to showing that the liberal conception of the self is a "metaphysical embarrassment."[10] Sandel's criticisms of the "liberal self" boil down to two. First, liberals (and Rawls is his exemplar) believe that the self is "prior to" and independent of its ends. Sandel claims that for liberals, the self is not "constituted" by its ends but rather "possesses" them: "The possessive aspect of the self means that I can never fully be constituted by my attributes." (20)[11] Second, Sandel insists that the liberal self can only come to "possess" its ends by making a deliberate and voluntary choice.

---

7. See, for example, Allen Buchanan, "Assessing the Communitarian Critique of Liberalism," *Ethics* 99, no. 4 (July 1989); Simon Caney, "Sandel's Critique of the Primacy of Justice: A Liberal Rejoinder," *The British Journal of Political Science* 40 (1992); Donald Herzog, "Some Questions for Republicans," *Political Theory* 14, no. 3 (Aug. 1986); Will Kymlicka, "Liberalism and Communitarianism," *The Canadian Journal of Philosophy* 18, no. 2 (June 1988); Amy Gutmann, "Communitarian Critics of Liberalism," *Philosophy and Public Affairs* 14, no. 3 (summer 1985).

8. Taylor, "Cross-Purposes," 181-182.

9. Taylor, "Cross-Purposes," 182.

10. Sandel, *Liberalism and the Limits of Justice*, 14. In this section, parenthetical remarks will be to this work (including the preface to the second edition).

11. Sandel admits that "this account is not offered by Rawls himself," but he claims it is "implicit in his theory." (20) Specifically, he believes it is implicit in the assumption of mutual disinterest among the parties in the original position. (54) What is odd is that Sandel recognizes that "the assumption of mutual disinterest . . . implies neither that these motivations hold for persons in real life, nor that they would hold for persons living in a well-ordered society governed by the two principles of justice." (42; cf. 61)

Both of these (alleged) assumptions are unacceptable to Sandel. The first thesis implies that there cannot be "constitutive attachments": it "rules out the possibility of any attachment (or obsession) able to reach beyond our values and sentiments to engage our identity itself." (62) But, Sandel argues, it is quite possible and often desirable for people to have commitments that literally make them who they are. The second thesis that he attributes to liberals implies that there are no ends or values that are truly binding unless they are deliberately chosen. But surely we are under a moral duty to treat strangers with basic decency, for example, and many people believe that they have strong moral obligations to their parents despite not having chosen them. The two theses attributed to liberalism are most clearly inadequate in situations in which people identify deeply with a particular system of values—their religious faith, say— without making a rational and deliberate choice.

The importance of unchosen social identities is a common theme among many communitarians.[12] Alasdair MacIntyre, for example, writes: "I am brother, cousin and grandson, member of this household, that village, this tribe. These are not characteristics that belong to human beings accidentally, to be stripped away in order to discover 'the real me.'"[13] Similarly, Charles Taylor, in the context of discussing Hegel, claims: "The state or the community has a higher life; its parts are related as the parts of an organism. Thus the individual is not serving an end separate from him; rather he is serving a larger goal which is the ground of his identity, for he only is the individual he is in this larger life."[14] Sandel seems squarely in this camp when he asserts

> we cannot regard ourselves as independent in this way [that the liberal account assumes] without great cost to those loyalties and convictions whose moral force consists partly in the fact that living by them is inseparable from understanding ourselves as the particular persons we are—as members of this family or community or nation or people, as bearers of this history, as sons and daughters of that revolution, as citizens of this republic. (179; cf. 172)

For Sandel, this comes down to a contrast between a "voluntarist" conception of the self and a "cognitive" conception. Rawls's account, Sandel claims, takes "the bounds of the self as given" and relates the self to its ends "by agency in its voluntarist sense, as willing subject to objects of choice." (152) According to Sandel's alternative, the self is related to its ends "not by choice but by reflection, as knowing (or inquiring) subject to object of (self-)

---

12. See the discussion in Andrew Jason Cohen, "Communitarianism, 'Social Constitution,' and Autonomy," *Pacific Philosophical Quarterly* 80, no. 2 (June 1999).

13. Alasdair MacIntyre, *After Virtue*, second edition (South Bend, Ind.: University of Notre Dame Press, 1984), 33.

14. Charles Taylor, *Hegel and Modern Society* (New York: Cambridge University Press, 1979), 86. See also *Sources of the Self* (Cambridge: Harvard University Press, 1989), especially 25-52.

understanding. . . . For the subject whose identity is constituted in the light of ends already before it, agency consists less in summoning the will than in seeking self-understanding." (152-153)

The contrast between these communitarian positions and that of liberals, however, amounts to less than at first may appear to be the case. All three of these communitarians—MacIntyre, Taylor, and Sandel—explicitly back off from the more radical interpretation of their claims of social embeddedness. Each recognizes an element of voluntarism. MacIntyre's description of a self that is identified by its participation in various social forms is his characterization of the self in "pre-modern, traditional societies," and he contrasts this sharply with the modern self-understanding. In fact, this contrast is the basis of his criticism of modern society: no longer embedded and constituted by our position in society, we are now free to choose our individual identities. Furthermore, he claims that while it is true that an individual's self-understanding properly begins as a member of some community, this "does not entail that the self has to accept the moral *limitation* of the particularity of those forms of community."[15] Taylor, for his part, grants that we are able to "re-evaluate" even our "most basic evaluations" so that "in principle no formulations are considered unrevisable."[16] Even Sandel acknowledges that, "As a self-interpreting being, I am able to reflect on my history and in this sense to distance myself from it, but the distance is always precarious and provisional, the point of reflection never finally secured outside the history itself." (179)

Still, if liberals really are committed to an extreme form of voluntarism, this more moderate communitarian view may be an attractive alternative. According to this moderate position, we have an ability to choose our conception of the good, but at any given moment, we typically find ourselves with ends that have not been deliberately chosen; we may have incorporated ends from our social environment, for example, without explicit reflection. The fact is, however, that Rawls is not committed to the kind of radically voluntarist picture that Sandel tries to foist upon him. Recall that Rawls's model of the person involves two moral powers, the second of which involves the capacity to form, to revise, and rationally to pursue a conception of the good. I emphasized in the previous two chapters that for political purposes this capacity is sufficient for an individual to be held responsible for her ends. There is no assumption that our conception of the good must be a product of a deliberate, self-conscious moment of choice.

Sandel quotes passages from *A Theory of Justice* like the following in order to attempt to establish that Rawls holds a radically "voluntarist" conception of the person:

---

15. MacIntyre, *After Virtue*, 221.

16. Charles Taylor, "What Is Human Agency?" in *Human Agency and Language*, vol. 1 of *Philosophical Papers* (New York: Cambridge University Press, 1985), 40; see also *Sources of the Self*, 37.

It is not our aims that primarily reveal our nature but rather the principles that we would acknowledge to govern the background conditions under which these aims are to be formed and the manner in which they are to be pursued. For the self is prior to the ends which are affirmed by it; even a dominant end must be chosen from among numerous possibilities. There is no way to get beyond deliberative rationality.[17]

Now first of all, we should remember that Rawls no longer speaks of "our nature" in contexts such as this. Instead, he emphasizes that the model of the person on which we rely is a political conception, designed to answer a specific question concerning basic social justice. Presumably the reason Sandel believes that this passage supports a voluntarist interpretation is Rawls's claim that "even a dominant end must be *chosen*." (my emphasis) However, as the next sentence reveals, his point concerns the limits of the formal principles of rational choice.

Rawls's point is that the formal principles of rational choice[18] are insufficient by themselves to determine a single rational conception of the good. In determining which specific conception of the good is rational for us, we must draw on more than these formal principles. This is what he means when he says that we must rely on deliberative rationality (and not only the formal principles) to identify our rational good. Notice that Rawls here says nothing about what further considerations might be relevant to this judgment; he says nothing, that is, about the content of an individual's rational deliberations. Rawls would now say that one's comprehensive doctrine provides this further content. It is simply a misreading, however, to think that Rawls believes that one's conception of the good must be the product of a voluntaristic choice. From the point of view of the formal principles of rational choice theory so to speak, an individual is left free to make her choice. But from her point of view—from the point of view of her comprehensive doctrine—these further considerations may dictate a single conception of the good and not leave any scope for individual choice.

Choice, for Sandel, seems only to be arbitrary, groundless, whimsical choice. This is clearly evident in his discussion of the inadequacy of liberal defenses of religious freedom, which, he claims, are predicated on a voluntarist picture of the self. Even in *A Theory of Justice*, Rawls explicitly denied this account of religious commitment, and recently Sandel has elaborated his critique by examining the decisions of the Supreme Court.[19] Even if the Court relies on such a form of voluntarism in some cases, it is unclear, of course, what implications this would have for liberal theory. However, in many of the

---

17. John Rawls, *A Theory of Justice* (Cambridge: Harvard University Press, 1971), 560 [491]. Sandel refers to Rawls's "voluntarism" and quotes this passage in *Liberalism and the Limits of Justice* on 186. However, Sandel fails to quote the final sentence that I have included.

18. For Rawls's discussion of these see *A Theory of Justice*, sections 63 and 64.

19. For Rawls's discussion of religious commitment in *A Theory of Justice*, see 206 [181], 214 [188], 243 [214].

decisions that Sandel cites, it is far from obvious that the Court is, in fact, relying on this voluntary model of the self. For example, Sandel cites *Cantwell v. Connecticut*, the 1940 decision that held that the Fourteenth Amendment incorporated the First Amendment's Establishment and Free Exercise Clauses and required, therefore, that they be applied to the state as well as to the federal government. The Court held: "Freedom of conscience and freedom to adhere to such religious organization or form of worship as the individual may choose cannot be restricted by law."[20] In a more recent case, the Court approved a city-sponsored display of a menorah alongside a Christmas tree because, in the words of Justice Sandra Day O'Connor, it conveyed "a message of pluralism and freedom to choose one's own beliefs."[21] Sandel believes that in both of these decisions, the Court assumes that religious beliefs are to be protected only because they are the products of choice. But surely there is a more natural reading.

In both cases, the Court was concerned that the government might restrict the range of religious faiths available to individuals. If the government does not dictate a single religious faith, individuals will be free to endorse a particular faith (or none) on the basis of other considerations. One natural way of expressing this is to say that from the point of view of the state, individuals are free to choose their own faith. This does not imply, of course, that their "choice" is arbitrary, groundless, or whimsical. From the point of view of a believer (and her comprehensive doctrine) there may be decisive reasons for her particular faith. On the basis of her acceptance of these reasons, she may not view it as a matter of (arbitrary) choice at all. This is perfectly compatible with saying that as a matter of law, or from the point of view of the basic structure of society, she has a choice. The point is precisely that her grounds for endorsing a particular religion, whatever they may be, are not dictated by the state. As Nancy Rosenblum has recently argued: "Voluntarism certainly does not mean that subjection to religious authority is the result of rational deliberation. How people arrive at their beliefs is a matter of indifference."[22]

Leaving aside the accuracy of the attribution of the voluntarist self to liberalism, why is Sandel concerned with this issue in the first place? The place to start is with Sandel's belief that the voluntarist model distorts the role of religious faith, at least for many true believers. By treating religious faith as a matter of choice, liberalism fails to appreciate the depth of commitment among believers and their understanding of their own faith:

---

20. *Cantwell v. Connecticut*, 310 U.S. 296, 303 (1940), quoted in Michael Sandel, *Democracy's Discontent* (Cambridge: Harvard University Press, 1996), 62.

21. *Allegheny County v. ACLU*, 492 U.S. 573, 634 (1989), quoted in Sandel, *Democracy's Discontent*, 63.

22. Nancy Rosenblum, *Membership and Morals* (Princeton: Princeton University Press, 1998), 84.

Construing all religious convictions as products of choice may miss the role that religion plays in the lives of those for whom the observance of religious duties is a constitutive end, essential to their good and indispensable to their identity. . . . To place religious convictions on a par with the various interests and ends an independent self may choose makes it difficult to distinguish between claims of conscience, on the one hand, and mere preferences, on the other. (xii-xiii)

Sandel's argument that the voluntarist picture of the self trivializes religion turns on two assumptions, each of which is questionable.

The first assumption is that our commitment to ends that come about from choices are weaker than our commitment to ends that we simply find given to us by our community or tradition, for example. It is unclear why Sandel thinks this. Perhaps he is thinking that what we choose one day we might abandon the next. Alternatively, perhaps he is assuming that we must view our unchosen ends as part of our conception of ourselves, and therefore we will be unable to abandon them. However, as we saw above, Sandel backs off from this stronger interpretation of the social constitution of the self when he grants that "As a self-interpreting being, I am able to reflect on my history and in this sense to distance myself from it." (179) In fact, we might be tempted to reject this first assumption in favor of its opposite: that the commitments that are the product of choice are stronger than those we have uncritically accepted on the basis of tradition alone. After all, if we do reflect on the grounds for these unchosen commitments, we may find that they are not worthy of our continued endorsement.

The second assumption that Sandel's argument depends on is that religious faith deserves a higher protection than mere preferences. The voluntarist defense of religious liberty "ignores the special concern of religious liberty with the predicament of conscientiously encumbered selves—claimed by duties they cannot choose to renounce, even in the face of civil obligations that may conflict." (xiii) But why does Sandel believe that we should give religious faith special protection? The answer is that in contrast to mere preferences, religion practices are accorded "special protection . . . either because they are admirable in themselves or because they foster qualities of character that make good citizens." (xiii-xiv) This account, he claims, will provide stronger protection to religious liberty than the assimilation of religious faith to mere preference. But this rather breathlessly assumes that it is obvious that a religious life is more admirable than other forms of life. Sandel nowhere attempts to demonstrate this. More significantly, his argument implies that only those religions that are intrinsically admirable or contribute to good citizenship are to be afforded protection: "Unless there were reason to think religious beliefs and practices contribute to morally admirable ways of life, the case for a right to religious liberty would be weakened." (xiv) It is hard to see how, in practice, this will result in anything but an undermining of the protection for unpopular religions. This hardly provides stronger protection than liberalism can offer.

Notice that in this discussion Sandel is not only concerned with an (allegedly) mistaken metaphysical picture. Contrary to Taylor's suggestion, Sandel is interested in the ontological status of the liberal self because he is interested in its normative implications.[23] The advocacy issues drive the ontology. Sandel believes that liberalism's voluntaristic picture provides insufficient protection to religious faith. For Sandel, this is but one instance of the fundamental problem: liberalism's commitment to the priority of right. A proper understanding of the self, he believes, will lead us to reject this commitment. Recently, Sandel has distinguished two senses in which liberalism holds that the right is prior to the good.[24]

> For Rawls, as for Kant, the priority of the right over the good stands for two claims, and it is important to distinguish them. The first is the claim that certain individual rights are so important that even the general welfare cannot override them. The second is the claim that the principles of justice that specify our rights do not depend for their justification on any particular conception of the good life or, as Rawls has put it more recently, on any "comprehensive" moral or religious conception. It is the second claim for the priority of right, not the first, that [*Liberalism and the Limits of Justice*] seeks to challenge. (x; cf. 185-188)

Here Sandel explains the first sense of the priority of right in terms of a commitment to "individual rights." It is more properly described, however, as a commitment to the normative priority of justice over other virtues. The second sense of the priority of right concerns the justification of the principles of justice. As Sandel explains, in this sense the priority of right requires that principles of justice not be tied strongly to any particular conception of the good or comprehensive doctrine. Notice, then, that even if we reject the priority of right in this second sense, as Sandel now advocates, we may still accept the priority of right in the first sense. That is, we might still believe, as Rawls does, that "justice is the first virtue of social institutions" and that "laws and institutions no matter how efficient and well-arranged must be reformed or abolished if they are unjust."[25] Contrary to Sandel's claim in the preface to the second edition of *Liberalism and the Limits of Justice*, I will argue below that the body of the text is concerned with rejecting the priority of right not only in the second sense, but in the first sense, as well. However, let us first consider the reasons Sandel has for rejecting the priority of right in the second sense.

We have just seen Sandel claim that the voluntarist self is unable to make sense of the deep commitment to religious faith that many believers have. No

---

23. Alan Ryan makes a similar point in his review of *Democracy's Discontent*. See "Republican Nostalgia," *Dissent* (winter 1997), especially 122.

24. For an excellent account of the priority of right and related issues, see Samuel Freeman, "Utilitarianism, Deontology, and the Priority of Right," *Philosophy and Public Affairs* 23, no. 4 (fall 1994).

25. Rawls, *A Theory of Justice*, 3 [3].

conception of justice based on the voluntarist model will be able to afford sufficient protection to religious faith, he argues, because such a model starts with a mistaken understanding of the relationship between an individual and the good. For Sandel the problems are not limited to protection of religious faith. The flawed model of the self leaves us unable to

> make sense of our moral experience, because it cannot account for certain moral and political obligations that we commonly recognize, even prize. These include obligations of solidarity, religious duties, and other moral ties that may claim us for reasons unrelated to a choice. Such obligations are difficult to account for if we understand ourselves as free and independent selves, unbound by moral ties we have not chosen. Unless we think of ourselves as encumbered selves, already claimed by certain projects and commitments, we cannot make sense of these indispensable aspects of our moral and political experience.[26]

A voluntarist picture of the self, Sandel claims, is unable to make sense of the moral importance of unchosen commitments. A conception of justice based on such an account of the self will inherit this defect and will undervalue the importance of such commitments. Since Sandel believes that the value of participating in a community is an example of such an unchosen, constitutive commitment, liberal conceptions of justice will systematically undervalue and distort the idea of civic virtue. It is in this sense that he is a communitarian.

According to Sandel, a liberal conception of justice will be unable to engage the full moral endorsement and commitment of citizens because it misidentifies a fundamental component of their moral experience. A society that "brackets morality and religion too completely soon generates its own disenchantment."[27] As we have seen, under certain conditions and for certain purposes, political liberalism does, indeed, require that we bracket our full comprehensive doctrine. It may seem, then, that Rawls's account of public reason may undermine the grounds for our commitment to the principles of justice. As Sandel asks rhetorically, "Why insist on separating our identity as citizens from our identity as persons more broadly conceived? Why should political deliberation not reflect our best understanding of the highest human ends?"[28] A failure to engage our deepest moral commitments and deepest identities means that a liberal society "cannot secure the liberty it promises because it cannot inspire the moral and civic engagement self-government requires."[29]

In fact, Rawls does not think that our sense of justice must be fully isolated from our comprehensive doctrine. Our comprehensive doctrine, if reasonable, will support our sense of justice. The requirements of public reason put restrictions on the kinds of justification it is appropriate to give in certain

---

26. Sandel, *Democracy's Discontent*, 13-14.
27. Sandel, *Democracy's Discontent*, 24.
28. Sandel, *Democracy's Discontent*, 322.
29. Sandel, *Democracy's Discontent*, 323.

circumstances for limited purposes. However, these restrictions are grounded precisely in the content of reasonable comprehensive doctrines and their commitment to the duty of civility. Rawls is relying on a certain complexity in the structure of reasonable comprehensive doctrines. Within such doctrines, we can distinguish one's sense of justice from one's conception of the good. A reasonable person's sense of justice guides his or her actions and arguments concerning the design of the basic structure and matters of basic social justice. In a well-ordered society, reasonable citizens share this sense of justice, while comprehensive doctrines and conceptions of the good vary from one person to the next. If a conception of justice is to be shared by those who endorse different comprehensive doctrines, its justification obviously cannot depend on any particular comprehensive doctrine (and conception of the good). Thus, justice as fairness is led to the priority of right in Sandel's second sense: it provides a justification of principles of justice without reference to any particular comprehensive doctrine or conception of the good.

I suspect that Sandel and other critics who charge that liberalism requires the alienation of the self from its ends have failed to understand the depth of Rawls's rejection of traditional instrumental models of practical reason. For Rawls, an individual's conception of the good does not exhaust the structure of his motivation or even of his moral motivation. A full account of an individual's character and motivational structure depends on both his conception of the good and his sense of justice. The classical instrumental account of rationality holds that practical reason is limited to the selection of efficient means in the pursuit of one's good. However, Rawls assumes the existence of a sense of justice that can motivate us to act and to reject the pursuit of ends that conflict with the demands of justice. As Edward McClennen notes, "The idea that the acquisition of a sense of justice implies an alteration in one's ends represents something of a departure from the ordinary way of thinking about the choice of principles or policies as instrumental to the personal goals of the participants."[30]

Communitarians claim that an account of the proper shape of society depends on a full account of the good. They hold that liberalism, which limits itself to a thin theory of the good, is inadequate. Charles Taylor, who has long argued that moral philosophy must be centered on a full conception of the human good, asserts that the liberal effort at self-limitation "is on the deepest level incoherent."[31] However, in modern circumstances, characterized by the reasonable pluralism described in chapter 2, resting justice on a full account of the good is to abandon all hope of a society that all reasonable citizens can

---

30. Edward McClennen, "Justice and the Problem of Stability," *Philosophy and Public Affairs* 18, no. 1 (winter 1989), 8.

31. Taylor, *Sources of the Self*, 89. Compare Taylor, "Cross-Purposes: The Liberal-Communitarian Debate," 190-191. See the discussion in J. B. Schneewind, "Book Review of *Sources of the Self*," *The Journal of Philosophy* 88, no. 8 (Aug. 1991); and Will Kymlicka, "The Ethics of Inarticulacy," *Inquiry* 34, no. 2 (June 1991).

recognize as just. As Rawls stresses repeatedly, in the absence of the most coercive forms of repression we have no choice but to suppose that a diversity of moral, religious, and philosophical doctrines, as well as conceptions of the good, will continue to flourish. In modern societies there simply is no hope of unanimous affirmation of a single set of values. If shared final ends are required, there is simply no realistic possibility of a just and stable society that wins the support of all of its reasonable citizens.

Rawls wants to resist this conclusion of hopelessness. He insists that there is at least the possibility of a just and virtuous society in the face of diverse comprehensive doctrines and conceptions of the good. He recognizes, however, that no society could hold together were there no ends which citizens collectively affirmed. The model conception of the person uses this insight to distinguish the ends that all citizens in a well-ordered society must share from those where such agreement is not required. It is precisely a sense of justice that citizens must have in common in order for a well-ordered society and its just institutions to hold together. Within the limits set by the demands of justice, the full diversity of conceptions of the good may be affirmed. It is worth recalling, as we saw in the discussion of the idea of a social union, that there is no requirement that citizens pursue their goals as individuals. They are perfectly free to pursue their ends as members of associations and communities with those who hold a similar comprehensive doctrine or conception of the good. What justice as fairness denies is that the whole society should be seen as such a community, devoted to a single conception of the good or to a unified comprehensive aim.[32]

As we have seen, the character of the institutions of the basic structure is dependent on the attitudes and actions of citizens. Therefore the requirements of institutional justice make demands on the conduct of individuals, and these may potentially conflict with an individual's conception of the good. The priority of right means that when such conflicts arise, we normally must follow the demands of justice. It is worth emphasizing, however, that although justice takes priority, it does not provide an exhaustive account of an individual's ends or motivations. As Rawls puts it near the end of *A Theory of Justice*: "It may be thought that once the principles of justice are given precedence, then there is a dominant end that organizes our life after all. Yet this idea is based on a misunderstanding." Although the claims that the principles of justice make on individuals are uncompromising, they are not "all controlling."[33] Justice rules out certain ends, and requires the adoption of others, but there is room left for the affirmation of a wide diversity of permissible goods. As Rawls explains:

---

32. See John Rawls, *Political Liberalism* (New York: Columbia University Press, 1993; paperback edition, 1996), 40-43.

33. Rawls, *A Theory of Justice*, 565 [495].

[I]n justice as fairness the priority of right implies that the principles of (political) justice set limits to permissible ways of life; hence the claims citizens make to pursue ends that transgress those limits have no weight (as judged by that political conception). But just institutions and the political virtues expected of citizens would serve no purpose—would have no point—unless those institutions and virtues not only permitted but also sustained ways of life that citizens can affirm as worthy of their full allegiance. A conception of political justice must contain within itself sufficient space, as it were, for ways of life that can gain devoted support.[34]

If it were not for the fact that each citizen affirms a particular conception of the good, there would be no reason to promote the justice of the basic structure. Citizens' sense of justice is what ensures both that these institutions remain fair and that they respect the diverse (permissible) goods that citizens affirm. But without a conception of the good, citizens would be indifferent to the distribution of the social primary goods in the first place.

Even though justice as fairness rejects the idea of an end that is all-controlling, it recognizes that we can speak, if we so choose, of the "common good" of society.[35] For justice as fairness, the linchpin of this common good is justice itself. After all, since citizens in a well-ordered society share a sense of justice, "they share one very basic political end, and one that has high priority: namely, the end of supporting just institutions and of giving one another justice accordingly, not to mention many other ends they must also share and realize through their political arrangements."[36] To repeat: since it is not all-controlling, a just basic structure will allow individuals and groups to affirm a wide variety of ends. Notice, too, that a just basic structure will allow the collective pursuit of more specific and concrete goals (even at the level of the state) when matters of basic social justice are not at stake. As we saw in chapter 2, Rawls holds that most political questions do not concern matters of basic social justice. In these ordinary political decisions, citizens and legislators need not respect the limits of public reason (or at least, need not respect them as strictly) and therefore may often act and vote according to their reasonable comprehensive doctrines.[37]

---

34. Rawls, "The Priority of Right and Ideas of the Good," *Philosophy and Public Affairs* 17, no. 4 (fall 1988), 251-252. See also Rawls, *Political Liberalism*, 174.

35. As Rawls does, for example, in *A Theory of Justice*, 226 [198]. Compare Stephen Holmes, *The Anatomy of Antiliberalism* (Cambridge: Harvard University Press, 1993), 198-200; and William Lund "Egalitarian Liberalism and Social Pathology: A Defense of Public Neutrality," *Social Theory and Practice* 23, no. 3 (fall 1997), 460.

36. Rawls, *Political Liberalism*, 202.

37. See Rawls, *Political Liberalism*, 214, and the discussion in my "Having It Both Ways: Justification and Application in Justice As Fairness," *Pacific Philosophical Quarterly* 75, no. 3&4 (Sept./Dec. 1994), 312-314; "The Reasonable in Justice As Fairness," *The Canadian Journal of Philosophy* 29, no. 1 (March 1999); and Peter de Marneffe, "Liberalism, Liberty, and Neutrality," *Philosophy and Public Affairs* 19, no. 3 (summer 1990).

If liberals can identify a common good of society, this suggests that perhaps some of the criticisms of the priority of right may simply be based on a misunderstanding. When William Galston claims that all "intelligible motives for action . . . invoke some conception of the good as the end of action,"[38] it seems that what we have here is, at least in part, merely a terminological dispute. For Rawls, both the good and the right can provide goals and motivation for action. What is important is not the labels we use but that we distinguish conceptually these two sources of motivation. This is because, to repeat, it would be too much to demand the complete agreement on comprehensive doctrines and conceptions of the good, but the stability of a well-ordered society requires that principles of justice be widely shared.[39]

Like other communitarians, Sandel argues that we should abandon the aspiration to defend principles of justice without reference to specific conceptions of the good. The obvious question then becomes: Which specific conception of the good are we to place at the base of our conception of justice? Sandel faces a dilemma. Either he must tell us which conception of the good is the correct one, or he must have us rely on the one which members of our community believe to be correct. We have already seen him explicitly reject the relativism implicit in the second option. Nevertheless, he has remarkably little to say about the specific conception of the good that he would place at the basis of society—which is the true (or best) one? Based on his criticisms of liberal justice, we can infer that it would give a prominent role to some combination of "solidarity, religious duties, and other moral ties that may claim us for reasons unrelated to a choice."[40] But this is speculative and, in any case, far from an adequate specification of a conception of the good. Sandel's unwillingness to engage the issue of which specific conception of the good should form the basis of our understanding of justice is not surprising. A detailed specification of a particular conception of the good will exclude some ways of life that reasonable people may take to be valuable. Without such a specific articulation of the good, we are left with no basis for evaluating social institutions at all. The other possibility, of course, is to rely on a general specification of what all reasonable conceptions of the good share, in which case we have a variant of liberalism's thin theory of the good (even if we call it something else).

Rejecting the priority of right in the second sense means that we base our conception of justice on a particular conception of the good. Sandel never tells

---

38. William Galston, "Equality of Opportunity and Liberal Theory," in *Justice and Equality Here and Now*, Frank Lucash, ed. (Ithaca, N.Y.: Cornell University Press, 1986), 92.

39. The extent to which a conception of justice is shared is not an all-or-nothing matter. A modus vivendi, even though potentially unstable, is more stable than no overlap at all, and a constitutional consensus is more stable still, although not as stable as an overlapping consensus. See Rawls, *Political Liberalism*, 158-168.

40. Sandel, *Democracy's Discontent*, 13.

us which conception of the good is the correct one, but he believes that a society that frames itself on the basis of a single conception of the good will be able to engage more fully the moral motivation of its citizens. In contrast, a liberal conception of justice that forces individuals to bracket their conceptions of the good (for certain purposes) will lead to a disenchanted and apathetic citizenry. This is not only because liberal justice forces them to ignore their deeply held, unchosen commitments. In addition, it will sometimes force them to subordinate their conception of the good to the requirements of justice. This is due to liberalism's commitment to the priority of right in the first sense. Against Sandel's account in the preface to the second edition, I will now argue that *Liberalism and the Limits of Justice* is concerned with rejecting the priority of right in this first sense.[41] Although in his new preface Sandel de-emphasizes this, in the body of the text he does set justice in competition with other virtues. This should be clear enough from the title: he is concerned, among other things, with the limits of justice. Sandel argues that by rejecting the priority of right (in the first sense) we will be able to leave behind liberalism's preoccupation with justice in the name of more noble virtues.

As we saw in chapter 2, Rawls claims that when assessing the design of the basic structure in the circumstances of justice, the virtue of justice should normally override other values when they conflict. Recall that the circumstances of justice are the "normal conditions under which human cooperation is both possible and necessary" for the pursuit of our individual and collective goals.[42] Sandel claims, ostensibly contrary to Rawls, that "we can readily imagine a range of more intimate or solidaristic associations in which the values and aims of the participants coincide closely enough that the circumstances of justice prevail to a relatively small degree." (30-31) He then quotes Hume approvingly to the effect that the family is an example of an institution within which ends should sufficiently coincide that justice will become unimportant. This shows, he claims, that "justice is the first virtue of social institutions not absolutely, as truth is to theories, but only conditionally, as physical courage is to a war zone." (31)

The comparison to a war zone is pointed, for Sandel hopes to portray the conditions in which justice comes to the fore as those in which individuals, isolated from one another, pursue their own private goals without concern for the welfare of others or the achievement of collective ends.[43] When we view it in

---

41. I am not the only reader who finds a rejection of the priority of right in the first sense in *Liberalism and the Limits of Justice*. Many reviewers focus on this point. See, for example, Brian Barry, "Review of *Liberalism and the Limits of Justice*," *Ethics* 94 (April 1984), especially 525; and C. Edwin Baker, "Sandel on Rawls," *University of Pennsylvania Law Review* 133 (April 1985), especially 917.

42. Rawls, *A Theory of Justice*, 126 [109].

43. This is a typical communitarian picture of liberal society. For MacIntyre, "Modern politics is civil war carried on by other means." (*After Virtue*, 253)

this way, he tells us, "justice appears as a remedial virtue, whose moral advantage consists in the repair it works on fallen conditions." (32) For Sandel, justice is only a virtue when people insufficiently identify with one another and when therefore their relations must be artificially mediated. In such a situation, individuals fail to see themselves as part of a collective body that dictates their ends, and thus their actions must be regulated by the "virtue" of justice. Sandel takes this to be a severe moral shortcoming: "One consequence of the remedial aspect of justice is that we cannot say in advance whether, in any particular instance, an increase in justice is associated with an overall moral improvement." (32) Later he tells us, "in some cases, justice is not a virtue but a vice." (34)

To convince us of this startling claim, Sandel argues that an increase in justice "can occur where before there was neither justice nor injustice but a sufficient measure of benevolence or fraternity such that the virtue of justice had not been extensively engaged." (32) The picture seems to be one in which an easy and natural fraternity is replaced by an increased reliance on rigid, abstract, and artificial standards of justice. This discussion suggests, perhaps, that Sandel is worried that frequent appeals to institutions of arbitration such as courts may undermine feelings of benevolence and solidarity between citizens. Whether or not this is a insightful social-psychological claim, it does not present a challenge to Rawls's claim that "justice is the first virtue of social institutions."

Recall that for Rawls, the basic structure is just when it satisfies the two principles of justice at least as well as any other feasible arrangement of basic institutions. An increase in the justice of the basic structure is not necessarily accompanied by an increase in appeals to rigid administrative procedures. Sandel appears to confuse the issue of whether the basic structure satisfies the demands of justice with the frequency of appeals to judicial and administrative institutions or rules within the society. It is not lack of fellow feeling or moral consideration that leads to the priority of justice. It is the fact that citizens do not generally share a single comprehensive doctrine. Mediating institutions are necessary not because of a lack of virtue but primarily because of honest disagreement about what virtue requires. Justice is not remedial; nor does it compete with the value of fraternity.

Contrary to Sandel's belief that justice may compete with community, I maintain not only that justice is compatible with the social virtues, but that it is a necessary precondition for an admirable form of community. Jeffrey Reiman's discussion on this point is instructive. Reiman argues that the circumstances in which Sandel claims justice is either unnecessary or is actually a vice (what Reiman calls the "circumstances of benevolence") are not actually beyond the circumstances of justice:

> [T]he circumstances of benevolence are not alternatives to the circumstances of justice; rather the former exist within and presuppose the latter. If, thinking they are in the circumstances of benevolence, people try to force someone to act

benevolently, they will find themselves in the circumstances of justice—conflicting aims and limited altruism. They have always been standing in those circumstances but did not notice it as long as everyone was acting benevolently voluntarily. . . . Since force is an ever-present possibility, so the circumstances of justice are ever present.[44]

Note two points about this account. First, justice here is taken as a virtue of individual conduct. This diverges from Rawls's primary usage, but, as we have seen, Rawls agrees that justice makes demands on individuals. Second, Reiman's account has the virtue of presenting justice as the condition of institutional non-subjugation. We might put it slightly differently: justice obtains in the social conditions of non-exploitation, understood in a non-technical sense.

The conditions of non-exploitation serve as a necessary background for a society to be morally admirable. Reiman makes the point eloquently:

We see thus the general mistake made by those who think the primacy of justice is opposed to the value of community. The community that is put forth as a moral value in competition with justice must be real community. . . . Real community exists only among people who share their relationship from within the very space that justice keeps clear of force. Sandel's benevolent community presupposes justice rather than posing an alternative to it.

Justice, then, is not only invoked by the enterprise of moralizing as its morality; it is invoked by community as its precondition. Since community can only really exist where people are voluntarily moved to act in pursuit of their shared ends, it cannot exist between people some of whom are being subjugated by others. People who believe they share real community must implicitly believe that their relations are not forms of subjugation and thus that they are compatible with justice.[45]

In fact, we can press this point a step further. Justice is indeed necessary for the possibility of a morally admirable community, but Sandel, like Taylor, is unable to see the possibility of justice in pluralistic societies.

Recall that in justice as fairness, the principles of justice apply to the "society's main political, social, and economic institutions, and how they fit together into one unified system of social cooperation from one generation to the next."[46] Rawls consistently includes the family as part of the basic structure of society.[47] This does not mean, however, that we must apply the principles of

---

44. Jeffrey Reiman, *Justice and Modern Moral Philosophy* (New Haven: Yale University Press, 1990), 211. This statement ignores the possibility of extreme scarcity, but this is not the direction of Sandel's objection.

45. Reiman, *Justice and Modern Moral Philosophy*, 211-212.

46. Rawls, *Political Liberalism*, 11.

47. See, for example, Rawls, *A Theory of Justice*, 7 [6]; *Political Liberalism*, 258; and most significantly, "The Idea of Public Reason Revisited," *University of Chicago Law Review* 64, no. 3 (summer 1997), 787-794. See the discussion in Susan Okin, *Justice, Gender, and the Family* (New York: Basic Books, 1989), chapter 2; Véronique Munoz-

justice directly to the internal arrangement of the family with the resulting absurdity that, say, allowances for children must be dictated by the difference principle. While they are not to be applied directly, the principles do put constraints on the institutional forms that are permissible. No matter what the marriage vows say, no matter what the traditional community values are, justice requires that no spouse is ever the legal possession of the other, that each has the right to vote and hold property, and that rape remains a serious moral violation. It is hard to see how one could reasonably believe that these guarantees of justice could possibly interfere with a valuable form of family life.

In fact, with these guarantees of basic social justice in place, individuals are better able to develop relationships that exemplify other communal virtues. As Jeremy Waldron observes, "Though marriage is certainly more than rights and correlative duties, and though one will not expect to hear claims of right in a happily functioning marriage, nevertheless the strength and security of the marriage commitment in the modern world depend in part on there being an array of legalistic rights and duties that the partners know they can fall back on, if ever their mutual affection fades."[48] The guarantee that all individuals receive a fair share of resources, to select another example, allows them to exercise the virtues of generosity and benevolence. Having a right to a certain share of wealth does not, of course, require that the individual either save that wealth or use it for consumption; it can be used to express generosity and care, for example. Indeed, a right to wealth need not be claimed in the first place. As John Tomasi points out, withholding a right-claim (which is only possible, of course, if a person has that right) can be a "profound expression of community."[49] Justice does not interfere with the virtues of benevolence or care, but rather by preventing exploitation, provides the condition under which these other virtues become possible and valuable.

It seems, then, that Sandel's remarkable claim that justice may sometimes be a vice actually amounts to an objection to a highly administered life. In reply, I have pointed out that for Rawls justice is not necessarily improved by more frequent appeals to such administrative or judicial procedures. Furthermore, I have argued that it is only against just background conditions that community is non-exploitative and admirable. Sometimes, however, it seems as though an overly rule-governed life is not exactly Sandel's complaint. Textual support is ambiguous. At times, it does seem to be over-officiousness that he sees as the

---

Dardé, "Rawls, Justice in the Family and Justice of the Family," *The Philosophical Quarterly* 48 (July 1998); and S. A. Lloyd, "Family Justice and Social Justice," *Pacific Philosophical Quarterly* 75, no. 3&4 (Sept./Dec. 1994).

48. Jeremy Waldron, "When Justice Replaces Affection: The Need for Rights," in *Liberal Rights* (New York: Cambridge University Press, 1993), 373-374.

49. See John Tomasi, "Individual Rights and Community Virtues," *Ethics* 101, no. 3 (April 1991), 536. This is not incompatible with the view that some rights (such as those mentioned above) are inalienable.

threat to community:

> Consider for example a more or less ideal family situation, where relations are governed in large part by spontaneous affection and where, in consequence, the circumstances of justice prevail to a relatively small degree. Individual rights and fair decision procedures are seldom invoked, not because injustice is rampant but because their appeal is preempted by a spirit of generosity in which I am rarely inclined to claim my fair share. (33)

Here it appears that the worry is that invoking fair procedures may be divisive while other procedures of distributing goods, because they are more spontaneous, would be more unifying and less competitive.

Immediately after this passage, however, Sandel continues as follows:

> Nor does this generosity necessarily imply that I receive out of kindness a share that is equal to or greater than the share I would be entitled to under fair principles of justice. I may get less. The point is not that I get what I would otherwise get, only more spontaneously, but simply that the questions of what I get and what I am due do not loom large in the overall context of this way of life. (33)

Here Sandel is clear that it is not simply the invocation of specific distributive mechanisms, but rather the willingness to reflect on whether institutions are fair that is the threat to community. It would be one thing if Sandel were merely to claim that under just background conditions the reliance on formal adjudicative mechanisms might undermine the trust between citizens, but his argument goes far beyond this. Sandel implies that even when background institutions are admittedly unjust, reflection on this situation may be a dangerous threat to the more important value of community.

Later in this chapter, we will consider the conservative argument that citizens should be reluctant to change their institutional structures, that is, that existing institutions have a claim to legitimacy simply because they already exist. Sandel's argument here is conservatism with a vengeance. He suggests that mere concern with the justice of current institutional arrangements can itself lead to a lowering of the moral standing of a community: other things equal, it would be better if people were not in the habit of reflecting on and questioning the justice of the institutions that they inherit.

On this point, the contrast with Rawls is especially stark. Recall that Rawls requires that his principles of justice satisfy a publicity condition. Citizens must be able to reflect on their institutions and publicly affirm that they meet the demands of justice. Far from weakening social union, he claims, the public knowledge that social institutions are just and treat all citizens fairly will strengthen citizens' support for their institutions. When social institutions do not meet the demands of justice, it is only by recognizing this fact that citizens will be able to struggle to reform them and eliminate exploitation and injustice.

Especially in circumstances marked by a plurality of conceptions of the good and by a variety of reasonable comprehensive religious, philosophical, and moral doctrines, a wide-ranging, spontaneous convergence of final ends cannot be expected. Justice as fairness attempts to uncover principles to regulate fairly the interaction of citizens who do not in general share each other's final ends. It is true that this may not be possible; ends may be too divergent to find any common ground. But this cannot be determined before the attempt is made. Justice as fairness isolates conceptually what may be difficult to distinguish empirically or phenomenologically—the right and the good—in order to reveal what is required for social union in modern pluralistic conditions. In a well-ordered society, citizens affirm a common conception of justice that regulates the basic structure of their society, while at the same time, beyond this shared core, they may affirm divergent conceptions of the good. Placing any one of these conceptions of the good at the foundation of society would be unacceptable to some individuals who reasonably reject it. If Sandel were to specify his favored conception of the good in the detail required, it would be clear that it would be inappropriate to play such a foundational role.

Complex Equality

While some critics believe that justice itself is dangerous because it is either in competition with communal virtues or is a threat to stability, others defend the concept of justice but believe that the specific conception advocated by Rawls is too abstract and disconnected from the values of particular societies. This type of criticism is well represented by Benjamin Barber who charges that "Rawls's formalism, his preoccupation with economic models and metaphors, his predilection for abstract reasoning, and, above all, his aspiration to endow muddy, much-contested politics with the clarity of a rational consensus rooted in philosophical theory—all combine to deter him from setting his emergent theory of justice in the context of historical and political reality."[50] One might have thought that the attempt "to endow muddy, much-contested politics with the clarity of a rational consensus" would be an admirable goal, but this type of criticism is extremely common. Michael Walzer's version of this critique is especially interesting for three reasons. First, Walzer's critique of Rawls is explicitly on the grounds that justice as fairness is too abstract and insensitive to local meanings. Second, Walzer does not believe that a conception of justice must be so abstract, and he is virtually unique in his attempt to construct a conception of justice which is sensitive to local meanings in a way that justice as fairness allegedly is not. Unlike Sandel, Walzer has no doubt that an increase in justice constitutes a moral improvement. Third, and finally, Walzer positions

---

50. Benjamin Barber, *The Conquest of Politics* (Princeton: Princeton University Press, 1988), 77.

himself on the political left and explicitly denies that his conception of justice is conservative. Therefore, he presents an important test case for the hypothesis that I develop below concerning the similarities between communitarians and conservatives.

The main thesis of Walzer's *Spheres of Justice* can be summarized rather easily: justice requires that different goods be distributed according to their particular social meanings. "Justice is relative to social meanings,"[51] he tells us. Thus: "When meanings are distinct, distributions must be autonomous." (10) This account leads to the idea of distinct spheres within which each social good is distributed according to mechanisms "entailed" by its meaning.[52] Injustice occurs when there is a distribution of some good contrary to its social meaning. Most frequently, this happens when one good is used to "dominate" (that is, influence or determine the distribution of) a good in a different sphere, or when some individual or group "monopolizes" a good by "successfully hold[ing] it against all rivals." "Dominance describes a way of using social goods that isn't limited by their intrinsic meanings or that shapes those meanings in its own image. Monopoly describes a way of owning or controlling social goods in order to exploit their dominance." (10-11) Walzer believes that cases of dominance are among the central problems we face in modern society, and he states that his "purpose in this book is to describe a society where no social good serves or can serve as a means of domination." (xiv)

Some critics have suggested that Walzer relies on two different standards of justice: the *shared meanings* criterion and the *different spheres* criterion.[53] This interpretation is misleading because each of the different spheres is identified by the meaning of the good with which it is associated. Without different meanings, there would be no basis for distinguishing different spheres, nor would there be any point in doing so. The only reason to keep the spheres distinct, for Walzer, is that a failure to do so would result in the distribution of some good by a mechanism contrary to its meaning. The idea of different spheres is only a metaphor for insuring the proper distribution of a good according to its social meaning. Thus for Walzer, to determine whether a society is just, we must first identify the social meaning of the various goods and then determine whether society distributes those goods according to their meanings or whether it allows their distribution to be dominated by some other good. For convenience, I will call the ideal of distribution according to social meanings Walzer's "general

---

51. Michael Walzer, *Spheres of Justice* (New York: Basic Books, 1983), 312. In this section, parenthetical references will be to this work.

52. Michael Walzer, *Thick and Thin* (South Bend, Ind.: University of Notre Dame Press, 1994), 33.

53. See, for example, Okin, *Justice, Gender, and the Family*, 62. Although she is skeptical of the idea of shared meanings, she believes that the idea of separate spheres can be a useful feminist tool.

conception of justice," but it is important to remember that this is a relativistic conception that does not itself specify any substantive principles of distribution.

An example may help clarify the idea. Throughout *Spheres of Justice*, Walzer often returns to one of the most important cases of dominance: the pervasive influence of wealth on the political process. For example, he writes:

> The most common form of powerlessness in the United States today derives from the dominance of money in the sphere of politics. The endless spectacle of property/power, the political success story of the rich, enacted and re-enacted on every social stage, has over time a deep and pervasive effect. Citizens without money come to share a profound conviction that politics offers them no hope at all. This is a kind of practical knowledge that they learn from experience and pass on to their children. With it comes passivity, deference, and resentment. (310-311)

Here is a case in which a certain good, wealth, is used to influence improperly another good, political power. The problem, as Walzer diagnoses it, is that the border between two spheres has been crossed; justice requires that wealth be confined to its proper sphere, and political power to its. In other words, cashing out the metaphor, political power is not being distributed according to its meaning, but is being dominated by another good, wealth. According to our understanding of political power, it must be distributed democratically: "What democracy requires is that property should have no political currency, that it shouldn't convert into anything like sovereignty, authoritative command, sustained control over men and women." (298)[54] On the other hand, given the meaning that money has in our society, once it is confined to its sphere, justice requires that it be distributed according to a pure market mechanism: "once we have blocked every wrongful exchange and controlled the sheer weight of money itself, we have no reason to worry about the answers the market provides." (107) No inequality in wealth that the market generates is unjust unless it is used to dominate other spheres, such as the political.

Walzer calls his conception *complex equality* in contrast to *simple equality*, which demands an equal distribution of each good. He explains complex equality this way:

> Imagine now a society in which different social goods are monopolistically held—as they are in fact and always will be, barring continual state intervention—but in which no particular good is generally convertible [to goods in other spheres]. . . . This is a complex egalitarian society. Though there will be many small inequalities, inequality will not be multiplied through the conversion process. (17)[55]

---

54. Walzer does not seem to doubt that we are all democrats. As we shall see, however, he does not believe that our democratic understanding of political power is the only possible one. In societies in which political power has a different meaning, justice may require that it be distributed undemocratically.

55. Unfortunately, this use of the term "monopolistically" seems flatly inconsistent

This he finds "an attractive picture." (17)

While it is true that in such a society goods will not be used to dominate others outside their sphere and "inequalities will not be multiplied," it is rather hard to see in what sense this can appropriately be called "complex *equality*" at all. As Richard Arneson observes:

> It is compatible with the definition of *autonomous distribution* that in a society the distribution of goods is fully autonomous, so that complex equality fully obtains, yet the same individuals always fall at the top end and bottom end of the distributional profile in every single sphere. Complex equality is also compatible with the supposition that the spread between the top and bottom of the distributional profile in every sphere is enormous. Winners win big, and losers get small crumbs, in each autonomous distribution, and furthermore the same individuals are the winners and losers in every separate sphere. Complex equality is only equality in Pickwickian sense.[56]

This seems exactly right, and Walzer's reply that complex equality's "egalitarianism [is] manifest[ed] in a radical decline in the dominance of some people over others" seems to miss the point.[57] Furthermore, he concedes in *Spheres of Justice* that it is possible that the same people might be "successful in one sphere after another, triumphant in every company, piling up goods without the need for illegitimate conversions," and that this "would certainly make for an inegalitarian society" without violating the demands of complex equality. (20)

One might attempt to salvage an egalitarian component of complex equality in the content of the social meanings themselves, but for Walzer social meanings are not necessarily egalitarian at all. Whether a social meaning involves egalitarian content in a particular case is a purely contingent matter. As we have seen, Walzer believes that our democratic understanding of political power, for example, does require its distribution to be egalitarian, but our understanding of wealth does not. This is simply a reflection of the meaning of these goods in our society. As Arneson observes, "This 'distribution according to social meanings' norm is an empty vessel, the content of which could be anything."[58] The "empty vessel" is to be filled not with a single account, but is supposed to retain a flexibility that allows it to reflect the specific social meanings that a good has in

---

with his definition six pages earlier: "Monopoly describes a way of owning or controlling social goods in order to exploit their dominance." (11)

56. Richard Arneson, "Against 'Complex Equality,'" *Public Affairs Quarterly* 4, no. 2 (April 1990), 103. A revised version of this paper appears in *Pluralism, Justice, and Equality*, David Miller and Michael Walzer, eds. (New York: Oxford University Press, 1995).

57. See Michael Walzer, "Response" in *Pluralism, Justice, and Equality*, Miller and Walzer, eds., 283.

58. Arneson, "Against 'Complex Equality,'" 107.

a particular community. It is precisely this flexibility and responsiveness to local meanings that is supposed to be the virtue of Walzer's theory. It is also what leads Brian Barry to dub complex equality a form of "conventionalism."[59] The general conception yields various specific principles of distribution in particular societies. Unlike justice as fairness, which relies on a single list of primary goods and proposes specific principles of justice, complex equality recognizes no specific standard for the just distribution of a particular good without first identifying the meaning of the good in question in the particular society. Walzer would not, therefore, think it a criticism to point out that complex equality, despite its name, does not necessarily require the egalitarian distribution of any good. In fact, he concedes the point: "In a society where social meanings are integrated and hierarchical, justice will come to the aid of [i.e., will support] inequality." (313) It is unclear how this amounts to "A Defense of Pluralism and Equality," as the subtitle of *Spheres of Justice* announces.

Still, there seem to be limits to Walzer's conventionalism. Recently he has emphasized that acceptable social meanings must be compatible with a minimal morality that is universally applicable: "Murder as a way of distributing life and death, for example, whether it is the work of a neighborhood thug or the secret police, is everywhere ruled out."[60] Even here, however, he appears to present this claim as an empirical generalization. Although he never spells out the content of this moral minimalism in any detail, it is clear that he intends it to be truly minimal. Although it prohibits "brutal repression," it does not, for example, require democracy.[61]

There is, however, a more serious problem with Walzer's account of justice. How are we to take the first step in the two-step procedure and identify the social meaning of a good? Recall that the main type of injustice with which he is concerned is dominance, which he defines as "a way of using social goods that isn't limited by their intrinsic meanings." (10-11) What does he mean by "intrinsic meanings"? It is certain that he cannot intend by "intrinsic meaning" the meaning which some good has in itself, independent of society. About this, Walzer is clear: "goods have different meanings in different societies. The same 'thing' is valued for different reasons, or it is valued here and disvalued there." (7) The quotation marks seem to indicate that Walzer has doubts as to whether we can even identify objects across societies, let alone assume their social meanings are fixed. More recently, Walzer has explained the "basic idea" of

---

59. Brian Barry, "Intimations of Justice," *Columbia Law Review* 84, no. 3 (April 1984), 807. A revised version of this paper appears in *Pluralism, Justice, and Equality*, Miller and Walzer, eds.

60. Walzer, *Thick and Thin*, 26.

61. Walzer, *Thick and Thin*, x. See also his insistence that the social meanings that determine the principles of just distribution must not "be the result of radical coercion." Thus, "the extorted agreement of slaves to their slavery . . . should not count in establishing the common understandings of a society." (*Thick and Thin*, 27)

complex equality this way: "since these goods have no essential nature, this means that [distributive justice] must stand in some relation to the place that these goods hold in the (mental and material) lives of the people among whom they are distributed."[62] So, what could he mean when he refers to the "intrinsic meaning" of an object? Walzer apparently thinks society (somehow) confers one unique meaning on each good. This social meaning is intrinsic (perhaps "latent" or "implicit" would be better choices for him here) because although society has the final say in what the meaning of any good will be, there may be a conflict between that true social meaning and the mechanism by which society in fact distributes it. It is precisely when these two come apart—when a society distributes a good contrary to the intrinsic meaning that the society gives to that good—that we have a case of injustice.

Given the centrality that the concept of social meaning plays in his account, Walzer has remarkably little to say about what exactly a social meaning is or how it is to be determined. Jon Elster has observed that despite a wealth of examples, Walzer's philosophical account is "disappointingly vague."[63] Walzer certainly does give many examples. However, Joshua Cohen, in an important review of *Spheres of Justice*, makes the following observation:

> In all these cases [that Walzer considers] the values of the political community *are identified through its practices*. . . . The existing practices serve as evidence—in fact as the only evidence—for the account of the "collective consciousness." . . . But this suggests a dilemma for the theorist who appeals to shared values as a critical perspective. If the values of a community are identified through its current distributive practices, then the distributive norms subsequently "derived" from those values will not serve as criticisms of existing practices.[64]

Cohen calls this circularity "the simple communitarian dilemma." We can identify a possible escape from the simplest form of this dilemma. Although Walzer himself may in fact only appeal to the existing institutions in determining the meaning of a good, it is open to him to make a different appeal. In addition to the existing institutions and practices, Walzer could appeal to the expressed attitudes and understandings of citizens toward each good. After all, as he points out, there is no guarantee that what citizens say about a good will be compatible with the existing mechanisms of distribution.

This is a potential escape from the simple communitarian dilemma, but it forces Walzer to face another question directly. When a society's distributive mechanism for some good diverges from what citizens say about that good, how are we to determine the true meaning? This is the crucial question because it is the only case in which we can avoid the circularity of the simple communitarian

---

62. Walzer, *Thick and Thin*, 26.

63. Jon Elster, *Local Justice* (New York: Russell Sage Foundation, 1992), 14.

64. Joshua Cohen, "Book Review of *Spheres of Justice*," *The Journal of Philosophy* 83 (1986), 463-464.

dilemma. It is, therefore, the only case in which complex equality might identify an instance of injustice. In cases in which such a conflict exists, one might think that we could simply rely on the expressed judgment of the citizens, criticizing the institutions in the name of the attitude of the majority. Walzer would seem to reject this approach however: "a majority of the citizens . . . might well misunderstand the logic of their own institutions or fail to apply consistently the principles they professed to hold." (99) Sometimes, it seems, institutions might distribute goods according to their meaning even when this is not recognized by the majority of citizens.

We can clarify this matter by looking at Walzer's treatment of a specific example. His discussion of health care is illustrative, and several commentators have chosen to focus on it. Walzer claims:

> Until recent times the practice of medicine was mostly a matter of free enterprise. . . . With regard to this practical outcome [namely, providing care on the basis of wealth] however, the profession has always had a collective bad conscience. For the distributive logic of the practice of medicine seems to be this: that care should be proportionate to illness and not to wealth. (86)

Notice that the "logic" of the distribution of medical resources is independent of the actual distributive practices of the society and, in fact, has remained the same through changing institutional practices. In this case, Walzer claims, the intrinsic social meaning can be seen not in the existing practices, nor in the beliefs of the general population, but rather in the collective conscience of those who participate professionally in those institutions.

It seems, however, that Walzer does not want to invest too much in this alleged "bad conscience" among medical practitioners. He quickly moves on to consider the obvious objection that "the refusal thus far to finance a national health service constitutes a political decision by the American people about the level of communal care [that should be provided outside the market]." He denies that this decision has been made, but more importantly, if it were made, "it would not necessarily be an unjust decision." (90)[65] If we (or they?) were to recognize and treat health care not as a need (as Walzer believes we already do) but as a luxury for example, the market would provide the just mechanism of distribution.

While he allows that the meaning of health care may vary among societies, Walzer insists that a society must determine this meaning on an all-or-nothing basis: "once communal provision begins, it is subject to further moral constraints: it must provide what is 'wanted' equally to all the members of the

---

65. This was published in 1983. Ten years earlier, Walzer had argued for removing heath care from the market without explicitly referring to its "social meaning." See "In Defense of Equality," in *Radical Principles* (New York: Basic Books, 1980), 242.

community." (88) In his review of *Spheres of Justice*, Ronald Dworkin observes this insistence and comments:

> We may find [the demand for a full national health service] attractive, but we need an argument for it, and merely constructing an ideal sphere and calling it the sphere of need, provides no argument. The point is a crucial one, because it might be that any genuine argument for a national health service would contradict Walzer's relativism. It might show that a society that leaves medical care entirely to the market would not be a just society, as he thinks, but would in fact be even more unjust than a society, like ours, that provides some but not enough free medical care.[66]

The first step in answering such a challenge would be for Walzer to clarify what would make one interpretation of the meaning of a good superior to a competing interpretation.

In an effort to provide such an account, Walzer has attempted to appropriate Dworkin's theory of judicial interpretation to serve his own purposes.[67] This initially appears to provide exactly what Walzer needs, since Dworkin's account denies the existence of any mechanical procedure for resolving hard cases, yet insists that there are standards for evaluating competing interpretations. Thus, while Dworkin thinks that some interpretations are better than others, they will often be contested, and there may be no way to establish to everyone's satisfaction which is superior.[68] Nevertheless, on closer examination Dworkin's model shows exactly the weakness of Walzer's account. Dworkin's theory is concerned not with the meaning of social goods, but rather with establishing the principles that underlie past political acts, principally legislative acts and judicial decisions. For Dworkin, the best interpretation is the one that provides the best justification for those actions. Interpretation, on his model, relies not only on standards of internal consistency but also on independent principles of political morality. This independent standard is precisely what is lacking in Walzer's account.

For Dworkin, the superiority of one interpretation is established, in part, by evaluating how well past decisions comport with independent principles of justice (or political morality generally). But Walzer's interpretations are

---

66. Ronald Dworkin, "To Each His Own," *New York Review of Books*, 14 April 1983, reprinted as "What Justice Isn't" in *A Matter of Principle* (Cambridge: Harvard University Press, 1985), 218.

67. Replying to Dworkin's criticism on this point, Walzer writes: "What is the best way of carrying on the argument [about the meaning of some social good]? Curiously, Dworkin has himself provided an excellent model in his account of how 'hard cases' ought to be decided in a legal system like our own." ("'Spheres of Justice': An Exchange," *New York Review of Books*, 21 July 1983, 43)

68. See, for example, Ronald Dworkin, *Law's Empire* (Cambridge: Harvard University Press, 1986).

attempting to establish those very principles. He has no basis on which to evaluate and compare interpretations: closeness of fit to practices alone is inadequate because this generates the "simple communitarian dilemma"; closeness of fit to the expressed attitudes of citizens is inadequate because they might "fail to apply consistently the principles they professed to hold." Walzer apparently has in mind some combination of these factors but he never explains how the balance is to be struck. This is a fatal weakness in those cases in which there is a conflict between institutional practice and the attitudes of the citizens—exactly the cases in which there might be an injustice. Brian Barry states the obvious solution when he suggests that the better interpretation "is not the one [that] can claim the *most* of the tradition but [that] can claim the *best* of it." But if this is the solution, he continues, "we cannot avoid asking: How does the critic decide which are the good bits, and how does he defend his decision to other members of his society?"[69] Cohen puts essentially the same criticism this way: "Walzer gives no *content* to the claim that one member of a set of competing interpretations, each of which fits our institutions and practices, might still be the right one."[70]

This criticism cuts to the core of Walzer's project because he provides no way to tell whether different accounts are competing interpretations of the same intrinsic meaning of a good or whether they are simply identifying different social meanings. This is a crucial issue, because Walzer believes that it is the social meaning that determines the just mechanism of distribution of each good. What are we to do when there are different meanings coexisting in a society? At one point in *Spheres of Justice* Walzer makes a parenthetical remark that apparently is supposed to address this issue:

A given society is just if its substantive life is lived in a certain way—that is, in a way faithful to the shared understandings of the members. (When people disagree about the meaning of social goods, when understandings are controversial, then justice requires that the society be faithful to the disagreements, providing institutional channels for their expression, adjudicative mechanisms, and alternative distributions.) (313)

In his review, Dworkin challenges Walzer on this point, claiming:

Our political arguments almost never begin in some shared understanding of the pertinent principles of distribution. Every important issue is a contest between competing models. . . .

If justice is only a matter of following shared understandings, then how can the parties be debating about justice when there is no shared understanding? In that

---

69. Brian Barry, "Social Criticism and Political Philosophy," *Philosophy and Public Affairs* 19, no. 4 (fall 1990), 369.

70. Cohen, "Review of *Spheres of Justice*," 466.

situation no solution can *possibly* be just, on Walzer's relativistic account, and politics can be only a selfish struggle.[71]

Walzer, in turn, replies as follows:

> In fact, two different kinds of disagreement are possible, which I have probably not sufficiently distinguished. First, people can disagree within a cultural tradition. They interpret meanings in somewhat different ways, or they take different positions on boundary disputes and on overlapping or entangled goods. . . .
>
> Second, people disagree because they come out of radically different cultural traditions, as in many third world states today. . . . If populations were mixed, as they most often are, then it might be (morally) necessary to work out a political accommodation. Politics must sometimes substitute for justice, providing a neutral frame within which a common life slowly develops.[72]

Remarkably enough, in this reply, Walzer grants Dworkin's central point: when social meanings are not shared, there can be no justice (or injustice). Note that by a "neutral framework," he does not mean a *just* structure, but rather a "political accommodation." Dworkin is wrong to claim that this must necessarily be a selfish struggle. He is correct, however, and Walzer concedes that according to complex equality, justice is a conceptual impossibility when there is not a widely shared consensus on the correct social meaning of a good.

What Walzer seems not to notice in this context—but what Dworkin and others have pointed out—is just how pervasive such disagreements are.[73] Elsewhere however (specifically, when arguing against Rawls's use of primary goods) Walzer himself recognizes this:

> A single necessary good, and one that is always necessary—food—for example—carries different meanings in different places. Bread is that staff of life, the body of Christ, the symbol of the Sabbath, the means of hospitality, and so on. Conceivably, there is a limited sense in which the first of these is primary, so that if there were twenty people in the world and just enough bread to feed the twenty, the primacy of bread-as-staff-of-life would yield a sufficient distributive principle. But that is the only circumstance in which it would do so; and even there, we can't be sure. If the religious uses of bread were to conflict with its nutritional uses—if the gods demanded that bread be baked and burned rather than eaten—it is by no means clear which use would be primary. How, then, is bread to be incorporated into the universal list? (8)

---

71. Dworkin, "What Justice Isn't," 216-217.

72. Michael Walzer, "'Spheres of Justice': An Exchange," 44. I discuss below Walzer's more recent attempts to develop this contrast between *internal* and *external* criticism. The reference to "third world states" is baffling. It is surely industrialized, cosmopolitan countries, at least as much as "third world states," that embody diverse cultural traditions and a plurality of social meanings.

73. See, for example, Amy Gutmann, "Justice across the Spheres," in *Pluralism, Justice, and Equality*, Miller and Walzer, eds.

The diverse social meanings that Walzer cites are all found in a single society. It follows that on his account there can be no just or unjust distribution of food in our society, but only a "political accommodation" in which we attempt to slowly develop a "common life" in which one of these meanings is dominant.

Recently Walzer has suggested that a society may have a diversity of mechanisms for the distribution of a good that has different meanings. His example is "soup kitchens and food stamps on the one hand and the grocery store on the other."[74] Instead of accommodating different meanings, however, this account assumes that there is a single, shared understanding of the meaning of the good of food with two components: it is a necessity up to a certain level, and a market good beyond that point. If either of these meanings is disputed, there will be no consensus on the meaning of this good and therefore no distributive mechanism or scheme of mechanisms can be either just or unjust.

In his reply to Dworkin, Walzer alludes to a distinction between two types of criticism, and in his more recent work he has developed this contrast. *Internal* criticism takes the form of interpreting the social meaning of some good and then arguing that the common practice in the society fails to live up to its meaning. A defender of complex equality would be an internal critic in this sense. *External* criticism attempts to bypass the interpretive stage in which the local social meaning determines the appropriate distribution of some social good. Instead, it appeals to some purportedly universal standard. Walzer does not often argue for internal criticism directly. Instead, he favorably contrasts the "connected social critic" with "the philosopher" who attempts to discover or invent a new moral world without reference to existing social meanings.[75]

According to Stephen Mulhall and Adam Swift, Walzer objects to external criticism because it is undemocratic (at least if it is not a disguised form of internal criticism).[76] An external critic ignores the values and ideals of the majority in the society. Of course, it is rare if ever, that philosophers are able to impose a social order on an unwilling populace. If, as is more plausible, a philosopher is simply trying to change people's minds about how to conceive of some social good—if she is not trying to force but to persuade—it is hard to see why this would necessarily be undemocratic or objectionable.[77]

---

74. Walzer, "Response," 282.

75. See Michael Walzer, *Interpretation and Social Criticism* (Cambridge: Harvard University Press, 1987), chapter 1, where he contrasts internal and external criticism; and *The Company of Critics* (New York: Basic Books, 1988), where he discusses his favorite connected critics. See also *Thick and Thin*, where he contrasts a "moral minimalism," which may be universal, with "maximalist morality," which includes matters of distributive justice and can only appropriately be pursued by an internal critic.

76. See Stephen Mulhall and Adam Swift, *Liberals and Communitarians*, second edition (Cambridge: Blackwell, 1996), 134-139.

77. Walzer concedes that "At the moment of publication, at least, he [the philosopher] is a proper democrat: his book is a gift to the people." (Michael Walzer, "Philosophy and Democracy," *Political Theory* 9, no. 3 (Aug. 1981), 389). On the other hand, he also

The problem, in part, is that Walzer is burdened by a brute majoritarian conception of democracy: "it is a feature of democratic government that the people have a right to act wrongly—in much the same way that they have a right to act stupidly."[78] By acting "wrongly," Walzer does not mean contrary to their own self-interest; that, presumably, would be acting "stupidly." He means what he says: within the limits of his unspecified minimal universal morality, the majority has a right to act contrary to any abstract principles that it does not choose to endorse. At the same time, however, Walzer does not unambiguously endorse democracy itself. Whether complex equality requires democracy depends on how political goods are understood by the members of a particular society. He is explicit on this point: the view he defends "won't be a universalism that requires democratic government in all times and places, but it opens the way for democracy wherever there are enough prospective and willing citizens."[79] Obviously one would also like to know what would count as evidence that there are "enough prospective and willing citizens" other than the existence of democratic institutions. Cohen's simple communitarian dilemma emerges once again at this point. In any event, it is peculiar to complain that external critics are undemocratic while denying that justice requires democracy.

Ultimately, Walzer seems to believe that the problem with external criticism is that if local social meanings are not the basis for a just distribution of goods, one society (or group) will be justified in imposing its social meanings on another society (or group). In one of the few passages where Walzer argues directly against the model of external criticism, he writes:

> The problem with disconnected criticism, and thus with criticism that derives from newly discovered or invented moral standards, is that it presses its practitioners toward manipulation and compulsion. Many, of course, resist the pressure; detachment and dispassion are built-in defenses against it. But insofar as the critic wants to be effective, wants to drive his criticism home (though the home is, in a sense, no longer his own) he finds himself driven to one or another version of an unattractive politics.[80]

On Walzer's account, if a critic defends political principles that are not widely accepted in her society she is "no longer at home" and is "disconnected."[81]

---

writes: "Enforcement is not, I admit, a common philosophical task, but those who believe that they have discovered the true moral law are likely enough to want or, whatever their private preferences, to believe themselves duty bound to enforce it." (*Interpretation and Social Criticism*, 18)

78. Walzer, "Philosophy and Democracy," 385. See also his hostility to judicial review on 388.

79. Walzer, *Thick and Thin*, x; cf. 68, and "Response," 289.

80. Walzer, *Interpretation and Social Criticism*, 64.

81. It is very odd, therefore, that Walzer would complain that in Foucault's work, "There would appear to be no independent standpoint, no possibility for the development

It is certainly true that such a critic has a more difficult task than one who believes existing practices and meanings are perfectly acceptable, but it simply does not follow that on that basis she is driven or even tempted towards "manipulation and compulsion," "force," or "coercion and uniformity."[82] As Brian Barry points out:

> one might consistently say that the institutions of a society are unjust but that if they rest on shared understandings it would be more unjust for anyone outside to intervene to change them. It seems fairly clear that Walzer wants to undercut even the judgment that the institutions are unjust in such a case. Yet there seems something paradoxical about a theory that implies a society with slavery, suttee, untouchability, or human sacrifice is a just society so long as the victims share the understandings that legitimize those institutions.[83]

All that needs to be added is that if there is a temptation to the use of force, it follows from the magnitude of the injustice. This is as it should be. Some injustices are so great that force ought to be used to prevent them. At this level of abstraction, of course, nothing can be settled concerning specific cases, but Walzer's suggestion that reliance on universal standards itself must lead to manipulation is simply unfounded.

When it comes to the specific principles of distribution that Walzer favors, he is certainly to the left of most Americans. In *Spheres of Justice*, in addition to public financing of health care, Walzer argues for, among other things, "a decentralized democratic socialism; a strong welfare state run, in part at least, by local and amateur officials; a constrained market; an open and demystified civil service; independent public schools; the sharing of hard work and free time; the protection of religious and familial life; a system of public honoring and dishonoring free from all considerations of rank or class; workers' control of companies and factories; a politics of parties, movements, meetings, and public debate." (318) Needless to say, most Americans do not think of themselves as democratic socialists. As Barry observes: "Walzer saddles himself with the highly unpromising task of trying to show that the major American institutions can be given a coherent justification only in ways that entail large changes in them—a strategy that is vulnerable to any plausible rationale for the internal

---

of critical principles." See Michael Walzer, "The Politics of Michel Foucault," in *Foucault: A Critical Reader*, David Hoy, ed. (New York: Blackwell, 1986), 64.

82. Walzer, *Thick and Thin*, 8, 29. For similar statements suggesting that external criticisms lead inexorably to coercion see *Thick and Thin*, 31, 33, 48, 60-61, 70.

83. Barry, "Intimations of Justice," 814. As I pointed out above (note 61), Walzer claims that the "extorted agreement of slaves" should not be taken as a shared understanding of slavery. (*Thick and Thin*, 27) Still, Barry's underlying point is correct, and he is far from alone among liberals in taking such a view. Compare J. S. Mill, *On Liberty*, Elizabeth Rapaport, ed. (Indianapolis: Hackett, 1978), 90.

consistency of the existing arrangements."[84] In *Spheres of Justice* Walzer claimed that his general conception was "radical," (10) and in his more recent works Walzer has attempted to show in more detail that complex equality is not inherently conservative.[85] Nonetheless, despite his repeated denials, I believe that the charge that his general conception is inherently conservative can be made to stick. This will become clear in the next section when we examine conservatism more closely.

Conservatism

The term *conservative* is used in contemporary discussions to cover a wide range of views. I use the term to describe a position concerning the desirability of social change or the rate of social change. Conservatives think that the fact that a certain social practice or institution is already in existence gives a strong, perhaps decisive reason for the continuation of that practice or institution.[86] Thus, I leave aside an important use of the term *conservative* in which it is used to describe a specific constellation of values associated with hierarchical social structures and certain forms of romanticism. Furthermore, given my definition, conservatives are not necessarily to be identified with today's political right-wing. Many libertarians, for example, are often considered to be part of the political right, but they are not conservative in my sense since they are not attempting to conserve existing institutional structures. In her recent history and analysis of the rightwing in the United States, Sara Diamond points out that "Rightists call themselves 'conservatives,' but they are not truly conservative in seeking just to preserve things as they are."[87] The contemporary right wing, in fact, is a rather incongruous mixture of traditionalists about values and quasi-libertarian defenders of the free market.[88] As Garry Wills commented on the ideology affirmed by Ronald Reagan: "According to the American myth he

---

84. Barry, "Social Criticism and Political Philosophy," 373.

85. See *Thick and Thin*, 41; *Interpretation and Social Criticism*, 3; and *The Company of Critics*, ix. On the selection of "connected critics" in *The Company of Critics*, see Barry, "Social Criticism and Political Philosophy," 363; and Joseph Raz, "Morality As Interpretation," *Ethics* 101, no. 2 (Jan. 1991).

86. Compare the definition in Torbjörn Tännsjö, *Conservatism for Our Time* (New York: Routledge, 1990), 4: "The conservative attitude . . . is characterized by two central tenets, to wit, (1) that, whatever exists as a well established fact ought to continue to exist and, (2) that, the reason why it ought to continue to exist is that it *is* well established."

87. Sara Diamond, *Roads to Dominion* (New York: Guilford, 1995), 313n2. Compare Anthony Quinton, "Conservatism" in *A Companion to Contemporary Political Philosophy*, Robert Goodin and Philip Pettit, eds., 258.

88. Such tensions may even be found within individuals. See, for example, John Judas, *William F. Buckley, Jr.: Patron Saint of the Conservatives* (New York: Simon and Schuster, 1988).

advances, capitalism is both individualistic and conservative, though the terms of that proposition are mutually contradictory."[89]

Many communitarians and conservatives share a distrust of principles of justice, which are judged to be too abstract and ahistorical. It is ironic, therefore, that contemporary communitarians are themselves apparently unaware of the affinities between their positions and conservative thought from Burke to the present. To see this, let us return to consider the charge that justice itself competes with the value of community. We have already seen a version of this claim when we considered Sandel's argument that since justice is a remedial virtue, "we cannot say in advance whether, in any particular instance, an increase in justice is associated with an overall moral improvement," and that "in some cases, justice is not a virtue but a vice."[90] Sandel stresses throughout his work, and the title of his book makes clear, that he believes that justice has its limits, and when it conflicts with the pursuit of some identity-constituting good, it may properly be sacrificed. As he concluded the first edition:

> justice finds its occasion because we cannot know each other, or our ends, well enough to govern by the common good alone. This condition is not likely to fade altogether, and so long as it does not, justice will be necessary. But neither is it guaranteed always to predominate, and in so far as it does not, community will be possible, and an unsettling presence for justice. . . . Liberalism . . . forgets the possibility that when politics goes well, we can know a good in common that we cannot know alone.[91]

Stephen Holmes provides the following rejoinder: "we can [also] know 'a bad' in common that we cannot know alone."[92] There are plenty of vices that are necessarily social. The goal of a racially pure society, for example, cannot be achieved by an isolated individual. The point is that the mere fact of community, even identity-conferring community, does not necessarily make social interaction good. We must evaluate the character of the interactions and identities.

Sandel expresses the view that justice is required only as a response to epistemic deprivation—a lack of knowledge of each other's ends. He does not explain how clearer knowledge of others or of ourselves would render justice unnecessary. It is as if he believes that knowledge of the true good would dissolve all potential conflicts. However, it is in part because of our clear awareness that modern societies are characterized by a diversity of reasonable

---

89. Garry Wills, *Reagan's America* (Garden City, N.Y.: Doubleday, 1987), 378.

90. Sandel, *Liberalism and the Limits of Justice*, 32, 34.

91. Sandel, *Liberalism and the Limits of Justice*, 183.

92. Stephen Holmes, "The Permanent Structure of Anti-Liberal Thought," in *Liberalism and the Moral Life*, Nancy Rosenblum, ed. (Cambridge: Harvard University Press, 1989), 286n24. See also Stephen Holmes, *The Anatomy of Anti-Liberalism* (Cambridge: Harvard University Press, 1993), 178-179.

but incompatible conceptions of the good that the question of justice emerges with such urgency. As I argued above, justice does not exhaust the virtues that a society may possess, but it does establish a necessary background within which others can be pursued. Sandel, however, is not alone in supposing that the good of community is "an unsettling presence for justice."

In recent years, perhaps the most visible critique of justice itself has come from certain feminist scholars. Following the work of Carol Gilligan, these authors contrast *the perspective of justice*, which they claim involves the application of decontextualized and abstract rules, with *the perspective of care*, which involves sympathetic attunement to the needs and perspectives of particular individuals in determinate contexts. Gilligan claims that her empirical research shows that women tend to be more attuned to the perspective of care, while men typically rely on the perspective of justice.[93] A subtext of her work, developed by some philosophers, is that moral philosophy has tended to embrace the perspective of justice while neglecting the importance of the perspective of care.[94] A singular focus on justice is taken to generate an inadequate and distorted account of morality. However, these critiques typically run together two different contrasts under the pair of labels *care* and *justice*.

First, consider the contrast between judgments regarding some particular action in which basic social institutions are not at stake (care) and judgments concerning the proper structure and functioning of the institutions of the basic structure (justice). In the first case, knowledge of the relations among the particular individuals involved, their past commitments, future expectations, hopes, and goals may all be relevant in identifying what morality permits or demands. Knowledge of the specifics of a friend's comprehensive doctrine and conception of the good is clearly relevant when determining which joint projects would be likely to strengthen the relationship, for example. All of these factors are relevant to care. On the other hand, when it comes to political judgments concerning the justice of the basic structure of society, it would be inappropriate partiality to attempt to tailor a social structure to one's particular situation and conception of the good. The approach that is suitable for each of these types of judgments is dictated by the subject matter in question. It is crucial to remember that liberal principles of justice do not require "universal, first-order impartiality."[95] Justice as fairness does not require that we view our entire lives from an impartial perspective. In contexts in which the institutional requirements

---

93. Carol Gilligan, *In a Different Voice* (Cambridge: Harvard University Press, 1982).

94. See, for example, the contributions to *Women and Moral Theory*, Eva Feder Kittay and Diana Meyers, eds. (Totowa, N.J.: Rowman and Littlefield, 1987), and *An Ethic of Care*, Mary Jeanne Larrabee, ed. (New York: Routledge, 1993).

95. The phrase is from Brian Barry, who argues that most of the participants in the justice-care debate, including both Gilligan and Kohlberg, mistakenly assume that justice requires "universal, first order impartiality." See chapter 10 of his *Justice As Impartiality* (New York: Oxford University Press, 1995).

of justice are securely in place, it is not unjust for individuals to pursue their particular goals. If *justice* and *care* designate different approaches to different kinds of questions, justice as fairness recognizes and embraces this contrast.

More often than not however, the contrast between *justice* and *care* is intended to mark not different types of questions but rather alternative approaches to the same moral dilemma. This is certainly the contrast that Gilligan herself has in mind. She claims that her empirical evidence reveals that boys and girls tend to approach the same problem differently, with boys more likely to embrace a perspective of justice and girls more likely to embrace a perspective of care. Gilligan affirms this understanding of the contrast when she argues, "Since all relationships can be characterized both in terms of equality and in terms of attachment or connection, all relationships—public and private—can be seen in two ways and spoken of in two sets of terms."[96] She suggests that these different perspectives correspond to two kinds of knowledge:

> One is the conception of knowledge as arising through the correspondence between mind and pure form, so that moral knowledge becomes the reflective equilibrium between the self and moral principles. One can then take the role of the other or assume Rawls' original position or play Kohlberg's game of moral musical chairs— all without specifically knowing anything about the other but simply by following the laws of perspective and putting oneself in his or her position. The other conception is of knowledge as gained through human connection, a conception conveyed in the Biblical passage: "And Adam knew Eve."[97]

Thus, Gilligan believes that any given moral dilemma can be approached in two different ways, approaches that are underwritten by two different kinds of knowledge. The perspective of justice tackles a problem in a formalistic and calculating manner while the perspective of care relies on an informal and more intuitive model of moral knowledge.

The two understandings of the contrast between justice and care can be seen clearly in the work of Seyla Benhabib. Her most famous contribution to the debate was a paper that introduced the terms "the generalized and the concrete other."[98] The perspective of the generalized other requires that "we abstract from

96. Carol Gilligan, "Prologue: Adolescent Development Reconsidered" in *Mapping the Moral Domain*, Carol Gilligan, Janie Victoria Ward, and Jill McLean, eds. (Cambridge: Harvard University Press, 1988), xviii.

97. Carol Gilligan and Grant Wiggins, "The Origins of Morality in Early Childhood Relationships," in *Mapping the Moral Domain*, Gilligan, et. al., eds., 125. A supposedly "natural" sensitivity among women has long been used by conservatives to argue that women must be restricted to nurturing roles in the home. See the discussion in Wendy Kaminer, *A Fearful Freedom* (Reading, Mass.: Addison-Wesley, 1988), chapter 6.

98. Seyla Benhabib, "The Generalized and Concrete Other" in *Women and Moral Theory*, Kittay and Meyers, eds. In this paragraph, parenthetical references will be to this work.

the individuality and concrete identity of the other." (163) This perspective informs all of the "Universalistic moral theories in the western tradition from Hobbes to Rawls" and "surreptitiously" assumes that all subjects are "white, male adults who are propertied or professional." (158) In contrast, when we adopt the perspective of the concrete other, we "view each and every rational being as an individual with a concrete history, identity, and affective-emotional constitution. . . . [We rely on] norms of friendship, love, and care." (164) These perspectives compete with one another, and the perspective of the concrete other helps us identify "the *ideological* limits of universalistic discourse." (168) In more recent work, however, she has moved away from her earlier view that these are competing perspectives:

> In retrospect, and as a result of further reflection on these matters, it would have been desirable for me to have distinguished more clearly between the *moral standpoint* and the *standpoint of justice*. The perspective of institutional justice, as embodied in the macro institutions of our societies, as John Rawls rightly points out, articulates rules of collective coexistence in the face of continuing and permanent disagreement about our conceptions of the good and different ways of life which we choose to pursue and cherish. Rules of justice articulate principles upon which we can agree when we know we cannot agree about our ethical conceptions concerning, for example, identity or the good life.[99]

She now believes that these perspectives complement one another and each is appropriate for addressing its own type of question.

Still, Gilligan's view (and Benhabib's earlier position) that the perspectives of justice and of care compete with one another is more common than the view that justice and care simply address different questions. What apparently has not been noticed in the literature concerning this debate is that a similar account of practical moral knowledge was made by the conservative Michael Oakeshott earlier this century. This connection has been neglected, perhaps, because Oakeshott did not correlate the perspectives with gender. His classic "Rationalism in Politics" was originally published in 1947. There, Oakeshott distinguishes two kinds of knowledge. On the one hand, there is "technical knowledge," the "chief characteristic" of which is that "it is susceptible of precise formulation, although special skill and insight may be required to give it that formulation."[100] In contrast,

> the second sort of knowledge I will call practical, because it exists only in use, is not reflective and (unlike technique) cannot be formulated in rules. This does not mean, however, that it is an esoteric sort of knowledge. It means only that the method by

---

99. Seyla Benhabib, "In Defense of Universalism—Yet Again! A Response to Critics of *Situating the Self*," *New German Critique* 62 (spring/summer 1994), 181.

100. Michael Oakeshott, "Rationalism in Politics" in *Rationalism in Politics and Other Essays*, new and expanded edition (Indianapolis: Liberty Press, 1991), 12.

which it may be shared and becomes common knowledge is not the method of formulated doctrine. And if we view it from this point of view, it would not, I think, be misleading to speak of it as traditional knowledge.[101]

Oakeshott frequently takes knowledge of language as a paradigm of this kind of intuitive, unreflective practical knowledge.

For Oakeshott, "rationalism" is an over-reliance on technical knowledge, and whatever else may be true, it is clear that he is opposed to rationalism in politics. He blames everything from war to the right of women to vote on "the kind of incompetence inherent in rationalist politics."[102] Furthermore, he believes that recognition of the importance of practical knowledge leads to a distinctively conservative political philosophy. What is rather unclear, however, is the connection he sees between a recognition of the importance of practices on the one hand, and the conservation of political structures on the other. We can give him an argument of the following sort. Some activities are based on technical knowledge while others require practical knowledge. Participation in political institutions, like the use of languages, requires the latter kind. Just as competent language use is not based on explicit rules, so too the effort to formulate explicit rules of justice mistakes the kind of knowledge that is required for functioning political institutions. What is actually required, instead, is the acquisition of practical knowledge through assimilation with a practice. And this requires participation in the existing social order, rather than obscure flights of fancy into some world where all knowledge is formulated explicitly in ideal rules. Thus, we are competent only to participate in existing practices, not to reform them in unknown directions.

The analogy appears to be a good one: neither the acquisition of linguistic knowledge nor knowledge of political practices typically is achieved through the formulation of explicit rules. Yet, notice that according to Oakeshott's definition, practical knowledge "is not reflective and . . . cannot be formulated in rules." This statement contains a crucial ambiguity. On the first interpretation, while we are able to formulate rules that characterize various aspects of a practice, these rules will be unhelpful because they will employ a vocabulary internal to the practice. That is, these rules will not be understood by someone not already competent within the practice. On this interpretation, what is denied is the possibility of formulating rules that reduce one practice to another. On the other, stronger interpretation, Oakeshott's claim is not that rule-formulation depends on the prior existence of practical knowledge of the practice (and therefore, presumably, will not be useful) but that practical knowledge, as he says, *cannot* be formulated in rules at all. It frequently looks as though Oakeshott inclines towards this second interpretation. In fact, however, only the

---

101. Oakeshott, "Rationalism in Politics," 12.
102. Oakeshott, "Rationalism in Politics," 11; 28; 34, n.33; and "Political Education," in *Rationalism in Politics and Other Essays*, 57, quoted below.

former interpretation is plausible. Furthermore, the more moderate interpretation has no particular political implications, conservative or otherwise. We cannot infer anything about the content of a practice or the appropriateness of various possible reforms from the importance of practical knowledge in the practice.

To see this, let us grant that the formulation of rules frequently cannot suffice to initiate someone without practical knowledge into a practice. Still, there might be other reasons to formulate them. Certainly language is a practice into which we are initiated without the explicit formulation of rules. Yet we are able to reflect on our linguistic practices and formulate the rules which govern them. And there can be many reasons to do this. For example, consider the recent increase in gender-neutral language in academic philosophy. This has been, at least in part, the result of criticism of the practice that previously existed in an unreflective way.[103] It is only once these practices are given explicit formulation that we are able to decide whether the contemplated change is one we want: whether (as some argue) the potentially sexist consequences to a continued use of masculine pronouns are weighty enough to require a change, or whether (as others reply) the aesthetic costs and the breaking of ties to tradition are more significant.

The reason for formulating such rules is not to reduce language to something else, nor (necessarily) to initiate someone into the practice for the first time. Rather, it may be to reflect on and evaluate the form the practice takes, or, indeed, the value of the practice as a whole. While not all linguistic principles can be made explicit at once, there is no reason to believe that any segment of our language necessarily must be excluded from explication and analysis. Consider another of Oakeshott's examples: games, which he says are inherently conservative.[104] Many games, take basketball as an example, involve practical knowledge in the sense that mastery does not (typically) require formulation of explicit rules. Yet here too, we have linguistic resources available to describe rules, plays, and techniques. If the need arose, we could develop further resources in order to describe additional subtleties of the game. This might happen not only in order to get better descriptions of the game, but also if controversy arose regarding the permissibility of a specific type of play, or if we wanted to alter the rules to eliminate or encourage certain techniques.

Contemporary communitarians have followed Oakeshott in arguing that there are some goods that are only recognizable as good from a perspective

---

103. The American Philosophical Association, for example, first published "Guidelines for Non-Sexist Use of Language" by Virginia Warren in 1986 (*Proceedings and Addresses of the APA* 59, no. 3 [Feb. 1986]). It now distributes reprints free of charge, although it does not formally endorse "any specific or compulsory set of rules."

104. See Oakeshott, "On Being Conservative" in *Rationalism in Politics and Other Essays*, 422. He concedes that "there are occasions when it is appropriate to reconsider them in the light of current experience" but he does not seem to see that this observation blocks the inference that he wants to make elsewhere.

internal to a practice. This is a central theme of MacIntyre's work, for example.[105] Sandel also emphasizes the importance of "a background of implicit practices and understandings" to our self-conceptions.[106] The problem is that nothing much follows from these observations; liberals as well as their critics can recognize these internal goods. What liberals point out is that even if some good is recognizable only to those who have the requisite practical knowledge, it is important to be able to evaluate the practice itself in order to decide whether to sustain and/or change it.[107] Indeed, the more important such practices are to our self-conceptions and pursuit of a good life, the more important it is that we be able to evaluate them. Reflection, evaluation, and discussion of our practices requires their explicit characterization, even when such characterizations are not necessary for actual participation.[108]

I asserted above that there are no particular political implications that follow from the emphasis on internal, practical knowledge of practices. Thomas McCarthy has given perhaps the definitive account of this fallacy, which he associates with Gadamer's philosophical hermeneutics:

> What we take for granted in any act of reflective critique is immeasurably vaster than what we call into question. From this ontological insight Gadamer tries to draw normative conclusions against enlightenment criticism and in favor of traditionalism, and that, of course, is a non sequitur. If we grant that we are always "more being than consciousness," as he says, this is no less true of the revolutionary critic than of the traditional conservative. Both will inevitably take much more for granted than they will consciously question, accept, or reject. But this does not tell us which to be or with respect to what we are to be either.[109]

If all criticism takes place within a shared discursive context, this tells us nothing about the nature and content of good criticism. Or, as Stephen Holmes puts it more briefly: "The social construction of the individual is worthless as an argument either for or against existing institutional arrangements."[110]

We have seen, therefore, that we are able to explicitly characterize our practices, and there may be reason to do so even though non-reflective practical

---

105. See MacIntyre, *After Virtue*, 187, 190, 191, 193.

106. See Sandel, *Liberalism and the Limits of Justice*, 172-173.

107. In fact, Rawls was a pioneer in investigating the idea of practices. One of his main points was that there could be standards of evaluation internal to a practice. But another important point was that there could also be external standards for evaluation of the practice that differed from the internal standards. See John Rawls, "Two Concepts of Rules," *The Philosophical Review* 64 (1955).

108. See Charles Larmore's contrast between "applying rules" and "acting on reasons that imply rules not given in advance" in *Patterns of Moral Complexity* (New York: Cambridge University Press, 1987), 8.

109. Thomas McCarthy, "Philosophy and Social Practice," in *Ideals and Illusions* (Cambridge: MIT Press, 1991), 18.

110. Holmes, *The Anatomy of Antiliberalism*, 179.

knowledge may be necessary for participation. If conservatives argue that we cannot reflect on and evaluate our practices, they are simply wrong. More typically, however, conservatives argue that even if we can, we should not engage in such reflection. To see why conservatives might think it dangerous to reflect explicitly on practices, let us begin at the beginning, with "the prophet—the Marx or the Mill—of conservatism,"[111] Edmund Burke. Conservative authors virtually without exception invoke Burke as the heroic founder of conservatism. Anthony Quinton for example, writes that conservatism is "above all, the political doctrine of Burke."[112] Russell Kirk attributes to Burke the following view, but he could equally well be describing Oakeshott's position:

> By and large, change is a process independent of conscious human endeavor, if it is beneficial change. Human reason and speculation can assist in the adjustment of the older order to new things if they are employed in a spirit of reverence, awake to their own fallibility.[113]

This suggests an explanation of conservatives' emphasis on practical knowledge: reflecting on our practices will only lead to an overzealous desire to destroy them, without the ability to reconstruct anything superior.

Burke's status among conservatives derives largely from his *Reflections on the French Revolution*, the famous polemical defense of "tradition" against the French Revolution.[114] Generations of conservatives have pointed to this work as providing the theoretical background necessary to establish the importance of community and tradition over radical change. As Don Herzog has argued, however, it is not at all clear what Burke's argument is, for he seems to have two conceptions of tradition.[115]

Most famous perhaps is Burke's belief that traditions embody the reason gained from past experience. When emphasizing this point, he argues that those who support radical change exhibit an unjustifiably extravagant assessment of their own reasoning powers. Thus, for example, he writes:

> We are afraid to put men to live and trade each on his own private stock of reason; because we suspect that the stock in each man is small, and that the individuals

---

111. Robert Nisbet, *Conservatism: Dream and Reality* (Minneapolis: University of Minnesota Press, 1986), x.

112. Quinton, "Conservatism," 244. He continues: "Since Burke it has taken the form of a continuous tradition, culminating for the time being in Oakeshott." See also Nisbet, *Conservatism: Dream and Reality*, 1.

113. Russell Kirk, *The Conservative Mind*, seventh revised edition (Chicago: Regnery Books, 1986), 45.

114. Edmund Burke, *Reflections on the Revolution in France*, J. G. A. Pocock, ed. (Indianapolis: Hackett, 1987).

115. Don Herzog, "Puzzling through Burke," *Political Theory* 19, no. 3 (Aug. 1991).

would do better to avail themselves of the general bank and capital of nations and of ages.[116]

The idea is that social orders are simply too complex for any individual or group of individuals to presume to be able to judge accurately. Therefore, we have to rely on "the general bank and capital of nations and of ages." Society's accumulated stock of knowledge is supposedly embedded in the social structures that have survived the test of time.[117] The fact of their continued existence is evidence that they are the rational structures: "It is a presumption in favor of any settled scheme of government against any untried project, that a nation has long existed and flourished under it."[118]

Thus, Burke turns against abstract reason because traditions themselves embody greater wisdom than any abstract formula. Contemporary conservatives frequently make reference to the following now classic argument:

What is the use of discussing a man's abstract right to food or medicine? The question is upon the method of procuring and administering them. In that deliberation I shall always advise to call in the aid of the farmer and the physician rather than the professor of metaphysics. The science of constructing a commonwealth, or renovating it, or reforming it, is, like every other experimental science, not to be taught *a priori*. Nor is it a short experience that can instruct us in that practical science, because the real effects of moral causes are not always immediate. . . . The science of government being therefore so practical in itself and intended for such practical purposes—a matter which requires experience, and even more experience than any person can gain in his whole life, however sagacious and observing he may be—it is with infinite caution that any man ought to venture upon pulling down an edifice which has answered in any tolerable degree for ages the common purposes of society, or on building it up again without having models and patterns of approved utility before his eyes.[119]

Contemporary conservatives and communitarians share Burke's hostility to abstract reason. Burke argues that the difficulties of the "science of government" are such that one cannot use a priori methods of reasoning but must rather rely on the practical experience of a society that is to be found in its history. Nisbet expresses the view this way: "Basic to conservative politics is its view of the role of history. 'History' reduced to its essentials is no more than experience, and it is from conservative trust in experience over abstract, and deductive thought in matters of human relationships that its trust in history is founded."[120]

116. Quoted in Herzog, "Puzzling through Burke," 344.

117. For skepticism concerning whether conservatives actually rely on the "test of time" as opposed to abstract theory, see Ted Honderich, *Conservatism* (Boulder, Colo.: Westview, 1991).

118. Quoted in Herzog, "Puzzling through Burke," 344.

119. Burke, *Reflections on the Revolution in France*, 53.

120. Nisbet, *Conservatism: Dream and Reality*, 23.

As Herzog points out, however, on this view reason is not in competition with tradition. Rather, tradition and experience provide evidence concerning what reason demands. As long as it is done in a spirit of modesty, there is nothing that prevents us from attempting to understand the reasons why past generations have chosen, deliberately or unintentionally, for better or worse, various institutions and why they have survived or been transformed. It follows that defenders of this view are not opposed to all reform whatsoever. Burke himself stakes out this position in the following passage: "A state without the means of some change is without the means of its conservation. Without such means it might even risk the loss of that part of the constitution which it wished the most religiously to preserve."[121]

Virtually all contemporary conservatives follow Burke on this point. They are at pains to deny that they are opposed to all change. As Nisbet claims:

> What Burke and his successors have fought is what he called "the spirit of innovation"; that is, the idle worship of change for its own sake; the shallow but pervasive need on the part of the masses for diversion and titillation through endless novelties. Particularly lethal is the spirit of innovation when it is applied to human institutions.[122]

Kirk formulates the point this way:

> Burke has no expectation that men can be kept from social change; neither is rigidity of form desirable. Change is inevitable, he says, and is designed providentially for the larger conservation of society; properly guided, change is a process of renewal. But let change come as the consequence of a need generally felt, not inspired by fine-spun abstractions. Our part is to patch and polish the old order of things, trying to discern the difference between a profound, slow, natural alteration and some infatuation of the hour. By and large, change is a process independent of conscious human endeavor, if it is beneficial change.[123]

Note especially the contrast between "conscious human endeavor" and "slow, natural alteration"—as if conscious human endeavor were always a result of "some infatuation of the hour" and slow alterations were "natural" as opposed to the result of deliberate human action.

In most cases, this official embrace of modest change is largely an empty rhetorical gesture. Conservatives simply are not convincing when they claim that they are not opposed to all reform. Their track record undermines their more moderate rhetoric. With the exception of a few isolated individuals,

---

121. Burke, *Reflections on the Revolution in France*, 19.

122. Nisbet, *Conservatism: Dream and Reality*, 26.

123. Kirk, *The Conservative Mind*, 45. Compare Roger Scruton, *The Meaning of Conservatism*, second edition (London: Macmillan, 1984), 22; and Quinton, "Conservatism," 247.

conservatives have found the argument "we've always done it that way" to be irresistible when it came to significant social change such as (to choose some of the more obvious examples): expanding the franchise to include, first, non-property owners and then women; introducing public education and child labor laws; the creation of social security; the abolition of slavery; and the development of civil rights for racial minorities, women, and homosexuals. It often seems as though the only circumstances in which conservatives accept even gradual and moderate reform are those in which others successfully clamor for more radical change.

Of course, there are cases in which conservatives favor radical changes to well-established practices, but these are almost always presented as the rejection of ill-conceived changes to the status quo ante. Conservative opposition to affirmative action, abortion rights, civil rights for accused criminals, and the ban on officially sanctioned prayer in public schools are cases in point, even though each of these practices or policies has been in place in the United States for well over a generation. Perhaps conservatives will say that these practices have not worked well enough. But this is just the point: well enough for whom and according to what standards? While conservatives tend to view such abstract questions as dangerous incitements to change, these are precisely the questions that concern liberals. Liberals, and even most radicals, agree that change for its own sake is a dangerous practice that potentially puts valuable social achievements in jeopardy. They do not support change based on the "infatuation of the hour," but only when it is necessary to correct injustice. As we will see in the next chapter, however, some postmodernists do seem to embrace the idea of change for its own sake.

When circumstances change, we are frequently driven to reflect on and evaluate our institutional arrangements. In such times of change and doubt the question is unavoidable: when should we rely on the "judgment" of our tradition, and when should we rely on our own judgment to remake our traditions and institutions? Surely we have little choice but to use our own reason to make such determinations. Understood in this way then, the conservative position reduces to the assertion that we should study and learn from history; political reforms should not be carried out in ignorance of the past. This is an impoverished conservatism to say the least—Marx would readily agree with it. Furthermore, it is reason itself that shows us our fallibility and that reckless experimentation can be dangerous. Changes that risk catastrophe will surely be unwarranted when the injustices they are intended to correct are not severe. On the other hand, significant injustice may demand risky strategies of change. The point is that it is we who must determine when a proposal is reckless and when it is required by the demands of justice. It is not possible to let tradition make such a judgment for us. We must evaluate the grounds for and against possible changes, taking into account the best reasons we can identify.

At times, however, Burke seems to invoke a different conception of tradition to make a different point, and as we shall see, this second idea of tradition also has been embraced in contemporary conservative thought. In this second sense, Herzog argues, tradition stands opposed to reason:

> Tradition here is not on the side of rational argument; it is the opposite of rational argument. When tradition reigns, people unthinkingly comply with the rules. They don't have any considered judgments, any mature grasp of the British constitution that leads them to assent to their role within it. Instead, they just do what they do because that's what they've always done. Or, more intriguingly, because they've been led to believe it's always been that way, even if it hasn't. The past is not to be combed carefully by discerning historians but to be constructed artfully by mythic poets. Or, to put the point as any self-respecting Jacobin would, by liars.[124]

Kirk, too, sometimes seems to find this position in Burke: "No one ever expressed more persuasively the impotence of human reason before divine mystery."[125] On this interpretation, Burke thought that the most important threat that the Jacobins posed was in their laying traditions open to rational scrutiny, whether historically informed or not. Thus, he complains: "All the pleasing illusions that made power gentle, and obedience liberal, which harmonized the different shades of life . . . are to be dissolved by this new conquering empire of light and reason. All the decent drapery of life is to be rudely torn off. . . . On this scheme of things, a king is but a man, a queen is but a woman."[126] As Herzog explains, "Burke thought illusions and veils were crucial in safeguarding social order."[127] The existing social structures can only be preserved and social disintegration prevented, on this view, by the unreflective acceptance of traditions and prejudices. Practical knowledge and the institutions it supports are under grave threat when the principles on which these institutions rest are subject to rational evaluation. In the preface to *A Vindication of Natural Society*, Burke asks rhetorically, "Even in Matters which are, as it were, just within our Reach, what would become of the World if the Practice of all moral Duties, and Foundations of Society, rested upon having their Reasons made clear and demonstrative to every Individual?"[128] Tradition, on this account, provides a way of guaranteeing social stability through a "noble lie" and is fundamentally at odds with reason.

By interpreting Burke to endorse a noble lie, Herzog is able to make sense of a wide range of puzzling and apparently contradictory texts.[129] But Herzog is

---

124. Herzog, "Puzzling through Burke," 356-357.

125. Kirk, *The Conservative Mind*, 31.

126. Burke, *Reflections on the Revolution in France*, 67.

127. Herzog, "Puzzling through Burke," 354.

128. Edmund Burke, *A Vindication of Natural Society*, Frank Pagano, ed. (Indianapolis: Liberty Classics, 1982), 9.

129. See Herzog, "Puzzling through Burke," 352-359.

also aware of (and takes apparent delight in) the great irony of Burke's exposure as a defender of a noble lie:

> Those base hairdressers are now aware of some dangerous conceptual possibilities: Witnessing the French Revolution, they can now talk about equality and natural rights; they can now suspect that the social and political order of Britain is contingent, not natural or necessary or providential, so it can be remade. They can see Burke's paeans to tradition as a clever subterfuge designed to keep them in their places; indeed, they can see through them.
>
> Can, and for that matter did. Burke often wrote as though he was talking about the workers, not to them. But the workers were eavesdropping, and for many of them, Burke became the very emblem of the hated inequalities of the *ancien regime*.[130]

The defender of a noble lie is, indeed, in an awkward position, for articulating a defense of this position threatens to undermine it.

In fact, this irony is not lost on at least one contemporary defender of conservatism, whom we shall now consider. Roger Scruton believes:

> Like Plato, a conservative may have to advocate the "Noble Lie". He might in all conscience seek to propagate the ideology which sustains the social order, whether or not there is a reality that corresponds to it. For even if there is no reality, the politician can in any case do no better than provide new myths for old.[131]

For Scruton, as for Burke, the stability of all social orders requires the propagation of myths. The efficacy of these myths requires that they be believed, and this, in turn, requires that they not be examined too closely or critically. The problem for the conservative then is that the very articulation of this view constitutes a threat to the social order, for it may lead people to question whether the existing myths should be believed. As Scruton observes, "It is hardly surprising therefore that, in a healthy nation, the constitution remains tacit, general, and inexplicit."[132] Scruton, on the final page of his *Meaning of Conservatism*, notes that the conservative,

> knows what he wants, and knows the social order that would correspond to it. But in becoming self-conscious he has set himself apart from things. The reasons that he observes for sustaining the myths of society are reasons which he cannot propagate; to propagate his reasons is to instill the world with doubt. Having struggled for articulacy, he must recommend silence.[133]

---

130. Herzog, "Puzzling through Burke," 360.
131. Scruton, *The Meaning of Conservatism*, 140; cf. 29.
132. Scruton, *The Meaning of Conservatism*, 51.
133. Scruton, *The Meaning of Conservatism*, 191.

This is a bitter pill to swallow: for the previous 200 pages Scruton violated his own recommendation and, more clearly than Burke, laid bare the justification for this conclusion. One cannot help but think of Plato's view in the *Phaedrus* that speaking is superior to writing because only then can one tailor one's spoken words to the nature of the audience—one never knows who will read what one has written.[134]

Here, then, we have a distinctively conservative position: citizens simply cannot be trusted to evaluate social institutions for themselves. The belief that there is, as Nisbet puts it, a "shallow but pervasive need on the part of the masses for diversion and titillation through endless novelties"[135] frequently underlies this fear. "Fine-spun abstractions," to repeat Kirk's phrase, only encourage people in their destructively arrogant belief that they can remake society as they choose. Avoidance of this catastrophic endeavor requires discouraging any reflective evaluation of the justice of society. We have seen that such a view is an implication of Sandel's critique of liberalism, but this esotericism is an explicit commitment in much conservative thought, starting with Joseph de Maistre and continuing perhaps most famously in the thought of Leo Strauss, for whom "In order to live, we have to silence the easily silenced voice of reason. . . . The more we cultivate reason, the more we cultivate nihilism: the less we are able to be loyal members of society."[136]

Here we see the contrast between conservative and liberal views at its most stark. For Rawls, stability is an important characteristic of a well-ordered society. But it is not an unconditional good: it is a virtue of just societies, and even in such societies Rawls insists on "stability for the right reasons."[137] Stability is to be achieved by constructing a basic structure that will "draw forth the willing cooperation of everyone taking part in it, including those less well situated."[138] As we have seen, in a just society "nothing need be hidden," and the

---

134. Plato, *Phaedrus*, 277b-e, in *Plato: The Collected Dialogues*, Edith Hamilton and Huntington Cairns, eds. (Princeton: Princeton University Press, 1961). In fact, Joseph de Maistre explicitly endorses exactly this conclusion. See Holmes, *The Anatomy of Antiliberalism*, 21. The fact that written language can also be detached from its initial context plays an important role in Jacques Derrida's thinking. See, for example, *The Post Card*, Alan Bass, trans. (Chicago: University of Chicago Press, 1987).

135. Nisbet, *Conservatism: Dream and Reality*, 26.

136. Leo Strauss, *Natural Right and History* (Chicago: University of Chicago Press, 1953), 6. This passage occurs in the context of describing modern liberalism. However, I believe that it accurately captures Strauss's belief that liberalism leads to nihilism because it places too much faith in the reason of the masses who, unlike the elite, are unable to understand natural law. See the discussion in Holmes, *The Anatomy of Antiliberalism*, 21-23, 61-87.

137. Rawls, *Political Liberalism*, xxxix. See my discussion in the first section of chapter 2.

138. Rawls, *A Theory of Justice*, 15 [13].

idea of publicity is a basic constraint on arguments for principles of justice.[139] A noble lie is ruled out from the beginning.

We are now in a position to examine the relationship between conservatives and communitarians. Oddly, this has not been systematically explored in the literature but has been relegated to a few passing comments or footnotes.[140] In part, I think, this is because philosophers have not frequently discussed conservatism itself, as opposed to other right wing ideologies such as libertarianism. The charge that communitarianism is actually a form of conservatism is liable to be misread as simply an ad hominem attack.[141] This, too, is in part due to a lack of attention to conservative thinkers. Communitarians in particular rarely mention conservatism, directing their criticisms toward liberalism and libertarianism instead. There is an apparent similarity between the more reflective, philosophical accounts of fascism and contemporary communitarians.[142] For example, Alfredo Rocco, a major ideologist of Italian fascism and Mussolini's minister of justice, criticizes liberalism in terms virtually identical to those used by communitarians such as Sandel, Taylor, and MacIntyre:

Society according to this [liberal] concept is merely a sum total of individuals, a plurality which breaks up into its single components. Therefore the ends of a society, so considered, are nothing more than the ends of the individuals which compose it and for whose sake it exists. An atomistic view of this kind is also necessarily anti-historical, inasmuch as it considers society in its spatial attributes and not in its temporal ones; and because it reduces social life to the existence of a single generation. Society becomes thus a sum of determined individuals, viz., the generation living at a given moment.[143]

---

139. Rawls, *Political Liberalism*, 68. Rawls continues: "We cannot guarantee that nothing is hidden, for there is always much we do not and perhaps cannot know, and many ways in which we can be misled by institutional appearances. But perhaps we can make sure that nothing need be hidden. . . . In this sense a well-ordered society may lack ideological, or false, consciousness." (Rawls, *Political Liberalism*, 68-69n21) See also 66-71; and Rawls, *A Theory of Justice*, 16 [15], 133 [115], 175 [153]. J. B. Schneewind discusses the history of a similar ideal in "Natural Law, Skepticism, and Methods of Ethics," *The Journal of the History of Ideas* 52, no. 2 (April-June 1991).

140. The most important exception is Stephen Holmes, "The Permanent Structure of Antiliberal Thought" and *The Anatomy of Antiliberalism*.

141. See Raz, "Morality and Interpretation," 396.

142. It is especially hard to know how to respond when Alasdair MacIntyre and Ronald Beiner condemn liberalism for its "rootless cosmopolitanism." Surely, they must know that this was the notorious phrase used by fascist anti-Semites to attack Jews. See Alasdair MacIntyre, *Whose Justice? Which Rationality?* (South Bend, Ind.: University of Notre Dame Press, 1988), 388; and Ronald Beiner, *What's the Matter with Liberalism?* (Berkeley: University of California Press, 1992), 24.

143. Alfredo Rocco, "The Political Doctrine of Fascism," in *Communism, Fascism, and Democracy*, third edition, Carl Cohen, ed. (New York: McGraw-Hill, 1997), 280.

The doctrine he recommends, in contrast, places the good of the community above that of individuals, or even their just treatment:

> The relations therefore between state and citizens are completely reversed by the Fascist doctrine. Instead of the liberal-democratic formula, "society for the individual," we have, "individuals for society" with this difference however: that while the liberal doctrines eliminated society, Fascism does not submerge the individual in the social group. It subordinates him, but does not eliminate him; the individual as a part of his generation ever remaining an element of society however transient and insignificant he may be. . . . For Fascism, society is the end, individuals the means, and its whole life consists in using individuals as instruments for its social ends. The state therefore guards and protects the welfare and development of individuals not for their exclusive interests, but because of the identity of the needs of individuals with those of society as a whole.[144]

It would seem that liberalism (in its Kantian formulation) has triumphed to the point that even contemporary communitarians would resist the claim that individuals ought to be used only as instruments of society, and certainly few would share Rocco's judgment concerning the content of those ends. Nonetheless, this critique of liberal individualism is common to both fascism and communitarianism.

More important than these similarities themselves is the reaction, or rather, the lack of reaction of the communitarians to them. Stephen Holmes highlights this peculiar inattention:

> By mentioning the fascist interlude in the history of antiliberalism, I do not mean to convict today's antiliberals of harboring dangerous thoughts. . . . I want to draw attention, instead, to the fundamentally ahistorical character of their thinking. Antiliberals talk endlessly about rootedness and tradition, but they nonchalantly disregard their own intellectual descent. They could easily distinguish themselves from their most unsavory precursors, I suppose. Yet they make no effort to do so— leaving readers perplexed. They blithely deplore what they consider the liberal individual's lack of "constitutive attachments," for example, but they never mention that this complaint was long the centerpiece of anti-Semitic propaganda, of political attacks on "uprooted" and cosmopolitan Jews. They apparently want to rehabilitate fascist rhetoric without fascist connotations. Their failure to consider the grim history of antiliberalism is therefore a serious mistake.[145]

Like Holmes, my point in raising the issue of fascism is not to say that the kind of community favored by communitarians is fascist. Rather, the point is that they typically fail even to raise the issue of how they might distinguish their position from fascism.

---

144. Rocco, "The Political Doctrine of Fascism," 284-285.
145. Holmes, "The Permanent Structure of Antiliberal Thought," 228.

In fact, I am aware of only one brief attempt by a contemporary communitarian to deal with the issue of fascism. At the end of an article on liberalism, Sandel attempts to deflect the charge that "Any attempt to govern by a vision of the good is likely to lead to a slippery slope of totalitarian temptation." Here is his answer:

> Communitarians reply, rightly in my view, that intolerance flourishes most where forms of life are dislocated, roots unsettled, traditions undone. In our day, the totalitarian impulse has sprung less from the convictions of confidently situated selves than from the confusions of atomized, dislocated, frustrated selves, at sea in a world where common meanings have lost their force.[146]

This reply is even more remarkable than the silence of other communitarians. Sandel seems completely oblivious to the fact that this is exactly the argument made by totalitarians, right down to the rhetoric of "atomized, dislocated, frustrated selves." In attempting to distance himself from fascists, he inadvertently reproduces precisely their position. Both the diagnosis and the general shape of the solution are shared by Rocco.

On the most charitable reading, Sandel is arguing that there is a tendency for highly "atomized" societies to swing back too far in the other direction, completely submerging the individual in grand social designs. To avoid this extreme, therefore, he recommends moving slightly (although he does not say this) in that direction to avoid a more violent reaction. I will not pursue here the question of whether a diverse society tolerant of the rights of individuals to affirm their own ways of life, or a homogeneous society in which individuals believe that their own way of life is the only one worth living is more likely to produce totalitarian impulses. The real difficulty with Sandel's reply is that he never explains what the problem is with the "totalitarian temptation." It is not at all clear that he thinks that the extreme submerging of the individual into grand social designs is actually dangerous.[147] In fact, Sandel fails to identify the objections to totalitarianism, and thus is left repeating the fascist diagnosis of and "solution" to the problems of liberalism. Sandel himself is not a fascist. This would be perfectly clear if he were to identify the conception of the good that he wants to place at the foundation of society. As we have seen, however, if he were to do that, it would highlight the contentious nature of excluding all other reasonable comprehensive doctrines.

Let us leave fascism aside and consider more respectable conservatives. Communitarians often seem as oblivious to conservatism as they are to fascism.

---

146. Michael Sandel, "Morality and the Liberal Ideal," *The New Republic*, 7 May 1988, 17.

147. As Baker points out: "the view suggested by Sandel's notion of a group subject, is entirely consistent with the coercive imposition of the particularities of the group on the person and with the coercive subordination of the individual." (C. Edwin Baker, "Sandel on Rawls," 904) See also Brian Barry, "Review of *Liberalism and the Limits of Justice*."

Yet Scruton's conservatism is strikingly similar to the view of many communitarians. For example, Scruton shares with communitarians a strong anti-individualist strain and distrust of individual rights.[148] Although they would not necessarily attribute the view to conservatives, most communitarians would agree with Scruton that "the conservative will be loath to found his political enterprise upon any doctrine of 'universal' or 'natural rights.'"[149] Even more important to note is Scruton's preference for local meanings over abstract principles. Once again, without the attribution to conservatives, the following statement could be a manifesto for contemporary communitarians:

> It is a *particular* country, a *particular* history, a *particular* form of life that commands the conservative's respect and energy. . . . Moral scruples may turn the conservative from condoning the practices of others of his kind; but his preferred form of political life will not be a deduction from abstract principles sufficient in themselves to forbid what he finds distasteful. . . . This is not to espouse the view (associated with such sociologists as Talcott Parsons) that alien "cultures" are in some way inaccessible to judgement. It is rather to emphasize that political understanding, as a form of practical judgement, does not readily translate itself into universal principles, and that conservatism, which takes its main inspiration from what *is*, has little competence to meddle in what is merely possible.[150]

Burke is similarly hostile toward abstract principles detached from local community practice.

As we have seen, Walzer rejects any identification with conservatism, and he certainly is not conservative in his views concerning specific social issues. Because of this, some commentators who have noted similarities between communitarianism and conservatism explicitly leave Walzer out of their discussions. There is, however, a striking similarity between Scruton and Walzer. I noted above that there was no reason to expect that inequalities in Walzer's complex equality will be minor. In fact, closely parallel to Walzer's "spheres" are Scruton's "autonomous institutions." Unlike Walzer's hope that the inequalities will be inconsequential, Scruton believes exactly the opposite:

> The persistence of autonomous institutions already points in the direction of a stratified society. The advantages conferred by education are to some extent transmissible across generations and, even if not so transmissible, are inevitably bound to divide those who can obtain them from those who cannot. The example shows, incidentally, the absurdity of the aim of "equality of opportunity." Such a thing seems to be neither possible nor desirable. . . . The attempt to provide equality of opportunity, unless it is to involve massive compulsory surgery of an unthinkable kind, is simply a confused stumble in the dark.[151]

---

148. See, for example, Scruton, *The Meaning of Conservatism*, 19.
149. Scruton, *The Meaning of Conservatism*, 49.
150. Scruton, *The Meaning of Conservatism*, 36.
151. Scruton, *The Meaning of Conservatism*, 157.

If there is no way to look beyond the horizons of particular spheres of distribution for Walzer, then for Walzer as for Scruton, there can be no way to evaluate the justice of schemes of institutions when taken together. There can be no possibility of taking compensatory steps to provide those deprived in one sphere with opportunity in another. As we have seen, Walzer grants that "In a society where social meanings are integrated and hierarchical, justice will come to the aid of [i.e., will support] inequality."[152]

We saw above that Walzer is especially concerned with the dominance of wealth over other spheres such as the political: "The dominance of capital outside the market makes capitalism unjust."[153] However, if Walzer wants dominance of a good outside its sphere always to be an instance of injustice, he must recognize that this is a two-way street. It is not only economic decisions, but political decisions as well that must be confined to their proper sphere. For Walzer, the political is just another sphere concerned with distributing its good according to its local meaning and it must not be allowed to dominate other spheres. I see no way for Walzer to avoid the conclusion that democratic political decisions that interfere with the free functioning of markets are objectionable cases of dominance—unless the good in question has a social meaning that requires it to be removed from the market altogether. Indeed, the political regulation of markets would seem to be as unjust as a wealthy capitalist's buying off a politician. Each would involve an equally unacceptable crossing of boundaries. To repeat (and extend) a passage from *Spheres of Justice* that I quoted earlier:

> once we have blocked every wrongful exchange and controlled the sheer weight of money itself, we have no reason to worry about the answers the market provides. . . . Given the right blocks, there is no such thing as a maldistribution of consumer goods. It just doesn't matter, from the standpoint of complex equality, that you have a yacht and I don't.[154]

It is understandable why Brian Barry would note that the implications of Rawls's theory for American society "are actually more radical than those reached by Walzer in *Spheres of Justice*, because he maintains, unlike Walzer, that the distribution of income is a matter of justice."[155] After all, Rawls's explicit concern with the influence of wealth on democratic political decisions has extended from *A Theory of Justice* to his most recent work.[156] He clearly recognizes that the political and economic realms are linked and argues not for

152. Walzer, *Spheres of Justice*, 313.
153. Walzer, *Spheres of Justice*, 315.
154. Walzer, *Spheres of Justice*, 107.
155. Barry, "Social Criticism and Political Philosophy," 373.
156. See, for example, Rawls, *A Theory of Justice*, 225-227 [197-200]; *Political Liberalism*, 284, 356-363; and Rawls, "The Idea of Public Reason Revisited," 772.

their isolation from one another, but rather for a certain priority between them. Economic institutions must be embedded within a democratic political structure.

In the last section, I quoted Joshua Cohen's observation that Walzer faces the "simple communitarian dilemma": "If the values of a community are identified through its current distributive practices, then the distributive norms subsequently 'derived' from those values will not serve as criticisms of existing practices."[157] Not everyone believes this is a dilemma, however. Some conservatives recognize these conservative implications and embrace them. Perhaps nowhere is this point more clear than in Oakeshott's discussion of the enfranchisement of women:

> [O]n the view of things I am suggesting, the only cogent reason to be advanced for the technical "enfranchisement" of women was that in all or most other important respects they had already been enfranchised. Arguments drawn from abstract natural right, from "justice," or from some general concept of feminine personality, must be regarded as either irrelevant, or as unfortunately disguised forms of the one valid argument; namely, that there was an incoherence in the arrangements of the society which pressed convincingly for remedy.[158]

For Oakeshott, it seems that it would be equally acceptable to attempt to disenfranchise women "in all or most other respects." It is inconceivable for him that a society should change unless it were in some way internally inconsistent. Similarly, on Walzer's model, the connected critic can only criticize the practices of a society on the basis of an internal inconsistency. Unlike Walzer, Oakeshott recognizes and embraces the profoundly conservative implications of this view.

Apparently in contrast to Oakeshott, Walzer insists that "criticism is a permanent possibility" since "every ruling class is compelled to present itself as a universal class."[159] There is always a gap, Walzer suggests, between the principles espoused in a society and the practice, and this leaves room for criticism: "The moral world and the social world are more or less coherent, but they are never more than more or less coherent. Morality is always potentially subversive of class and power."[160] Walzer thinks that he can always find an inconsistency on which to hang the demand for progressive political change. But the existence of an inconsistency, even if one can always be found, does not tell us which direction reform should take. When there is such an inconsistency, Walzer's account of justice cannot tell us how the conflict should be resolved: by reforming the institutions of distribution, or by revising the social meanings—by distributing health care on an egalitarian basis, or by allowing it

---

157. Cohen, "Book Review of *Spheres of Justice*," 464.
158. Oakeshott, "Political Education," 57.
159. Walzer, *Interpretation and Social Criticism*, 40.
160. Walzer, *Interpretation and Social Criticism*, 22.

to be controlled more fully by the market; by constraining the influence of wealth in the political process, or by giving up our democratic commitments.

I have already argued that if justice depends on the shared meaning of a good, in circumstances of diversity there can be neither justice nor injustice. Walzer, in effect, admits this. Under such circumstances, recall, he says we must rely on a "political accommodation" within which "a common life slowly develops." It is clear that such a common life does not currently exist in our society. As Rawls emphasizes, and as Walzer recognizes in other contexts, there is virtually no good that has a single meaning to all citizens. A consistent application of Walzer's theory would render him silent on virtually all issues of justice in our society. Unlike other communitarians, however, and to his credit, Walzer does discuss in detail what he believes justice demands for us. In order to do this however, he must ignore the diversity of meanings within our society and simply assert what he thinks the "intrinsic" social meaning of each of the various goods is. As I pointed out above, it seems clear that Walzer's understanding of the meaning of many such goods is far from that held by the majority of Americans. As Barry observes, in arguing for the reforms he advocates, Walzer is "fatally hampered by his own theory of justice."[161]

Ultimately, Walzer's complex equality is conservative because it is a form of relativism. We can clarify the sense in which most forms of relativism have conservative implications by looking at an argument made by Richard Rorty, whose views we will examine in detail in the next chapter. Rorty quotes Walzer approvingly that "A given society is just if its substantive life is lived . . . in a way faithful to the shared understandings of the members."[162] To illustrate this point, Rorty criticizes certain "intellectuals . . . [who] attempted to rehabilitate Kantian notions in order to say, with Chomsky, that the [Vietnam] War not merely betrayed America's hopes and interests and self-image, but was *immoral*, one which we had had no *right* to engage in in the first place."[163] Rorty's point is that moral claims are literally empty unless they are understood as reflecting a society's "hopes and interests and self-image."

But many citizens (not only "intellectuals") who were critical of the war in Vietnam, like Chomsky thought that it was all too consistent with America's traditions, hopes and self-image in foreign policy. Yet, they still insisted it was wrong. Will Kymlicka makes the point nicely with a different example:

When a Muslim woman in Egypt says "sexual discrimination is wrong" she does *not* mean [as Rorty claims] "we don't do that around here." On the contrary, she is saying that precisely because it *is* done around there, and always has been done, and

---

161. Barry, "Intimations of Justice," 813.

162. Richard Rorty, "Postmodern Bourgeois Liberalism," in *Objectivity, Relativism, and Truth*, vol. 1 of *Philosophical Papers* (New York: Cambridge University Press, 1991), 198.

163. Rorty, "Postmodern Bourgeois Liberalism," 201.

is very firmly embedded in all the myths, symbols and institutions of their history and society. She is saying "discrimination is wrong, although it is approved around here."[164]

There is simply no reason to accept Rorty's view that social criticism must be based on the charge of local inconsistency. Yet this is exactly what Walzer believes. Judith Shklar puts the point as a *reductio ad absurdum*:

> If primary justice is wholly a matter of enduring local customs that are shared by all, especially in the absence of political meaningful dissent and complaint, then the South's case for slavery was as just as any. In fact, the best case made before the Civil War was not that slaves had always been recognized as property and that the rights of property were sacred to all American citizens. It was that abstract justice was socially meaningless, that the entire culture and social fabric of the South entailed slavery, and that even the republican virtues of its citizens were dependent upon it.[165]

Although as we have seen, Walzer grants that "the extorted agreement of slaves to their slavery . . . should not count in establishing the common understandings of a society,"[166] he also claims that a caste system would be just if the citizens accept the values that support it.[167] He allows that an outsider may try to convince members of such a society that their beliefs are false. But, on Walzer's account, this argument could not be based on the demands of justice.

Shklar's reference to slavery reminds us that some of the most fully articulated defenses of local social meanings come from frequently overlooked Southern theorists.[168] Starting most famously with John Calhoun, these theorists developed arguments for the preservation of a distinctively Southern culture. Calhoun's main theoretical concern was the potential for "conflict among [a society's] different interests—each striving to obtain possession of its powers, as the means of protecting itself against the others—or of advancing its respective interests, regardless of the interests of others."[169] His idea of a *concurrent*

---

164. Kymlicka, "Liberalism and Communitarianism," 199-200; see also Will Kymlicka, *Liberalism, Community, and Culture* (New York: Oxford University Press, 1989), 66.

165. Judith Shklar, *The Faces of Injustice* (New Haven: Yale University Press, 1990), 116. Compare Jean Hampton, "Feminist Contractarianism," in *A Mind of One's Own*, Louise Antony and Charlotte Witt, eds. (Boulder, Colo.: Westview, 1993), 236.

166. Walzer, *Thick and Thin*, 27.

167. See Walzer, *Spheres of Justice*, 313-315.

168. For overviews, see Paul Conkin, *The Southern Agrarians* (Knoxville: University of Tennessee Press, 1988); Eugene Genovese, *The Slaveholders' Dilemma: Freedom and Progress in Southern Conservative Thought, 1820-1860* (Columbia: University of South Carolina Press, 1992); *The Southern Tradition: The Achievement and Limitations of an American Conservatism* (Cambridge: Harvard University Press, 1994).

169. John C. Calhoun, "A Disquisition on Government" in John C. Calhoun, *Union*

majority was designed "to prevent any one interest, or combination of interests, from using the powers of government to aggrandize itself at the expense of the others."[170] It did this by giving "to each division or interest, through its appropriate organ, either a concurrent voice in making and executing the laws, or a veto on their execution."[171] The fear that the bourgeois, market-driven North would come to dominate the South was a motivating concern for Southerners from Calhoun to those opposed to the Civil Rights movement. "The South," the historian Eugene Genovese writes, "virtually alone, stood for progress and modernity without the terrible evils that plagued the bourgeois societies."[172] Their concern was real. But if we allow our attention to focus narrowly on the issues of local meanings and internal consistency, we will miss the injustice in the heart of Southern society: its vicious racism.[173]

Although one of the most sustained and powerfully articulated defenses of localism that the United States has produced was based in part on the inherent inequality of individuals based on race, this is not to say that all forms of localism and communitarianism are racist. They are not. On the other hand, this singular case should serve as an eternal reminder of the need to reflect on the content of particular social forms and not to embrace them blindly. As Amy Gutmann has pointed out, "Even when the dominant understanding is widely shared, it may still, causally speaking, be the standard of the most powerful ('dominant') groups in society, who by virtue of dominating socialization and education also shape social understandings." She continues:

> While presupposing a single shared cultural understanding is false, relying upon the dominant understanding is dangerous. The danger follows not from our always knowing that a dominant understanding is the standard of a dominant group or groups, but rather from our rarely knowing it is *not* and often having reason to think that it is (even if we cannot prove it). . . . If cultural relativism relies upon the standard of dominant understandings, it threatens to identify justice with the social understandings of dominant groups, and in so doing, implicitly denies that justice can serve as a critical standard to assess dominant understandings.[174]

---

and Liberty, Ross Lence, ed. (Indianapolis: Liberty Fund, 1992), 15.

170. Calhoun, "A Disquisition on Government," 21.

171. Calhoun, "A Disquisition on Government," 21.

172. Genovese, *The Slaveholders' Dilemma*, 7.

173. Genovese says of nineteenth-century Southern theorists: "most of these southerners defended slavery, and even St. George Tucker and George Tucker, who did not, staunchly defended 'southern rights' and the political principles and policies of the slaveholders' regime." (Genovese, *The Slaveholders' Dilemma*, 2-3) And he observes that "Most of the Agrarians believed in the inferiority of blacks." (Genovese, *The Southern Tradition*, 122n77)

174. Amy Gutmann, "The Challenge of Multiculturalism in Political Ethics," *Philosophy and Public Affairs* 22, no. 3 (summer 1993), 176. See also Shklar, *The Faces of Injustice*, 114-115.

Even when a social meaning is widely shared, it is important that we be able to evaluate that consensus.

As we saw in chapter 2, justice as fairness is an attempt to resolve an "impasse in our recent political history; namely, that there is no agreement on the way basic social institutions should be arranged if they are to conform to the freedom and equality of citizens as persons."[175] The commitment to treating citizens as free and equal implies respecting their different reasonable comprehensive doctrines and conceptions of the good. Sandel and Walzer disagree concerning which conception of the good should be placed at the foundation of society, but neither can cope with the diversity of the reasonable comprehensive doctrines that exist within a single society. Like many conservatives, Sandel devalues justice itself in the mistaken belief that the good of community may conflict with the demands of justice. Walzer's relativism renders his theory unable to determine how internal conflicts concerning social meanings should be resolved.

Oakeshott emphasizes the importance of practical knowledge and claims that this recognition leads him to distinctly conservative conclusions. But a recognition of the importance of internal goods does not tell us anything about the nature or content of those practices, nor whether they should be conserved, changed, or eliminated. Similarly, Burke sometimes argues that political reason is embedded in our inherited social forms. At other times, however, he heaps scorn on reason in the name of our inherited institutions. Again, the more moderate position that reason must be informed by historical experience does not lead to any particular conclusions. Conservative conclusions only follow from the more extreme position—that we ought not to reflect on and evaluate our institutions. We have seen that many conservatives and some communitarians embrace this position. They believe that social stability depends precisely on not allowing people to understand the principles on which their institutions are founded. Many communitarians are driven to this position because they do not see how critical reflection could possibly proceed without a shared conception of the good.

Part of the hostility to justice as fairness comes from the belief that Rawls's principles are too abstract and detached from the real experiences of actual individuals. Comments like the following are ubiquitous in the secondary literature, even among those sympathetic to the basic liberal perspective: "Rawls's goal was to rise above the hurly-burly of particularistic interests in search of an untainted standard that would be of use in all cultures and polities. But his is not the world we live in."[176] From this perspective, a theory such as Walzer's complex equality has obvious attractions. After all, unlike other communitarians, Michael Walzer has attempted to construct an account of

---

175. Rawls, *Political Liberalism*, 300.

176. James Young, *Reconsidering American Liberalism* (Boulder, Colo.: Westview, 1996), 275.

justice that is sufficiently sensitive to local goods. I argued, however, that this attempt fails for a number of reasons. Most importantly it presupposes widespread agreement concerning the meaning of various social goods. Without such agreement, on his account no distribution is possibly just or unjust. This renders the theory inapplicable to modern situations, in which we cannot expect agreement concerning conceptions of the good. All Walzer can recommend in such circumstances is to attempt to build consensus about the meaning of the good. But it is precisely in circumstances in which the meanings of particular goods are contested that justice becomes a pressing and urgent matter.

In addition, I argued that despite his vigorous denials Walzer's general conception is inevitably conservative. Either there is agreement between the institution and the common attitude of the citizens, in which case the institution is just, or there is a conflict, in which case justice cannot adjudicate the dispute. There is simply no reason to insist that critics limit themselves to finding internal inconsistencies. As Rawls observes: "Now there are two ways in which injustice can arise: current arrangements may depart in varying degrees from publicly accepted standards that are more or less just; or these arrangements may conform to a society's conception of justice, or to the view of the dominant class, but this conception itself may be unreasonable, and in many cases clearly unjust."[177]

As we saw in chapter 2, justice as fairness is committed to the liberal principle of legitimacy, which requires that we defend the principles of justice in terms that all reasonable citizens can accept. When there is a diversity of reasonable comprehensive doctrines, respecting this requirement forces us to rely on rather abstract arguments:

> The work of abstraction, then, is not gratuitous: not abstraction for abstraction's sake. Rather, it is a way of continuing public discussion when shared understandings of lesser generality have broken down. We should be prepared to find that the deeper the conflict, the higher the level of abstraction to which we must ascend to get a clear and uncluttered view of its roots. Since the conflicts in the democratic tradition about the nature of toleration and the basis of cooperation for a footing of equality have been persistent, we may suppose they are deep.[178]

The need to abstract away from particular understandings of the good follows directly from the commitment to public justification in a context of reasonable pluralism. Although these abstract principles rule out certain conceptions of the good as unreasonable, they do not identify a single way of life as best or as required. Citizens are free to affirm whichever reasonable comprehensive doctrine they believe best, for whatever reasons they take to be most powerful, and they are ensured a fair share of resources with which to pursue it. There is

---

177. Rawls, *A Theory of Justice*, 352 [309].
178. Rawls, *Political Liberalism*, 46.

no requirement that there be a single moment of choice or that citizens engage in a high level of critical reflection on their ways of life. Furthermore, having identified these abstract principles of justice, the specific institutions that they permit or require often depend on the particular social, economic, and historical conditions of the society in question.[179] But when it comes to the justification of the principles, abstraction is necessary precisely because of the diversity of the reasonable comprehensive doctrines held by the citizens to whom we aim to justify the principles.

The commitment to the publicity condition implies that we must rely on our own reason when we evaluate our inherited traditions. We must, of course, be aware of our fallibility and the risks associated with radical change, but this is a requirement of reason itself. Finally, the commitment to public reason in circumstances of reasonable pluralism means that we cannot rely on any single comprehensive doctrine and conception of the good, whether endorsed by the majority of citizens or held only by a single philosopher. Instead, as we have seen, justice as fairness proceeds from what all reasonable comprehensive doctrines share.

---

179. See my "Having It Both Ways: Justification and Application in Justice As Fairness."

Chapter 5
The Politics of Postmodernism

If communitarians are unable to address the inevitable diversity of modern societies, the same cannot be said of the other political perspective that has recently been attractive to the left. Those who take inspiration from postmodern perspectives often emphasize the depth of human diversity. In this chapter I consider whether a postmodernist approach can generate a useful and progressive political perspective. I will focus primarily on the work of the two authors who are most commonly associated with the idea of postmodernism: Jacques Derrida and Michel Foucault. Despite the fact that postmodernism is often associated with the left, one of the trenchant philosophical critiques of postmodernism has come from Jürgen Habermas, who is himself a philosopher of the left. We will consider Habermas's theory as a reply to postmodernism before concluding by comparing his work to that of Rawls. There has been a growing interest in the relationship between these two theorists, and I believe that their work is much more complementary than is commonly believed.

While both Derrida and Foucault insist on the political implications of their work, it is often extremely difficult to draw any concrete implications or principles that would be at all useful for political engagement. In part, this is due to the notoriously obscure writing that characterizes much postmodern writing. This obscurity has had unfortunate consequences, not least among them the phenomenon Martha Nussbaum observes: "Some precincts of the continental philosophical tradition, though surely not all of them, have an unfortunate tendency to regard the philosopher as a star who fascinates, and frequently by obscurity, rather than as an arguer among equals. . . . In this way obscurity creates an aura of importance."[1] In some cases, there may be a more principled reason for this admitted obscurity. For some postmodernists, simply making claims about justice involves unacceptable coercion and implicates one in an objectionable hierarchy. In order to avoid such self-undermining, these theorists are often forced into cryptic moves of indirection, refusing to acknowledge explicitly any principled basis on which to make political judgments. As Stephen White has observed, "A thoroughly poststructuralist approach to

---

1. Martha Nussbaum, "The Professor of Parody," *The New Republic*, 22 Feb. 1999, 39. Compare Luc Ferry and Alain Renaut, *French Philosophy of the Sixties*, Mary Cattani, trans. (Amherst: University of Massachusetts Press, 1990; originally published in 1985), 12-15.

political thinking would be one dominated by what is in effect a perpetual withholding gesture."[2] This avoidance of concrete political theorizing is often an integral part of their work.

The term *postmodernism* often seems to describe an attitude rather than any particular doctrine. As with communitarianism, many of those most associated with the attitude have sought to distance themselves from this label. In an interview conducted shortly before his death, for example, Michel Foucault replied to a question about postmodernism with an ironic question of his own: "What are we calling postmodernity? I'm not up to date. . . . I do not understand what kind of problem is common to the people we call post-modern or post-structuralist."[3] In order to clarify the different ideas associated with the term *postmodernism*, let us begin by distinguishing three contexts in which the term is commonly used: social and historical; cultural and artistic; and philosophical.[4] Jean-François Lyotard's 1979 book, *The Postmodern Condition* attempted to bring these elements together under his famous definition: "Simplifying to the extreme, I define *postmodern* as incredulity toward metanarratives."[5] The thought is that in each of these areas, there has been a rejection of foundational and legitimating discourses. In one way or another, each area has fragmented into a plurality of local practices, ungrounded in any overarching scheme or structure.

Although our main concern will be with philosophical developments, I will begin by saying something about each of these other areas first. However, one word of warning must be retained throughout: we must remember that our goal is to provide an overview and assessment of some of the main elements of postmodernism that may seem to make it attractive as a perspective from which to address political issues. We will venture into other areas, but we will do so always with an eye toward the political implications of the doctrine.

---

2. Stephen White, *Political Theory and Postmodernism* (New York: Cambridge University Press, 1991), 19.

3. Michel Foucault, "Critical Theory/Intellectual History" (originally published in 1983) in *Michel Foucault: Politics, Philosophy, Culture: Interviews and Other Writings 1977-1984*, Lawrence Kritzman, ed. (New York: Routledge, 1988), 33-34.

4. Compare Alex Callinicos, "Reactionary Postmodernism?" in *Postmodernism and Society*, Roy Boyne and Ali Rattansi, eds. (London: Macmillan, 1990), 100-101.

5. Jean-François Lyotard, *The Postmodern Condition*, Geoff Bennington and Brian Massumi, trans. (Minneapolis: University of Minnesota Press, 1984; originally published in 1979), xxiv. His examples of "metanarratives" or "grand narratives" include "the dialectics of Spirit, the hermeneutics of meaning, the emancipation of the rational or working subject, or the creation of wealth." (xxiii) For an effort to distinguish foundational metanarratives from non-foundational "large narratives about changes in social organization and ideology" see Nancy Fraser and Linda Nicholson, "Social Criticism without Philosophy," in *Feminism/Postmodernism*, Linda Nicholson, ed. (New York: Routledge, 1989). (This phrase occurs on 26.)

Before the term *postmodern* gained prominence in the areas of cultural criticism and philosophy, it was used by historians and sociologists. The first use of the term "post-Modern" is often attributed to Arnold Toynbee in 1954, although Steven Best and Douglas Kellner have cited earlier uses.[6] In Toynbee's theory of history, the end of the modern age in 1875 was followed by a "post-Modern age" characterized by anarchy, relativism, and nihilism. In 1959, C. Wright Mills had a similarly negative characterization of our "post-modern period" as one in which "our basic definitions of society and of self are being overtaken by new realities" since it was no longer clear that increased rationality would provide increased freedom.[7]

In the 1960s and 1970s, many more historians and sociologists began to use the term *postmodern* (and a variety of other "posts-") to describe what was widely believed to be a fundamental break in the organization of society.[8] Indeed, many argued that the traditional frameworks used to explain historical change or the operation of society, such as functionalism or Marxism, were no longer applicable. Others, of course, rejected the idea of such a fundamental break. But even among theorists who agreed that traditional forms of social organization were being displaced, there was no consensus concerning what attitude to take toward those fundamental changes. Does throwing off the stifling weight of tradition open up the possibility of realizing unprecedented social improvements, or does it imply that we have lost our orientation and ability to assess competing social forms? For some like Amitai Etzioni, postmodernism was a fundamentally hopeful development, resulting from the introduction of new forms of communication and organizations of production after World War II.[9] For others, such as Daniel Bell, the changes were brought about by the imperatives of bureaucratic, corporate capitalism and resulted in a displacement of traditional values that unleashed unrestrained hedonism.[10]

The second main sense in which the term *postmodernism* has been used is to describe certain cultural and artistic developments. In the introduction to an influential account of postmodern art, Stanley Trachtenberg writes that "postmodernism describes a sensibility, a feeling for innovation, for experiment

---

6. Steven Best and Douglas Kellner, *Postmodern Theory: Critical Interrogations* (New York: Guilford, 1991). They identify a reference to "postmodern painting" from 1870. (5) They also point out that the term was used in D. C. Somervell's summary of Toynbee's history, and then subsequently adopted by Toynbee, himself.

7. C. Wright Mills, *The Sociological Imagination* (New York: Oxford University Press, 1959), quoted in Best and Kellner, *Postmodern Theory*, 8.

8. See Daniel Bell, *The Coming of Post-Industrial Society* (New York: Basic Books, 1973), 51-54, where he cites many such terms to illustrate the widespread sense of deep structural changes in Western societies.

9. Amitai Etzioni, *The Active Society* (New York: Free Press, 1968); see Best and Kellner, *Postmodern Theory*, 12-13.

10. Daniel Bell, *The Cultural Contradictions of Capitalism* (New York: Basic Books, 1976); see Best and Kellner, *Postmodern Theory*, 13-14.

with conventional ways of framing experience so that it is at once removed from recognizable relationships and from the locations in which they exist."[11] This is manifested in various ways in different arts. In literature, for example, works like John Fowles's *The French Lieutenant's Woman*, Umberto Eco's *The Name of the Rose*, and E. L. Doctorow's *Ragtime* are often described as postmodern novels in part because they challenge traditional narrative structures. Sometimes the so-called magical realism of authors such as Salman Rushdie and Gabriel García Márquez is also included.[12]

It is in the field of architecture, however, that the term first gained widespread prominence. There, it represented a reaction to Modernism and what is often thought to be the culmination of Modernism in the International Style. This form of late Modernism attempted to eliminate historical references, decoration, and meaning in favor of a more "honest" functionalism. Reacting against such an approach, architects such as Robert Venturi argued that architects should take into account the existing environment—both natural and built.[13] Others began to re-incorporate decorative elements and historical references. Postmodernist architects often inserted these familiar design elements into non-traditional roles. Charles Jencks, one of the key proponents of postmodern architecture, finds in it "an underlying schizophrenia" since it relies on two codes of meaning: a traditional, familiar code, and a rapidly changing, technologically advanced code.[14] During the 1970s architects became more concerned, as Diane Ghirardo puts it, with "the questions of meaning and how individuals order the world."[15] Mary McLeod agrees: "Underlying . . . the development of postmodernism in architecture in all its diverse and contradictory manifestations, is a search for meaning."[16] According to Ghirardo, the poststructuralist philosophies of Derrida and Foucault were important in convincing many postmodernist architects that meaning could not be grounded in any traditional source. Thus, these architects attempted to "embrace notions of fragmentation, dispersion and discontinuity through formal means."[17]

As Lyotard argues, there does seem to be something of a family resemblance among the themes used to characterize postmodernism in these very different social and cultural areas. In each case, meaningful elements are

---

11. Stanley Trachtenberg, introduction to *The Postmodern Moment* (Westport, Conn.: Greenwood Press, 1985), 6.

12. See Philip Stevick, "Literature," in *The Postmodern Moment*, Trachtenberg, ed.

13. See, for example, Robert Venturi, Denise Scott Brown, and Steven Izenour, *Learning from Las Vegas*, revised edition (Cambridge: MIT Press, 1977).

14. Charles Jencks, *The Language of Post-Modern Architecture*, revised enlarged edition (New York: Rizzoli, 1977), 130. This is his famous idea of "double-coding."

15. Diane Ghirardo, *Architecture after Modernism* (London: Thames and Hudson, 1996), 32.

16. Mary McLeod, "Architecture," in *The Postmodern Moment*, Trachtenberg, ed., 24.

17. Ghirardo, *Architecture after Modernism*, 36.

set free from the traditional structures that gave them meaning and/or legitimacy. As a result, these elements are often treated by postmodernists with a certain playfulness or irony—not to say cynicism. Still, there is room to question the usefulness of the term *postmodern* in characterizing the changes in the social/historical and cultural/artistic arenas. What often gets lost in such discussions is that the characteristics most frequently taken to be definitive of postmodernity are virtually identical to the terms that describe *modernism*.[18] Thus, Marshall Berman appropriates Marx's slogan and claims: "To be modern . . . is to experience personal and social life as a maelstrom, to find one's world and oneself in perpetual disintegration and renewal, trouble and anguish, ambiguity and contradiction: to be part of a universe in which all that is solid melts into air."[19] As Callinicos observes, the "appropriation of Modernist motifs is absolutely typical of accounts of Postmodernist art."[20] A hallmark of the modernist movement of surrealism and the avant-garde was the self-conscious use of traditional elements in non-traditional contexts. Berman puts the point this way: modernists "sometimes call themselves 'post-modernists'" when they take an affirmative (and typically apolitical) vision toward modernity.[21] Lyotard's touchstone of postmodernism, the rejection of meta-narratives and foundations, thus is equally the core of modernism itself. Even Lyotard himself acknowledges that postmodernism "is undoubtedly a part of the modern. . . . Postmodernism thus understood is not modernism at its end but in the nascent state, and this state is constant."[22]

There is room to doubt, therefore, the usefulness of the term *postmodern* as a blanket characterization of recent social and cultural changes. A full assessment of the utility of the concept of the postmodern would have to distinguish carefully its use in different arts and social theories.[23] This is far beyond what we can consider here, but at least it is clear that there are serious grounds for doubting the uniform usefulness of this concept across all areas of

---

18. Alex Callinicos makes this case very strongly in *Against Postmodernism* (New York: St. Martin's, 1989), especially chapters 1 and 5.

19. Marshall Berman, *All That Is Solid Melts into Air* (New York: Simon and Schuster, 1982; reprint, New York: Penguin, 1988), 345.

20. Callinicos, *Against Postmodernism*, 12.

21. Berman, *All That Is Solid Melts into Air*, 32. Berman includes as modernists many of the authors and artists typically identified as postmodernists. See 24, 31-32.

22. Lyotard, *The Postmodern Condition*, 79.

23. McLeod argues: "Thus, postmodernism in architecture is not, as it is in some fields, a more sophisticated and comprehensive exploration of the formal discoveries of modernism: fragmentation, dispersion, interpenetration, shear, the grid, and continuous space. Rather, it is a reaction against those very discoveries and their resultant destruction of accepted styles and compositional modes. Unlike many postmodern writers, postmodern architects ordinarily accept the canons of premodernist humanism: representation, figuration, content, and meaning." ("Architecture," in *The Postmodern Moment*, Trachtenberg, ed., 24.)

culture and social theory. As Callinicos argues, what needs to be explained is not so much the development of a new epoch in either art or society, but rather the widespread belief that such a transformation has occurred. The attraction of the idea of the postmodern (especially for the left) does call for explanation, and we will return to this issue in the Conclusion.

In contrast to the lingering doubts about the usefulness of the term *postmodern* in the social/historical and cultural/artistic areas, it seems clear that poststructuralist philosophy has raised a series of fundamental challenges to the traditional goals and methods of Western philosophy.[24] While Callinicos believes that most attempts to characterize a postmodern epoch in society or culture are "of small calibre intellectually, usually superficial, often ignorant, sometimes incoherent," even he concedes that the work of poststructuralist philosophers must be confronted on their own terms and not simply dismissed.[25] Drawing on insights originating in structural linguistics, poststructuralism has challenged traditional attempts to ground both theoretical and practical reason on an account of the subject. Lyotard, for example, argues that for postmodernism, "justice is consigned to the grand narrative in the same way as truth."[26] Our concern will focus on the practical side, specifically, the challenge poststructuralism poses to liberal political theory.

Poststructuralism

To begin to understand poststructuralism, we need a brief account of structuralism, which originated with the work of the Swiss linguist Ferdinand de Saussure. One approach to the understanding of language is to think of it as a system of correspondences between words and either ideas or objects. Corresponding to the word *tree* for example, is the idea of a tree (or perhaps an actual tree); corresponding to the word *horse* is the idea of a horse (or perhaps an actual horse). This starting point suggests a program for determining how more complicated linguistic entities relate to the world. Saussure, however, objects that this approach "assumes that ideas already exist independently of words. . . . Furthermore, it leads one to assume that the link between a name and a thing is something quite unproblematic, which is far from being the case."[27] In

---

24. As Peter Dews shows, there are many similarities between these challenges and the reaction of the German idealists to Kant. See Peter Dews, *The Logics of Disintegration* (New York: Verso, 1987), 19-24, and *The Limits of Disenchantment* (New York: Verso, 1995), chapter 6.

25. Callinicos, *Against Postmodernism*, 5.

26. Lyotard, *The Postmodern Condition*, xxiv.

27. Ferdinand de Saussure, *Course in General Linguistics*, Charles Bally and Albert Sechehaye, eds., Roy Harris, trans. (La Salle, Ill.: Open Court, 1986), 65-66. Parenthetical references in this and the next three paragraphs will be to this work.

contrast, Saussure calls the combination of a signal (a sound pattern) and a signification (a concept) a *sign*, and he proposes to understand signs holistically:

> [I]t is a great mistake to consider a sign as nothing more than the combination of a certain sound and a certain concept. To think of a sign as nothing more would be to isolate it from the system to which it belongs. It would be to suppose that a start could be made with individual signs, and a system constructed by putting them together. On the contrary, the system as a united whole is the starting point, from which it becomes possible, by a process of analysis, to identify its constituent elements. (112)

Saussure's holism operates at both the material level (the phonetic level of signals) and the conceptual level (the semantic level of significations). To be able to identify any of a language's constituent elements, whether material or conceptual, requires "the system as a united whole."

Saussure points out that the choice of which sound will signify which concept is arbitrary. In itself, the sound "horse" does not have any meaning at all. "No one disputes the fact that linguistic signs are arbitrary," Saussure writes. "But it is often easier to discover a truth than to assign it to its correct place." (68) The insight that Saussure places at the core of his work is that signs (both signals and significations) do not come individuated and distinguished prior to language. It takes a system of language in order to be able to identify what is a meaningless noise, what is a meaningful sound, and what is a sequence of distinct meaningful sounds. Signs are individuated precisely through their contrasts with one another: "The sound of a word is not in itself important, but the phonetic contrasts which allow us to distinguish that word from any other. That is what carries the meaning." (116) Similarly, the signification of a sign is also determined holistically through determinate contrasts with other significations. Thus: "The content of a word is determined in the final analysis not by what it contains but by what exists outside it." (114)

Saussure summarizes his particular form of holism this way: "*In language itself, there are only differences.*" (118) It is crucial to recognize that Saussure does not draw any skeptical conclusions from this thesis—quite the contrary, in fact. He presents his form of structuralism precisely as an attempt to show how language works and is able to generate meaning. Taken as a whole, a system of signals (given their identities through contrasts with one another) and a system of significations (again, given their particular identities through contrasts with one another) together "gives rise to a system of values." (118)

Two more points about Saussure's structuralism are important for us. First, the linguistic system within which particular sounds have meanings is a social product. The point of saying that a sign is arbitrary "must not be taken to imply that a signal depends on the free choice of the speaker." In fact, "the individual has no power to alter a sign in any respect once it has become established in a linguistic community." (68) The second and related point is that Saussure insists that thought itself depends on language:

> Philosophers and linguists have always agreed that were it not for signs, we should be incapable of differentiating any two ideas in a clear and constant way. In itself, thought is like a swirling cloud, where no shape is intrinsically determinate. No ideas are established in advance, and nothing is distinct, before the introduction of linguistic structure. (110)

Together with his meaning holism, this is a powerful combination. If thought depends on language and language is a social creation, it implies that our thought is largely beholden to the system of signs that our linguistic community bequeaths to us. Eric Matthews explains the radical results of such an approach this way:

> it undermines the view of language (and so of thought) as a transparent representation of an objective reality: it is not the nature of the world which determines the concepts which we can have of it, but the reverse. The structures of our language determine the kinds of distinction which we make between types of objects, the sorts of categorization of things which we use in our thought.[28]

Based on this combination of views, structuralism extended its influence beyond the study of language, first into anthropology and then into philosophy.

Jacques Derrida begins with, but radicalizes this structuralist account in order to challenge what he takes to be central tenets of the Western philosophical tradition. Jonathan Culler explains Derrida's approach to meaning by pointing to a "paradox" that arises within traditional philosophy of language:

> We tend to think that what we call the meaning of a word depends on the fact that it has been used by speakers on various occasions with the intention of communicating or expressing this meaning, and we thus might want to argue that what can in general be called the structure of a language—the general system of its rules and regularities—is derived from and determined by events: by acts of communication. But if we took this argument seriously and began to look at the events which are said to determine structures, we would find that every event is itself already determined and made possible by prior structures. . . . The structures, of course, are themselves always products, but however far back we try to push, even when we think about the birth of language itself and try to describe an originating event which might have produced the first structure, we discover that we must assume prior organization, prior differentiation.[29]

---

28. Eric Matthews, *Twentieth-Century French Philosophy* (New York: Oxford University Press, 1996), 138.

29. Jonathan Culler, "Jacques Derrida" in *Structuralism and Since*, John Sturrock, ed. (New York: Oxford University Press, 1979), 163-164.

This point was already made explicitly by Saussure: "At any given period, however far back in time we go, a language is always an inheritance from the past. . . . In fact, no society has ever known its language to be anything other than something inherited from previous generations, which it has no choice but to accept."[30] Derrida radicalizes this insight by arguing that since meaning depends on what always remains in the background, it can never be determined finally and definitively. As with the structuralists, meaning is dependent on a system of differences. Derrida, however, stresses that a final resolution of meaning is always being deferred by elements that are not present—by the structure that is presupposed as background. This combination of difference and deferment are fused in Derrida's term *différance*.[31]

This account of meaning lies at the heart of the idea of deconstruction. If meaning is always deferred and never simply present, this implies that there is a sense in which every text fails in its implicit attempt to reach beyond itself in a fixed and determinate way. Deconstructing a text shows this failure. As David Hoy explains:

> Deconstruction reveals not only how the text gives the impression of working, but insofar as the text can be found to have rhetorical devices deliberately perpetuating this illusion, how it really works against itself. A text would work (and would be a work) if it succeeded in being a unified, coherent whole, perhaps communicating a message, but in some more general way representing or recreating a reality external to it. Deconstruction shows the failure of a work's attempt at representation and, by implication, the possibility of comparable failure by any such work, or by any text whatsoever.[32]

Revealing the inevitability of such failures has important philosophical implications. Since ancient Greece, philosophers have attempted to distinguish logic, in which an argument is conducted through reason, from rhetoric, in which the speaker or author attempts to induce a belief or attitude in the audience through other means. Because logic works through reason, it aims at establishing a conclusion based on the free assent of the audience. Rhetoric, in contrast, may attempt to go behind the back of reason, so to speak, and manipulate the audience. But if, as deconstruction seeks to demonstrate, rhetoric and manipulation are always at work in any text when it attempts to go beyond itself, the traditional contrast between a realm of freedom and non-coercive logical relations, on the one hand, and violent manipulations, on the other, is not tenable. Deconstruction, therefore, aims to undermine the centrality of

---

30. Saussure, *Course in General Linguistics*, 71-72.

31. See, for example, Jacques Derrida, "Différrance," in *Margins of Philosophy*, Alan Bass, trans. (Chicago: University of Chicago Press, 1982).

32. David Hoy, "Jacques Derrida" in *The Return of Grand Theory in the Human Sciences*, Quentin Skinner, ed. (New York: Cambridge University Press, 1985), 44.

"logocentrism" or the "metaphysics of presence" in the history of Western philosophy.

If his ultimate target is the logocentrism that he finds throughout the history of Western philosophy—in the privileging of logic over rhetoric and of speech over writing, for example—Derrida most frequently attacks it in the form of phenomenology. In the early part of the century, Edmund Husserl developed a phenomenology which attempted to bracket all known facts about the world and proceed from a subject certain only of itself and its experiences. The central claim of Husserl's phenomenology was that our experiences in themselves are intentional—they purport to be about or of something that is not itself present in experience. We need not concern ourselves with how this movement developed through the middle part of the century. It will suffice to point out, as Foucault and many others have observed, that French social philosophy after World War II was dominated by an attempt to combine phenomenology and Marxism.[33] The towering figure in this project was Jean-Paul Sartre.

Structuralists and then poststructuralists attacked this project head-on. Structuralism showed that the sharp contrast between content that was entirely present to a subject and that which was not present but merely represented could not be sustained. Introspection alone was not a suitable method for philosophical insight or, indeed, for the determination of meaning. Content—meaning—was only generated by an element's participation in a system, most of which was not present in (or to) the subject. For some, such as Louis Althusser, this became the basis for a structuralist version of Marxism.[34] Others, such as Maurice Merleau-Ponty attempted to adapt the phenomenological project to the requirements of a more adequate account of language (and content) by developing an understanding of subjectivity as emerging from and as part of both the natural and social worlds. The poststructuralists went in the opposite direction: rather than attempting to understand subjectivity in a more naturalistic way, poststructuralism takes the form of anti-humanism in the sense of denying the coherence of the subject. As Callinicos puts it, for Derrida, "The subject is subordinated to the endless play of difference, but his move takes us not into, but beyond, history."[35] And Peter Dews argues that on Derrida's view,

there could never be an emergence of meaning: there would be nothing but an unstoppable mediation of signs by other signs. The majority of Derrida's interpreters

---

33. Foucault, "Critical Theory/Intellectual History," 21. Alexandre Kojève's famous lectures between 1933 and 1939, on Hegel's *Phenomenology* were also formative for the next generation of French philosophers. See Matthews, *Twentieth-Century French Philosophy*, 112-119; and Paul Berman, *A Tale of Two Utopias* (New York: Norton, 1996), 257-262.

34. For a brief introduction to Althusser, see Susan James, "Louis Althusser" in *The Return of Grand Theory in the Human Sciences*, Quentin Skinner, ed.

35. Callinicos, *Against Postmodernism*, 75. Compare Dews, *Logics of Disintegration*, 19.

have, of course, resisted this implication of his position: Derrida is portrayed as merely suggesting that meaning is far more insecure, elusive, undecidable than philosophers had previously imagined. Yet the logical consequence of his argument is not the volatilization of meaning, but its destruction.[36]

Poststructuralism, we might say, accepts structuralism's undermining of the self-certain subject, but does not accept the coherence and stability of the structures with which the structuralists sought to replace it.

Whatever one thinks of Derrida's philosophy of language and his deconstruction of phenomenology and metaphysics, one might reasonably ask whether his work has any particular political or ethical implications. In the Anglo-American philosophical context, no one has been a greater champion of Derrida's work than Richard Rorty, calling him "the most intriguing and ingenious of contemporary philosophers."[37] According to Rorty, Derrida (at least in his work since the mid-1970s) shows how "to break with the temptation [of Heidegger and, by implication, most philosophers] to identify himself with something big—something like 'Europe' or the 'call of Being' or 'man.'"[38] For Rorty, this is a great achievement, even if "a lot of Derrida's arguments . . . are just awful."[39] But this is only useful or interesting for those (mostly professional philosophers) who are interested in such metaphysical notions in the first place.

> Derrida talks as if . . . there were a terrible, oppressive force called "the metaphorics of philosophy" or the "history of metaphysics" which is making life impossible not only for playful punsters like himself but for society as a whole. . . . This idea repeats Heidegger's claim that the history of the genre which has sought a total, unique, and closed language is central to the entire range of human possibilities in the contemporary West. This claim seems very implausible.[40]

Although Derrida's work may be important for those philosophers (like Rorty) who like to debunk certain philosophical errors and read the history of

---

36. Dews, *Logics of Disintegration*, 30, note omitted.

37. Richard Rorty, "Habermas, Derrida, and the Functions of Philosophy," in *Truth and Progress*, vol. 3 of *Philosophical Papers* (New York: Cambridge University Press, 1998), 307.

38. Richard Rorty, *Contingency, Irony, and Solidarity* (New York: Cambridge University Press, 1989), 122.

39. Richard Rorty, "Deconstruction and Circumvention," in *Essays on Heidegger and Others*, vol. 2 of *Philosophical Papers* (New York: Cambridge University Press, 1991), 93n12. His indifference to Derrida's "awful" arguments is due to the fact that Rorty does not take Derrida to be offering refutations of old theories but inventing a new way to write. See Richard Rorty, "Is Derrida a Transcendental Philosopher?" in *Essays on Heidegger and Others*, especially 121; and Richard Rorty, "Habermas, Derrida, and the Functions of Philosophy," in *Truth and Progress*.

40. Rorty, "Deconstruction and Circumvention," 100-101.

philosophy in a new light, Rorty believes that this is essentially a private affair, unrelated to political issues. Derrida's ideas

> may be useful to some of us in our individual quests for private perfection. When we take up our public responsibilities, however, the infinite and the unrepresentable are merely nuisances. . . . Emphasizing the impossibility of meaning, or of justice, as Derrida sometimes does, is a temptation to Gothicize—to view democratic politics as ineffectual, because unable to cope with preternatural forces.[41]

For Rorty, it would be better simply to drop the false political aspirations and take Derrida for what he is: a "playful punster" who shows us how not to take philosophy's traditional aspirations too seriously.

In contrast, however, Derrida has been consistent and explicit in emphasizing the centrality of political concerns to his work. In a 1993 conference, he commented:

> My hope, as a man of the left, is that certain elements of deconstruction will have served or—because the struggle continues, particularly in the United States—*will* serve to politicize or repoliticize the left with regard to positions which are not simply academic. I hope—and if I can continue to contribute a little to this I will be very content—that the political left in universities in the United States, France and elsewhere, will gain politically by employing deconstruction. To a certain extent, and in an unequal way, this is a movement that is already under way.[42]

Elsewhere, he is even more emphatic, if more cryptic: "Deconstruction is justice."[43] Presumably, as he explains elsewhere, the thought is that "Without a call for justice we would not have any interest in deconstructing the law."[44] Some of his followers have taken this insistence on the political implications of deconstruction to rather preposterous extremes, arguing that anyone critical of deconstruction is complicit in the worst kinds of political atrocities. In the aftermath of the bitter debate over J. L. Austin's philosophy of language between Derrida and John Searle, Michael Ryan with apparent seriousness was able to refer to "the circuit that leads from John Searle's reactionary philosophic study to David Rockefeller's bank office, to the torture chambers of Santiago de

---

41. Richard Rorty, *Achieving Our Country* (Cambridge: Harvard University Press, 1998), 96-97.

42. Jacques Derrida, "Remarks on Deconstruction and Pragmatism," in *Deconstruction and Pragmatism*, Chantal Mouffe, ed. (New York: Routledge, 1996), 85-86.

43. Jacques Derrida, "Force of Law: The 'Mystical Foundation of Authority,'" in *Deconstruction and the Possibility of Justice*, Drucilla Cornell, Michel Rosenfeld, and David Gray Carlson, eds. (New York: Routledge, 1992), 15.

44. Jacques Derrida, *Deconstruction in a Nutshell*, John Caputo, ed. (New York: Fordham, 1997), 16.

Chile."[45] Here we have a position opposite to that of Rorty: Derrida's work is supposed to have extremely deep and profound political implications.

All sides, however, admit that the political implications of deconstruction are at least elusive. As Peter Dews observes,

> Derrida has not been noticeably successful in articulating the relationship between "deconstruction" in its initial discursive sense, as concerned with the analysis of "logocentrism" and the "metaphysics of presence", and his more concrete political concerns. Throughout his work, Derrida hints at a complicity between the fundamental assumptions of Western thought and the violences and repressions which have characterized Western history, but the nature of this complicity is never truly clarified.[46]

Indeed, Derrida himself points out: "There are no doubt many reasons why the majority of texts hastily identified as 'deconstructionist'—for example, mine— *seem*, I do say *seem*, not to foreground the theme of justice (as theme, precisely), or the theme of ethics or politics."[47] There is a reason for this elusiveness. Deconstruction must be indirect in this way if it is to avoid trapping itself in the logocentrism that it diagnoses as the (purportedly political) failure of other texts. Any attempt to explicate the idea of justice will necessarily undermine itself.

For Derrida, "Justice in itself, if such a thing exists, outside or beyond law, is not deconstructable."[48] This is because "one cannot speak *directly* about justice, thematize or objectivize justice, say 'this is just' and even less 'I am just,' without immediately betraying justice, if not law (*droit*)."[49] In contrast to justice itself, any claim about justice can be deconstructed. Critics of Derrida, such as Mark Lilla, therefore charge that Derrida's position leaves him no room for anything but "revelation":

> He simply cannot find a way of specifying the nature of the justice to be sought through left-wing politics without opening himself to the very deconstruction he so gleefully applies to others. Unless, of course, he places the "idea of justice" in the

---

45. Michael Ryan, *Marxism and Deconstruction* (Baltimore: Johns Hopkins University Press, 1982), 46. Ryan is pointing out that a full analysis of these connections "requires supplementing Derrida's fine micrological critique of the structural principles and operations of the institutions of power and domination in philosophy with a more macrological and social mode of analysis." Derrida himself was responsible for initiating this mode of attack when he suggested that Searle's philosophy of language implicates him with "the police [that] is always waiting in the wings." See Jacques Derrida, "Limited Inc. a b c . . ." in *Limited Inc* (Chicago: Northwestern University Press, 1988), 105.

46. Dews, *Logics of Disintegration*, 35.

47. Derrida, "Force of Law," 7.

48. Derrida, "Force of Law," 14.

49. Derrida, "Force of Law," 10.

eternal, messianic beyond where it cannot be reached by argument, and assumes that his ideologically sympathetic readers won't ask too many questions.[50]

Even those sympathetic to Derrida concede that the political implications of his thought are indirect. As Richard Beardsworth, in a book entitled *Derrida and the Political*, writes:

> In its affirmative refusal to advocate a politics, deconstruction forms, firstly, an account of why all political projects fail. Since the projection of any decision has ethical implications, deconstruction in fact generalizes what is meant by the political well beyond the local sense of politics.[51]

But how is this refusal to advocate a politics any kind of affirmation at all?

One answer is provided by Richard Bernstein. For Bernstein, it is true that "There is scarcely anything resembling a straightforward analysis of such concepts as right, good, obligation, justice, and virtue—or anything stable enough to label Derrida's ethical-political 'position.'"[52] Yet, he insists: "Few contemporary thinkers have been so alert and perceptive about the temptations and dangers of violently crushing or silencing differences, otherness, alterity— in 'others' or even the 'other' in ourselves. Few writers have written with such nuanced understanding about the suffering, mourning 'other.'"[53] By showing us that the things we take to be stable and clear, including meaning and a sense of self, are actually unstable and never fully determined, we are spurred on to reconsider and recreate them. Here, then, are the political implications. As Bernstein argues:

> The danger with any political code is that it can become rigidified or reified—a set of unquestioned formulas that we rely on to direct our actions. More important, no code is ever *sufficient* to justify or legitimate a decision in any specific context. No code can close the gap or diminish the undecidability that confronts us in making an ethical-political decision or choice.[54]

Deconstruction may serve a valuable political purpose, on this view, by undermining our tendency to believe that political codes are written in the metaphysical substratum of nature or of the subject. It continuously reveals to us that nothing—not subjects, not objects, not meaning—is fully determinate or stable.

---

50. Mark Lilla, "The Politics of Jacques Derrida," *New York Review of Books*, 25 June 1998, 39, 40.

51. Richard Beardsworth, *Derrida and the Political* (New York: Routledge, 1996), 19.

52. Richard Bernstein, "Serious Play: The Ethical-Political Horizon of Derrida," in *The New Constellation* (Cambridge: MIT Press, 1992), 173.

53. Bernstein, "Serious Play," 184.

54. Richard Bernstein, "An Allegory of Modernity/Postmodernity: Habermas and Derrida," in *The New Constellation*, 214.

The danger of a code becoming rigidified or reified may well be a danger, but it is not the only one. Having observed our inability to provide some kind of "final justification" that relieves us of the burden of all further questioning and doubt, we are still left with the practical question of what to do and which institutions to defend or construct. Good politics is not only about avoiding complacency. It is about judging which changes, if any, would be improvements and which would only be destructive. Bernstein recognizes this point when he observes, in criticism of Derrida:

> We want *some* understanding of what kinds of institutions and practices should be developed for "a democracy to come." Or even more minimally, we want some orientation about what changes "here and now" are needed in our present institutional structures. Derrida, thus far, has very little to say about any of this. Consequently there is a danger that, for all the evocative power of the very idea of a "democracy to come," the idea of such a democracy can become an impotent, vague abstraction.[55]

The problem is that if the primary focus on one's political concerns is that a political code might become "regidified or reified," it is hard to see how one could avoid relying on anything but "impotent, vague abstraction[s]."

Chantal Mouffe's understanding of the political implications of Derrida's work is similar to that of Bernstein's interpretation. She believes that the "consensus approach" to political institutions (she names Habermas and Rawls, although Rorty is her main target) "must postulate the availability of a consensus without exclusion, i.e. a consensus that is the expression of a rational agreement and that would have completely eliminated antagonism."[56] This false and politically dangerous illusion is corrected by deconstruction:

> This privileging of the "consensus" with the different forms that it currently takes in the numerous versions of "deliberative democracy" represents in my view a serious misconception of the nature of democracy. This is why an approach like deconstruction, which reveals the impossibility of establishing a consensus without exclusion is of fundamental importance for grasping what is at stake in democratic politics. Because it warns us against the illusion that Justice could ever be instantiated in the institutions of any society, deconstruction forces us to keep the democratic contestation alive.[57]

To repeat Bernstein's criticism: even if we assume that it is impossible to establish a consensus without exclusion, there still remains the problem of what

---

55. Bernstein, "An Allegory of Modernity/Postmodernity," 223.

56. Chantal Mouffe, "Deconstruction, Pragmatism and the Politics of Democracy," in *Deconstruction and Pragmatism*, Mouffe, ed., 8-9.

57. Mouffe, "Deconstruction, Pragmatism and the Politics of Democracy," 9.

institutions we should have. Mouffe assumes that deliberative democracy is the obvious choice.

There is, however, a large gap in this argument. It is by no means obvious why the rejection of the aspiration to consensus lends any support to democracy as opposed to, say, purely market-based relations or, indeed, anarchy. As far as I can tell, this issue is not addressed in any of Derrida's work. Derrida himself seems to recognize this, at least at one point:

> Once it is granted that violence is *in fact* irreducible, it becomes necessary—and this is the moment of politics—to have rules, conventions and stabilizations of power. All that a deconstructive point of view tries to show, is that since convention, institutions and consensus are stabilizations (sometimes stabilizations of great duration, sometimes micro-stabilizations), this means that they are stabilizations of something essentially unstable and chaotic. Thus, it becomes necessary to stabilize precisely because stability is not natural; it is because there is instability that stabilization becomes necessary; it is because there is chaos that there is a need for stability. Now, this chaos and instability, which is fundamental, founding and irreducible, is at once naturally the worst against which we struggle with laws, rules, conventions, politics and provisional hegemony, but at the same time it is a chance, a chance to change, to destabilize.[58]

If "stability is not natural," if we can change or destabilize our institutions, once we point that out we have a responsibility to decide which institutions to support, defend, and construct. The fact is, however, that Derrida has not provided (nor even endorsed) any tools with which to make these judgments.

Perhaps the most insightful critic of this political reading of Derrida's work is Thomas McCarthy, who writes:

> Deconstructive practices seem here to be necessarily complementary to practices of constructing and reconstructing the ideals, norms, principles, laws and institutions we live by. Thus the more Derrida has insisted on the practical-political import of deconstruction, the more he has been confronted with the objection that it has little to offer in the way of positive ethicopolitical proposals. His standard responses to this objection have not been convincing.[59]

If Derrida occasionally announces the need for a constructive project to complement deconstruction, his failure to develop such a positive account is worse that incomplete or unhelpful. Mouffe may believe that benign democratic institutions follow from a recognition of instability and conflict, but this is not the only possibility. As McCarthy continues:

---

58. Jacques Derrida, "Remarks on Deconstruction and Pragmatism," 83-84.

59. Thomas McCarthy, "The Politics of the Ineffable: Derrida's Deconstruction" in *Ideals and Illusions* (Cambridge: MIT Press, 1991), 107.

It is sheer romanticism to suppose that uprooting and destabilizing universalist structures will of itself lead to letting the other be, in respect and freedom, rather than to intolerant and aggressive particularism, a war of all against all in which the fittest survive and the most powerful dominate. Enlarging the social space in which otherness can be, establishing and maintaining a multifarious and spacious pluralism, seem, on the contrary, to require that we inculcate universal principles of tolerance and respect and stabilize institutions that secure rights and impose limits. Otherwise, how is the tolerance of difference to be combined with the requirements of living *together* under *common* norms?[60]

The problem for Derrida is that if he were to elaborate what justice requires, this would threaten to undo the point that deconstruction reveals: the radical instability of all constructions. He would lose what, according to Bernstein and Mouffe, is most distinctive and valuable in his approach. He must remain silent concerning positive norms or risk suggesting that a consensus could be formed around the reified, unquestioned formula that he proposes.

On rare occasions, Derrida has taken this risk and addressed more concrete political issues. For example, he contributed a text to a catalog for an exhibit of anti-apartheid art which opened in Paris is 1983. Among other things, Derrida is concerned in this essay with the term *apartheid*, as well as with the role of art, when he imagines the works of art in the exhibition reflecting back from a post-apartheid South Africa. But in addition, Derrida condemns apartheid with surprisingly conventional vocabulary. He pleads: "save humanity from this evil." He reminds us (twice) that the United Nations General Assembly judged apartheid to be a "crime against humanity." He condemns the hypocrisy of countries which do not let the U.N.'s finding disrupt "diplomatic, economic or cultural exchanges, the deliveries of arms, and geopolitical solidarity." He cites statistics from Amnesty International concerning the distribution of wealth, and urges that we not allow these abstract measures to distract us from the "daily suffering, oppression, poverty, violence, [and] torture." He approves of "The white resistance movement in South Africa [which] deserves our praise."[61]

Perhaps most remarkably, however, in a later reply, Derrida excoriates his critics for "the enormous blunder that led you to take a *prescriptive* utterance for a *descriptive* (theoretical and constative) one."[62] Despite his insistence that

---

60. McCarthy, "The Politics of the Ineffable," 112-113. Compare Bernstein, "An Allegory of Modernity/Postmodernity," 222.

61. Jacques Derrida, "Racism's Last Word," *Critical Inquiry* 12, no. 1 (autumn 1985), 295, 298, 293, 297.

62. Jacques Derrida, "But, beyond . . ." *Critical Inquiry* 13, no. 1 (autumn 1986), 158. He is replying to Anne McClintock and Rob Nixon, "No Names Apart," *Critical Inquiry* 13, no. 1 (autumn 1986). McClintock and Nixon provide a brief but useful overview of elements of the history of South Africa including the official use of the term *apartheid*. Although they are critical of Derrida's failure to recognize this history, they note the obvious good faith in Derrida's opposition to apartheid. This good faith is lost in

"deconstructive practices are also and first of all political and institutional practices" and, indeed, that they are "perhaps more radical and certainly less stereotyped than others,"[63] it is hard to see how Derrida's analysis of apartheid relies on deconstructive practices at all. Indeed, one critic notes that Derrida's "personal political commitments . . . do not seem . . . to rise much above a fairly commonplace left liberalism."[64] I should note that the "commonplace" nature of his condemnation of apartheid may be either a good thing or a bad thing. For those who look to Derrida to provide a new perspective from which to engage in political practice, this certainly would be a disappointment. Rorty is correct: deconstruction does not hold the secret to unlocking a new realm of value or political criticism. On the other hand, the commonplace nature of these political judgments reveals that Derrida's understanding of poststructuralism is at least compatible with sound political judgment—something that may seem more questionable when we discuss Foucault.

It is significant, however, that even in this case Derrida does not articulate a vision of a post-apartheid society. Nor, despite the standard liberal pieties, does Derrida make explicit the grounds of his condemnation. Quite the contrary, in fact: he observes that the "silence" of the paintings "is just. A discourse would once again compel us to reckon with the present state of force and law. It would draw up contracts, dialecticize itself, let itself be reappropriated again."[65] As Callinicos comments: "So the resistance to apartheid must remain inarticulate, must not seek to formulate a political programme and strategy: any attempt to do so would simply involve reincorporation into 'the present state of law and force' and perhaps even into the 'European discourse of racism.'"[66]

There is a sense in which by selecting the case of apartheid, Derrida has made things too easy on himself. We do not need a fully elaborated theory of justice in order to see the manifest injustice of apartheid. If all cases of injustice were equally transparent, elaboration of a complex theory might seem less necessary. It is interesting to consider Rorty in more detail because he often seems to imply that there is no real difficulty in identifying where injustice lies and what is to be done about it. Philosophical reflection is not needed for such an endeavor and should properly be confined to the realm of private enrichment. Good politics simply requires that we "help the poor resist the rich" or "redeem [sic] the balance of power between the strong and the weak."[67] Deep

Derrida's reply, which is rather overwhelming in its viciousness and hostility.

63. Derrida, "But, beyond . . ." 168.

64. Callinicos, *Against Postmodernism*, 79.

65. Derrida, "Racism's Last Word," 299.

66. Callinicos, *Against Postmodernism*, 78.

67. Richard Rorty, "Intellectuals in Politics," *Dissent* (fall 1991), 489; Richard Rorty, "Reply," *Dissent* (spring 1992), 267. I should note that I am sympathetic with the main point of these articles which is to criticize the idea (often associated with postmodernism) that social progress can be based on the idea of transgressive stands within the academy.

philosophical reflection is likely only to interfere with this process since political criticism is most effectively carried on by simply repeating the "statistics about income distribution, per-pupil expenditure in school districts, and so on."[68] Instead of elaborate philosophical theories of justice (Rorty has Habermas in mind) we should "drop this idea, privatise philosophy, and say that when it comes to the communal self-reassurance of the modern democratic societies, most of the work gets done not by deep thinkers (e.g. people attracted by Plato and Kant) but by superficial dreamers—people like Edward Bellamy, Henry George, H. G. Wells, Michael Harrington, Martin Luther King."[69]

Rorty claims that he has "no wish to diminish" the power of the idea of human solidarity, "but only to disengage it from what has often been thought of as its 'philosophical presuppositions'."[70] The fact is, however, that despite his claim that moral progress consists in expanding the scope of solidarity, Rorty expresses a strikingly skeptical attitude toward the idea of solidarity. Of the idea of identifying with "humanity" or "all rational beings" he writes: "no one, I have been claiming, *can* make *that* identification." Identifying with "humanity as such" is "impossible—a philosopher's invention, an awkward attempt to secularize the idea of becoming one with God."[71] To support this speculation, Rorty hypothesizes that rescuers of Jews from the Holocaust would have explained their actions not in terms of helping their "fellow human beings" but in "more parochial terms" like this: "that this particular Jew was a fellow Milanese, or a fellow Jutlander, or a fellow member of the same union or profession, or a fellow bocce player, or a fellow parent of small children."[72] As it happens, Norman Geras shows in detail that this is not how most rescuers view their own behavior—most view their actions in universal terms.[73] Furthermore, when any theorist calls for a high degree of solidarity, Rorty cries "foundationalism." Recall from the previous chapter, he criticizes Chomsky's argument that "the [Vietnam] War not merely betrayed America's hopes and interests and self-image, but was *immoral*, one which we had had no *right* to engage in in the first place."[74] The objectionable idea that Chomsky seems to be proposing is that of a universalistic morality in which even unknown individuals on the other side of the world have basic human rights that must be respected.

---

68. Rorty, "Reply," *Dissent* (spring 1992), 267.

69. Richard Rorty, "Posties," *London Review of Books* (21 July 1983), 13.

70. Rorty, *Contingency, Irony, and Solidarity*, 192.

71. Rorty, *Contingency, Irony, and Solidarity*, 198.

72. Rorty, *Contingency, Irony, and Solidarity*, 190-191.

73. Norman Geras, *Solidarity in the Conversation of Humankind* (New York: Verso, 1995). Geras handles the evidence quite carefully and displays clear awareness of the possibility of selective recollections and retrospective justifications.

74. Richard Rorty, "Postmodern Bourgeois Liberalism," in *Objectivity, Relativism, and Truth*, 201.

On the one hand, Rorty sometimes endorses particular political struggles in the name of increased solidarity. On the other hand, he does not believe that people can be moved by any universalistic concern even for the most elementary human rights and he criticizes those who invoke such a standard. Let me propose an explanation for this incongruity. Much of Rorty's writing is devoted to debunking various foundational projects, especially in epistemology. In the area of ethics, this leads him to focus on foundational projects that aim to convince the radical skeptic that morality is a requirement of reason. As Richard Bernstein observes: "Rorty is concerned (one is tempted to say 'obsessed') with variations on a single theme—the metatheoretical question of whether Rawls' enterprise is one of 'articulation' of common intuitions and shared beliefs or a 'justification' of liberal democracy."[75] Because of this nearly exclusive focus, Rorty seems to assume that the only reason one might want to identify moral principles is to refute a radical skeptic by finding an unassailable foundation. This is why he often frames the debate in terms of whether philosophy or literature is more effective at converting non-liberals to the liberal cause.

Rorty's obsession with showing the impossibility of refuting a radical skeptic blinds him to the possibility of any other project. It also leads him to conflate universalism (the content of a moral view) with foundationalism (the grounding of such a view). Initially, Rorty took Rawls to be engaged in a "neo-Kantian," foundational project.[76] Gradually, over time, Rorty came to realize that this interpretation was mistaken:

> Many people, including myself, initially took Rawls's *A Theory of Justice* to be such an attempt. We read it as a continuation of the Enlightenment attempt to ground our moral intuitions on a conception of human nature (and, more specifically, as a neo-Kantian attempt to ground them on the notion of "rationality"). However, Rawls's writings subsequent to *A Theory of Justice* have helped us realize that we were misinterpreting his book, that we had overemphasized the Kantian and underemphasized the Hegelian and Deweyan elements.[77]

Rorty now sees Rawls as a theorist who is "thoroughly historicist and antiuniversalist."[78] If Rawls turns out not to be interested in the foundational project, for Rorty this implies that he is engaged in the "superficial" project of "communal self-reassurance." If we properly reject foundationalism, "the most philosophy can hope to do is to summarize our culturally influenced intuitions about the right thing to do in various situations" as a way of "heightening the

---

75. Richard Bernstein, "One Step Forward, Two Steps Backward: Rorty on Liberal Democracy and Philosophy," in *The New Constellation*, 238.

76. See, for example, Richard Rorty, "Philosophy As a Kind of Writing," in *Consequences of Pragmatism* (Minneapolis: University of Minnesota Press, 1982), 92.

77. Richard Rorty, "The Priority of Democracy to Philosophy," in *Objectivity, Relativism, and Truth*, 184-185.

78. Rorty, "The Priority of Democracy to Philosophy," 180.

sense of shared moral identity that brings us together in a moral community."[79] For Rorty, there is no real difficulty in identifying injustice. The only contribution that philosophy can make is to summarize our views in a way that may make them more attractive to others. On this view, philosophy really does become just another form of writing, and not a particularly powerful one. Literature and the arts are much more effective in awakening the moral sense in those who seem to be lacking one.

What this picture leaves out is exactly the project that Rawls wants to pursue and what makes his work interesting and important. Rorty is correct that Rawls is not concerned with refuting the radical skeptic. He assumes the existence of a sense of justice, but one which is full of uncertainties, tensions, and complications. He takes his job to be to clarify and to critically reflect on its content. Neither Rorty nor Derrida seem to have room for such a project. As Bernstein points out in criticism of Rorty: "We do not settle issues by the appeal to 'our political practices'—we need to confront the issues of which practices are to be favored and which are to be modified or eliminated."[80]

Near the end of *A Theory of Justice*, Rawls considers the nature of the justification on which he has relied, and he observes:

> justification is argument addressed to those who disagree with us, or to ourselves when we are of two minds. It presumes a clash of views between persons or within one person, and seeks to convince others, or ourselves, of the reasonableness of the principles upon which our claims and judgments are founded. Being designed to reconcile by reason, justification proceeds from what all parties to the discussion hold in common.[81]

This is not the project of converting a radical skeptic to the moral point of view. Instead, it is designed to address two closely related possible situations: first, those in which we are unsure what justice requires; second, those in which we disagree about what justice requires with others whom we recognize to be reasonable (in the technical sense outlined in chapter 2).

In the first case, our aim is to try to reach reflective equilibrium and resolve our uncertainties. This involves reflecting on our provisional fixed points and considering what reasons there are to endorse one conception of justice rather than another. As we saw in chapter 2, Rawls hypothesizes that considering the choice from the original position may help with this process. In the second case, we recognize significant points of agreement with others, yet disagree with them on some matter concerning basic social justice. The duty of civility says that in these matters we must attempt to provide justifications within the limits of

---

79. Richard Rorty, "Human Rights, Rationality, and Sentimentality," in *Truth and Progress*, 171.

80. Bernstein, "One Step Forward, Two Steps Backward," 241.

81. John Rawls, *A Theory of Justice* (Cambridge: Harvard University Press, 1971), 580 [508].

public reason so that all reasonable individuals can accept them. This is what justice as fairness aspires to do in its search for full reflective equilibrium. Where there is disagreement on matters of basic social justice, therefore, justice as fairness attempts to "reconcile by reason" rather than imposing a resolution by force.

But what if this contrast between reason and force is itself unfounded? What if every attempted justification through reason is itself implicated in power relations no different in kind than that involved in coercion? At least some of Michel Foucault's work can be read as raising this challenge, and it is to his work that we now must turn. I should point out, however, that this challenge seems much less compelling in the case of our own uncertainty. Indeed, from a first-person point of view, if we have not (yet) reached reflective equilibrium, it is hard to see how this presents any challenge at all. If we are trying to determine which conception of justice we should endorse, we have no choice but to consider reasons for one or another conception. The general charge that all such reasons are really a kind of force does not seem to get any critical grip at all. If there is a reason—any reason—to reject a certain consideration, this may itself be included as part of our effort to reach reflective equilibrium. Rawls's second case, in which there is disagreement among reasonable persons and the duty of civility leads us to offer reasons that all reasonable people could accept, does seem to depend on a contrast between force and reason. We can see Foucault's challenge, therefore, as being directed against the coherence of the contrast implicit in the duty of civility.

Foucault

Michel Foucault's work is commonly divided into three periods, corresponding to three broad methodological approaches. In his early work through the 1960s, he developed an approach that he called "archaeological." In the 1970s, he characterized his method as "genealogical." Finally, prior to his death in 1984, he began on a new course of investigation sometimes characterized as "ethics" or "problematizations" in which he investigated, among other things, the "care of the self." There is a debate in the secondary literature concerning the relationship among these methods.[82] What is important for us is simply to observe that Foucault's approach changed over the course of his career. Specifically, with the development of genealogy, Foucault becomes more explicitly aware of the social structures and power relationships within

---

82. Compare Arnold Davidson, "Archaeology, Genealogy, Ethics," in *Foucault: A Critical Reader*, David Couzens Hoy, ed. (New York: Blackwell, 1986), who argues for continuity, with Hubert Dreyfus and Paul Rabinow, *Michel Foucault: Beyond Structuralism and Hermeneutics*, second edition (Chicago: University of Chicago Press, 1983), who argue for a more radical transformation. Even Dreyfus and Rabinow recognize a certain complementarity, however. See, e.g., xxv, 104.

which various discourses are developed, maintained and transformed. Foucault himself traces this change to his reaction to the events in Paris of May 1968.[83] Foucault's most explicitly political discussions came largely in the form of interviews and lectures conducted during this genealogical period. In his early and late work, he tends not to address political questions as directly.

In his early archaeological works, Foucault is concerned with the history and sociology of the human sciences—what he calls "the sciences of man." Specifically, he examines the systems of concepts and linguistic structures within which authoritative scientific claims are made and validated.[84] These frameworks are not explicitly formulated by those working within them. They constitute what Foucault calls, with evident irony, a "historical a priori."[85]

> The positivities that I have tried to establish must not be understood as a set of determinations imposed from the outside on the thought of individuals, or inhabiting it from the inside, in advance as it were; they constitute rather the set of conditions in accordance with which a practice is exercised, in accordance with which that practice gives rise to partially or totally new statements, and in accordance with which it can be modified. These positivities are not so much limitations imposed on the initiative of subjects as the field in which that initiative is articulated.[86]

As Arnold Davidson explains, archaeology attempts to understand truth claims as part of "a system of ordered procedures for the production, regulation, distribution, circulation, and operation of statements."[87] Gary Gutting puts the point this way: "Foucault suggests (and shows how the suggestion is fruitful) that the play of individuals' thought, in a given period and disciplinary context, takes place in a space with a structure defined by a system of rules more fundamental than the assertions of the individuals thinking in the space."[88]

Thus, in *Madness and Civilization*, for example, he considers the framework in which individuals are classified either as rational or as mad.[89] And

---

83. See Michel Foucault, "Truth and Power," (originally published in 1977) in *Power/Knowledge*, Colin Gordon, ed. (New York: Pantheon, 1980), 115-116; and "Revolutionary Action: 'Until Now,'" (originally published in 1971) in *Language, Counter-Memory, Practice*, Donald Bouchard, ed. (Ithaca, N.Y.: Cornell University Press, 1977), 222-223.

84. In *Madness and Civilization* he was concerned with institutional structures of confinement. But this institutional emphasis was dropped as he developed his archaeological method in a more structuralist direction. See Dreyfus and Rabinow, *Michel Foucault: Beyond Structuralism and Hermeneutics*, 16-17.

85. Michel Foucault, *The Archaeology of Knowledge*, A. M. Sheridan Smith, trans. (New York: Pantheon, 1972; originally published in 1969), 127.

86. Foucault, *The Archaeology of Knowledge*, 208-209.

87. Davidson, "Archaeology, Genealogy, Ethics," 221.

88. Gary Gutting, "Michel Foucault: A User's Manual" in *The Cambridge Companion to Foucault*, Gary Gutting, ed. (New York: Cambridge University Press, 1994), 9-10.

89. Michel Foucault, *Madness and Civilization*, Richard Howard, trans. (New York:

in *The Order of Things*, he identifies a specific conception of *man* as a central element in the human sciences.[90] This modern understanding of man, Foucault claims, is of a being who stands apart from and represents the external world. He argues that it was only in the modern period, as humans began to reconceive themselves as representors, that the nature of representation itself first became an object of concern.[91] The contrast between rationality and madness and the nature of representation are themselves part of the background structures within which scientific questions are formed and truth claims made and validated. They establish the conditions under which it makes sense to talk about the truth or falsehood of specific claims.

As an historian of these frameworks, Foucault himself brackets the question of the truth of specific claims made within them.[92] In the preface to *The Birth of the Clinic*, for example, he writes:

> I should like to make it plain once and for all that this book has not been written in favour of one kind of medicine as against another kind of medicine, or against medicine and in favour of an absence of medicine. It is a structural study that sets out to disentangle the conditions of its history from the density of discourse, as do others of my works.[93]

And in his most explicit methodological discussion of archaeology, he writes:

> This unity certainly does not enable us to say of Linnaeus or Buffon, Quesnay or Turgot, Broussais or Bichat, who told the truth, who reasoned with rigour, who most conformed to his own postulates; nor does it enable us to say which of these *œuvres* was closest to a primary, or ultimate, destination, which would formulate most radically the general project of a science. But what it does reveal is the extent to which Buffon and Linnaeus (or Turgot and Quesnay, Broussais and Bichat) were talking about "the same thing," by placing themselves at "the same level" or at "the same distance," by deploying "the same conceptual field," by opposing one another on "the same field of battle"; and it reveals, on the other hand, why one cannot say that Darwin is talking about the same thing as Diderot, that Laennec continues the work of Van Swieten, or that Jevons answers the Physiocrats. It defines a limited space of communication.[94]

Vintage Books, 1988; originally published in 1961).

90. Michel Foucault, *The Order of Things*, Alan Sheridan, trans. (New York: Vintage Books, 1994; originally published in 1966).

91. See Dreyfus and Rabinow, *Michel Foucault: Beyond Structuralism and Hermeneutics*, 28.

92. Indeed, Dreyfus and Rabinow argue that archaeology attempts to bracket the *meaning* of these claims as well as their truth. See *Michel Foucault: Beyond Structuralism and Hermeneutics*, 13, 49.

93. Michel Foucault, *The Birth of the Clinic*, A. M. Sheridan Smith, trans. (New York: Vintage, 1994; originally published in 1963), xix.

94. Foucault, *The Archaeology of Knowledge*, 126.

Defenders of Foucault argue that this bracketing of truth is appropriate since Foucault is not engaged in the underlying scientific investigation but rather in exploring the history of the frameworks within which such investigations operate. Arnold Davidson, for example, contends that "Foucault's aim, in those of his books that worked out his archaeological method, was a thoroughly descriptive one."[95] Thus, these defenders argue, despite the risk of being read as a relativist or nihilist, Foucault's archaeological histories should not be read as undermining or even as attempting to evaluate the soundness of the practices under investigation. Against the notion that an archaeology is necessarily a kind of debunking, Foucault asks in a 1977 interview, "Why should an archaeology of psychiatry function as an 'anti-psychiatry', when an archaeology of biology does not function as an anti-biology?"[96]

Despite such disclaimers, Foucault has been widely read as a relativist or nihilist.[97] For any historian or sociologist of science, there is always a risk that the bracketing of the question of truth will be understood either as denying the ground-level truth claims under investigation or as a form of relativism according to which there are no rational grounds for the evaluation of the different frameworks. Of course, in principle historians need not adopt either stance. But it is very difficult not to read Foucault as attempting to stand outside of the tradition under examination and to argue that the contrast between madness and reason and a particular understanding of man are fundamentally mistaken. Despite his protestations that he is not interested in evaluating the underlying practice, there are many cases in which he cannot resist revealing his attitude toward these discourses. Most famously, perhaps, at the end of *The Order of Things* he seems to look forward to a new discourse in which *man* (understood, as above, as one who represents the external world) played no role: "As the archaeology of our thought easily shows, man is an invention of recent date. And one perhaps nearing its end."[98] It is also impossible to read numerous passages in *Madness and Civilization* as anything but condemnations. After initial quotes from Pascal and Dostoevsky, he begins his preface this way: "We have yet to write the history of that other form of madness, by which men, in an act of sovereign reason, confine their neighbors, and communicate and recognize each other through the merciless language of non-madness; to define the moment of this conspiracy before it was permanently established in the

---

95. Davidson, "Archaeology, Genealogy, Ethics," 223.

96. Michel Foucault, "The History of Sexuality" (first published in 1977) in *Power/Knowledge*, 192.

97. For the charge that Foucault is a relativist, see Hilary Putnam, *Reason, Truth, and History* (New York: Cambridge University Press, 1981), 155. For the charge that he is a nihilist, see Hayden White, "Michel Foucault" in *Structuralism and Since*, John Sturrock, ed. (New York: Oxford University Press, 1979), 81; and Michael Walzer, "The Politics of Michel Foucault," in *Foucault: A Critical Reader*, Hoy, ed., 61.

98. Foucault, *The Order of Things*, 387.

realm of truth, before it was revived by the lyricism of protest."[99] Later, he writes: "What is traditionally called 'progress' toward madness's attaining a medical status was in fact made possible only by a strange regression."[100] In the end, there is little doubt that Jon Simons is right: "Foucault's descriptive analyses of the limits of humanism are impassioned denunciations of the modern humanist regime."[101]

For better or worse, this attitude of oppositional condemnation solidified as Foucault moved into the next phase of his work. While in his archaeological period Foucault's principal concern was the operation of various discourses of knowledge, in the genealogies he becomes interested in how power relations shape those and other practices. No longer do linguistic practices appear to be autonomous; instead they are presented as the product of the exercise of power. The sciences of man are now understood as part of a wider operation of power in which modern society seeks to "normalize" human beings. Foucault focuses his attention on the operation of various forms of incarceration and surveillance, for example. Just as archaeology investigates the background conditions under which specific claims produced by subjects engaged in a discursive practice, genealogy investigates the background power structures within which the subject emerges. As Foucault explains:

> One has to dispense with the constituent subject, to get rid of the subject itself, that's to say, to arrive at an analysis which can account for the constitution of the subject within a historical framework. And this is what I would call genealogy, that is, a form of history which can account for the constitution of knowledges, discourses, domains of objects etc., without having to make reference to a subject which is either transcendental in relation to the field of events or runs in its empty sameness throughout the course of history.[102]

Genealogies, which attempt to identify the power relations through which subjects are constituted, cannot rely on the prior existence of such subjects.

J. G. Merquior, among others, detects a change in Foucault's attitude toward truth in the early 1970s, as his concerns became more overtly political. Foucault begins to "cast suspicion upon the very concept of truth, which was merely 'suspended' in the *Archaeology*. Hereafter, epistemological categories tended to be frankly 'politicized'. . . . [H]ere we have no welding of theory and practice, but rather a *collapse* of theory into practice."[103] Foucault begins to understand truth itself as a form of normalization and control, or even of violence: "We must conceive discourse as a violence that we do to things, or, at all events, as a practice we impose upon them. It is in this practice that the

---

99. Foucault, *Madness and Civilization*, ix.
100. Foucault, *Madness and Civilization*, 206.
101. Jon Simons, *Foucault and the Political* (New York: Routledge, 1995), 42.
102. Foucault, "Truth and Power," 117.
103. J. G. Merquior, *Foucault* (Modern Masters) (London: Fontana Press, 1985), 85.

events of discourse find the principle of their regularity."[104] As William Connolly explains: "The claim, in short, is that the will to truth that governs modernity is the will to extend discipline, to impose form over that which was not designed to receive it."[105] This reconceptualization of truth as merely the result of the play of power is central to Foucault's understanding of genealogy. In his most explicit statement of the genealogical method he comments that "all knowledge rests upon injustice."[106] In retrospect, it was easy for Foucault to reinterpret his earlier archaeological works as incomplete attempts to theorize the operation of power. In a 1977 interview he reflected: "When I think back now, I ask myself what else it was that I was talking about, in *Madness and Civilisation* or *The Birth of the Clinic*, but power? Yet I'm perfectly aware that I scarcely ever used the word and never had such a field of analyses at my disposal."[107]

As is the case with archaeology, the concern with power relations and institutional structures does not imply relativism or the reduction of truth to power. History, even genealogical history, need not be taken to reveal the emptiness of a discursive practice. But Foucault often takes it in just this way— an unmasking that reveals that behind a practice there lurks nothing but a power relation. As Joseph Rouse writes of Foucault's work in this period:

> The tone of Foucault's portrayal suggests that these new forms of power/knowledge ought to be resisted. Yet he resolutely rejects the idea that there is any ground or standpoint from which such a call to resistance could be legitimated. The connection he proposes between power and knowledge is not just a particular institutional *use* of knowledge as a means to domination. Foucault objects to the very idea of a knowledge or a truth outside of networks of power relations. The scope of his objection thus also encompasses the possibility of a critical knowledge that would speak the truth to power, exposing domination for what it is, and thereby enabling or encouraging effective resistance to it.[108]

This is most clear when Foucault attempts to draw normative or political implications from his work, especially in his interviews and lectures from the 1970s. Recall that genealogies aim to uncover the power relations that generate the subject. This gives them a more political aim as well, for Foucault suggests

---

104. Michel Foucault, "The Discourse on Language" (originally published in 1971) appendix to *The Archaeology of Knowledge*, 229.

105. William Connolly, "Taylor, Foucault, and Otherness," *Political Theory* 13, no. 3 (Aug. 1985), 366.

106. Michel Foucault, "Nietzsche, Genealogy, History" (originally published in 1971) in *Language, Counter-Memory, Practice*, 163.

107. Foucault, "Truth and Power," 115.

108. Joseph Rouse, "Power/Knowledge," in *The Cambridge Companion to Foucault*, Gutting, ed., 99.

that they will help us in to undermine the idea of the subject. For example, in one discussion published in 1971, he observes:

> The theory of the subject . . . can be attacked in two ways: either by a "desubjectification" of the will to power (that is, through political struggle in the context of class warfare) or by the destruction of the subject as a pseudosovereign (that is, through an attack on "culture": the suppression of taboos and the limitations and divisions imposed upon the sexes; the setting up of communes; the loosening of inhibitions with regard to drugs; the breaking of all the prohibitions that form and guide the development of a normal individual).[109]

Clearly he intends genealogy to contribute to the latter project. "Genealogical analyses," William Connolly declares, "disturb the sense of ontological necessity, historical inevitability, and purity of discrimination in established dualities of identity/difference, normality/abnormality, innocence/guilt, crime/accident, and responsible agent/delinquent offender."[110] They do this by showing that these apparently stable and permanent dualities are themselves merely the result of power relations.

It is in the works of Foucault's genealogical period—principally in *Discipline and Punish* and the first volume of *The History of Sexuality* together with various lectures and interviews—that we get a direct challenge to the contrast between reason and power that is implicit in the liberal principle of legitimacy. If genealogy reveals that power is always in the background (at least) of our knowledge claims, we must think of them not as in opposition to each other, but as together forming a new complex: power/knowledge. In a late interview published in 1983, Foucault denied that he identified knowledge with power: "studying their *relation* is precisely my problem."[111] But here is what he wrote about their relation in *Discipline and Punish*:

> We should admit rather that power produces knowledge (and not simply by encouraging it because it serves power or by applying it because it is useful); that power and knowledge directly imply one another; that there is no power relation without the correlative constitution of a field of knowledge, nor any knowledge that does not presuppose and constitute at the same time power relations. . . . In short, it is not the activity of the subject of knowledge that produces a corpus of knowledge, useful or resistant to power, but power-knowledge, the processes and struggles that traverse it and of which it is made up, that determines the forms and possible domains of knowledge.[112]

---

109. Foucault, "Revolutionary Action: 'Until Now,'" 222.

110. William Connolly, "Beyond Good and Evil: The Ethical Sensibility of Michel Foucault," *Political Theory* 21, no. 3 (Aug., 1993), 367

111. Foucault, "Critical Theory/Intellectual History," 43.

112. Michel Foucault, *Discipline and Punish*, Alan Sheridan, trans. (New York: Vintage, 1977; originally published in 1975), 27-28.

To be sure there is not a simple identification of knowledge and power: they "directly imply one another." The claim is that activities of knowledge, which one might have thought to be the product of subjects, are in fact the result of power relations.

Foucault argues that instead of evaluating the content of claims and their truth, we should focus on the power structures that generate those claims. In a revealing passage, he observes that "one's point of reference should not be to the great model of language (*langue*) and signs, but to that of war and battle. The history which bears and determines us has the form of a war rather than that of a language: relations of power, not relations of meaning."[113] There are immediate political implications that Foucault is eager to draw: "It's not a matter of emancipating truth from every system of power (which would be a chimera, for truth is already power) but of detaching the power of truth from the forms of hegemony, social, economic and cultural, within which it operates at the present time."[114]

At this point it becomes difficult not to ask: Why should we attempt to detach the power of truth from the current power relations within which it operates? Which system of power would be superior to the one(s) we have at the present time? But to ask these questions is already to miss Foucault's point. The lack of explicit normative grounding is not a mere oversight. It is an integral part of his genealogical method, as it was for Derrida. Thus, in one of his more amazing statements, remarkable for making explicit what is only implicit in so much poststructuralist work, he claims that "to imagine another system is to extend our participation in the present system."[115] We can make sense of this paradoxical position when we recall that for Foucault, "We must conceive discourse as a violence that we do to things."[116]As Peter Dews explains: "For Foucault, the mere fact of becoming an object of knowledge represents a kind of enslavement. Cognition is itself a form of domination."[117] But how is Foucault himself to escape from his own participation in such a form of domination?

Connolly attempts to defend Foucault this way:

> But Foucault, conceiving discourse as "a violence we do to things," cannot endorse [the] quest for attunement and self-realization. He proceeds at the second level, then, as a genealogist, deploying rhetorical devices to incite the experience of discord or discrepancy between the social construction of self, truth, and rationality and that

---

113. Foucault, "Truth and Power," 114. Compare, however, his hatred of polemics expressed in a late interview, "Polemics, Politics, and Problemizations," in *The Foucault Reader*, Paul Rabinow, ed. (New York: Pantheon, 1984), 381-382.

114. Foucault, "Truth and Power," 133.

115. Foucault, "Revolutionary Action: 'Until Now,'" 230. He continues: "Reject theory and all forms of general discourse. This need for theory is still part of the system we reject." (231)

116. Foucault, "The Discourse on Language," 229.

117. Dews, *Logics of Disintegration*, 177.

which does not fit neatly within their folds. And the recurrent experience of discord eventually shakes the self loose from the quest for a world of harmonization, a world in which the institutional possibilities for personal identity harmonize with a unified set of potentialities in the self, and the realization of unity in the self harmonizes with the common good realized by the social order. . . . Genealogy is not a claim to truth . . .; it exercises a claim upon the self that unsettles the urge to give hegemony to the will to truth.[118]

Instead of aiming at truth, genealogy has a strategic goal: precisely to disrupt the will to truth, the commitment to identity and permanence, and the goal of harmonizing the individual and common good. Given this goal, there is no need for any explicit reference to normative standards of evaluation or construction of a (potentially) superior system of power relations. Jon Simons defends an interpretation of Foucault similar to the political reading of Derrida we saw above: "Foucault offers an ethic of permanent resistance. The point is not that humanism can never be overcome, or that it can be replaced only by another system of domination, but that any mode of government entails limits that are apt to harden, tending to become permanent and rigid."[119] Like Connolly, Simons is untroubled by the fact that "Foucault is not systematic or explicit about what is wrong with that which arouses his oppositional passion. A great deal of the persuasive power of his work rests on the effect of his language and style rather than the elaboration of normative reasons for resistance."[120] These defenders of Foucault argue, therefore, that the positive political value of his work is not to be found in the content of the claims he makes but rather in the rhetorical effect which inspires us to recognize the radical contingency of our institutions, our ways of thinking, and our self-conceptions. Simons is explicit: "What matters [for Foucault] is frustration with and resentment of the present, including ourselves, rather than a better alternative."[121]

Indeed, any attempt to make explicit a political goal, such as a more just society, will be counterproductive—it will merely "extend our participation in the current situation." Foucault's insistence on this position is demonstrated very clearly in his debate with Noam Chomsky, published in 1974.[122] For Foucault, "the real political task in a society such as ours is to criticise the workings of institutions, which appear to be both neutral and independent; to criticise and attack them in such a manner that the political violence which has always exercised itself obscurely through them will be unmasked, so that one can fight

---

118. Connolly, "Taylor, Foucault, and Otherness," 368.

119. Simons, *Foucault and the Political*, 6. By "government" Foucault and Simons mean not only political institutions, but also self-governance.

120. Simons, *Foucault and the Political*, 42.

121. Simons, *Foucault and the Political*, 86.

122. Michel Foucault and Noam Chomsky, "Human Nature: Justice versus Power" in *Reflexive Water: The Basic Concerns of Mankind*, Fons Elders, ed. (London: Souvenir Press, 1974). Parenthetical references in this paragraph will be to this work.

against them." (171) Chomsky believes that this approach to political engagement is incomplete. In fact, he thinks, there are "two intellectual tasks." One is "to try to create the vision of a future just society." (172) Chomsky favors a form of "anarcho-syndicalism" in which all individuals can satisfy their "need for creative work, for creative inquiry, for free creation without the arbitrary limiting effect of coercive institutions." (169) The other task is "to understand very clearly the nature of power and oppression and terror and destruction in our own society." (172) That is, to understand how our institutions fail to live up to the ideal of a just society. He observes that simply unmasking the hidden operations of power is by itself no guide to political action: "it is of critical importance that we know what impossible goals we're trying to achieve, if we hope to achieve some of the possible goals." (175) With this, we come to the core of their disagreement:

> Foucault: One makes war to win, not because it is just.
>
> Chomsky: I don't personally, agree with that.
>   For example, if I could convince myself that attainment of power by the proletariat would lead to a terrorist police state, in which freedom and dignity and decent human relations would be destroyed, then I wouldn't want the proletariat to take power. In fact the only reason for wanting any such thing, I believe, is because one thinks, rightly or wrongly, that some fundamental human values will be achieved by that transfer of power.
>
> Foucault: When the proletariat takes power, it may be quite possible that the proletariat will exert towards the classes over which it has just triumphed, a violent, dictatorial and even bloody power. I can't see what objection one could make to this. (182)

What underlies this stark and startling contrast is Foucault's belief that since justice is an ideal that has been "formed within our civilisation, within our type of knowledge and our form of philosophy," it cannot be used "to describe or justify a fight which should—and shall in principle—overthrow the very fundaments of our society." (187)

It is perhaps unsurprising that during this period Foucault's work is at its most explicitly political. Foucault's tone in this period is often apocalyptic as he describes a completely controlled society in which everything and everyone is subject to surveillance and is normalized on the model of Bentham's panopticon.[123] As David Hoy observes: "Foucault paints the picture of a totally normalized society, not because he believes our present society is one, but because he hopes we will find the picture threatening."[124] To be sure, Foucault

---

123. See Foucault, *Discipline and Punish*, 195-228.

124. David Hoy, introduction to *Foucault: A Critical Reader*, Hoy, ed., 14. Notice the agreement with Connolly's and Simons's reading that Foucault is less interested in the accuracy or soundness of his account than in its rhetorical effect.

often includes a carefully placed qualification: "It is not that life has been totally integrated into techniques that govern and administer it; it constantly escapes them."[125] But even so, it is hard to see how there could be anything like genuine progress when "humanity installs each of its violences in a system of rules and thus proceeds from domination to domination."[126] At best, there might be room for local pockets of resistance. Indeed, he sometimes calls for the "reactivation of local knowledges" as a way of escaping "the established régimes of thought."[127] Yet, at other times, as Michael Walzer observes, "Foucault seems to see a grand alternative: the dismantling of the whole thing, the fall of the carceral city, not revolution but abolition."[128] What this alternative might be, of course, we cannot know since "to imagine another system is to extend our participation in the present system."[129]

This vacillation between nearly complete resignation and radical restructuring in unknown and unpredictable ways lies at the root of what can only be described as a series of appalling political judgments. Consider three examples which may seem to be little more than embarrassing lapses, yet are expressed with great urgency and conviction. First, in "A Discussion with Maoists," Foucault takes the position that "popular justice" cannot and should not be institutionalized in any system of courts: "the revolution can only take place via the radical elimination of the judicial apparatus, and anything which could reintroduce the penal apparatus, anything which could reintroduce its ideology and enable this ideology to surreptitiously creep back into popular practices, must be banished."[130] In reply to the query, "Then how is it to be regularised?" Foucault answers the only way he can: "it remains to be discovered. . . . The masses will discover a way of dealing with the problems of their enemies, of those who individually or collectively have harmed them, methods of retribution which will range from punishment to reeducation, without involving the form of the court which . . . is to be avoided."[131]

Next, consider this description of his well-known participation as a prison activist: "The ultimate goal . . . was not to extend the visiting rights of prisoners to thirty minutes or to procure flush toilets for the cells, but to question the social and moral distinction between the innocent and the guilty."[132] Foucault

---

125. Michel Foucault, *An Introduction*, vol. 1 of *The History of Sexuality*, Robert Hurley, trans. (New York: Random House, 1978; originally published in 1976), 143.

126. Foucault, "Nietzsche, Genealogy, History," 151.

127. Michel Foucault, "Two Lectures" (originally presented in 1976) in *Power/Knowledge*, 85, 81. Compare his "Revolutionary Action: 'Until Now,'" 227.

128. Walzer, "The Politics of Michel Foucault," 60.

129. Foucault, "Revolutionary Action: 'Until Now,'" 230.

130. Michel Foucault, "On Popular Justice: A Discussion with Maoists" (originally published in 1972) in *Power/Knowledge*, 16.

131. Foucault, "On Popular Justice," 28.

132. Foucault, "Revolutionary Action: 'Until Now,'" 227.

later turned on his former colleagues in the prison movement who, it seems, were attempting to follow his lead. In a 1977 interview he complains that the movement "has allowed itself to be penetrated by a whole naive, archaic ideology which makes the criminal at once into the innocent victim and the pure rebel—society's scapegoat—and the young wolf of future revolutions."[133] Now strictly speaking, questioning "the social and moral distinction between the innocent and the guilty" does not imply that we are all innocent. But surely in context, it was predictable that this would be the implication drawn. Furthermore, without some kind of normative guidance it is unclear how Foucault distinguishes between the transgressions of ordinary criminals and those whom he admires for their resistance to "the established régimes of thought" and goal of "overthrow[ing] the very fundaments of our society."

Finally, consider his admiration for the Iranian revolution in 1979. The revolution, Foucault believes, "has brought out . . . an absolutely collective will," and in light of this absolute unity: "Well, you have to salute it, it doesn't happen every day."[134] Foucault seems oddly untroubled by his cool observation that "There were demonstrations, verbal at least, of violent anti-semitism. There were demonstrations of xenophobia and directed not only at the Americans, but also at foreign workers who had come to work in Iran."[135] Apparently, we are to accept this in stride because "They don't have the same regime of truth as ours."[136]

Not surprisingly, Foucault's groundless militancy has found many critics. We will examine Habermas's critique and response in detail below, but briefly consider Nancy Fraser's important discussion.[137] For Fraser, Foucault's understanding of power is insightful and useful primarily for three reasons. First, Foucault understands that in the modern period power "does not emanate from some central source, but circulates throughout the entire social body down even to the tiniest and apparently most trivial extremities." (278) Second, in his genealogical period he emphasizes that an understanding of power is a matter of social institutions, not only of ideology. His position "rules out, that is, the view that given the appropriate objective material conditions, the only or main thing that stands in the way of social change is people's ideologically distorted perception of their needs and interests." (279) Finally, as Foucault understands power, it is not only repressive. It does not only "say no to what are defined as

---

133. Foucault, "Truth and Power," 130.

134. Michel Foucault, "Iran: The Spirit of a World without Spirit" (originally published in 1979) in *Michel Foucault: Politics, Philosophy, Culture*, 215.

135. Foucault, "Iran: The Spirit of a World without Spirit," 222.

136. Foucault, "Iran: The Spirit of a World without Spirit," 223.

137. Nancy Fraser, "Foucault on Modern Power: Empirical Insights and Normative Confusions," *Praxis International* 1, no. 3 (Oct. 1981). Parenthetical references in this and the next paragraph will be to this work.

illicit desires, needs, acts, and speech." Rather, "modern power is equally involved in *producing* all of these things." (281)

Nonetheless, despite these insights, for Fraser there is a crucial weakness: "Foucault's work ends up, in effect, inviting questions which it is structurally unequipped to answer." (281) Specifically:

> Foucault calls in no uncertain terms for resistance to domination. But why? Why is struggle preferable to submission? Why ought domination to be resisted? Only with the introduction of normative notions of some kind could Foucault begin to answer such questions. . . . Clearly what Foucault needs and needs desperately are normative criteria for distinguishing acceptable from unacceptable forms of power. (283, 286)

As we will see, this lack of attention to the norms with which to distinguish legitimate from illegitimate power forms part of Habermas's critique as well. In fact, many have raised similar questions, including, somewhat surprisingly, Dreyfus and Rabinow, who conclude their study of Foucault with several questions that they leave unanswered, including: "What is wrong with carceral society? Genealogy undermines a stance which opposes it on the grounds of natural law or human dignity, both of which presuppose the assumptions of traditional philosophy. . . . What are the resources which enable us to sustain a critical stance?"[138]

Before turning to Habermas's work, it is worth briefly pursuing Foucault's thinking into his final works. These developments were prematurely cut short by his death, and it is therefore unsurprising that there is considerable controversy in the secondary literature concerning how they should be understood. It may very well be that Foucault took the criticisms of people like Fraser and Habermas to heart. In a late interview he comments, "Now, obviously, if I had been familiar with the Frankfurt School, if I had been aware of it at the time, I would not have said a number of stupid things that I did say and I would have avoided many of the detours which I made while trying to pursue my own humble path—when, meanwhile, avenues had been opened up by the Frankfurt School."[139] In that interview, Foucault does not specify which "stupid things" he wishes he might have avoided, but in a recently published lecture originally delivered in 1980 he comments:

---

138. Dreyfus and Rabinow, *Michel Foucault: Beyond Structuralism and Hermeneutics*, 206.

139. Foucault, "Critical Theory/Intellectual History," 26. Compare his ironic comment: "I am interested in what Habermas is doing. I know that he does not agree with what I say—I am a little more in agreement with him." (Michel Foucault, "The Ethic of the Care for the Self As a Practice of Freedom," originally published in 1984, in *The Final Foucault*, James Bernauer and David Rasmussen, eds. [Cambridge: MIT Press, 1994], 18.)

When I was studying asylums, prisons, and so on, I insisted, I think, too much on the techniques of domination. What we can call discipline is something really important in these kinds of institutions, but it is only at one aspect of the art of governing people in our society. We must not understand the exercise of power as pure violence or strict coercion. Power consists in complex relations: these relations involve a set of rational techniques, and the efficiency of those techniques is due to a subtle integration of coersion-technologies and self-technologies.[140]

In his later work, Foucault's emphasis shifted from coercion-technologies, which involve violence or the threat of violence, to self-technologies, which involve techniques of self-mastery. What is especially striking about this late emphasis on self-mastery of the subject is that it implies a measure of freedom which (at a minimum) Foucault neglected to emphasize in his earlier work. In fact, he was able to write:

Power is exercised only over free subjects, and only insofar as they are free. By this we mean individual or collective subjects who are faced with a field of possibilities in which several ways of behaving, several reactions and diverse comportments may be realized. Where the determining factors saturate the whole there is no relationship of power; slavery is not a power relationship when man is in chains. (In this case it is a question of a physical relationship of constraint.)[141]

Since power works through free subjects, "There is no power without potential refusal or revolt."[142]

The degree to which this late work constitutes a major shift in his emphasis is a matter of dispute. Foucault himself has not helped in this matter. On the one hand, in the introduction to the second volume of *The History of Sexuality*, first published in 1984, he emphasizes the important shift that his thinking had undergone, and how his conception of this project changed since the publication of the first volume in 1976. He compares this shift to the development of his archaeology and genealogy: "It appeared that I now had to undertake a third shift, in order to analyze what is termed 'the subject.' It seemed appropriate to look for the forms and modalities of the relation to self by which the individual constitutes and recognizes himself *qua* subject."[143] On the other hand, as he often did before, he attempted to reinterpret his earlier work in light of these more recent concerns:

---

140. Michel Foucault, "About the Beginning of the Hermeneutics of the Self," (originally presented in 1980) *Political Theory* 21, no. 2 (May 1993), 204.

141. Michel Foucault, "The Subject and Power" in Dreyfus and Rabinow, *Michel Foucault: Beyond Structuralism and Hermeneutics*, 221.

142. Michel Foucault, "Politics and Reason" (Tanner Lectures, delivered in 1979) in *Michel Foucault: Politics, Philosophy, Culture*, 84.

143. Michel Foucault, *The Use of Pleasure*, vol. 2 of *The History of Sexuality*, Robert Hurley, trans. (New York: Vintage, 1990; originally published in 1984), 6.

I would like to say, first of all, what has been the goal of my work during the last twenty years. It has not been to analyze the phenomena of power, nor to elaborate the foundations of such an analysis.

My objective, instead, has been to create a history of the different modes by which, in our culture, human beings are made subjects.[144]

As Foucault became more interested in the creation of subjects, he also became interested in care of subjects and this introduces explicitly normative elements into consideration.[145] As Peter Dews writes in an article titled "The Return of the Subject in Late Foucault": "It is impossible not to read this [late] work both as an attempt to overcome the ambiguity of his earlier relation to concepts of power and emancipation, and an admission of the limits of the 'postmodern' thought which attempts to bypass the concept of the subject, and consequently destroys any coherent notion of freedom at all."[146]

The focus on the self-constitution of subjects gave Foucault the opportunity to ask new and important questions. How, for example, did Greek society think of its ethical concerns? Not, Foucault claims, as normalizing imperatives to be applied universally. Rather, "the principal target of this kind of ethics was an aesthetic one . . . [and] it was reserved for a few people in the population; it was not a question of giving a pattern of behavior for everybody."[147] Foucault is here approaching the issue of norms. Indeed, he goes on to ask rhetorically, "What strikes me is the fact that in our society, art has become something which is related only to objects and not to individuals, or to life. . . . But couldn't everyone's life become a work of art? Why should the lamp or the house be an art object, but not our life?"[148] Still, in an interview, Dreyfus and Rabinow press Foucault on whether he takes the aesthetic practices of the Greeks to be "an attractive and plausible alternative." His answer is unequivocal:

No! I am not looking for an alternative; you can't find the solution of a problem in the solution of another problem raised at another moment by other people. You see, what I want to do is not the history of solutions, and that's the reason why I don't accept the world "alternative." I would like to do genealogy of problems, of *problématiques*. My point is not that everything is bad, but that everything is dangerous, which is not exactly the same as bad. If everything is dangerous, then we

---

144. Foucault, "The Subject and Power," 208.

145. See, for example, Michel Foucault, *The Care of the Self*, vol. 3 of *The History of Sexuality*, Robert Hurley, trans. (New York: Vintage, 1986; originally published in 1984); and Michel Foucault, "The Ethic of Care for the Self As a Practice of Freedom," in *The Final Foucault*, Bernauer and Rasmussen, eds.

146. Peter Dews, "The Return of the Subject in Late Foucault," *Radical Philosophy* 51 (1989), 38.

147. Foucault, "On the Genealogy of Ethics: An Overview of Work in Progress," in Dreyfus and Rabinow, *Michel Foucault: Beyond Structuralism and Hermeneutics*, 230.

148. Foucault, "On the Genealogy of Ethics," 236.

always have something to do. So my position leads not to apathy but to a hyper- and pessimistic activism.[149]

Right up to the end, Foucault steadfastly refused to make explicit the grounds of his normative judgments.

When Foucault says that everything is dangerous and that we must remain active, he sets up a problem that he does not answer: What are the greatest dangers and in what direction should our activism be directed? As Chomsky pointed out in their debate, it is not enough to simply identify dangers, especially if everything is dangerous—we need to identify and assess feasible alternatives. If we focus on social and political institutions, our attention cannot help but be directed to the danger of the state (although it is clearly not the only source of danger). Is the state necessary to avoid even greater dangers and, if so, which forms best avoid those dangers and are least dangerous themselves? In other words, by the end of his life, Foucault had managed to work his way to the questions that have been the starting point of liberal political theory for the last 300 years.

In response to the charge that Foucault has failed even to address these basic issues in the evaluation of alternative arrangements, defenders of Foucault have two strategies. First, they may reply that Foucault's perspective allows us to open up new and different questions neglected by the Anglo-American moral philosophy.[150] For example, he raises the question of how "individuals are urged to constitute themselves as subjects of moral conduct . . . [by] setting up and developing relationships with the self, for self-reflection, self-knowledge, self-examination."[151] This very well may be, but it concedes the point: Foucault has little to offer in thinking about how our basic political and social institutions should be constituted. Indeed, in a late interview, he seems to agree: "I would more or less agree with the idea that in fact what interests me is much more morals than politics."[152] The problem, of course, is not that Foucault focuses on different questions—there is plenty of important intellectual work to be done beyond political theory. The problem is with the suggestion, which Foucault himself often encourages, that his work opens up new ways of doing political theory without having to engage in critical and explicit reflection on the norms with which one is making one's evaluations.

The other strategy adopted by some of Foucault's defenders is to go on the offensive. There is no need to make one's normative principles explicit, some claim, and the demand that we do so itself exhibits a dangerous attachment to *theory*. What Foucault's work allegedly shows is that we can have political

149. Foucault, "On the Genealogy of Ethics," 231-232.

150. See, for example, Davidson, "Archaeology, Genealogy, Ethics," 228-232.

151. Foucault, *The Use of Pleasure*, 29.

152. Michel Foucault, "Politics and Ethics: An Interview" (conducted in 1983) in *The Foucault Reader*, Rabinow, ed., 375.

engagement without being wed to the impossible goal of giving transparent foundations for our judgments. Dreyfus and Rabinow, for example, admit that "Foucault does not propound a normative theory, yet as Habermas points out, Foucault's work certainly has a normative thrust."[153] In their view, this is just the point: "maturity would consist in at least being willing to face the possibility that action cannot be grounded in universal, ahistorical theories of the individual subject and of writing, or in the conditions of community and speaking, and that, in fact, such attempts promote what all parties agree is most troubling in our current situation."[154] Foucault is supposed to offer a way out because his "interpretive approach consists in identifying what he takes to be our current problem, describing with detachment how this situation arose and, at the same time, using his rhetorical skills to reflect and increase shared uneasiness in the face of the ubiquitous danger as he extrapolated it."[155] But why is *theory* the greatest danger of our current situation?

As we saw, during his middle, most explicitly political period, Foucault attacked theory as inherently violent—indeed, at one point he associates it with genocide[156]—because he believed "all knowledge rests upon injustice" since "discourse is a violence that we do to things."[157] In his later work, however, he differentiated power from violence. But even with this differentiation, he still resisted making his normative principles explicit and subjecting them to critical reflection. Why, if language involves "power" in a non-violent sense, would he continue to resist such explication of his normative principles? According to Niko Kolodny, Foucault's point is no longer that theory is inherently totalitarian. Rather, his point is merely that philosophers' "faith in theory can blind them to its limitations and risks."[158] "Theory is risky," he writes, "because its practical effects are uncertain." (67) Thus: "Criticism should be guided by an 'attitude', Foucault suggests, not a system of principles." (70) For Kolodny, there is no doubt that Foucault made normative judgments without making their grounds explicit; he was, in Habermas's phrase, a "cryptonormativist." There is, however, a point to his evasions: "Foucault was reluctant to avow a normative theory, because he believed it would suggest to his critics that that was all that was at stake." (79) Instead of relying on principles, we must cultivate the proper ethos.

---

153. Hubert Dreyfus and Paul Rabinow, "What Is Maturity? Habermas and Foucault on 'What Is Enlightenment?'" in *Foucault: A Critical Reader*, Hoy, ed., 115.

154. Dreyfus and Rabinow, "What Is Maturity?" 118.

155. Dreyfus and Rabinow, "What Is Maturity?" 115.

156. Foucault, *An Introduction*, vol. 1 of *The History of Sexuality*, 137.

157. Foucault, "Nietzsche, Genealogy, History," 163; Foucault, "The Discourse on Language," 229.

158. Niko Kolodny, "The Ethics of Cryptonormativism: A Defense of Foucault's Evasions," *Philosophy and Social Criticism* 22, no. 5 (Sept. 1996), 67. Parenthetical references in this paragraph will be to this work.

Ian Hacking also illustrates the dictum that the best defense is a good offense. He suggests that the proper reply to those "self-styled pragmatists or Critical Theorists or academic social democrats" who "harass Foucault" about his lack of normative principles is that they should "start their critique with Kant" who, after all, "made freedom something that is necessarily outside the province of knowledge."[159] Kant is indeed the key figure in this debate, but Hacking's observation can be turned against him. While Kant is often identified as the classical exemplar of a theory-builder and exponent of rules, as Hacking points out he was also keenly aware of the limits of reason. Despite the way in which Kant is presented to generations of introductory philosophy students, Kant was very clear that the ability to follow a rule was insufficient for moral maturity: "Rules and formulas, those mechanical aids to the rational use, or rather misuse, of his natural gifts, are the shackles of a permanent immaturity."[160] Specifically, judgment is required since rules do not apply themselves:

> If understanding in general is to be viewed as the faculty of rules, judgment will be the faculty of subsuming under rules; that is, of distinguishing whether something does or does not stand under a given rule (*casus datae legis*). General logic contains, and can contain, no rules for judgment. . . . If it sought to give general instructions how we are to subsume under these rules, that is, to distinguish whether something does or does not come under them, that could only be by means of another rule. This in turn, for the very reason that it is a rule, again demands guidance from judgment. . . . A physician, a judge, or a ruler may have at command many excellent pathological, legal, or political rules . . . and yet, none the less, may easily stumble in their application.[161]

Kant, therefore, was well aware that theory alone—rules alone—were insufficient since a non-rule-governed judgment was necessary for a rule to be applied. Nonetheless, Kant did not let this insight prevent him from advocating critical reflection on our principles of action. Indeed, for Kant this was necessary for an action to have moral worth.[162] The point is simply this: the demand for

---

159. Ian Hacking, "Self-Improvement" in *Foucault: A Critical Reader*, Hoy, ed., 238, 239.

160. Immanuel Kant, "An Answer to the Question: What Is Enlightenment?" in *Perpetual Peace and Other Essays*, Ted Humphrey, trans. (Indianapolis: Hackett, 1983), 41 [Ak.36].

161. Immanuel Kant, *Critique of Pure Reason*, Norman Kemp Smith, trans. (St. Martin's, 1965), A132/B171 - A134/B173. See also *Groundwork of the Metaphysics of Morals*, Mary Gregor, ed. (New York: Cambridge University Press, 1997), 3 [Ak.389]; and "On the Proverb: That May Be True in Theory, but Is of No Practical Use" in *Perpetual Peace and Other Essays*, 61 [Ak.275].

162. See Christine Korsgaard, "From Duty and for the Sake of the Noble: Kant and Aristotle on Morally Good Action" in *Aristotle, Kant, and the Stoics*, Stephen Engstrom and Jennifer Whiting, eds. (New York: Cambridge University Press, 1996), especially

critical and explicit reflection on the normative standards on which one bases one's judgments need not be motivated by an objectionable fetish for theory.[163]

Contrary to the defenders of Foucault who attempt to denigrate the explication of normative principles, we do not have to choose between explicit rules or the correct ethos. In fact, as Kant argued, the correct ethos involves critical reflection on our principles of action. Making our normative principles explicit is a first step not only for a foundational philosophy to which Rorty (among others) objects. Instead, it may be a first step in the critical reflection on ourselves, our conduct, and our institutions. If Foucault truly abandoned the view that language was itself a form of violence, there could be no further objection to making explicit the principles on which he based his political judgments. To fail to make them explicit is simply to avoid critical scrutiny, and as we have seen, his political judgments were not beyond reproach. A recognition of our own fallibility leads to the need for critical reflection. I repeat: this need not be motivated by the futile search for a foundational grounding beyond dispute, but rather by the desire to push back the limits of what is taken for granted and unexamined. In fact, as we saw in chapter 2, this process is precisely what Rawls calls wide reflective equilibrium. With this thought, we turn to consider the work of Jürgen Habermas.

Habermas

There is little doubt that Jürgen Habermas is the most persistent and insightful left critic of poststructuralism.[164] This is not only because of the large volume of material that he has produced, much of it concerned explicitly with issues of modernity and postmodernity. It is also because Habermas has not been content merely to point out the shortcomings of the poststructuralists; he has attempted to develop a positive account of reason that escapes their criticisms. In this section, I cannot hope to provide a complete account of this

---

210.

163. Compare the discussion in Charles Larmore, *Patterns of Moral Complexity* (New York: Cambridge University Press, 1987), especially 1-21.

164. In this section, references to the following works by Habermas will be made parenthetically in the text using the following abbreviations: *TCA1—Reason and the Rationalization of Society*, vol. 1 of *The Theory of Communicative Action*, Thomas McCarthy, trans. (Boston: Beacon, 1984; originally published in 1981); *TCA2—Lifeworld and System: A Critique of Functionalist Reason*, vol. 2 of *The Theory of Communicative Action*, Thomas McCarthy, trans. (Boston: Beacon, 1987; originally published in 1981); *PDM—The Philosophical Discourse of Modernity*, Frederick Lawrence, trans. (Cambridge: MIT Press, 1987; originally published in 1985); *MCCA—Moral Consciousness and Communicative Action*, Christian Lenhardt and Shierry Weber Nicholsen, trans. (Cambridge: MIT Press, 1990; originally published in 1983); *BFN—Between Facts and Norms*, William Gehg, trans. (Cambridge: MIT Press, 1996; originally published in 1992).

project—to say nothing of Habermas's many other concerns. My discussion, therefore, will be guided by the relationship of Habermas's work to two poles: the poststructuralists on one side and Rawls on the other.

The core of Habermas's work is his theory of "communicative action" which was given its most complete articulation in two massive volumes first published in 1981. These volumes span the fields of philosophy, linguistics, and sociology. Predecessors to this project include Kant, Hegel, Marx, Durkheim, Weber, Mead, the Frankfurt School, Austin, Parsons, and Searle. For the most part, however, this work is not directly political. Habermas himself has called it "hopelessly academic."[165] Thus, it might be surprising that the motivation for this work was explicitly, albeit, indirectly political: "my real motive in beginning the book in 1977 was to understand how the critique of reification, the critique of rationalization, could be reformulated in a way that would offer a theoretical explanation of the crumbling of the welfare-state compromise and of the potential for a critique of growth in new movements, without surrendering the project of modernity or descending into post- or anti-modernism, 'tough' new conservatism or 'wild' young conservatism."[166]

A useful starting point for approaching Habermas's diagnosis of and alternative to poststructuralism is Max Weber's theory of the rationalization of society. For Weber, modernity is characterized by a "disenchanted" view of the world. Associated with the triumph of the scientific world view, Weber postulates the triumph of *Zweckrationalität*, or "instrumental reason," as the primary mode of practical reasoning. On this view, the rational subject deploys scientific knowledge to identify efficient means with which to pursue her ends. But in restricting the authority of reason to questions of efficiency alone, our capacity rationally to evaluate ends withers. We become trapped in an "iron cage," endlessly pursuing the expansion of wealth and power without the ability to identify the ends that these should properly serve. Of the culmination of this process, Weber famously remarks: "For of the last stage of this cultural development, it might well be truly said: 'Specialists without spirit, sensualists without heart; this nullity imagines that it has attained a level of civilization never before achieved.'"[167]

Obviously for Weber there is a high cost to this process of rationalization—most importantly, the loss of freedom and meaning as individuals participate in complex systems that are driven by their own instrumental imperatives. But he recognizes benefits as well—principally increased efficiency in the organization

---

165. Jürgen Habermas, "The Dialectics of Rationalization" (interview conducted in 1981) in *Autonomy and Solidarity*, revised edition, Peter Dews, ed. (New York: Verso, 1992), 108.

166. Habermas, "The Dialectics of Rationalization," 108; cf. 106. Habermas often refers to the poststructuralists as "young conservatives."

167. Max Weber, *The Protestant Ethic and the Spirit of Capitalism*, Talcott Parsons, trans. (London: Unwin Hyman, 1930), 182.

of an exceedingly complex society and a huge expansion in productivity. As Habermas explains: "Weber is full of admiration for the organizational accomplishments of modern bureaucracies, but when he adopts the perspectives of members and clients, and analyzes the objectification of social relations in organizations as depersonalizing, he describes the rationality of bureaucracies that have been cut loose from vocational-ethical attitudes, from value-rational attitudes in general, and have developed their own internal dynamics, in terms of the image of a rationally operating machine." (*TCA2*, 307)

For many theorists, especially on the left, this temperate assessment of the gains and losses of modern social organization was upset by the horrors of the twentieth century. In the aftermath of the Holocaust, Stalinism, and Hiroshima, their balance sheets tipped strongly against instrumental reason. If this is what the rationalization of society meant—increasingly efficient killing machines and inhuman bureaucracy—there was a serious question whether we might be better off without it. (See *TCA1*, 366-367.) The classic statement of such a view is the *Dialectic of Enlightenment*, written by Max Horkheimer and Theodor Adorno in exile from Nazi Germany in 1944. It begins this way: "In the most general sense of progressive thought, the Enlightenment has always aimed at liberating men from fear and establishing their sovereignty. Yet the fully enlightened earth radiates disaster triumphant."[168] As Habermas points out, in the aftermath of the "political disappointments at the absence of revolution in the West, the development of Stalinism in Soviet Russia, and the victory of fascism in Germany . . . it becomes intelligible how the impression could indeed get established in the darkest years of the Second World War that the last sparks of reason were being extinguished from this reality and had left the ruins of a civilization in collapse without any hope." (*PDM*, 116-117)

As Habermas reconstructs it, Horkheimer and Adorno's position is a radicalization of *ideology critique*. For Habermas, ideology critique can be understood as follows:

> Critique becomes ideology critique when it attempts to show that the validity of a theory has not been adequately dissociated from the context in which it emerged; that behind the back of the theory there lies hidden an inadmissible *mixture of power and validity*, and that it still owes its reputation to this. (*PDM*, 116)

The radical move proposed by Horkheimer and Adorno is to suspect that ideology critique does not have clean hands itself. The thought is that ideology critique is implicated in an unholy mixture of power and validity: "Then doubt reaches out to include reason, whose standards ideology critique had found already given in bourgeois ideals and had simply taken at their word." (*PDM*,

---

168. Max Horkheimer and Theodor Adorno, *Dialectic of Enlightenment*, John Cumming, trans. (New York: Herder and Herder, 1972; reprint, New York: Continuum, 1999; originally published in 1944), 1.

116) Specifically, it is charged: "As instrumental, reason assimilated itself to power and thereby relinquished its critical force—that is the *final* disclosure of ideology critique applied to itself." (*PDM*, 119) In fact, as Habermas sees it, this is the core charge that virtually all critics of modernity have embraced:

> In the discourse of modernity, the accusers raise an objection that has not substantially changed from Hegel and Marx down to Nietzsche and Heidegger, from Bataille and Lacan to Foucault and Derrida. The accusation is aimed against a reason grounded in the principle of subjectivity. And it states that this reason denounces and undermines all unconcealed forms of suppression and exploitation, of degradation and alienation, only to set up in their place the unassailable domination of rationality. Because this regime of a subjectivity puffed up into a false absolute transforms the means of consciousness-raising and emancipation into just so many instruments of objectification and control, it fashions for itself an uncanny immunity in the form of a thoroughly concealed domination. (*PDM*, 55-56)

Habermas distinguishes several strategies that critics of modernity adopt in light of this analysis. For us, the relevant strategy is that of those who attempt to take "critique out of the hands of reason." (*PDM*, 59)[169] The proponents of this strategy are "easily recognizable by a prefix, by the neologisms formed with the prefix 'post.'" (*PDM*, 59)

Although he defends the enlightenment project broadly conceived, Habermas feels the pull of the critiques of Weber, Horkheimer and Adorno, and Foucault. He agrees that there is a danger, one which Foucault in particular helps us to identify, of "a humanism that has been brought down from heaven to earth and has become a normalizing form of violence." (*PDM*, 283) But for Habermas, the belief that the rationalization of society must inevitably generate an "iron cage" and loss of freedom itself reveals an inadequate understanding of reason. Specifically, he argues that this understanding of reason is based on "the philosophy of consciousness" which is now "exhausted." (*PDM*, 296; cf. *TCA1*, 386) The philosophy of consciousness, or the philosophy of the subject, begins with a picture of the individual subject confronting the objective world. When this subject engages in practical deliberation, she imposes purposes or ends on the world and attempts to identify means with which to accomplish them. Rationalization, on this model, results in an exclusive focus on efficiency without any room for the rational assessment or adjustment of the ends served. It is simply a matter of manipulation and control—an expression of an underlying will to power and domination.

---

169. Compare Jürgen Habermas, "Modernity versus Postmodernity," *New German Critique* 22 (winter 1981), 13-14; and Jürgen Habermas, "Modernity: An Unfinished Project," in *Habermas and the Unfinished Project of Modernity*, Maurizio Passerin d'Entrèves and Seyla Benhabib, eds. (Cambridge: MIT Press, 1996; originally published in 1981), 53-54.

If the instrumental conception of reason is to be resisted, we must look for an alternative model other than that of the individual subject attempting efficiently to realize her arbitrary ends. Habermas's alternative is to understand reason as *intersubjective*. This is most clearly revealed in communicative action. This is the core and the most strikingly original element of Habermas's work—the idea that by unpacking what is implicit in ordinary communication, we will reveal the hidden norms of a rationality neglected by the philosophy of consciousness. Furthermore, these norms are presupposed by the very theorists working within the assumptions of the philosophy of consciousness. The theory of communicative action "studies the suppositions of rationality inherent in ordinary communicative practice and conceptualizes the normative content of action oriented to mutual understanding in terms of communicative rationality." (*PDM*, 76)

To understand how Habermas attempts to capture the normativity implicit in communicative action, we must distinguish different orientations that an individual may adopt toward interaction with others:

> We call an action oriented to success *strategic* when we . . . assess the efficiency of influencing the decisions of a rational opponent. . . . By contrast, I shall speak of *communicative* action whenever the actions of the agents involved are coordinated not through egocentric calculations of success but through acts of reaching understanding. In communicative action participants are not primarily oriented to their own individual successes; they pursue their individual goals under the condition that they can harmonize their plans of action on the basis of common situation definitions. (*TCA1*, 285-286; cf. 101; and *MCCA*, 58, 133-134)

If two (or more) subjects undertake communicative action, they orient themselves not to achieving a pre-given goal but toward establishing a rational consensus as the basis for their interaction. With this as their aim, a speaker making a claim must be prepared (at least in principle) to redeem that claim by being able to give reasons in its defense. In fact, the speaker must be able to respond to three possible challenges: to the truth of the claim, to its appropriateness, and to its sincerity.[170] Focusing on the first dimension, Habermas explains: "A speech-act offer has a coordinating effect because the speaker, by raising a validity claim, concomitantly takes on a sufficiently credible guarantee to vindicate the claim with the right kind of reasons, should this be necessary." (*BFN*, 18)[171] Indeed, for Habermas this potential for asking for and giving reasons is necessary for even understanding a claim: "A hearer

---

170. See *TCA1*, 99, 307, and *MCCA*, 58. As we shall see, Habermas adopts Weber's view that modern societies (unlike pre-modern ones) differentiate arguments concerned with each of these dimensions of assessment.

171. See the discussion in William Hohengarten, translator's introduction to Jürgen Habermas, *Postmetaphysical Thinking*, (Cambridge: MIT Press, 1992; originally published in 1988), x.

understands the meaning of an utterance when . . . he knows those *essential conditions* under which he could be motivated by a speaker to take an affirmative position." (*TCA1*, 298, notes omitted; cf. *BFN*, 19) The key to communicative action is that it aims at uncoerced agreement. "The rationality inherent in this practice is seen in the fact that a communicatively achieved agreement must be based *in the end* on reasons. And the rationality of those who participate in this communicative practice is determined by whether, if necessary, they could, *under suitable circumstances*, provide reasons for their expressions." (*TCA1*, 17)

Habermas believes that those working within the philosophy of consciousness fail to attend sufficiently to the rationality implicit in communicative action. For Weber, for example, "What counts as fundamental is not the interpersonal relation between at least two speaking and acting subjects—a relation that refers back to reaching understanding in language—but the purposive activity of a solitary acting subject." (*TCA1*, 279) Thus, for Weber, "the only aspects of action open to objective appraisal are the *effectiveness* of a causal intervention into an existing situation and the *truth* of the empirical assumptions that underlie the maxim or the plan of action—that is, the subjective belief about a purposive-rational organization of means." (*TCA1*, 281) In contrast, "In communicative action, the very outcome of interaction is even made to depend on whether the participants can come to an agreement among themselves on an *intersubjectively valid* appraisal of their relations to the world." (*TCA1*, 106)

Despite his emphasis on communicative action, Habermas does not believe that all actions are instances of this type. Sometimes we simply take our goal for granted and attempt to determine the best way to achieve it. Furthermore, not all actions involving language are instances of communicative action. Sometimes we take a use of language to be the most effective way of achieving our goal. Habermas makes this point explicitly:

> On the other hand, not every linguistically mediated interaction is an example of action oriented to reaching understanding. Without doubt, there are countless cases . . . [in which,] on the basis of an already habitual communicative practice of everyday life, one subject inconspicuously harnesses another for his own purposes, that is, induces him to behave in a desired way by manipulatively employing linguistic means and thereby instrumentalizes him for his own success. (*TCA1*, 288)

But if we aim at achieving mutual understanding and agreement, we commit ourselves to at least being able to give reasons rather than treating one another as means only and manipulating each other in an effort to bring about a pre-given goal. "From the perspective of the participants, coming to an understanding is not an empirical event that causes de facto agreement; it is a process of mutually convincing one another in which the actions of participants are coordinated on the basis of motivating by reasons. 'Coming to an understanding' refers to communication aimed at achieving a valid agreement." (*TCA1*, 392; cf. 287)

Although not all uses of language are instances of communicative action, Habermas thinks that it is clear that sometimes, at least, we really do aim at mutual understanding and not strategic manipulation. Furthermore, Habermas argues that the effectiveness of strategic uses of language depends on the existence of communicative uses. Cases in which "one subject inconspicuously harnesses another for his own purposes, that is, induces him to behave in a desired way by manipulatively employing linguistic means" are "parasitic" on the existence of a linguistic community with established practices of communicative reason.[172] And to repeat, when we do engage in communicative action, we commit ourselves to providing reasons for our claims in terms that others could recognize as good reasons and adjusting our own commitments in light of the reasons that others cite.

When we engage in communicative reason, we reject manipulating others through power relations or mere rhetoric. In the ideal, participants rely only on the "unforced force of the better argument." (*PDM*, 130) In particular:

> Anyone who seriously engages in argumentation must presuppose that the context of discussion guarantees in principle freedom of access, equal rights to participate, truthfulness on the part of participants, absence of coercion in adopting positions, and so on. If the participants genuinely want to convince one another, they must make the pragmatic assumption that they allow their "yes" and "no" responses to be influenced solely by the force of the better argument.[173]

Now this ideal speech situation is never fully realized in practice. Yet in order to engage in communicative action, participants must assume that these ideal conditions have been implemented to a sufficient degree:

> Once participants enter into argumentation, they cannot avoid supposing, in a reciprocal way, that the conditions for an ideal speech situation have been sufficiently met. And yet they realize that their discourse is never definitively "purified" of the motives and compulsions that have been filtered out. As little as we can do without the supposition of a purified discourse, we have equally to make do with "unpurified" discourse. (*PDM*, 323)[174]

---

172. The initial quote is from *TCA1*, 288. The term "parasitic" is from *PDM*, 199. See also Habermas, *Postmetaphysical Thinking*, 153, quoted below. Compare the structurally similar account that Kant provides of false promises in the *Groundwork*, 15 [Ak.403].

173. Jürgen Habermas, *Justification and Application: Remarks on Discourse Ethics*, Ciaran Cronin, trans. (Cambridge: MIT Press, 1993; first published in 1991), 31.

174. Compare Jürgen Habermas, *Communication and the Evolution of Society*, Thomas McCarthy, trans. (Boston: Beacon Press, 1979; originally published in 1976), 3; and Habermas, *Justification and Application*, 55-56.

This point has been misunderstood, and it is important to emphasize that the ideal speech situation is a regulative ideal. Habermas is well aware that all actual speech acts are incomplete realizations of the standards to which speakers are implicitly committed. In any actual dialogue, there will always be rhetorical elements, for example, which cannot fully be redeemed by reasons: "the pure types of action oriented to mutual understanding are merely limit cases. In fact, communicative utterances are always embedded in various world relations at the same time." (*TCA2*, 120)[175] The point is that we can use this ideal speech situation as the basis for criticism of the failure of actual arguments to respond to the "unforced force of the better argument." Actual breakdowns may be nefarious, as when one participant lies strategically, or they may be unintended, as when there is an unrecognized difference in the understanding of a term or disagreement about a relevant fact. In either case, the ideal speech situation functions as a critical reference point, although never fully attainable in practice.

The payoff for analyzing the "inescapable presuppositions" (*MCCA*, 89) of certain kinds of interactions is Habermas's identification of an ineliminable idealizing or universalizing element. As we have just seen, every actual interaction among real persons, whether strategic or communicative, will be made in a context of specific power relations among the participants. But when participants adopt the attitude of communicative reason, they commit themselves to abstracting beyond those particularities and to a structure of communication that "rules out all external or internal coercion other than the force of the better argument and thereby also neutralizes all motives other than that of the cooperative search for truth." (*MCCA*, 89) Communicative action, although instantiated in particular contexts, aspires to transcend them. As Habermas dramatically puts it:

> There is no pure reason that might don linguistic clothing only in the second place. Reason is by its very nature incarnated in contexts of communicative action and in structures of the lifeworld. . . . Agreement arrived at through communication, which is measured by the intersubjective recognition of validity claims, makes possible a networking of social interactions and lifeworld contexts. Of course, these value claims have a Janus face: As claims, they transcend any local context; at the same time, they have to be raised here and now and be de facto recognized if they are going to bear the agreement of interaction participants that is needed for effective cooperation. The transcendent moment of *universal* validity bursts every provinciality asunder; the obligatory moment of accepted validity claims renders them carriers of a *context-bound* everyday practice. (*PDM*, 322)

---

175. Compare Habermas, *Postmetaphysical Thinking*, 205, and Habermas, *Justification and Application*, 55-56.

The analysis of communicative reason reveals how our ordinary interactions carry with them a transcendent element in their aspiration to intersubjective validity.

It is important to recognize, however, that despite Habermas's identification of an ideal speech situation, he rejects the traditional aspiration of "first philosophy" or "ultimate justification."[176] As we will see, Habermas emphasizes that *as a philosopher* he has nothing to contribute to the content of instances of communicative reason. The validity of a claim is to be redeemed through an actual discourse that aims to approximate the ideal as closely as is possible. In other words, it is not Habermas's claims about the ideal speech situation, but rather the claims made by participants in such a discourse that carry the justificatory weight: "Communicative reason thus makes an orientation to validity claims possible, but it does not itself supply any substantive orientation for managing practical tasks—it is neither informative nor immediately practical." (*BFN*, 5) Habermas is not himself telling us how to go about justifying validity claims beyond (trivially) telling us to look for the better reasons and then (not trivially) pointing out what we must presuppose if we are to do that. The claims made in such a dialogue, while fallible and therefore not beyond challenge, aspire to a transcendent status: "The theory of communicative action aims at the moment of unconditionality that, with criticizable validity claims, is built into the conditions of processes of consensus formation. *As claims* they transcend all limitations of space and time, all the provincial limitations of the given context." (*TCA2*, 399) As Peter Dews observes, "For Habermas, in other words, it is not the *universality* of philosophical truth-claims which is to be abandoned, but rather their non-fallibilist aspect."[177]

We can now turn to Habermas's account of the poststructuralists. Consider, first, Derrida. Habermas can agree with Derrida that meaning is never fully resolved by elements currently present to subjects. As we have seen, Habermas insists that meaning depends on the hypothetical ability to answer challenges with reasons. That is, meaning depends, in part, on what would be said, and these hypothetical elements, as Derrida insists are never fully present. Furthermore, Habermas would even agree that every actual speech act may involve elements of rhetoric and manipulation. Nonetheless, in opposition to Derrida, he insists that communicative action involves a commitment to being able to redeem claims by reason when challenged. As Habermas puts it, Derrida "overgeneralizes this one linguistic function—namely, the poetic." (*PDM*, 207) Finding rhetorical elements always to be present, Derrida collapses language into a strategic tool for the instrumental manipulation of others. Derrida's emphasis on rhetoric prevents him from seeing the possibility of using language

---

176. See Jürgen Habermas, "Questions and Counterquestions," in *Habermas and Modernity*, Richard Bernstein, ed. (Cambridge: MIT Press, 1985), 196; and *MCCA*, 95-98.

177. Peter Dews, editor's introduction in *Autonomy and Solidarity*, 24.

in a cooperative search for the truth. Although there is always a mix, Habermas insists that we can differentiate speech acts in which rhetorical and poetic elements are dominant from those in which they have a minor role. As Thomas McCarthy explains:

> As Habermas reconstructs it, the heart of this argument is whether or not it is possible to draw a viable distinction between everyday speech (as it functions within contexts of communicative action) and poetic discourse. If not, then the aestheticizing of language proposed by Derrida carries, with the consequence that any given discourse can properly be analyzed by rhetorical-literary means. . . . In the communicative practice of everyday life, language functions as a medium for dealing with problems that arise within the world. . . . In Derrida and his followers, Habermas argues, language's capacity to solve problems disappears behind its world-creating capacity.[178]

Furthermore, for Habermas even the highly rhetorical, poetic uses of language depend on the existence of meaning, which in turn depends on the structures of communicative action. Habermas gives "primacy to world-disclosing language—as the medium for the possibility of reaching understanding, for social cooperation, and for self-controlled learning processes—over world-generating subjectivity."[179] Even if Derrida and his followers conceive of his work as highly rhetorical and eschewing reason giving, it is ultimately dependent on the structures of communicative reason for its sense.

Habermas believes that at their core, the positions of Derrida and Foucault are caught in a "performative contradiction." (*MCCA*, 80-81) In making their claims, they must presuppose what they are explicitly denying: "The radical critique of reason exacts a high price for taking leave of modernity. In the first place, these discourses can and want to give no account of their own position." (*PDM*, 336) In the last section, we saw Nancy Fraser's criticism that Foucault "needs desperately . . . normative criteria for distinguishing acceptable from unacceptable forms of power."[180] Habermas agrees and calls Foucault's position a form of "cryptonormativism." (*PDM*, 284) It implicitly relies, that is, on normative standards that it refuses to recognize explicitly. In a challenge similar to that of Fraser, Habermas asks: "if [genealogy] is just a matter of mobilizing counter-power, of strategic battles and wily confrontations, why should we muster any resistance at all against this all-pervasive power circulating in the bloodstream of the body of modern society, instead of just adapting ourselves to it? . . . why fight at all?" (*PDM*, 283-284)

Habermas's account actually cuts deeper than Fraser's, however. Fraser argues that Foucault relies on evaluative norms that he does not make explicit

---

178. Thomas McCarthy, introduction to Jürgen Habermas, *The Philosophical Discourse of Modernity*, xii-xiii. See also *PDM*, 209.

179. Habermas, *Postmetaphysical Thinking*, 153.

180. Fraser, "Foucault on Modern Power," 286.

when he considers different practices involving power relations. The key point for Habermas, however, is not simply that Foucault makes ungrounded evaluations of various social institutions and practices. Rather, the point is that there are covert (and some rather explicit) evaluations of reason itself. And because of this, Foucault is involved in a performative self-contradiction—he must assume implicitly what he is denying explicitly:

> [Foucault's] investigations are caught exactly in the self-referentiality that was supposed to be excluded by a naturalistic treatment of the problematic of validity. . . . That is to say, [according to Foucault] the meaning of validity claims consists in the power effects they have. On the other hand, this basic assumption of the theory of power is self-referential; if it is correct, it must destroy the foundations of the research inspired by it as well. But if the truth claims that Foucault himself raises for his genealogy of knowledge were in fact illusory and amounted to no more than the effects that this theory is capable of releasing within the circle of its adherents, then the entire undertaking of a critical unmasking of the human sciences would lose its point. (*PDM*, 279)

That is, if everything—including Foucault's own speech acts—are merely the result of a play of power, then there is no validity claim implicit in Foucault's linguistic actions. He is merely trying to influence his readers strategically, not trying to give them reasons to believe his claims. If this is correct, then he can offer us no reason to engage in the project of unmasking the power relations behind reason in the first place. But that is precisely what he apparently is attempting to do. As with Derrida, Habermas shares a good deal with Foucault, but rejects his most important conclusions. Foucault has done important historical work in unmasking the power relations behind sciences that claim to have none. For Habermas, however, this "critique of the domineering thought of subject-centered reason" must be "diagnosed not as an excess but as a deficit of rationality." (*PDM*, 310) Because the poststructuralists remain trapped in the philosophy of consciousness, they fail to see communicative reason as the untapped source for a critique of instrumental reason.

One might suspect that Habermas, at this point, would attempt to deduce moral norms from those implicit in communicative action. After all, the presumptions of the ideal speech situation have a decidedly moral flavor: freedom of all to participate on equal terms without coercion. Thus, he would attempt to show that Foucault not only implicitly makes assumptions about the non-coercive force of reason, but that this commits him to a moral point of view. Remarkably, in an interview conducted just before his death, Foucault seems to endorse this kind of position: "In the serious play of questions and answers, in the work of reciprocal elucidation, the rights of each person are in some sense immanent in the discussion. They depend only on the dialogue situation."[181]

---

181. Michel Foucault, "Polemics, Politics, and Problemizations," in *The Foucault Reader*, Rabinow, ed., 381-382. Foucault explains his dislike of polemics: "The

Many people have thought that Habermas makes this argument, but it is not the path he takes.

Habermas insists explicitly and repeatedly that moral norms cannot simply be read off of the presuppositions of the ideal speech situation. Rather, they are the substantive product of such a dialogue. In other words, the validity of moral claims is to be redeemed through the actual use of communicative reason, not by examining its presuppositions:

> One cannot demonstrate a transfer of this kind as Apel and Peters try to do, namely by deriving basic ethical norms *directly* from the presuppositions of argumentation. Basic norms of law and morality fall outside the jurisdiction of moral theory; they must be viewed as substantive principles to be justified in practical discourses. Since historical circumstances change, every epoch sheds its own light upon fundamental moral-practical ideas. Nevertheless, in such practical discourses we always already make use of substantive normative rules of argumentation. It is *these rules* alone that transcendental pragmatics is in a position to derive. (*MCCA*, 86)[182]

There is no way for a philosopher (or anyone) to identify ahead of time how such dialogues will turn out and what norms will be justified in the end. On the other hand, as we shall see, there is no prohibition on philosophers (or anyone) taking part in such dialogues which, in principle, are open to universal participation. Recall that for Habermas the ideal speech situation is not supposed to provide a foundational or deductive basis that short-circuits the actual discussion—precisely the contrary. The weight of justification is carried by the reasons identified in such a discourse. We need actually to make the moral arguments for or against certain norms, citing good moral reasons.

Thus, the structure of communicative reason and the model of the ideal speech situation applies not only to the redemption of empirical claims that aspire to truth but also claims that certain norms are valid. Here Habermas believes "everyday life," in fact, has an edge on "philosophical ethics":

> In philosophical ethics, it is by no means agreed that the validity claims connected with norms of action, upon which commands or "ought" sentences are based, can, analogously to truth claims, be redeemed discursively. In everyday life, however, no one would enter into moral argumentation if he did not start from the strong presupposition that a grounded consensus could in principle be achieved among those involved. (*TCA1*, 19)

---

polemicist, on the other hand, proceeds encased in privileges that he possesses in advance and will never agree to question. On principle, he possesses rights authorizing him to wage war and making that struggle a just undertaking; the person he confronts is not a partner in the search for the truth, but an adversary, an enemy who is wrong, who is harmful and whose very existence constitutes a threat." (382)

182. See also Habermas, *Justification and Application*, 57-58; and *BFN*, 4-5.

Accordingly, Habermas's metaethics is a form of cognitivism. This might suggest that normative claims are true or false in the same way that empirical claims are. Habermas rejects this inference. (See, e.g., *MCCA*, 52, 54, 59-62, 68, 76) Claims about norms are not true or false of an independent order, but rather assert what forms of cooperative interaction would themselves be the product of communicative reason. Specifically, "the validity of any norm means in the end only that it *could* be accepted with good reasons by *everyone* involved." (*TCA2*, 94) More technically, Habermas formulates the following "principle (D)" to identify valid moral (and legal) norms: "Just those action norms are valid to which all possibly affected persons could agree as participants in rational discourses." (*BFN*, 107)[183] This is the core of Habermas's project of "discourse ethics" which attempts "to reformulate Kant's ethics by grounding moral norms in communication." (*MCCA*, 195)

For Habermas, then, moral norms are to be redeemed discursively, in actual dialogues that aim to approximate the ideal speech situation. Moral norms, like empirical claims, aspire to universal validity (although not in the same way). But not all evaluative claims can be redeemed in this way. The simple fact is that "There is an indissoluble element of arbitrariness (*Willkür*) in the choice of a life project." (*TCA2*, 109) It is crucial, therefore, to distinguish between claims concerning the evaluation of a good life, which will be tied to arbitrary and contingent factors, and claims concerning the norms of coordination among individuals, which aspire to unconditional universality. Accordingly, Habermas distinguishes between *evaluative* and *moral* claims:

> Thus the development of the moral point of view goes hand in hand with a differentiation within the practical into *moral questions* and *evaluative questions*. Moral questions can in principle be decided rationally, i.e., in terms of *justice* or the generalizability of interests. Evaluative questions present themselves at the most general level as issues of the *good life* (or of self-realization); they are accessible to rational discussion only *within* the unproblematic horizon of a concrete historical form of life or the conduct of an individual life. (*MCCA*, 108; cf. 121, 178, 180-181, 196-197, and *TCA2*, 397)

Principles of justice are based on generalizable interests, while evaluative questions are tied to interests that may vary for different individuals and communities. What is motivating Habermas is not a belief that we cannot or should not evaluate our conceptions of the good life. We can and should do so within various particular groups and communities. However, we cannot expect to be able to provide a full defense of our evaluative judgments that could be accepted by all in an ideal speech situation, because such judgments are tied to

---

183. Compare *MCCA*, 197. This principle is not to be confused with the related principle (U) which is a "bridging principle" from specific arguments to validity of moral claims. See *BFN*, 107-109, 459-460. Compare this recent view to that in *MCCA*, 63, 65-66, 86-94.

particular ways of life.

> A deontological moral theory that concentrates on questions of justice pays for the presumptive general validity of moral judgments with a narrow concept of morality. But it does not thereby banish questions of the good or unfailed life from the pale of rational treatment. It need only maintain that ethical discussions, in contrast to moral arguments, are always already embedded in the traditional context of a hitherto accepted, identity-constituting form of life. Moral judgments differ from ethical judgments only in their degree of contextuality.[184]

It is an appreciation of the diversity of conceptions of the good, therefore, that lies at the heart of Habermas's distinction between evaluative questions about the nature of the good life and moral questions about the nature of justice.

Thomas McCarthy describes Habermas's discourse ethics as follows:

> If taking modern pluralism seriously means giving up the idea that philosophy can single out a privileged way of life, or provide an answer to the question "How should I (we) live?" that is valid for everyone, it does not, in Habermas's view, preclude a general theory of a much narrower sort, namely a theory of justice. The aim of the latter is to reconstruct the moral point of view as the perspective from which competing normative claims can be fairly and impartially adjudicated.[185]

What is striking about this passage is that it reveals how very close discourse ethics is to justice as fairness. Both see justice as the fair adjudication of conflicting but permissible conceptions of the good. Unsurprisingly, given this perspective, Habermas, like Rawls, asserts that the principles of justice constrain permissible conceptions of the good, but do not determine a unique one: "If it is to be a good life, these identities may not contradict moral demands, but their substance cannot itself be justified from universalistic points of view." (*TCA2*, 110) Neither Rawls nor Habermas denies that we can reflect critically on our conception of the good, but both insist that reflection on justice carries a higher burden of universality, since it will be imposed on all in the face of diverse conceptions of the good life. The treatment of the relationship between the right and the good, therefore, constitutes an especially deep point of contact between the two theories.

There are also important points of agreement between the two at the institutional level, but to see this we must return to Habermas's relation to Weber. Habermas agrees with Weber that the process of modernization has been problematic. For Habermas, however, these problems cannot be laid at the feet of modernity. Rather, they are the result of a distorted or incomplete process of modernization. As we have seen, Habermas rejects Weber's characterization of

---

184. Habermas, *Justification and Application*, 105; cf. 2, 62-63.
185. Thomas McCarthy, introduction to *Moral Consciousness and Communicative Action*, viii.

"the iron cage" of modernization since he holds out the possibility of the growth not only of instrumental rationality but of communicative rationality as well. But Habermas does share Weber's characterization of pre-modern societies. Such societies are typically organized around a religious or quasi-religious world view in which normative imperatives are taken to be holy, that is, beyond rational dispute. Furthermore, there is no differentiation of the value spheres that we take for granted:

> From Durkheim to Lévi-Strauss, anthropologists have repeatedly pointed out the peculiar *confusion between nature and culture*. We can understand this phenomenon to begin with as a mixing of two object domains, physical nature and the sociocultural environment. Myths do not permit a clear, basic, conceptual differentiation between things and person, between objects that can be manipulated and agents—subjects capable of speaking and acting to whom we attribute linguistic utterances. . . . Moral failure is conceptually interwoven with physical failure, as is *evil* with *harmful*, and *good* with the *healthy* and the *advantageous*. (*TCA1*, 48)

The process of modernization and de-mythologization leads to a differentiation of types of validity claims and cultural value spheres. Specifically, modern societies differentiate reasons relating to empirical truth, normative rightness, and sincerity or authenticity. (*TCA1*, 249)[186] For Weber, this differentiation generates a loss of meaning as these spheres compete with one another in the absence of any comprehensive framework of understanding. In contrast, for Habermas, the process of modernization opens up the possibility of a critical and productive deployment of reason: "the authority of the holy is gradually replaced by the authority of an achieved consensus. This means a freeing of communicative action from sacrally protected normative contexts." (*TCA2*, 77) Or at least this potential emerges in modern societies. We can rely on instrumental reasons when determining how to manipulate the world to achieve our ends, on moral reasons when reflecting on our social relations, and on aesthetic reasons when dealing with our own expressive authenticity. In its place, each of these types of reasoning is appropriate.

With the eclipse of traditional world views, a diversity of incompatible comprehensive doctrines emerges. When this happens, social coordination can no longer be based on the assumption of a shared and unquestioned system of meanings. At this point Habermas distinguishes between *social integration* and *system integration*: "In one case [social integration] the action system is integrated through consensus, whether normatively guaranteed or communicatively achieved; in the other case [system integration] it is integrated through the nonnormative steering of individual decisions not subjectively coordinated." (*TCA2*, 150) The former is achieved in traditional societies where

---

186. See also Habermas, "Modernity: An Unfinished Project," 45. Notice that these correspond to the three dimensions according to which a speech act can be challenged. See note 170, above.

a shared world view is in place as background—what Habermas calls a "lifeworld"—or when consensus is achieved through communicative action. Markets, on the other hand, are the most important mechanism for system integration. Actions are coordinated not on the basis of a communicatively achieved consensus concerning shared ends, but rather through the use of the non-linguistic "steering medium" of money. (The other example Habermas frequently discusses is the steering medium of power, especially in bureaucratic organizations.) Unfortunately, Habermas sometimes describes such non-linguistically mediated interactions as "norm-free." (See, e.g., *TCA2*, 150, 171.) This is surely mistaken and gives the impression that the market is somehow the natural condition of interaction. As Habermas himself shows, however, the norms of the market are themselves social accomplishments. The real point of the contrast is that markets allow interactions to occur with a minimal overlap among the lifeworlds of the interacting parties. Market interaction requires consensus only about what counts as money and a valid contract and the like, rather than requiring the introduction of complete systems of values. System integration allows regular interaction without requiring the resolution of disagreements concerning the worth of the ends being pursued.

It is crucial to recognize that Habermas does not object to the development of media-steered systems, per se. In fact, he is critical of Marx for failing to recognize "the *intrinsic* evolutionary *value* that media-steered sub-systems possess." (*TCA2*, 339; cf. 318) Habermas has a subtle appreciation of the gains and losses associated with system integration:

> If responsibility means that one can orient one's actions to criticizable validity claims, then action coordination that has been detached from communicatively achieved consensus no longer requires responsible participants. This is one side of the matter. The other side is that relieving interaction from yes/no positions on criticizable validity claims—which actors themselves have to defend and for which they hold one another accountable—also enhances the degrees of freedom of action oriented to success. (*TCA2*, 263; cf. 184-185)

In complex and diverse societies, markets are absolutely crucial in order to relieve individuals of the burden of identifying a shared set of ends. When interactions are mediated by money, individuals may participate in such systems without reaching a consensus on ends and there is no requirement that they defend their goals to one another. But precisely because of this, no individual views him- or herself as responsible for the collective outcome of the interactions. Furthermore, when individuals interact on the basis of non-linguistic steering media, they adopt a strategic attitude toward one another.

Again, Habermas recognizes the necessity of relying on non-linguistic steering media and "bureaucratization has to be viewed, to begin with, as a normal component of modernization processes." (*TCA2*, 318) However, there is a risk of "internal colonization" of the lifeworld when steering media and instrumental reason crowd out communicative action:

> To the degree that the economic system subjects the life-forms of private households and the life conduct of consumers and employees to its imperatives, consumerism and possessive individualism, motives of performance, and competition gain the force to shape behavior. The communicative practice of everyday life is one-sidedly rationalized into a utilitarian life-style; this media-induced shift to purposive-rational action orientations calls forth the reaction of a hedonism freed from the pressures of rationality. As the private sphere is undermined and eroded by the economic system, so too is the public sphere by the administrative system. (*TCA2*, 325)

One of the troubling results of such colonization is the attitude that citizens develop toward their political and legal institutions. Strategically oriented toward their own ends alone, relieved of the burden of providing justifications that all can share, individuals begin to view their political participation in narrowly instrumental terms. Law comes to be viewed merely as an external imposition, limiting one's ability to pursue one's subjective ends. For Habermas, such an attitude is dangerous to the stability of society. Although force is the immediate guarantor of the authority of laws, in the end the stability of a political regime can only be achieved by a general recognition of its legitimacy by its citizens: "No stable social order can emerge from the contingent clashes of different expected interest-positions and competing calculations of success." (*BFN*, 67; cf. *TCA2*, 188) When individuals generally take an exclusively external perspective on their own laws, society faces a "legitimation crisis."

Now we can see that while Habermas does not dispute Weber's claim that modern capitalistic societies have been characterized by a loss of meaning and freedom, he does not attribute this to modernization as such. Rather it is due to an incomplete modernization in which system integration has dominated social integration; that is, the lifeworld has been colonized:

> The deformations that interested Marx, Durkheim, and Weber—each in his own way—ought not be attributed either to the rationalization of the lifeworld as such or to increasing system complexity as such. . . . It is not the uncoupling of media-steered subsystems and of their organizational forms from the lifeworld that leads to the one-sided rationalization or reification of everyday communicative practice, but only the penetration of forms of economic and administrative rationality into areas of action that resist being converted over to the media of money and power because they are specialized in cultural transmission, social integration, and child rearing, and remain dependent on mutual understanding as a mechanism for coordinating action. (*TCA2*, 330)

In *The Theory of Communicative Action* Habermas presents the incursion of economic and administrative rationality into domains where communicative reason should hold sway as a problem endemic to capitalism:

Between capitalism and democracy there is an *indissoluble* tension; in them two opposed principles of societal integration compete for primacy. . . . The normative meaning of democracy can be rendered in social-theoretical terms by the formula that the fulfillment of the functional necessities of *systemically* integrated domains of action shall find its limits in the integrity of the lifeworld, that is to say, in the requirements of domains of action dependent on *social* integration. . . . The internal systemic logic of capitalism can be rendered in social-theoretical terms by the formula that the functional necessities of systemically integrated domains of action shall be met, if need be, even at the cost of *technicizing* the lifeworld. (*TCA2*, 345)

Habermas looks to the "new social movements"—such as the antinuclear, environmental, and feminist movements—to resist the incursion of system imperatives (of markets and bureaucracies) into the communicative structures of the lifeworld. (*TCA2*, 392-395)

In his more recent work on law, Habermas has continued to investigate the relationship between system integration, which relies on strategic reasoning, and social integration, which relies on communicative reasoning.[187] The law, Habermas now emphasizes, can be viewed from two points of view. On the one hand, compliance is enforced and so individuals may view it as an external constraint on their pursuit of their good. On the other hand, it claims legitimacy for itself and therefore maintains that its imperatives could be redeemed through communicative reason.

Depending on the chosen perspective, the legal norm presents a different kind of situational element: for the person acting strategically, it lies at the level of social facts that externally restrict her range of options; for the person acting communicatively, it lies at the level of obligatory expectations that, she assumes, the legal community has rationally agreed on. . . . The legal validity of a norm—and this is its point—means, now, that *two things* are guaranteed *at the same time*: both the legality of behavior, in the sense of an average norm compliance that, if necessary, is enforced by sanctions; and the legitimacy of the rule itself, which always makes it possible to follow the norm out of respect for the law. (*BFN*, 31; cf. 448)

Thus, the law occupies a position touching both system rationality and communicative reason. But why do we need such institutional mechanisms that can be viewed from both points of view? Habermas answers: "Under the modern conditions of complex societies, which require self-interested and hence normatively neutralized action in broad spheres, the paradoxical situation arises in which *unfettered* communicative action can neither unload nor seriously bear the burden of social integration falling to it." (*BFN*, 37) As we have seen, Habermas believes that because of the differentiation of value spheres in modern societies and the resulting diversity of lifeworlds, system integration is

---

187. Some have argued that Habermas's recent work downplays the dangers of system integration which he previously highlighted. See the discussion in Peter Dews, *The Limits of Disenchantment*, 195, 200.

necessary. Furthermore: "Both media of systemic integration, money and power, are anchored via legal institutionalization in orders of the lifeworld, which is in turn socially integrated through communicative action." (*BFN*, 40) In other words, it is through law that citizens "*come to some understanding* about the *normative regulation of strategic interactions.*" (*BFN*, 26-27) Because law has a foot in media-steered subsystems as well as in communicatively redeemable norms, we can view it from either of these perspectives: as an external constraint on our strategic actions or as a normatively valid expression of our communicative action.

From this understanding of law, Habermas argues for two conclusions. First, from the side of social integration, "the concept of modern law . . . already harbors the *democratic idea* developed by Rousseau and Kant: the claim to legitimacy on the part of a legal order built on rights can be redeemed only through the socially integrative force of the 'concurring and united will of all' free and equal citizens." (*BFN*, 32) Second, from the side of system integration, "We can then also see, from a historical perspective, that the core of modern law consists of private rights that mark out the legitimate scope of individual liberties and are thus tailored to the strategic pursuit of private interests." (*BFN*, 27) In other words, implicit in this understanding of law is a commitment both to democracy and to individual rights. For Habermas, there is an "internal relation between the rule of law and democracy" since "the individual liberties of the subjects of private law and the public autonomy of enfranchised citizens make each other possible." (*BFN*, 454)

Law reveals how both social and system integration—communicative and strategic interaction—are necessary in modern societies. When exercising public autonomy, that is, when exercising their rights to democratic participation in the political process, citizens must orient themselves to the common good and aim to "*reach an understanding* about the rules for their living together," rather than taking a strategic attitude and using their political power for their own narrow interests. (*BFN*, 84) On the other hand,

> private autonomy extends as far as the legal subject does *not* have to give others an account or give publicly acceptable reasons for her action plans. Legally granted liberties entitle one to *drop out of* communicative action, to refuse illocutionary obligations; they ground a privacy freed from the burden of reciprocally acknowledged and mutually expected communicative freedoms. (*BFN*, 120)

In other words, law protects "private autonomy" which "forms a protective cover for the individual's ethical freedom to pursue his own existential life project or, in Rawls's words, his current conception of the good." (*BFN*, 451) A just society allows individuals considerable scope to engage in strategic interactions with one another (for example, through markets); this allows them to coordinate their actions without having to reach consensus concerning their value orientations. The laws which regulate these strategic interactions, however, are to be established and justified through communicative reason.

This point can be made in terms of the relationship between two kinds of liberties: the so-called liberties of the ancients (including rights of political participation and in the establishment of law) and the liberties of the moderns (including liberties of conscience, thought, expression, and property). It is often claimed that liberalism gives priority to the liberties of the moderns by starting with a notion of atomistic individuals with their natural individual rights. These rights are supposed to set limits on what laws sovereign power can enact and also to generate a right to democratic participation since democracy is supposed to afford the best protection for the natural rights.[188] Other theorists, often called "civic republicans," grant priority to the liberties of the ancients. They attempt to generate rights purely from the requirements of active participation in civic institutions and democratic structures. Rights which do not make such a contribution, or hinder the collective decision-making ability of the community, are given a low priority. As Habermas observes, "From both perspectives, human rights and popular sovereignty do not so much mutually complement as compete with each other." (*BFN*, 99)

Habermas claims that since on his analysis both sets of rights originate in the dual structure of modern law, he is able to generate "a system of rights that gives *equal weight* to both the private and the public autonomy of the citizen." (*BFN*, 118) Although Rousseau and Kant attempted to identify a common source for both sets of rights, they failed in opposite directions: "On the whole, Kant suggests more of a liberal reading of political autonomy, Rousseau a republican reading." (*BFN*, 100) Indeed, Habermas goes so far as to claim that "Thus far no one has succeeded in satisfactorily reconciling private and public autonomy at a fundamental conceptual level." (*BFN*, 84) Habermas apparently treats Rawls as a typical liberal who grants priority to the liberties of the moderns. Yet, although there may be some uncertainty about what Habermas would count as a reconciliation "at a fundamental conceptual level," I believe his account is strikingly similar to that of Rawls.

For Rawls, as for Habermas, both sets of liberties are co-original—neither derives from nor is reducible to the other. All of the basic liberties are specified in terms of the model of the person (which is itself determined by the

---

188. Rawls claims that Isaiah Berlin holds such a view. See *Political Liberalism* (New York: Columbia University Press, 1993; paperback edition, 1996), 299. Habermas misreads this passage, believing that Rawls is himself endorsing this view. See Jürgen Habermas, "Reconciliation through the Public Use of Reason: Remarks on John Rawls's Political Liberalism," in *The Inclusion of the Other*, Ciaran Cronin and Pablo de Greiff, eds. (Cambridge: MIT Press, 1998; originally published in 1996), 70; and Rawls, *Political Liberalism*, 404n39. Compare *A Theory of Justice*, 233 [205], where Rawls is already explicit: "Of course, the grounds for self-government are not solely instrumental."

requirements of a stable and fair system of cooperation), and they are chosen by the parties in the original position. Unlike classical liberals, Rawls does not grant priority to the liberties of the moderns.[189] Justice as fairness recognizes no pre-social state in which individuals have natural rights that constrain the system of rights and liberties in a just society. Nor does justice as fairness attempt to deduce all basic liberties from the requirements of a democratic procedure. Recently, Joshua Cohen has defended justice as fairness against "proceduralist" critics who argue that many liberal rights illegitimately interfere with democracy. These critics recognize that the right to vote, for example, is a necessary component of a democratic procedure and so must be protected from the will of the majority. But they hold that religious liberties, in contrast, are simply restrictions on the majority, not required by the democratic procedure itself and therefore not worthy of a high level of protection.

In reply, Cohen argues that democracy should be understood as "a substantive, not simply a procedural, ideal."[190] This ideal conceives of political justification as the result of "free public reasoning among equals."[191] On this approach, the basic liberties are not limited to those that are necessary for participation in the political procedures. They also include those rights that make political decisions legitimate and binding. The legitimacy of law requires not only rights of participation (the liberties of the ancients), but also a guarantee that the political process will not infringe on certain core liberties (the liberties of the moderns). These are basic liberties that reasonable citizens would not be willing to subject to a binding collective decision. If the political process fails to recognize and protect basic religious liberties, for example, it is no less illegitimate than one which arbitrarily excludes some individuals from participation. Because of its fundamental commitment to public justification and the liberal principle of legitimacy, justice as fairness holds a substantive conception of democracy, and it generates both political and non-political liberties from a common source: the original position.

Furthermore, like Habermas, Rawls recognizes a fundamental contrast between the models of the instrumental reason, embodied in the market, and communicative reason—Rawls's "public reason"—embodied in democratic political institutions. For Rawls, the market gives space within which individuals and associations may pursue their own (permissible) conception of the good, "secure in the knowledge that elsewhere in the social system the necessary

---

189. This is not to say that there cannot be conflicts among basic liberties. Even Habermas concedes this. See *BFN*, 180. Rawls discusses the resolution of such conflicts in Lecture 8 of *Political Liberalism*, "The Basic Liberties and Their Priority."

190. Joshua Cohen, "Pluralism and Proceduralism," *Chicago-Kent Law Review* 69, no. 3 (1994), 594.

191. Joshua Cohen, "Procedure and Substance in Deliberative Democracy," in *Democracy and Difference*, Seyla Benhabib, ed. (Princeton: Princeton University Press, 1996), 99.

corrections to preserve background justice are being made."[192] It relieves them of the burden of providing a full justification for (as opposed merely to establishing the permissibility of) their goals. But, Rawls insists, such market mechanisms must be embedded within broader political institutions: "Free market arrangements must be set within a framework of political and legal institutions which regulates the overall trends of economic events and preserves the social conditions necessary for fair equality of opportunity."[193] And, of course, for Rawls, these political structures must be democratic.

It is often asserted that liberals understand democracy as a system of aggregating private interests or preferences.[194] Certainly this is how some see it, but not Rawls. Democratic institutions are not merely mechanisms for the expression and aggregation of private interests. When addressing matters of basic social justice, justice as fairness requires that citizens, as well as legislators and other officials, act (and specifically vote) according to their judgment of the requirements of the public reason.[195] Rawls's picture, like that of Habermas, is one in which individuals have liberties to participate in institutions within which they may reason instrumentally in pursuit of their diverse conceptions of the good. These institutions are regulated by political structures, and individuals also have the right to participate in these institutions. When they participate in these political institutions to address matters of basic social justice, however, they must act on the basis of reasons not tied to their own particular conception of the good but only on those that can be shared by all (reasonable) citizens. Thus, for both Rawls and Habermas politics is (in part) concerned with establishing a public consensus shared by all reasonable citizens concerning the scope of permissible strategic action by individuals and groups.

For many years, despite the important points of contact between their theories, it was rare to find a detailed comparison of Rawls and Habermas. Recently, this situation has dramatically reversed. Thanks to the important work of Kenneth Baynes and Thomas McCarthy among others, we now have important studies of the relationship between Rawls and Habermas.[196] Both Baynes and McCarthy emphasize their common Kantian heritage and many important points of agreement. But both tend to read Rawls as presenting an incompletely developed variation of Habermas's approach. Although there have

---

192. Rawls, *Political Liberalism*, 269.

193. Rawls, *A Theory of Justice*, 73 [63].

194. On the contrast between aggregative and deliberative models of democracy see Cohen, "Procedure and Substance in Deliberative Democracy," 98-102.

195. See Rawls, *Political Liberalism*, 215, 219-220. See also Rawls's discussion of the contrast between the market and democratic political procedures in *A Theory of Justice*, 359-360 [316-317].

196. See, for example, Kenneth Baynes, *The Normative Grounds of Social Criticism* (Albany: SUNY Press, 1992), and Thomas McCarthy, "Kantian Constructivism and Reconstructivism: Rawls and Habermas in Dialogue," *Ethics* 105, no. 1 (Oct. 1994).

been various criticisms that Habermas and his followers have pressed against Rawls, there is one that cuts to the heart of justice as fairness. It has been raised by Habermas for many years right up though the recent exchange between them in the *Journal of Philosophy*, and it has also been repeated by numerous commentators.[197] Before discussing this point, I should stress however, that both Habermas and Rawls recognize the deep affinities between their theories. There is every reason to take seriously the words with which Habermas prefaced his recent remarks on *Political Liberalism*: "Because I admire this project, share its intentions, and regard its essential results as correct, the dissent I express here will remain within the bounds of a family quarrel."[198]

Habermas has expressed the criticism I will examine in various ways, but essentially the charge is that although Rawls purports to identify principles that can be accepted by all reasonable persons, he presents himself as the sole judge of what is acceptable. Real dialogue, Rawls allegedly thinks, is not necessary:

> Like Kant, Rawls operationalizes the standpoint of impartiality in such a way that every individual can undertake to justify basic norms on his own. . . . It is only logical, therefore, that Rawls views the substantive parts of his study (e.g., the principle of average utility), not as the *contribution* of a participant in argumentation to a process of discursive will formation regarding the basic institutions of late capitalist society, but as the outcome of a "theory of justice," which he as an expert is qualified to construct. (*MCCA*, 66)

Habermas insists that actual discourses "have to be carried through *in fact* and cannot be replaced by monological mock dialogue." (*TCA2*, 95) As we have seen, Habermas contends that there is no way to determine ahead of time what reasons would be cited in an ideal speech situation. We must actually engage in such argumentation in order to test the validity of the claims and results that would be identified there. Rawls, Habermas suggests, remains trapped in the philosophy of consciousness that he inherits from Kant.

In fact, I think Habermas exaggerates the extent to which Kant is properly described as working within the philosophy of consciousness.[199] Indeed, if there is a connection between the philosophy of consciousness and an instrumental conception of reason, even Habermas should be suspicious of this description.[200] For Kant, reason is, at its core, public.[201] Describing the idea of a critique of

---

197. See *The Journal of Philosophy* 92, no. 3 (March 1995).

198. Habermas, "Reconciliation through the Public Use of Reason," 50.

199. A similar criticism is made by Tracy Strong and Frank Andreas Sposito, "Habermas's Significant Other," in *The Cambridge Companion to Habermas*, Stephen White, ed. (New York: Cambridge University Press, 1995), 267-273.

200. Habermas is obviously aware that Kant rejects an instrumental conception of reason. See *TCA1*, 345.

201. As I explain in the conclusion, Kant does contrast public and private uses of reason, but both are essentially intersubjective.

reason, he writes: "Reason depends on this freedom for its very existence. For reason has no dictatorial authority; its verdict is always simply the agreement of free citizens, of whom each one must be permitted to express, without let or hindrance, his objections or even his veto."[202] Elsewhere, in a passage that could serve as the founding principle for Habermas's work, he distinguishes objective validity from illusion this way: "The touchstone whereby we decide whether our holding a thing to be true is conviction or mere persuasion is therefore external, namely, the possibility of communicating it and of finding it to be valid for all human reason."[203] Finally, as we will see in the conclusion, Kant insists on the importance of the "public use of reason" in the project of enlightenment.[204]

Our main concern, however, is with Rawls. Why would Habermas assume that Rawls conceives of justice in a "monological" fashion? The answer, I think, is because of an analogy between their theories that is almost impossible to resist: the comparison between the ideal speech situation and the original position. Habermas makes this analogy explicit: "The general presuppositions of argumentation have the same status in discourse ethics as the construction of the original position in Rawls's theory of justice."[205] After all, each theorist conceives of principles of justice as being generated from some kind of hypothetical choice situation. Rawls's account does, it might seem, rely on a monological choice in the original position. As Rawls points out, since the parties in the original position are "equally rational and similarly situated . . . we can view the choice in the original position from the standpoint of one person selected at random. If anyone after due reflection prefers a conception of justice to another, then they all do, and a unanimous agreement can be reached."[206] If we focus on this comparison, it is hard not to side with Habermas since the ideal speech situation seems better to capture the idea that the principles of justice are those that real citizens—not artificial representatives for them—would choose from a fair choice situation.

I want to suggest, however, that the comparison between the ideal speech situation and the original position is misconceived from the start. Recall that the original position is a device that is introduced to help us reach reflective equilibrium:

> The original position is an analytic device used to formulate a conjecture. . . . That the principles so agreed to [in the original position] are indeed the most reasonable ones is a conjecture, since it may of course be incorrect. We must check it against the fixed points of our considered judgments at different levels of

---

202. Kant, *Critique of Pure Reason*, A739/B767.
203. Kant, *Critique of Pure Reason*, A820/B848.
204. Kant, "What Is Enlightenment?" 41-42 [Ak.36]. I should also mention the centrality of publicity in Kant's understanding of justice. See "To Perpetual Peace: A Philosophic Sketch" in *Perpetual Peace and Other Essays*, 135-136 [Ak.381].
205. Habermas, *Justification and Application*, 163. Compare *MCCA*, 198.
206. Rawls, *A Theory of Justice*, 139 [120].

generality. We also must examine how well these principles can be applied to democratic institutions and what their results would be, and hence ascertain how well they fit in practice with our considered judgments on due reflection.[207]

For Rawls, what ultimately justifies a conception of justice is the arguments that we use to reach full reflective equilibrium. These include not only the considerations available to the parties in the original position, but also the reasons we have for setting up the original position in the first place.

As we have seen, participants in Habermas's ideal speech situation do not simply repeat to each other that whatever principles they endorse will be valid. Instead, they give reasons to adopt one view or another. They aim at getting it right. This is exactly what Rawls himself is doing and what he would have us do in our effort to reach full reflective equilibrium. It is not, however, what the parties in the original position are doing. This suggests that the proper comparison is between the participants in the ideal speech situation (searching for the most favored principles of justice that they can identify) and what Rawls sometimes calls the perspective "of you and me" in our effort to reach full reflective equilibrium.[208]

Understood in this way, justice as fairness is not monological.[209] Rawls is simply making a proposal concerning which conception of justice is most favored and which arguments for and against that conception are good arguments. In other words, he is making a substantive proposal to the public at large, assuming that the conditions for dialogue are realized here and now to a sufficient degree. Sometimes Habermas, too, reads Rawls this way, for example, when he writes: "To the extent to which a moral theory touches on substantive areas—as Rawls's theory of justice does, for example—it must be understood as a contribution to a discourse among citizens." (*MCCA*, 94) Oddly, however, as we have seen, Habermas denies that Rawls sees his own work that way: "Rawls views the substantive parts of his study . . . not as the *contribution* of a participant in argumentation . . . but as the outcome of a 'theory of justice,' which he as an expert is qualified to construct." (*MCCA*, 66)

In any event, for Habermas, contributions to the debate concerning substantive principles of morality or justice are not the proper goal of philosophy. It is not that philosophers should not engage in such debates. For decades Habermas himself has been an active participant in debates about practical political issues in Germany,[210] and he admires Rawls for seeking to make such a practical contribution. His point is simply that we should not confuse this with philosophy:

---

207. Rawls, *Political Liberalism*, 381; cf. 72.

208. See, for example, *Political Liberalism*, 28.

209. Rawls points this out in *Political Liberalism*, 383.

210. See Max Pensky, "Universalism and the Situated Critic," in *The Cambridge Companion to Habermas*, White, ed.

[Philosophers] can sometimes—if only rarely—be useful people. If they are, they may write books like that of Rawls, for instance. Rawls hasn't systematically cared when he speaks as a philosopher and when he speaks simply as a committed liberal in his society. This is what I think philosophers should also do: forget about their professional role and bring what they can do better than others into a common business. But the common business of political discourses among citizens nevertheless stays what it is. It is not a philosophical enterprise.[211]

It is true that Rawls has not distinguished when he speaks "as a philosopher" and when as a member of the public. But why should Habermas insist on making this distinction in the first place?

The answer, in part, concerns Habermas's narrow understanding of the role of philosophy. For Habermas, philosophy has nothing to contribute to our understanding of the content of morality. Rather, it is concerned only with the possibility and nature of the moral point of view: "What moral *theory* can do and should be trusted to do is to clarify the universal core of our moral intuitions and thereby to refute value skepticism. What it cannot do is make any kind of substantive contribution." (*MCCA*, 211) The thought seems to be that if philosophy addressed itself to the substantive content of the requirements of morality, it would be usurping tasks for its own experts that are properly reserved for the public at large. This suggests that unlike substantive reflection on the content of morality, the clarification of the moral point of view and the refutation of skepticism is properly undertaken by philosophical experts and not by the general public. It seems to me that this contrast is overdrawn. Although language and arguments may be more or less technical or specialized, there is no qualifying test that individuals must pass in order to be allowed to enter into dialogues concerning the matters Habermas regards as philosophy proper. Even Habermas's most technical claims have no privileged status. They are open to evaluation and criticism from anyone willing to put in the work to understand them.

In the end, despite Habermas's emphasis on the distinction, it may seem that not much hangs on whether we call contributions to reflection on the substance of justice "philosophy" or not. Indeed, disagreement on this matter may simply reflect differences in the cultural significance of philosophy in German and American societies. But it seems to me there may be a more substantive disagreement between Rawls and Habermas that is relevant here. Consider the following expression of Habermas's views on the contribution that philosophy can make:

The *moral* intuitions of everyday life are not in need of clarification by the philosopher. . . . Moral philosophy does have an enlightening or clarificatory role to play vis-à-vis the confusions that it has created in the minds of the educated, that is,

---

211. Jürgen Habermas, "Life-Forms, Morality and the Task of the Philosopher" (interview from 1984) in *Autonomy and Solidarity*, 199-200.

to the extent to which value skepticism and legal positivism have established themselves as professional ideologies and have infiltrated everyday consciousness by way of the educational system. (*MCCA*, 98)[212]

In contrast, for Rawls, the moral intuitions of everyday life are in need of clarification. This is not because most people are mistaken and philosophers must correct their erroneous views. It is for the simple reason that when it comes to issues of basic social justice, our intuitions are typically indeterminate and conflicting. For Rawls, this does not mean that we are to abandon them and look for some kind of external foundation that philosophical experts alone can provide: "In justice as fairness there are no philosophical experts. Heaven forbid!"[213] But it does mean that there is hard work to be done in identifying which conception of justice is the most reasonable. These arguments must in principle be accessible by all reasonable citizens. Justice as fairness requires "full publicity": "everything that we would say—you and I—when we set up justice as fairness and reflect why we proceed in one way rather than another" must be "publicly available."[214] But this does not mean that the arguments will be easy or obvious. Unfortunately, that is simply a reflection of the nature of the subject. When we attempt to resolve a deep conflict, we will often have to identify a rather abstract perspective from which to "get a clear and uncluttered view of its roots."[215] Attempting to resolve the deep conflicts in our tradition requires the construction of a perspective that may seem far removed from the immediate conflicts, but these devices are always at the service of the resolution of practical uncertainties and conflicts.

I suspect that there is one final misunderstanding lurking beneath Habermas's objections to Rawls's attempting to generate substantive principles of justice. After all, in *Between Facts and Norms*, Habermas argues for, among others, "*the right to the greatest possible measure of equal individual liberties*"; "Basic rights to equal opportunities to participate in [the] processes . . . through which they generate legitimate law"; and "Basic rights to the provision of living conditions that are socially, technologically, and ecologically safeguarded,

---

212. Compare Immanuel Kant, *The Metaphysics of Morals*, Mary Gregor, ed. (New York: Cambridge University Press, 1996), 134 [Ak. 378]: "People who are accustomed merely to explanations by natural sciences will not get into their heads the categorical imperative from which these [moral] laws proceed dictatorially, even though they feel themselves compelled irresistibly by it. Being unable to *explain* what lies entirely beyond that sphere (*freedom* of choice) . . . they are stirred by the proud claims of speculative reason, which makes its power so strongly felt in other fields, to band together in a general *call to arms*, as it were, to defend the omnipotence of theoretical reason. And so now, and perhaps for a while longer, they assail the moral concept of freedom and, wherever possible, make it suspect; but in the end they must give way."

213. Rawls, *Political Liberalism*, 427; cf. 383.

214. Rawls, *Political Liberalism*, 67.

215. Rawls, *Political Liberalism*, 46.

insofar as the current circumstances make this necessary if citizens are to have equal opportunities to utilize the civil rights [elaborated previously]." (*BFN*, 122-123) To be sure, Habermas insists that the detailed elaboration and application of these rights cannot be done ahead of time by the philosopher. They should be conceived of as "unsaturated placeholders for the specification of particular basic rights; they are thus more like legal principles that guide the framers of constitutions." (*BFN*, 126)[216] So, for Habermas philosophy can contribute a general framework that is to have its details filled in based on the particular circumstances of application. Why does Habermas think that Rawls is doing anything different?

The clue to answering this question, I believe, is Habermas's recent suggestion that instead of relying on a "consistently worked-out proceduralism," Rawls's theory "lays down the complete design of a well-ordered society for . . . citizens."[217] This common belief is simply mistaken. The original position is only designed to generate the most abstract, fundamental principles of justice.[218] In justice as fairness, the application of these principles to determine specific institutional arrangements takes place in the subsequent stages of the four-stage sequence, where the parties have additional information about the circumstances to which they are applying the principles.[219] Like the original position, these subsequent stages are not supposed to be historical events but rather ideal specifications of perspectives suitable for the application of the principles. But unlike the original position, Rawls does not suppose that the parties will be likely to reach unanimous agreement, even in the ideal.[220] This is because "the question whether legislation is just or unjust, especially in connection with economic and social policies, is commonly subject to reasonable differences of opinion."[221] Therefore, when assessing whether a law or proposal is consistent with the principles of justice, it is necessary that we provide public justifications of our judgment since "the exchange of opinion with others checks our partiality and widens our perspective; we are made to see things from their standpoint and the limits of our vision are brought home to us."[222] Compare the reason that

---

216. He treats the final right to the provision of living standards differently.

217. Habermas, "'Reasonable' versus 'True,' or the Morality of Worldviews" in *The Inclusion of the Other*, 95.

218. Habermas argues that law may depart from the moral point of view and "give expression to the particular wills of members of a particular legal community." (*BFN*, 152). However, he also points out that "the more [disputes] focus on constitutional essentials and underlying conceptions of justice, the more they *resemble* moral discourses." (Habermas, "'Reasonable' versus 'True,' or the Morality of Worldviews" in *The Inclusion of the Other*, 87)

219. See the discussion in my "Having It Both Ways: Justification and Application in Justice As Fairness," *Pacific Philosophical Quarterly* 75, no. 3&4 (Sept./Dec. 1994).

220. See Rawls, *A Theory of Justice*, 357 [314].

221. Rawls, *A Theory of Justice*, 198-199 [174].

222. Rawls, *A Theory of Justice*, 358 [315].

Habermas gives when arguing that actual dialogue is necessary: "For only when the self-understanding of each individual reflects a transcendental consciousness, that is, a universally valid view of the world, would what from my point of view is equally good for all actually be in the equal interest of each individual. But this can no longer be assumed under conditions of social and ideological pluralism."[223] It seems that there is little difference between them concerning the importance of and reasons for actual public dialogue on matters of basic social justice.[224]

In some places Rawls elaborates what he believes the principles of justice require, and it may be these discussions that Habermas and others have in mind when they claim that Rawls is trying to present a "complete design of a well-ordered society." For example, Rawls argues that the Supreme Court's decision in *Buckley v. Valeo* striking down limitation on expenditures in political campaigns was "profoundly dismaying" since it failed "to recognize the essential point that fair value of the political liberties is required for a just political procedure, and that to insure their fair value it is necessary to prevent those with greater property and wealth . . . from controlling the electoral process to their advantage."[225] When he considers the application of his principles in cases like this, it is clear that he is making a public argument concerning the proper shape of the basic liberties in the contemporary United States. It is hard to see, however, what could be construed as monological, exclusionary, or undemocratic about such an argument; Rawls is obviously participating in a public debate.

In fact, Rawls has been even more severely criticized for failing to elaborate fully the application of his principles. This is especially the case with his second principle. He has been very reluctant to enter into debates concerning which economic arrangements are most likely to satisfy the second principle. In comparing a property-owning democracy and a form of liberal market socialism, Rawls writes:

---

223. Habermas, "Reconciliation through the Public Use of Reason" in *The Inclusion of the Other*, 57. Ironically, Habermas is here arguing against the device of the original position. I should also note that recently Habermas has taken to characterizing valid moral norms as serving the "equal interest" or "equal good" of all. See, e.g., Habermas, *Justification and Application*, 51, 59, 124; "Reconciliation through the Use of Public Reason," 49, 52, 57, 66; *BFN*, 103, 108, 152, 306. Moon complains, rightly in my view, that "it is not obvious that there could be a metric that could be used to measure the extent to which a norm served the interest of the good of people whose values differ significantly." (J. Donald Moon, "Practical Discourse and Communicative Ethics" in *The Cambridge Companion to Habermas*, White, ed., 162n38) See my discussion in the fourth section of chapter 2.

224. In fact, Stephen Holmes has argued that the emphasis on public dialogue "was a staple of liberal theory from Milton to Mill." See Stephen Holmes, *The Anatomy of Antiliberalism* (Cambridge: Harvard University Press, 1993), 209.

225. Rawls, *Political Liberalism*, 359-360.

Which of these systems and the many intermediate forms most fully answers to the requirements of justice cannot, I think, be determined in advance. There is presumably no general answer to this question, since it depends in large part upon the traditions, institutions, and social forces of each country, and its particular historical circumstances.[226]

On the basis of this passage, Rawls is often read by the left as "having nothing to say" about the choice of economic institutions. This charge is made, for example, by Benjamin Barber (who, oddly enough, also criticizes Rawls for attempting to take political decisions out of the hands of citizens and put them into the hands of philosophers): "To assert that, so far as a theory of justice is concerned, there is nothing to choose between capitalism and socialism is so striking a claim that to cite it nearly obviates the need to comment on it."[227] In the few places that Rawls has commented upon economic institutions, he has rejected the view that is nearly universally attributed to him and argued that the welfare state capitalism is not likely to be the best arrangement to satisfy the second principle of justice.[228] In any event, the conclusion to be drawn is that when Rawls has selectively taken up the concrete application of his principles, it is not from a "privileged position of philosopher" trying to preempt public debate but as a contribution to that debate.

All of this suggests that many of the differences in emphasis between Rawls and Habermas can be traced to their attention to different questions. And this suggests, as J. Donald Moon has put it: "Although their theories are often seen as competing, they might be seen as pursuing complementary projects. Where Rawls *assumes* 'the moral point of view,' using it to derive substantive principles of a just political and social order, Habermas aims to ground the moral point of view itself."[229] I think this is correct. For Habermas, the ideal speech situation grounds the moral point of view; for Rawls, the original position is designed to elaborate certain implications of that point of view.

---

226. Rawls, *A Theory of Justice*, 274 [242].

227. Benjamin Barber, *The Conquest of Politics* (Princeton: Princeton University Press, 1988), 81. Compare similar charges by John Gray, "Contractarian Method, Private Property and the Market Economy" in his *Liberalisms: Essays in Political Philosophy* (New York: Routledge, 1989), 161; and Barry Clark and Herbert Gintis, "Rawlsian Justice and Economic Systems," *Philosophy and Public Affairs* 7, no. 4 (fall 1978), 304.

228. See the "Preface for the French Edition of *A Theory of Justice*," his *Collected Papers*, Samuel Freeman, ed. (Cambridge: Harvard University Press, 1999), 419-420. And compare the preface for the revised edition of *A Theory of Justice* [xiv-xvi]. See also Richard Krouse and Michael McPherson, "Capitalism, 'Property-Owning Democracy,' and the Welfare State," in *Democracy and the Welfare State*, Amy Gutmann, ed. (Princeton: Princeton University Press, 1988); and my "Rawls and the Left," *Socialist Review* 21, no. 3&4 (July-Dec. 1991).

229. Moon, "Practical Discourse and Communicative Ethics," 145; cf. 158.

To clarify the different focuses of Rawls and Habermas, consider two senses in which a theory may be termed *postmetaphysical*. Habermas says that he makes the following assumptions about society throughout *Between Facts and Norms*:

> a predominantly secular society in which normative orders must be maintained without metasocial guarantees. Even lifeworld certainties, which in any case are pluralized and ever more differentiated, do not provide sufficient compensation for this deficit. As a result, the burden of social integration shifts more and more onto the communicative achievements of actors for whom validity and facticity—that is, the binding force of rationally motivated beliefs and the imposed force of external sanctions—have parted company as incompatible. (*BFN*, 26)

Within such a society, Habermas claims, the justification of norms would have to be postmetaphysical. But there is a crucial ambiguity in this phrase. Is it that no individual or group believes there are any "metasocial guarantees" or is it that there are no metasocial guarantees that all citizens accept? Political liberalism accepts the latter, while Habermas assumes the former.[230] As Charles Larmore points out: "The political doctrine of liberalism is 'postmetaphysical' only in a trivial sense: metaphysical and religious assumptions are too controversial to have a place at its base. But the same is equally true for general philosophical conceptions of so-called postmetaphysical thought."[231]

From Rawls's point of view, the grounding of the moral point of view and the principles of justice in discourse ethics and the theory of communicative action may certainly be an appropriate one. But it is only one of many possible such groundings, no one of which is shared by all reasonable citizens. Rawls is correct when he claims that Habermas offers a partially comprehensive view.[232] Justice as fairness simply does not take a stand on, for example, Habermas's "radically anti-Platonic insight that there is neither a higher nor a deeper reality to which we could appeal." (*BFN*, xli)

If followers of Habermas present justice as fairness as an incomplete realization of an approach based on an analysis of communicative action, from Rawls's point of view Habermas's theory of communicative action provides one of many reasonable comprehensive doctrines within which justice as fairness can be embedded. This is exactly what justice as fairness expects and needs from reasonable comprehensive doctrines. Recall that a political conception has multiple foundations provided by reasonable comprehensive doctrines, no one of

---

230. Sometimes he seems very close to Rawls's view, for example, when he endorses Rawls's understanding of the pluralism of reasonable comprehensive doctrines in *Justification and Application*, 94, and Jürgen Habermas, "Remarks on Legitimation through Human Rights," *Philosophy and Social Criticism* 24, no. 2/3 (April 1998), 169.

231. Charles Larmore, *Morals of Modernity* (New York: Cambridge University Press, 1996), 213-216.

232. See Rawls, *Political Liberalism*, 376-379.

which is endorsed by the political conception itself. Habermas's theory is a nearly perfect example of how this can be done. As Habermas puts it, we can think of features of the original position as being "ultimately anchored in the symmetries of the mutual recognition of communicatively acting subjects in general." (*BFN*, 63) Indeed, we can. But we can also look at it as the realization of indefinitely many other reasonable comprehensive doctrines. Justice as fairness, as a political conception, takes no stand on these further matters, aiming to include as many reasonable comprehensive doctrines as possible within an overlapping consensus on the principles of justice.

Although justice as fairness does not endorse any particular comprehensive doctrine, it does depend on reasonable comprehensive doctrines in a rather strong way. An overlapping consensus of reasonable comprehensive doctrines may be rejected by comprehensive doctrines that are not reasonable in the technical sense.[233] Some of these—for example, those that we saw earlier in this chapter—will reject the core commitment to public reason and the liberal principle of legitimacy. They will reject the aim of attempting to reconcile by reason, believing that such efforts are merely covert expressions of the will to power and domination. They believe that all knowledge rests upon injustice; that discourse is a violence that we do to things; that to imagine another system is to extend our participation in the present system; that what matters is frustration with and resentment of the present rather than a better alternative.

A political conception of justice is in no position to refute such charges itself. At most, it can attempt to illustrate how public reason might operate, but it has no resources with which to engage such skepticism directly. To do so would require that it endorse a specific comprehensive doctrine. This would take it beyond the realm of the political and threaten the loss of support from other reasonable comprehensive doctrines. But that does not mean that reasonable comprehensive doctrines cannot themselves attempt to refute those skeptical challenges. Since justice as fairness cannot itself engage the poststructuralists directly, it depends on Habermas and the defenders of other reasonable comprehensive doctrines to do so. The projects of Rawls and Habermas, therefore, truly are complementary, each investigating areas on which the other depends.

---

233. See, for example, Rawls, *Political Liberalism*, xviii-xix. See also the discussion in my "The Reasonable in Justice As Fairness," *Canadian Journal of Philosophy* 29, no. 1 (March 1999).

Conclusion

Enlightenment is man's emergence from his self-imposed immaturity. Immaturity is the inability to use one's understanding without guidance from another. This immaturity is *self-imposed* when its cause lies not in lack of understanding, but in lack of resolve and courage to use it without guidance from another. *Sapere Aude!* "Have courage to use your own understanding!"—that is the motto of enlightenment.[1]

With these words, Kant begins his 1784 essay, "An Answer to the Question: What Is Enlightenment?" He points out that enlightenment in this sense is difficult for people to achieve individually. Many forces conspire to keep most individuals in their dependent condition, including self-appointed leaders who profit from "making their domestic livestock dumb." (41, [Ak.35]) In contrast, he is more optimistic that "the public" as a whole may be able to enlighten itself: "indeed, if it is only allowed freedom, enlightenment is almost inevitable." (41-42 [Ak.36]) More specifically, what is required for enlightenment is "the freedom to use reason *publicly* in all matters." (42 [Ak.36])

Kant contrasts this public use of reason with "the *private use* of reason," which may "often be very narrowly restricted, without otherwise hindering the progress of enlightenment." (42 [Ak.37]) This contrast between the public and private use of reason may not be entirely clear, and things become even more puzzling when Kant gives examples of each type. An officer on duty, he says, must obey the commands of a superior, but "as a scholar" he may criticize "errors in military service." (42-43 [Ak.37]) It may seem that Kant is suggesting that public reason is not practical but only theoretical. This would mean, however, that public reason buys its freedom at the price of confining itself to a purely speculative realm and therefore isolating itself from practice. This certainly does not sound very Kantian, and in any event it does not explain why Kant would call the officer's obedience to his commander a "private" use of reason.

Kant gives a similar example concerning a pastor. The pastor, he says, must instruct his congregation according to church dogma and symbols. "But as a scholar he has complete freedom, indeed, even a calling, to impart to the public

---

1. Immanuel Kant, "An Answer to the Question: What Is Enlightenment?" in *Perpetual Peace and Other Essays*, Ted Humphrey, trans. (Indianapolis: Hackett, 1983), 41 [Ak.35]. Parenthetical references in the first three paragraphs will be to this work. My interpretation is indebted to Onora O'Neill, "The Public Use of Reason," in *Constructions of Reason* (New York: Cambridge University Press, 1989).

all of his carefully considered and well-intentioned thoughts concerning mistaken aspects of that symbol, as well as his suggestions for the better arrangement of religious and church matters." (43 [Ak.38]) As Kant explains:

> What he teaches in consequence of his office as a servant of the church he sets out as something with regard to which he has no discretion to teach in accord with his own lights; rather, he offers it under the direction and in the name of another. . . . Thus an appointed teacher's use of his reason for the sake of his congregation is merely *private*, because, however large the congregation is, this use is always only domestic; in this regard, as a priest, he is not free and cannot be such because he is acting under instructions from someone else. By contrast, the cleric—as a scholar who speaks through his writings to the public as such, i.e., the world—enjoys in this *public use* of reason an unrestricted freedom to use his own rational capacities and to speak his own mind. (43 [Ak.38])

Here we have the key to the contrast between public and private uses of reason. The relevant factor is not where reason is deployed or by whom; it is not whether the reason is theoretical or practical. The decisive contrast concerns the shared background assumptions or goals of the audience to whom the argument is addressed.

The pastor deploys private reason when he reasons from church dogma. Similarly, the officer who follows orders and pursues the ends given to him by his superior relies on private reason. Both of these uses of private reason, Kant claims, have their place, but they occur only when shared background assumptions or goals are accepted without question. However, rational creatures can also break out of the limitations that private reason imposes and call into question the premises or goals that private reason takes for granted. They can question and evaluate the goals of the superior officer and the dogmas of the church. This deployment of reason is public not because it is used "in public." Rather, it is public because it is addressed not only to those who share dogmatically accepted premises or goals, but also to the public at large, including those who reject those dogmas. Any use of reason which puts premises or goals off limits to the critical scrutiny of reason, no matter how many individuals accept them, is never an instance of public reason but is "only domestic." Enlightenment is not a goal in which all of our questions have been answered. Rather it is the project of trusting ourselves to use our reason in its public employment without the external imposition of dogmatic assumptions or goals.

Both communitarianism and poststructuralism reject the Kantian model of enlightenment, but they do so for opposite reasons. Communitarians believe that Kantian public reason provides an inadequate basis from which to assess the basic structure of society since it does not start from a shared conception of the good. Poststructuralists, on the other hand, believe that its reliance on reason is itself a dogmatic commitment that should be rejected. Both deny the possibility of identifying principles of justice that respect the diversity of reasonable conceptions of the good characteristic of modern societies. Neither position, therefore, is conducive to a commitment to social justice in circumstances of pluralism. I now want to offer hypotheses concerning why, nonetheless, the left has been attracted by them. I will then conclude by discussing one further point of contact between justice as fairness and Kant's view of reason.

Communitarians argue that practical deliberation must begin with a specific conception of the good. For some, such as Sandel, the proper conception of the good from which to consider the organization of basic social institutions is the true (or best) conception of the good, regardless of what citizens of a particular society happen to think. For others, such as Walzer, the proper starting point is whichever conception of the good is widely accepted in society. In both cases, they reject the possibility of generating principles of justice that are not based on a full conception of the good. They are aware, of course, that justice as fairness claims to do exactly this. They conclude, therefore, that justice as fairness's neutrality is bogus. Under the heading *individualism*, critics of liberalism charge that liberalism covertly smuggles in a conception of the good.

We need to distinguish two versions of this charge. First, communitarians sometimes claim that liberalism is individualistic in that it only supports individualistic conceptions of the good. Terry Eagleton may have his tongue in cheek, but he expresses a widespread misconception when he writes that liberals argue that the state must not enforce a communitarian conception of the good "since this might constitute an undue infringement of the rights of those who wished to pursue happiness by sitting in a darkened room with a paper bag over their head."[2] Liberals are not concerned only with those who hold an individualistic conception of the good. Rather, they focus on those who do not share the dominant understanding of the character of a good community. If, as communitarians sometimes suggest, it is important to put religious faith at the center of social organization, liberals will certainly be worried about atheists and agnostics. But they will also be worried about those whose understanding of religious faith conflicts with the one placed at the center of society, whether or not it is shared by the majority. To be sure, liberals hold that not all conceptions of the good are permissible. But ruling out unjust or unreasonable conceptions of the good must not be confused with placing one particular conception at the basis of society. The exclusionary nature of the communitarian proposal would become clear if they were to specify which conception of the good they would give pride of place.

Second, some critics recognize that liberalism is not committed to conceptions of the good that are individualistic in content. However, they claim that it is still individualistic in valuing individual choice over all else. Eagleton, once again, expresses this charge with great clarity: "What is wrong with the

2. Terry Eagleton, *The Illusions of Postmodernism* (New York: Blackwell, 1996), 82.

disinterestedness of the liberal state is not that it speciously masks some interest, but that it quite explicitly enshrines one: the all-important interest of individual choice."[3] While it may be true that some classical liberals traced the value of an end to its deliberate selection, this simply is not true of Rawls. Although Rawls argues that participation in a system of fair cooperation requires the capacities to form, to revise, and rationally to pursue a conception of the good, this does not imply that a conception of the good is only valuable because it was deliberately chosen. From the first-person point of view, citizens will typically have many reasons for endorsing the particular conception of the good that they hold, beyond the brute fact that they chose it. Justice as fairness in no way denies this.

Why, then, does the charge of individualism stick so doggedly to political liberalism? One answer, I think, is that there is a persistent tendency to confuse liberal political philosophy with the institutions and culture of the United States. Often this is only an implicit identification, but sometimes it is explicit. Before going on to criticize liberalism, Ronald Beiner actually defines it this way: "a liberal is someone who sees nothing *fundamentally* questionable, morally or metaphysically, in the kind of social order that has currently been developed in the United States of America."[4]

To illustrate the mistaken inference from the practice of the United States to the theory of political liberalism, consider the left's long-standing critique of what it perceives to be the rampant consumerism in the United States.[5] Consumerism embodies both of the forms of individualism mentioned above: it involves goals that an individual can pursue in relative isolation without concern for others and it places the highest value on individual choice. Obviously, I cannot here consider either the extent to which this is an accurate characterization of the culture of the United States, or the ways in which this might be objectionable if it is. As this charge relates to Rawls, however, recall that Rawls rejects the model of a private society. Unlike the communitarians, he develops an account of how a social union is possible when there is a diversity of reasonable conceptions of the good. Furthermore, recall that a Rawlsian well-ordered society requires citizens to be motivated by a normally effective sense of justice that is itself not reducible to their self-interested calculations. In summary, I can do no better than simply to quote Jeremy Waldron's recent comments on Rawls's reputation as an apologist for American institutions:

> It's not complete nonsense: he does show a certain amount of pride in the local Constitution and in things like the separation of church and state. But it's mostly nonsense, and it cannot survive even the most cursory reading of *A Theory of*

---

3. Eagleton, *The Illusions of Postmodernism*, 80.

4. Ronald Beiner, *Philosophy in a Time of Lost Spirit* (Toronto: University of Toronto Press, 1997), 10.

5. A recent example is Juliet Schor, "The New Politics of Consumption," *The Boston Review* 24, no. 3-4 (summer 1999).

Justice. If there is an apology for America in Rawls's work, it is an apology at most for the American impulse to think and talk in terms of freedom and equality for all, and to use that as an organising framework for debates in politics and Constitutional law. Certainly, Rawls knows that this impulse is honoured most often in the breach, and that principles of rights, toleration and opportunity for all remain a cruel mockery for millions of US citizens. Still, the existence of the impulse shows that he is not doing anything odd or alien when he tries to figure out what making good on these promises would actually amount to.[6]

I suspect that the communitarian hostility toward liberalism has an additional source, especially for those who incline toward relativism and conservatism. Many seem to believe that although reason is able to unmask inherited conceptions of the good and show them to be groundless, it will be unable to generate support for any replacement. If people are encouraged or even allowed to reflect on their conceptions of the good and the organization of society, they will eventually slip into a self-indulgent hedonism. Better then to discourage such critical reflection with myths in the name of a harmonious and stable community. This type of argument is explicit in conservatives from Burke to Strauss to Scruton. We will return to this point below, but let me assert, once again, that while political liberalism assumes that citizens have the capacity to reflect on their conceptions of the good, it does not require that they be either the product of deliberate choice or constructed from reason alone.

In contrast to communitarians, poststructuralists believe that Kant's understanding of enlightenment does not go far enough in its unmasking since it continues to rely on public reason itself. Of course, Kant does not simply accept reason dogmatically, but subjects it to a critique, as we will see below. The scouring skepticism of postmodernism deprives its adherents of any grounds for reconstructing an alternative to what is criticized. Joshua Cohen has described the task of political criticism this way:

> Believing that the principles they use in criticism could be satisfied by an alternative form of social cooperation, political critics must indicate the political arrangements that their criticism aims to advance—what alternatives there are and how they might work as a stable set of institutions. The force of their criticism of current institutions ultimately depends on the power and the plausibility of those alternatives.[7]

If political criticism is ultimately practical in this sense—if it is ultimately tied to providing guidance in the construction of institutional arrangements—we should consider poststructuralism to be a form of anti-politics. There are two

---

6. Jeremy Waldron, "The Plight of the Poor in the Midst of Plenty," *London Review of Books* 21, no. 14 (15 July 1999); <http://www.lrb.co.uk/v21/n14/wald2114.htm>.

7. Joshua Cohen, "Reflections on Rousseau," *Philosophy and Public Affairs* 15, no. 3 (summer 1986), 297. Compare John Rawls, *A Theory of Justice* (Cambridge: Harvard University Press, 1971), 52 [45].

senses in which this may be true. Either poststructuralism simply has nothing to say about political reflection or it says that political engagement should occur without explicit reflection.

Richard Rorty, for example, argues that poststructuralism has nothing to contribute to political reflection. Indeed, this is one of the reasons he embraces it. According to Rorty, if poststructuralism aimed at developing a political theory, it would be far less interesting and important. This is not because he believes political philosophy is especially dangerous, but rather because there is nothing important for it to do. It is unable to provide foundations for political judgments since there are no foundations to be found. When we say that something is wrong, we simply mean that we do not do that around here. Nor is political philosophy particularly effective, when compared to literature for example, in cajoling people into behaving morally or reforming their institutions in the direction of justice. Nor, finally, is there any real difficulty in figuring out what justice requires. Political theory might make a small contribution to this task, but only in a very limited way: "the most philosophy can hope to do is to summarize our culturally influenced intuitions about the right thing to do in various situations."[8] Rorty believes that theory is largely superfluous. It only becomes problematic or dangerous when it aspires to reach beyond itself to provide foundations or to generate substantive political or moral principles.

Others, however, believe that poststructuralism has a lot to teach us about the dangers of political theory. It shows us that we should fight any political philosophy that attempts to identify explicitly the principles we should use when evaluating the justice of our basic social institutions. Any such theory would only contribute to the mistaken belief that there are stable meanings and principles on which we can rely. Suggesting that we can make objective and normative claims about the world, theory lulls us into thinking that there are stable realities to which we can appeal when making our judgments. Worse still, theorizing is an expression of the will to dominate and normalize. It recreates the world in its own image through violence.

On this reading, poststructuralism achieves its political ends without co-opting itself since it does not defend any explicit principles of justice. The real force of the poststructuralist position, it is claimed, is not found in the content of the arguments they make, but rather in the overwhelming rhetorical force of the work itself. Stephen White observes that the "maximally 'impertinent'" tone of much postmodern writing is intended "to shock or jolt the addressee into seeing the contestable quality of what he takes as a certainty."[9] The point is not to argue that what the addressee believes is false, but only that it is "contestable." The

---

8. Richard Rorty, "Human Rights, Rationality, and Sentimentality," in *Truth and Progress*, vol. 3 of *Philosophical Papers* (New York: Cambridge University Press, 1998), 171.

9. Stephen White, *Political Theory and Postmodernism* (New York: Cambridge University Press, 1991), 6-7.

problem is that when the "shock" wears off, there quite literally is nothing left. We still must decide whether to accept or reject what we previously believed. Poststructuralism steadfastly refuses to participate in this project. It therefore gives the impression that such reconstruction is unnecessary and that the content of our commitments is unimportant as long as we see that they are contestable.

Jon Simons argues that "Foucault's thought is . . . timely because it . . . proceeds without proposing a viable alternative system." This is because, "Given the decline of the socialist alternatives, there is the distinct danger that actually existing liberal democracy will become increasingly dogmatic in the absence of credible challenges." Since it does not propose an alternative, he concludes, "Foucault's is a critical thought for a Western present without an alternative."[10] This is perhaps more telling than Simon intends. If it is important to show that what we often take for granted is contestable and contingent, there is no better way to do this than to propose a superior alternative. Criticism without an alternative is a certain recipe for complacency and despair as soon as the thrill of transgression recedes.

This, in fact, is our clue to why the left is attracted to postmodernism. I am far from the first to suggest that the left's flirtation with postmodernism is itself an expression of despair and hopelessness. The symbolic turning point was 1968. In May, student led protests threatened to topple French society. They did so without the help of the French Communist Party which, up to that point, had been the central organization of left intellectual life. Indeed, the party intervened to bring the general strike to an end. Coming hard on the heels of the Prague Spring, these events convinced many left intellectuals that Marxism could no longer provide an adequate framework for social progress. If any remained to be convinced, the events of 1989 made this unmistakable.

The intellectual left's disillusionment with Marxism was compounded by their perception of what the movements of 1968 both succeeded and failed to accomplish. Nobody could possibly claim that the left succeeded in its traditional aim of a radical transformation of the basic institutions of society. The true significance of the movement, therefore, would have to be found elsewhere. For thinkers such as Foucault, Lyotard, and Derrida, what the left achieved in 1968 was the transformation of its own understanding of what politics should be about. Instead of aiming to transform institutions in a progressive way, it would aim to take transgressive stances, especially within the academy, and produce new meanings. While the events of 1968 were more dramatic in France, and the subsequent embrace of poststructuralism deeper, the left in the United States followed a similar path. The perceived failures of the late 1960s led to a turning away from political engagement in the direction of various forms of self-creation and identification. The focus of concern shifted from creating just social institutions to various forms of identity politics.

---

10. John Simons, *Foucault and the Political* (New York: Routledge, 1995), 124.

Alex Callinicos certainly over-simplifies, but he captures more than a grain of truth when he writes: "Ten years on, the millenial [sic] expectations of imminent revolution that ha[d] flourished in 1968 had been dashed. . . . Twenty years after, in 1988, with Western capitalism seemingly restabilized under the leadership of the New Right, the retreat of the generation of 1968 from the revolutionary beliefs of their youth had gone even further."[11] In such a context, the attractions of what I have called an anti-politics to a disillusioned and disheartened left are clear enough. Marshall Berman attempts to explain Foucault's popularity among the left this way: he "offers a generation of refugees from the 1960s a world-historical alibi for the sense of passivity and helplessness that gripped so many of us in the 1970s. There is no point in trying to resist the oppressions and injustices of modern life, since even our dreams of freedom only add more links to our chains."[12]

In retrospect, we can distinguish two possible lessons that the left could learn from 1968. The first is that the reform and improvement of social institutions through the deployment of public reason is hopeless at best, and complicit with violence at worst. This is the lesson that postmodernists take. Lyotard summarizes this perspective in his slogan: "'May 1968' refutes the doctrine of parliamentary liberalism."[13] The other possible lesson is that millennial aspirations for total revolution were exactly the problem. What was lacking was precisely principled reflection on which institutional structures might be superior to those already in place. We are led back, therefore, to consider how justice as fairness understands critical reflection.

Unlike communitarianism and poststructuralism, justice as fairness embraces something quite like Kant's view of enlightenment. Reflective equilibrium puts nothing off limits to critical assessment. It does not start from a unchallenged conception of the good, nor does it attempt to move beyond reason itself. It is important to remember, however, that it is not foundational. Reflective equilibrium works from our most secure convictions, whatever they are, but it does so without assuming that those starting points are themselves immune from criticism: "Moral philosophy is Socratic: we may want to change our present considered judgments once their regulative principles are brought to light. And we may want to do this even though these principles are a perfect fit."[14] Reason is employed in critical reflection on the commitments we already have, not in reconstructing all of our beliefs from scratch.

---

11. Alex Callinicos, *Against Postmodernism* (New York: St. Martin's Press, 1989), 165.

12. Marshall Berman, *All That Is Solid Melts into Air* (New York: Simon and Schuster, 1982; reprint, New York: Penguin, 1988), 35.

13. Jean-François Lyotard, *The Differend*, Georges Van Den Abbeele, trans. (Minneapolis: University of Minnesota Press, 1988; originally published in 1983), 179.

14. Rawls, *A Theory of Justice*, 49. See chapter 2, note 80 above.

These thoughts lead us to one final point of contact between political liberalism and Kant. For Kant, the idea of a *critique* of reason aims at the vindication of reason as its own ultimate arbiter. Kant insists that this vindication can only succeed within certain limits. There can be no way to identify these limits, however, except through the use of reason itself. So for Kant, reason is vindicated within the limits that it establishes for itself. This requires giving up on traditional rationalist aspirations. As Onora O'Neill puts it,

> He constantly rejects conceptions of reason, such as the Principle of Sufficient Reason, which supposedly give sufficient instructions for all thinking and acting (for example, see [*The Critique of Pure Reason*] A783/B811). His insistence that "reason is no dictator" reiterates the thought that there is no algorithm that fully determines the content of reasoned thought and action. Nor should we "expect from reason what obviously exceeds its power" (A786/B814). Reason offers only necessary conditions for thought and action—in Kant's terminology a "Canon" for thought and action (A795/B823 ff.; *Groundwork*, [Ak.] 4:424)[15]

"To those who expect reason to determine everything," she continues, "this may seem a deeply disappointing failure. If Kant is right, such disappointment is itself a symptom of undisciplined metaphysical passions (cf. A786/B814)."[16]

Consistent with the requirements of a political conception of justice, Rawls is agnostic concerning the limits of reason as such. However, he insists that public reason alone cannot definitively answer all questions, or even all practical and moral questions. It can, however, identify its own limits and give guidance for proceeding within them. Specifically, all reasonable people can recognize that public reason cannot identify a single comprehensive doctrine as the true (or best) one. This is not to be confused with the metaphysical thesis that there is a plurality of fundamental values in the universe. Rather, it is a thesis concerning the limits of what public reason is able to establish.

Our inability to answer a practical question within the limits of public reason may be more or less troubling depending on the case. For example, there is no great urgency to identify the correct form of religious practice within the limits of public reason. This is not because such questions are unimportant, but rather because we can adopt a principle of religious toleration which allows us to continue to function in the face of unresolved disagreements concerning the ultimate nature of religious truth. The adopting of such a principle is an accomplishment of liberal societies that is not to be underestimated. Each of us can go beyond the limits of public reason and embrace religious commitments (or none) that others reasonably reject. More generally, each of us can go beyond the limits of public reason and embrace a particular comprehensive doctrine and conception of the good that others reasonably reject. Again, this is

---

15. Onora O'Neill, "Vindicating Reason," in *The Cambridge Companion to Kant*, Paul Guyer, ed. (New York: Cambridge University Press, 1992), 296.

16. O'Neill, "Vindicating Reason," 304.

not because such matters are unimportant, but because we can interact with others with whom we do not share comprehensive doctrines. Furthermore, it is possible for us to do this on terms that we all can recognize as fair.

The basic structure of society is a very different case, however. We cannot each have our own basic structure, whatever that would mean. If we are living in one society, we share a single basic structure—a single set of fundamental background institutions within which we interact with one another. Because of this, reasonable people respect the limits of public reason when they defend principles for the evaluation of the justice of the basic structure. When it comes to the basic structure, to violate the limits of public reason would be quite unlike exceeding them in adopting a religion or conception of the good, since one's choice of a basic structure dictates everyone else's choice, too. Justice as fairness responds by generating a political conception of justice, relying only on the resources of public reason. It aims to create a system of reciprocity without denying or undermining the diversity that gives rise to the need for justice in the first place. In order to fulfill the demands of reciprocity, it directs our attention to the least advantaged social position that is generated by the basic structure.

In the preface I quoted Ronald Dworkin's 1973 review of *A Theory of Justice*, where he challenges the left's assumption that justice as fairness is "a particularly subtle rationalization of the political status quo, which may safely be disregarded by those who want to offer a more radical critique of the liberal tradition."[17] Unfortunately, this continues to be the attitude held by much of the left. The development of poststructuralist and communitarian theories has tempted and distracted the left enough that we still have yet to see a serious engagement with political liberalism at either a theoretical or practical level. It would be too much to say that the hopelessness and resignation, the valorization of one's oppressed status and the aggrandizement of difference that characterizes so much of the left are blessings. These conditions, however, do provide us an opportunity to reflect on our fundamental commitments. Now is the time to do the spade work that will prepare us to help move society in the direction of greater social justice. Some authors such as Todd Gitlin and Ira Katznelson are beginning to take such steps. If the argument of this book is correct, the conservatism of communitarianism and the normative dead end of poststructuralism are ill-suited to a revitalized progressive political engagement. It is time to remove our ideological blinders and to give political liberalism serious consideration as a framework for reflecting on matters of basic social justice. We could do no better than to start with the work of John Rawls.

---

17. Ronald Dworkin, "The Original Position," in *Reading Rawls*, Norman Daniels, ed. (New York: Basic Books, 1975; reprint Stanford: Stanford University Press, 1989), 52.

Bibliography

Ackerman, Bruce. *The Future of Liberal Revolution*. New Haven: Yale University Press, 1992.

———. "Political Liberalisms." *The Journal of Philosophy* 91, no. 7 (July 1994).

Alejandro, Roberto. *The Limits of Rawlsian Justice*. Baltimore: Johns Hopkins University Press, 1998.

Alexander, Larry. "Fair Equality of Opportunity: John Rawls' (Best) Forgotten Principle." *Philosophy Research Archives* 11 (1986).

Amdur, Robert. "Rawls and His Radical Critics." *Dissent* (summer 1980).

"Americans with Disabilities Act of 1990." <http://www.eeoc.gov/laws/ada.html>.

Anderson, Elizabeth. *Value in Ethics and Economics*. Cambridge: Harvard University Press, 1993.

———. "What Is the Point of Equality?" *Ethics* 109, no. 2 (Jan. 1999).

Anonymous. "The Good of Justice As Fairness." *Times Literary Supplement*, 5 May 1972, no. 3662.

Arneson, Richard. "Against 'Complex Equality.'" *Public Affairs Quarterly* 4, no. 2 (April 1990).

———. "Against Rawlsian Equality of Opportunity." *Philosophical Studies* 93, no. 1 (Jan. 1999).

———. "Equality and Equal Opportunity for Welfare." *Philosophical Studies* 56, no. 1 (May 1989).

———. "Primary Goods Reconsidered." *Nous* 24, no. 3 (June 1990).

Arrow, Kenneth. "Some Ordinalist-Utilitarian Notes on Rawls's Theory of Justice." *The Journal of Philosophy* 70, no. 9 (May 1973).

Baier, Kurt. "Justice and the Aims of Political Philosophy." *Ethics* 99, no. 4 (July 1989).

Baker, C. Edwin. "Sandel on Rawls." *University of Pennsylvania Law Review* 133 (April 1985).

Barber, Benjamin. *The Conquest of Politics*. Princeton: Princeton University Press, 1988.

Barry, Brian. "Intimations of Justice." *Columbia Law Review* 84, no. 3 (April 1984).

———. "John Rawls and the Search for Stability." *Ethics* 105, no. 4 (July 1995).

———. *Justice As Impartiality*. New York: Oxford University Press, 1995.

———. *The Liberal Theory of Justice*. New York: Oxford University Press, 1973.

———. "Review of Liberalism and the Limits of Justice." *Ethics* 94, no. 3 (April 1984).

———. "Social Criticism and Political Philosophy." *Philosophy and Public Affairs* 19, no. 4 (fall 1990).

———. "Utilitarianism and Preference Change." *Utilitas* 1 (1989).

Baynes, Kenneth. *The Normative Grounds of Social Criticism*. Albany: State University of New York Press, 1992.

Beardsworth, Richard. *Derrida and the Political*. New York: Routledge, 1996.

Beckley, Harlan. "A Christian Affirmation of Rawls's Idea of Justice As Fairness—Part I." *The Journal of Religious Ethics* 13 (1985).

——. "A Christian Affirmation of Rawls's Idea of Justice As Fairness—Part II." *The Journal of Religious Ethics* 14 (1986).

Beiner, Ronald. *Philosophy in a Time of Lost Spirit*. Toronto: University of Toronto Press, 1997.

——. *What's the Matter with Liberalism?* Berkeley: University of California Press, 1992.

Bell, Daniel. *The Coming Post-Industrial Society*. New York: Basic Books, 1973.

——. *The Cultural Contradictions of Capitalism*. New York: Basic Books, 1976.

Bellah, Robert. *The Broken Covenant*. Second edition. Chicago: University of Chicago Press, 1975.

Benhabib, Seyla. *Critique, Norm, and Utopia*. New York: Columbia University Press, 1986.

——. "The Generalized and Concrete Other." In *Women and Moral Theory*, Kittay and Meyers, ed.

——. "In Defense of Universalism—Yet Again! A Response to Critics of *Situating the Self*." *New German Critique*, no. 62 (spring/summer 1994).

——. "Judith Shklar's Dystopic Liberalism." In *Liberalism without Illusions*, Bernard Yack, ed. Chicago: University of Chicago Press, 1996.

——. "The Methodological Illusions of Modern Political Theory." *Neue Hefte für Philosophie* 21 (1982).

Berlin, Isaiah. *The Crooked Timber of Humanity*. Henry Hardy, ed. New York: Knopf, 1991.

——. "Does Political Theory Still Exist?" In *Philosophy, Politics and Society* (second series), Peter Laslett and W. G. Runciman, eds. Oxford: Basil Blackwell, 1962.

——. "Two Concepts of Liberty." In *Four Essays on Liberty*. New York: Oxford University Press, 1969.

Berman, Marshall. *All That Is Solid Melts into Air*. New York: Simon and Schuster, 1982; reprint, New York: Penguin, 1988.

Berman, Paul. *A Tale of Two Utopias*. New York: Norton, 1996.

Bernauer, James, and David Rasmussen, eds. *The Final Foucault*. Cambridge: MIT Press, 1994.

Bernstein, Richard. "An Allegory of Modernity/Postmodernity: Habermas and Derrida." In *The New Constellation*.

——. *The New Constellation*. Cambridge: MIT Press, 1992.

——. "One Step Forward, Two Steps Backward: Rorty on Liberal Democracy and Philosophy." In *The New Constellation*.

——. "Serious Play: The Ethical-Political Horizon of Derrida." In *The New Constellation*.

Best, Steven, and Douglas Kellner. *Postmodern Theory: Critical Interrogations*. New York: Guilford, 1991.

Bird, Colin. "Mutual Respect and Neutral Justification." *Ethics* 107, no. 1 (Oct. 1996).

Bloom, Allan. "Justice: John Rawls versus the Tradition of Political Philosophy." In *Giants and Dwarfs*. New York: Simon and Schuster, 1990.

Bork, Robert. *Slouching towards Gomorrah*. New York: Regan Books, 1996.

Boxill, Bernard. "The Culture of Poverty." *Social Philosophy and Policy* 11, no. 1 (winter 1994).

Brandt, Richard. *A Theory of the Good and the Right*. New York: Oxford University Press, 1979.

Braybrooke, David. "Utilitarianism with a Difference: Rawls's Position in Ethics." *The Canadian Journal of Philosophy* 3, no. 2 (Dec. 1973).

Brighouse, Harry. "Civic Education and Liberal Legitimacy." *Ethics* 108, no. 4 (July 1998).

Buchanan, Allen. "Assessing the Communitarian Critique of Liberalism." *Ethics* 99, no. 4 (July 1989).

——. *Marx and Justice.* Totowa, N.J.: Rowman & Allanheld, 1982.

——. "Revisability and Rational Choice." *The Canadian Journal of Philosophy* 5, no. 3 (Nov. 1975).

Burke, Edmund. *Reflections on the Revolution in France.* J. G. A. Pocock, ed. Indianapolis: Hackett, 1987.

——. *A Vindication of Natural Society.* Frank Pagano, ed. Indianapolis: Liberty Classics, 1982.

Calhoun, John. "A Disquisition on Government." In *John C. Calhoun, Union and Liberty*, Ross Lence, ed. Indianapolis: Liberty Fund, 1992.

Callinicos, Alex. *Against Postmodernism.* New York: St. Martin's Press, 1989.

——. *Making History.* Ithaca, N.Y.: Cornell, 1988.

——. "Reactionary Postmodernism?" In *Postmodernism and Society*, Roy Boyne and Ali Rattansi, eds. London: Macmillan, 1990.

Caney, Simon. "Sandel's Critique of the Primacy of Justice: A Liberal Rejoinder." *The British Journal of Political Science* 40 (1992).

Carter, Stephen. *The Culture of Disbelief.* New York: Basic Books, 1993.

Chang, Ruth, ed. *Incommensurability, Incomparability, and Practical Reason.* Cambridge: Harvard University Press, 1998.

Choptiany, Leonard. "A Critique of John Rawls's Principles of Justice." *Ethics* 83, no. 2 (Jan. 1973).

Clark, Barry, and Herbert Gintis. "Rawlsian Justice and Economic Systems." *Philosophy and Public Affairs* 7, no. 4 (fall 1978).

Cohen, Andrew Jason. "Communitarianism, 'Social Constitution,' and Autonomy." *Pacific Philosophical Quarterly* 80, no. 2 (June 1999).

Cohen, G. A. "Incentives, Inequality, and Community." In *The Tanner Lectures on Human Values*, vol. 13, Grethe Peterson, ed. Salt Lake City: University of Utah Press, 1992.

——. "On the Currency of Egalitarian Justice." *Ethics* 99, no. 4 (July 1989).

——. "The Pareto Argument for Inequality." *Social Philosophy and Policy* 12, no. 1 (winter 1995).

——. "Self-Ownership, World-Ownership, and Equality." In *Self-Ownership, Freedom, and Equality.* New York: Cambridge University Press, 1995.

——. "Where the Action Is: On the Site of Distributive Justice." *Philosophy and Public Affairs* 26, no. 1 (winter 1997).

Cohen, Joshua. "Book Review of *Spheres of Justice*." *The Journal of Philosophy* 83 (1986).

——. "Democratic Equality." *Ethics* 99, no. 4 (July 1989).

——. "Freedom of Expression." *Philosophy and Public Affairs* 22, no. 3 (summer 1993).

——. "Moral Pluralism and Political Consensus." In *The Idea of Democracy*, David Copp, Jean Hampton, and John Roemer, eds. New York: Cambridge University Press, 1993.

——. "A More Democratic Liberalism." *Michigan Law Review* 92, no. 6 (May 1994).

——. "Pluralism and Proceduralism." *Chicago-Kent Law Review* 69, no. 3 (1994).

——. "Procedure and Substance in Deliberative Democracy." In *Democracy and Difference*, Seyla Benhabib, ed. Princeton: Princeton University Press, 1996.

——. "Reflections on Rousseau: Autonomy and Democracy." *Philosophy and Public Affairs* 15, no. 3 (summer 1986).

Cohen, Marshall. "Review of *A Theory of Justice*." *New York Times Book Review*, 16 July 1972.

Coleman, Joe. "Civic Pedagogies and Liberal-Democratic Curricula." *Ethics* 108, no. 4 (July 1998).

Conkin, Paul. *The Southern Agrarians*. Knoxville: University of Tennessee Press, 1988.

Connolly, William. "Beyond Good and Evil: The Ethical Sensibility of Michel Foucault." *Political Theory* 21, no. 3 (Aug. 1993).

——. "Taylor, Foucault, and Otherness." *Political Theory* 13, no. 3 (Aug. 1985).

Crick, Bernard. "On Justice." *New Statesman*, 5 May 1972.

Culler, Jonathan. "Jacques Derrida." In *Structuralism and Since*, John Sturrock, ed.

D'Souza, Dinesh. *Illiberal Education*. New York: Free Press, 1991.

Daniels, Norman. "Equality of What: Welfare, Resources, or Capabilities?" In *Justice and Justification*.

——. "Health-Care Needs and Distributive Justice." In *Justice and Justification*.

——. *Just Health Care*. New York: Cambridge University Press, 1985.

——. *Justice and Justification*. New York: Cambridge University Press, 1996.

——. "The Prudential Lifespan Account of Justice across Generations." In *Justice and Justification*.

——, ed. *Reading Rawls*. New York: Basic Books, 1975; reprint, Stanford: Stanford University Press, 1989.

——. "Reflective Equilibrium and Justice As Political." In *Justice and Justification*.

——. "Wide Reflective Equilibrium and Theory Acceptance in Ethics." In *Justice and Justification*.

Darwall, Stephen. *Impartial Reason*. Ithaca, N.Y.: Cornell University Press, 1983.

Davidson, Arnold. "Archaeology, Genealogy, Ethics." In *Foucault: A Critical Reader*, David Hoy, ed.

Derrida, Jacques. "But, beyond . . ." *Critical Inquiry* 13, no. 1 (autumn 1986).

——. *Deconstruction in a Nutshell*. John Caputo, ed. New York: Fordham University Press, 1997.

——. "Différrance." In *Margins of Philosophy*, Alan Bass, trans. Chicago: University of Chicago Press, 1982.

——. "Force of Law: The 'Mystical Foundation of Authority.'" In *Deconstruction and the Possibility of Justice*, Drucilla Cornell, Michel Rosenfeld, and David Gray Carlson, eds. New York: Routledge, 1992.

——. "Limited Inc. a b c . . ." In *Limited Inc.* Chicago: Northwestern University Press, 1988.

——. *The Post Card*. Alan Bass, trans. Chicago: University of Chicago Press, 1987.

——. "Racism's Last Word." *Critical Inquiry* 12, no. 1 (autumn 1985).

——. "Remarks on Deconstruction and Pragmatism." In *Deconstruction and Pragmatism*. Chantal Mouffe, ed.

Dews, Peter. Editor's introduction in Habermas, *Autonomy and Solidarity*.

——. *The Limits of Disenchantment*. New York: Verso, 1995.

——. *Logics of Disintegration*. New York: Verso, 1987.

——. "The Return of the Subject in Late Foucault." *Radical Philosophy* 51 (1989).

Diamond, Sara. *Roads to Dominion*. New York: Guilford, 1995.

DiQuattro, Arthur. "Rawls and Left Criticism." *Political Theory* 11, no. 1 (Feb. 1983).

Douglass, R. Bruce, and David Hollenbach, eds. *Catholicism and Liberalism*. New York: Cambridge University Press, 1994.

Dreyfus, Hubert, and Paul Rabinow. *Michel Foucault: Beyond Structuralism and Hermeneutics*. Second edition. Chicago: University of Chicago Press, 1983.

——. "What Is Maturity? Habermas and Foucault on 'What Is Enlightenment?'" In *Foucault: A Critical Reader*, David Hoy, ed.

Dworkin, Ronald. *Law's Empire*. Cambridge: Harvard University Press, 1986.

——. "Liberalism." In *Public and Private Morality*, Stuart Hampshire, ed. New York: Cambridge University Press, 1978.

——. "Objectivity and Truth: You'd Better Believe It." *Philosophy and Public Affairs* 25, no. 2 (spring 1996).

——. "The Original Position." In *Reading Rawls*, Norman Daniels, ed.

——. "To Each His Own." *New York Review of Books*, 14 April 1983; reprinted as "What Justice Isn't." In *A Matter of Principle*. Cambridge: Harvard University Press, 1985.

——. "What Is Equality? Part I: Equality of Welfare." *Philosophy and Public Affairs* 10, no. 3 (summer 1981).

——. "What Is Equality? Part II: Equality of Resources." *Philosophy and Public Affairs* 10, no. 4 (fall 1981).

Eagleton, Terry. *The Illusions of Postmodernism*. New York: Blackwell, 1996.

Elshtain, Jean Bethke. "Cardinal Virtue." *The New Republic*, 9 Dec. 1996.

Elster, Jon. *Local Justice*. New York: Russell Sage Foundation, 1992.

——. *Making Sense of Marx*. New York: Cambridge University Press, 1985.

Elster, Jon, and John Roemer, eds. *Interpersonal Comparisons of Well-Being*. New York: Cambridge University Press, 1991.

English, Jane. "Justice between Generations." *Philosophical Studies* 31 (1977).

Estlund, David. "Liberalism, Equality, and Fraternity in Cohen's Critique of Rawls." *The Journal of Political Philosophy* 6, no. 1 (March 1998).

Etzioni, Amitai. *The Active Society*. New York: Free Press, 1968.

Ferry, Luc, and Alain Renaut. *French Philosophy in the Sixties*. Mary Cattani, trans. Amherst: University of Massachusetts Press, 1990. (Originally published in 1985.)

Fishkin, James. *Justice, Equal Opportunity, and the Family*. New Haven: Yale University Press, 1983.

Foucault, Michel. "About the Beginning of the Hermeneutics of the Self." *Political Theory* 21, no. 2 (May 1993). (Originally presented in 1980.)

——. *The Archaeology of Knowledge*. A. M. Sheridan Smith, trans. New York: Pantheon, 1972. (Originally published in 1969.)

——. *The Birth of the Clinic*. A. M. Sheridan Smith, trans. New York: Vintage, 1994. (Originally published in 1963.)

——. *The Care of the Self*. Vol. 3 of *The History of Sexuality*. Robert Hurley, trans. New York: Vintage, 1986. (Originally published in 1984.)

——. "Critical Theory/Intellectual History." In *Michel Foucault: Politics, Philosophy, Culture*. (Originally published in 1983.)

——. *Discipline and Punish*. Alan Sheridan, trans. New York: Vintage, 1977. (Originally published in 1975.)

——. "The Discourse on Language." Appendix to *The Archaeology of Knowledge*. (Originally published in 1971.)

——. "The Ethic of Care for the Self As a Practice of Freedom." In *The Final Foucault*. James Bernauer and David Rasmussen, eds. (Interview conducted in 1984.)

——. *The Foucault Reader*. Paul Rabinow, ed. New York: Pantheon, 1984.

——. "The History of Sexuality." In *Power/Knowledge*. (Originally published in 1977.)

——. *An Introduction*. Vol. 1 of *The History of Sexuality*. Robert Hurley, trans. New York: Random House, 1978. (Originally published in 1976.)

——. "Iran: The Spirit of a World without Spirit." In *Michel Foucault: Politics, Philosophy, Culture*. (Originally published in 1979.)

——. *Language, Counter-Memory, Practice: Selected Essays and Interviews*. Donald Bouchard, ed. Ithaca, N.Y.: Cornell University Press, 1977.

——. *Madness and Civilization*. Richard Howard, trans. New York: Vintage, 1988. (Originally published in 1961.)

——. *Michel Foucault: Politics, Philosophy, Culture: Interviews and Other Writings, 1977-1984*. Lawrence Kritzman, ed. New York: Routledge, 1988.

——. "Nietzsche, Genealogy, History." In *Language, Counter-Memory, Practice*. (Originally published in 1971.)

——. "On Popular Justice: A Discussion with Maoists." In *Power/Knowledge*. (Originally published in 1972.)

——. "On the Genealogy of Ethics: An Overview of Work in Progress." In Hubert Dreyfus and Paul Rabinow, *Michel Foucault: Beyond Structuralism and Hermeneutics*.

——. *The Order of Things*. Alan Sheridan, trans. New York: Vintage, 1994. (Originally published in 1966.)

——. "Polemics, Politics, and Problemizations." In *The Foucault Reader*. (Interview conducted in 1983.)

——. "Politics and Ethics: An Interview." In *The Foucault Reader*. (Interview conducted in 1983.)

——. "Politics and Reason." In *Michel Foucault: Politics, Philosophy, Culture*. (Tanner Lectures, delivered in 1979.)

——. *Power/Knowledge: Selected Interviews and Other Writings, 1972-1977*. Colin Gordon, ed. New York: Pantheon, 1980.

——. "Revolutionary Action: 'Until Now.'" In *Language, Counter-Memory, Practice*. (Originally published in 1971.)

——. "The Subject and Power." In Hubert Dreyfus and Paul Rabinow, *Michel Foucault: Beyond Structuralism and Hermeneutics*.

——. "Truth and Power." In *Power/Knowledge*. (Originally published in 1977.)

——. "Two Lectures." In *Power/Knowledge*. (Lectures originally presented in 1976.)

——. *The Use of Pleasure*. Vol. 2 of *The History of Sexuality*. Robert Hurley, trans. New York: Vintage, 1990. (Originally published in 1984.)

Foucault, Michel, and Noam Chomsky. "Human Nature: Justice versus Power." In *Reflexive Water: The Basic Concerns of Mankind*, Fons Elders, ed. London: Souvenir Press, 1974.

Fraser, Nancy. "Foucault on Modern Power: Empirical Insights and Normative Confusions." *Praxis International* 1, no. 3 (Oct. 1981).

Fraser, Nancy, and Linda Nicholson. "Social Criticism without Philosophy." In *Feminism/Postmodernism*, Linda Nicholson, ed. New York: Routledge, 1989.

Frazer, Elizabeth, and Nicola Lacey. *The Politics of Community*. Toronto: University of Toronto Press, 1993.

Freeman, Samuel. "Political Liberalism and the Possibility of a Just Constitution." *Chicago-Kent Law Review* 69, no. 3 (1994).

——. "Symposium on John Kekes's 'A Question for Egalitarians.'" <http://www.brown.edu/Departments/Philosophy/bears/9802free.html>

——. "Utilitarianism, Deontology, and the Priority of Right." *Philosophy and Public Affairs* 23, no. 4 (fall 1994).

Galston, William. "Defending Liberalism." *American Political Science Review* 72 (1982).

——. "Equality of Opportunity and Liberal Theory." In *Justice and Equality Here and Now*, Frank Lucash, ed. Ithaca, N.Y.: Cornell University Press, 1986.

Gauthier, David. *Morals by Agreement*. New York: Oxford University Press, 1986.

Genovese, Eugene. "The Question." *Dissent* (summer 1994).

——. *The Slaveholders' Dilemma*. Columbia: University of South Carolina Press, 1992.

——. *The Southern Tradition: The Achievement and Limitations of an American Conservatism*. Cambridge: Harvard University Press, 1994.

Geras, Norman. *Solidarity in the Conversation of Humankind*. New York: Verso, 1995.

Ghirardo, Diane. *Architecture after Modernism*. London: Thames and Hudson, 1996.

Giddens, Anthony. *The Constitution of Society*. Berkeley: University of California Press, 1984.

Gilligan, Carol. *In a Different Voice*. Cambridge: Harvard University Press, 1982.

——. "Prologue: Adolescent Development Reconsidered." In *Mapping the Moral Domain*, Carol Gilligan et al., eds.

Gilligan, Carol, Janie Victoria Ward, and Jill McLean, eds. *Mapping the Moral Domain*. Cambridge: Harvard University Press, 1988.

Gilligan, Carol, and Grant Wiggins. "The Origins of Morality in Early Childhood Relationships." In *Mapping the Moral Domain*, Carol Gilligan et al., eds.

Gitlin, Todd. "The Future of Progressive Politics" (speech in New York, 6 March 1997, "Alternative Radio").

——. *The Twilight of Common Dreams*. New York: Metropolitan, 1995.

Goodin, Robert, and Philip Pettit, eds. *A Companion to Contemporary Political Philosophy*. New York: Blackwell, 1993.

Gould, Carol. *Rethinking Democracy*. New York: Cambridge University Press, 1988.

Grasso, Kenneth, Gerard Bradley, and Robert Hunt, eds. *Catholicism, Liberalism, and Communitarianism*. Lanham, Md.: Rowman and Littlefield, 1995.

Gray, John. "Contractarian Method, Private Property and the Market Economy." In *Liberalisms: Essays in Political Philosophy*. New York: Routledge, 1989.

——. *Mill on Liberty: A Defense*. Second edition. New York: Routledge, 1996.

Gutmann, Amy. "The Challenge of Multiculturalism in Political Ethics." *Philosophy and Public Affairs* 22, no. 3 (summer 1993).

——. "Civic Education and Social Diversity." *Ethics* 105, no. 3 (April 1995).

——. "Communitarian Critics of Liberalism." *Philosophy and Public Affairs* 14, no. 3 (summer 1985).

——. "Justice across the Spheres." In *Pluralism, Justice, and Equality*, David Miller and Michael Walzer, eds.

Gutting, Gary, ed. *The Cambridge Companion to Foucault*. New York: Cambridge University Press, 1994.

——. "Michel Foucault: A User's Manual." In *The Cambridge Companion to Foucault*. Gary Gutting, ed.

Habermas, Jürgen. *Autonomy and Solidarity*. Revised edition. Peter Dews, ed. New York: Verso, 1992.

——. *Between Facts and Norms*. William Gehg, trans. Cambridge: MIT Press, 1996. (Originally published in 1992.)

——. *Communication and the Evolution of Society*. Thomas McCarthy, trans. Boston: Beacon Press, 1979. (Originally published in 1976.)

——. "The Dialectics of Rationalization." In *Autonomy and Solidarity*. (Interview conducted in 1981.)

——. *The Inclusion of the Other*. Ciaran Cronin and Pablo de Greiff, eds. Cambridge: MIT Press, 1998. (Originally published in 1996.)

——. *Justification and Application: Remarks on Discourse Ethics*. Ciaran Cronin, trans. Cambridge: MIT Press, 1993. (Originally published in 1991.)

——. "Life-Forms, Morality and the Task of the Philosopher." In *Autonomy and Solidarity*. (Interview conducted in 1984.)

——. *Lifeworld and System: A Critique of Functionalist Reason*. Vol. 2 of *The Theory of Communicative Action*. Thomas McCarthy, trans. Boston: Beacon, 1987. (Originally published in 1981.)

——. "Modernity: An Unfinished Project." In *Habermas and the Unfinished Project of Modernity*, Maurizio Passerin d'Entrèves and Seyla Benhabib, eds. Cambridge: MIT Press, 1996. (Originally published in 1981.)

——. "Modernity versus Postmodernity." *New German Critique*, no. 22 (winter 1981).

——. *Moral Consciousness and Communicative Action*. Christian Lenhardt and Shierry Weber Nicholsen, trans. Cambridge: MIT Press, 1990. (Originally published in 1983.)

——. *The Philosophical Discourse of Modernity*. Frederick Lawrence, trans. Cambridge: MIT Press, 1987. (Originally published in 1985.)

——. *Postmetaphysical Thinking*. William Hohengarten, trans. Cambridge: MIT Press, 1992. (Originally published in 1988.)

——. "Questions and Counterquestions." In *Habermas and Modernity*, Richard Bernstein, ed. Cambridge: MIT Press, 1985.

——. *Reason and the Rationalization of Society*. Vol. 1 of *The Theory of Communicative Action*. Thomas McCarthy, trans. Boston: Beacon, 1984. (Originally published in 1981.)

——. "'Reasonable' versus 'True,' or the Morality of Worldviews." In *The Inclusion of the Other*.

——. "Reconciliation through the Public Use of Reason: Remarks on John Rawls's Political Liberalism." *The Journal of Philosophy* 92, no. 3 (March 1995); reprinted in *The Inclusion of the Other*.

——. "Remarks on Legitimation through Human Rights." *Philosophy and Social Criticism* 24, no. 2/3 (April 1998).

Hacking, Ian. "Self-Improvement." In *Foucault: A Critical Reader*, David Hoy, ed.

Hampshire, Stuart. "A New Philosophy of the Just Society." *The New York Review of Books*, 24 Feb. 1972.

Hampton, Jean. "The Common Faith of Liberalism." *Pacific Philosophical Quarterly* 75, nos. 3/4 (Sept./Dec. 1994).

——. "Contracts and Choices: Does Rawls Have a Social Contract Theory?" *The Journal of Philosophy* 77, no. 6 (June 1980).

——. "Feminist Contractarianism." In *A Mind of One's Own*, Louise Antony and Charlotte Witt, eds. Boulder, Colo.: Westview, 1993.

——. "Rethinking Reason." *American Philosophical Quarterly* 29, no. 3 (July 1992).

Hardimon, Michael. *Hegel's Social Philosophy: The Project of Reconciliation*. New York: Cambridge University Press, 1994.

——. "Role Obligations." *The Journal of Philosophy* 91, no. 7 (July 1994).

Hare, R. M., "Ethical Theory and Intuitionism." In *Utilitarianism and Beyond*, Amartya Sen and Bernard Williams, eds.

——. *Moral Thinking: Its Levels, Method, and Point*. New York: Oxford University Press, 1981.

——. "Rawls' Theory of Justice." In *Reading Rawls*, Norman Daniels, ed.

Harman, Gilbert. *The Nature of Morality*. New York: Oxford University Press, 1977.

Harsanyi, John. "Can the Maximin Principle Serve As a Basis for Morality? A Critique of John Rawls's Theory." In *Essays on Ethics, Social Behavior, and Scientific Explanation*. Boston: D. Reidel, 1976.

——. "Cardinal Utility in Welfare Economics and the Theory of Risk-Taking." *The Journal of Political Economy* 61 (1953).

Hart, H. L. A. "Rawls on Liberty and Its Priority." In *Reading Rawls*, Norman Daniels, ed.

Hayek, Friedrich. *The Mirage of Social Justice*. Vol. 2 of *Law, Legislation and Liberty*. (Chicago: University of Chicago Press, 1976).

Held, Virginia. *Rights and Goods*. Chicago: University of Chicago Press, 1984.

Herzog, Don. "Puzzling through Burke." *Political Theory* 19, no. 3 (Aug. 1991).

——. "Some Questions for Republicans." *Political Theory* 14, no. 3 (Aug. 1986).

Hobbes, Thomas. *Leviathan*. C. B. Macpherson, ed. New York: Penguin, 1968.

Hohengarten, William. Translator's introduction in Jürgen Habermas, *Postmetaphysical Thinking*.

Holmes, Stephen. *The Anatomy of Antiliberalism*. Cambridge: Harvard University Press, 1993.

——. "The Permanent Structure of Anti-Liberal Thought." In *Liberalism and the Moral Life*, Nancy Rosenblum, ed. Cambridge: Harvard University Press, 1989.

Honderich, Ted. *Conservatism*. Boulder, Colo.: Westview, 1991.

Horkheimer, Max, and Theodor Adorno. *Dialectic of Enlightenment*. John Cumming, trans. New York: Herder and Herder, 1972; reprint, New York: Continuum, 1999. (Originally published in 1944.)

Hoy, David, ed. *Foucault: A Critical Reader*. New York: Basil Blackwell, 1986.

——. Introduction to *Foucault: A Critical Reader*, David Hoy, ed.

——. "Jacques Derrida." In *The Return of Grand Theory in the Human Sciences*, Quentin Skinner, ed.

Jackson, Timothy. "To Bedlam and Part Way Back: John Rawls and Christian Justice." *Faith and Philosophy* 8, no. 4 (Oct. 1991).

Jacoby, Russell. *Dogmatic Wisdom*. New York: Doubleday, 1994.

——. *The Last Intellectuals*. New York: Noonday Press, 1987.

James, Susan. "Louis Althusser." In *The Return of Grand Theory in the Human Sciences*, Quentin Skinner, ed.

Jencks, Charles. *The Language of Post-Modern Architecture*. Revised enlarged edition. New York: Rizzoli, 1977.

Judas, John. *William F. Buckley, Jr.: Patron Saint of the Conservatives*. New York: Simon and Schuster, 1988.

Kaminer, Wendy. *A Fearful Freedom*. Reading, Mass.: Addison-Wesley, 1988.

Kant, Immanuel. "An Answer to the Question: What Is Enlightenment?" In *Perpetual Peace and Other Essays*.

——. *Critique of Pure Reason*. Norman Kemp Smith, trans. New York: St. Martin's Press, 1965.

——. *Groundwork of the Metaphysics of Morals*. Mary Gregor, ed. New York: Cambridge University Press, 1997.

——. *The Metaphysics of Morals*. Mary Gregor, ed. New York: Cambridge University Press, 1996.

——. "On the Proverb: That May Be True in Theory, but Is of No Practical Use." In *Perpetual Peace and Other Essays*.

——. *Perpetual Peace and Other Essays*. Ted Humphrey, trans. Indianapolis: Hackett, 1983.

——. "To Perpetual Peace: A Philosophic Sketch." In *Perpetual Peace and Other Essays*.

Katznelson, Ira. *Liberalism's Crooked Circle*. Princeton: Princeton University Press, 1996.

Kekes, John. *Against Liberalism*. Ithaca, N.Y.: Cornell University Press, 1997.

——. *Facing Evil*. Princeton: Princeton University Press, 1990.

——. *Moral Wisdom and Good Lives*. Ithaca, N.Y.: Cornell University Press, 1995.

——. "A Question for Egalitarians." *Ethics* 107, no. 4 (July 1997).

Kirk, Russell. *The Conservative Mind*. Seventh revised edition. Chicago: Regnery Books, 1986.

Kittay, Eva Feder. "Human Dependency and Rawlsian Equality." In *Feminists Rethink the Self*, Diana Meyers, ed. Boulder, Colo.: Westview, 1997.

Kittay, Eva Feder, and Diana Meyers, eds. *Women and Moral Theory*. Totowa, N.J.: Rowman & Littlefield, 1987.

Kolodny, Niko. "The Ethics of Cryptonormativism: A Defense of Foucault's Evasions." *Philosophy and Social Criticism* 22, no. 5 (Sept. 1996).

Korsgaard, Christine. "Commentary [on Cohen and Sen]." In *The Quality of Life*, Martha Nussbaum and Amartya Sen, eds. New York: Oxford University Press, 1993.

——. "From Duty and for the Sake of the Noble: Kant and Aristotle on Morally Good Action." In *Aristotle, Kant, and the Stoics*, Stephen Engstrom and Jennifer Whiting, eds. New York: Cambridge University Press, 1996.

——. "The Normativity of Instrumental Reason." In *Ethics and Practical Reason*, Garrett Cullity and Berys Gaut, eds. New York: Oxford University Press, 1997.

Kronman, Anthony. "Talent Pooling." In *Human Rights (NOMOS XXIII)*, J. Roland Pennock and John Chapman, eds. New York: NYU Press, 1981.

Krouse, Richard, and Michael McPherson. "Capitalism, 'Property-Owning Democracy,' and the Welfare State." In *Democracy and the Welfare State*, Amy Gutmann, ed. Princeton: Princeton University Press, 1988.

Kukathas, Chandran, and Philip Pettit. *Rawls: A Theory of Justice and Its Critics*. Stanford: Stanford University Press, 1990.

Kymlicka, Will. "Community." In *A Companion to Contemporary Political Philosophy*, Robert Goodin and Philip Pettit, eds.

——. "The Ethics of Inarticulacy." *Inquiry* 34, no. 2 (June 1991).

——. "Liberal Individualism and Liberal Neutrality." *Ethics* 99, no. 4 (July 1989).
—— "Liberalism and Communitarianism." *The Canadian Journal of Philosophy* 18, no. 2 (June 1988).
——. *Liberalism, Community, and Culture*. New York: Oxford University Press, 1989.
——. "Two Models of Pluralism and Tolerance." In *Toleration: An Elusive Virtue*, David Heyd, ed. Princeton: Princeton University Press, 1996.
Laden, Anthony. "Games, Fairness, and Rawls's *A Theory of Justice*." *Philosophy and Public Affairs* 20, no. 3 (summer 1991).
Langan, John. "Catholicism and Liberalism." In *Liberalism and the Good*, R. Bruce Douglass, Gerald Mara, and Henry Richardson, eds. New York: Routledge, 1990.
Larmore, Charles. *The Morals of Modernity*. New York: Cambridge University Press, 1996.
——. *Patterns of Moral Complexity*. New York: Cambridge University Press, 1987.
Larrabee, Mary Jeanne, ed. *An Ethic of Care*. New York: Routledge, 1993.
Laslett, Peter. Introduction to *Philosophy, Politics and Society* (first series), Peter Laslett, ed. New York: Basil Blackwell, 1956.
Levine, Andrew. "Beyond Justice: Rousseau against Rawls." *The Journal of Chinese Philosophy* 4, no. 2 (Aug. 1977).
Lilla, Mark. "The Politics of Jacques Derrida." *New York Review of Books*, 25 June 1998.
Lloyd, S. A. "Family Justice and Social Justice." *Pacific Philosophical Quarterly* 75, nos. 3/4 (Sept./Dec. 1994).
——. "Relativizing Rawls." *Chicago-Kent Law Review* 69, no. 3 (1994).
Lukes, Steven. *Individualism*. New York: Basil Blackwell, 1973.
Lund, William. "Egalitarian Liberalism and Social Pathology: A Defense of Public Neutrality." *Social Theory and Practice* 23, no. 3 (fall 1997).
Lyons, Paul. *New Left, New Right and the Legacy of the Sixties*. Philadelphia: Temple University Press, 1996.
Lyotard, Jean-François. *The Differend*. Georges Van Den Abbeele, trans. Minneapolis: University of Minnesota, 1988. (Originally published in 1983.)
——. *The Postmodern Condition*. Geoff Bennington and Brian Massumi, trans. Minneapolis: University of Minnesota, 1984. (Originally published in 1979.)
Macedo, Stephen. "Liberal Civic Education and Religious Fundamentalism: The Case of God v. John Rawls?" *Ethics* 105, no. 3 (April 1995).
MacIntyre, Alasdair. *After Virtue*. Second edition. South Bend, Ind.: University of Notre Dame Press, 1984.
——. "I'm Not a Communitarian, but . . ." *The Responsive Community* 1 (1991).
——. *Whose Justice? Which Rationality?* South Bend, Ind.: University of Notre Dame Press, 1988.
Mackie, J. L. *Ethics: Inventing Right and Wrong*. New York: Penguin, 1977.
Macpherson, C. B. *Democratic Theory: Essays in Retrieval*. New York: Oxford University Press, 1973.
——. *The Political Theory of Possessive Individualism*. New York: Oxford University Press, 1962.
——. "Rawls's Models of Man and Society." *Philosophy of the Social Sciences* 3 (1973).
Mandle, Jon. "Having It Both Ways: Justification and Application in Justice As Fairness." *Pacific Philosophical Quarterly* 75, nos. 3/4 (Sept./Dec. 1994).
——. "Justice, Desert, and Ideal Theory." *Social Theory and Practice* 23, no. 3 (fall 1997).

——. "Rawls and the Left." *Socialist Review* 21, nos. 3-4 (July-Dec. 1991).

——. "The Reasonable in Justice As Fairness." *The Canadian Journal of Philosophy* 29, no. 1 (March 1999).

de Marneffe, Peter. "Liberalism, Liberty, and Neutrality." *Philosophy and Public Affairs* 19, no. 3 (summer 1990).

Martin, Rex. *Rawls and Rights*. Lawrence: University Press of Kansas, 1985.

Matthews, Eric. *Twentieth-Century French Philosophy*. New York: Oxford University Press, 1996.

McCarthy, Thomas. *Ideals and Illusions*. Cambridge: MIT Press, 1991.

——. Introduction to Jürgen Habermas, *The Philosophical Discourse of Modernity*.

——. "Kantian Constructivism and Reconstructivism: Rawls and Habermas in Dialogue." *Ethics* 105, no. 1 (Oct. 1994).

——. "Philosophy and Social Practice." In *Ideals and Illusions*.

——. "The Politics of the Ineffable: Derrida's Deconstruction." In *Ideals and Illusions*.

McClennen, Edward. "Justice and the Problem of Stability." *Philosophy and Public Affairs* 18, no. 1 (winter 1989).

McClintock, Anne, and Rob Nixon. "No Names Apart," *Critical Inquiry* 13, no. 1 (autumn 1986).

McLeod, Mary. "Architecture." In *The Postmodern Moment*, Stanley Trachtenberg, ed.

Merquior, J. G. *Foucault* (Modern Masters). London: Fontana Press, 1985.

Mill, J. S. *On Liberty*. Elizabeth Rapaport, ed. Indianapolis: Hackett, 1978.

Miller, David, and Michael Walzer, eds. *Pluralism, Justice, and Equality*. New York: Oxford University Press, 1995.

Millgram, Elijah. "Incommensurability and Practical Reason." In *Incommensurability, Incomparability, and Practical Reason*, Ruth Chang, ed. Cambridge: Harvard University Press, 1997.

——. *Practical Induction*. Cambridge: Harvard University Press, 1997.

Mills, C. Wright. "The Decline of the Left." In *Power, Politics and People*, Irving Horowitz, ed. New York: Ballantine Books, 1963.

——. *The Sociological Imagination*. New York: Oxford University Press, 1959.

Minow, Martha. *Making All the Difference*. Ithaca, N.Y.: Cornell University Press, 1990.

Moon, J. Donald. *Constructing Community*. Princeton: Princeton University Press, 1993.

——. "Practical Discourse and Communicative Ethics." In *The Cambridge Companion to Habermas*, Stephen White, ed.

Mouffe, Chantal, ed. *Deconstruction and Pragmatism*. New York: Routledge, 1996.

——. "Deconstruction, Pragmatism and the Politics of Democracy." In *Deconstruction and Pragmatism*, Chantal Mouffe, ed.

Mulhall, Stephen, and Adam Swift. *Liberals and Communitarians*. Second edition. Cambridge: Blackwell, 1996.

Munoz-Dardé, Véronique. "Rawls, Justice in the Family and Justice of the Family." *The Philosophical Quarterly* 48, no. 192 (July 1998).

Musgrave, R. A. "Maximin, Uncertainty, and the Leisure Trade-Off." *The Quarterly Journal of Economics* 88 (1974).

Nagel, Thomas. "Libertarianism without Foundations." *The Yale Law Journal* 85, no. 136 (1975).

——. *Mortal Questions*. New York: Cambridge University Press, 1979.

——. "Rawls on Justice." In *Reading Rawls*, Norman Daniels, ed.

——. *The View from Nowhere*. New York: Oxford University Press, 1986.

Neal, Patrick. "Does He Mean What He Says? (Mis)Understanding Rawls' Practical Turn." In *Liberalism and Its Discontents*. New York: NYU Press, 1997.

Nisbet, Robert. *Conservatism: Dream and Reality*. Minneapolis: University of Minnesota Press, 1986.

Nozick, Robert. *Anarchy, State, and Utopia*. New York: Basic Books, 1974.

Nussbaum, Martha. "The Professor of Parody." *The New Republic*, 22 Feb. 1999.

Oakeshott, Michael. "On Being Conservative." In *Rationalism in Politics and Other Essays*.

———. "Political Education." In *Rationalism in Politics and Other Essays*.

———. "Rationalism in Politics." In *Rationalism in Politics and Other Essays*.

———. *Rationalism in Politics and Other Essays*. New and expanded edition. Indianapolis: Liberty Press, 1991.

Okin, Susan. *Justice, Gender, and the Family*. New York: Basic Books, 1989.

O'Neill, Onora. "The Public Use of Reason." In *Constructions of Reason*. New York: Cambridge University Press, 1989.

———. "Vindicating Reason." In *The Cambridge Companion to Kant*, Paul Guyer, ed. New York: Cambridge University Press, 1992.

Peffer, R. G. *Marxism, Morality, and Social Justice*. Princeton: Princeton University Press, 1990.

Pensky, Max. "Universalism and the Situated Critic." In *The Cambridge Companion to Habermas*, Stephen White, ed.

Plato. *Phaedrus*. In *Plato: The Collected Dialogues*, Edith Hamilton and Huntington Cairns, eds. Princeton: Princeton University Press, 1961.

Pogge, Thomas. *Realizing Rawls*. Ithaca, N.Y.: Cornell University Press, 1989.

Putnam, Hilary. *Reason, Truth, and History*. New York: Cambridge University Press, 1981.

Quinton, Anthony. "Conservatism." In *A Companion to Contemporary Political Philosophy*, Robert Goodin and Philip Pettit, eds.

Rawls, John. "Constitutional Liberty and the Concept of Justice." In *Justice (NOMOS VI)*, C. J. Friedrich and John Chapman, eds. New York: Atherton, 1963.

———. "Fairness to Goodness." *The Philosophical Review* 84 (1975).

———. "The Idea of Public Reason Revisited." *University of Chicago Law Review* 64, no. 3 (summer 1997).

———. "The Independence of Moral Theory." *Proceedings and Addresses of the American Philosophical Association* 48 (1975).

———. "Justice As Fairness." *The Philosophical Review* 67 (1958).

———. "Justice As Fairness: A Brief Restatement" (unpublished manuscript, 1989).

———. "The Justification of Civil Disobedience." In *Civil Disobedience: Theory and Practice*, Hugo Adam Bedau, ed. New York: Pegasus, 1969.

———. "Kantian Constructivism in Moral Theory: The Dewey Lectures 1980." *The Journal of Philosophy* 77, no. 9 (Sept. 1980).

———. *Political Liberalism*. New York: Columbia University Press, 1993. Paperback edition, 1996.

———. "Preface for the French Edition of *A Theory of Justice*." In *Collected Papers*, Samuel Freeman, ed. Cambridge: Harvard University Press, 1999.

———. "The Priority of Right and Ideas of the Good." *Philosophy and Public Affairs* 17, no. 4 (fall 1988).

——. "Reply to Alexander and Musgrave." *The Quarterly Journal of Economics* 88 (1974).

——. "Reply to Habermas." *The Journal of Philosophy* 92, no. 3 (March 1995). Reprinted in *Political Liberalism.*

——. "Reply to Lyons and Teitelman." *The Journal of Philosophy* 69, no. 18 (Oct. 1972).

——. "The Sense of Justice." *The Philosophical Review* 72 (1963).

——. "Social Unity and Primary Goods." In *Utilitarianism and Beyond*, Amartya Sen and Bernard Williams, eds.

——. "Some Reasons for the Maximin Criterion." *American Economic Review* 64 (1974).

——. *A Theory of Justice.* Cambridge: Harvard University Press, 1971. Revised edition, 1999.

——. "Two Concepts of Rules." *The Philosophical Review* 64 (1955).

——. "A Well-Ordered Society." In *Philosophy, Politics and Society* (fifth series), Peter Laslett and James Fishkin, eds. New Haven: Yale University Press, 1979.

Raz, Joseph. "Morality As Interpretation." *Ethics* 101, no. 2 (Jan. 1991).

——. *The Morality of Freedom.* New York: Oxford University Press, 1986.

Reiman, Jeffrey. *Justice and Modern Moral Philosophy.* New Haven: Yale University Press, 1990.

Richards, David. "Public Reason and Abolitionist Dissent." *Chicago-Kent Law Review* 69, no. 3 (1994).

Rocco, Alfredo. "The Political Doctrine of Fascism." In *Communism, Fascism, and Democracy.* Third edition. Carl Cohen, ed. New York: McGraw-Hill, 1997.

Roemer, John. "A Pragmatic Theory of Responsibility for the Egalitarian Planner." In *Egalitarian Perspectives.* New York: Cambridge University Press, 1996.

——. *Theories of Distributive Justice.* Cambridge: Harvard University Press, 1996.

Rorty, Richard. *Achieving Our Country.* Cambridge: Harvard University Press, 1998.

——. *Contingency, Irony, and Solidarity.* New York: Cambridge University Press, 1989.

——. "Deconstruction and Circumvention." In *Essays on Heidegger and Others.*

——. *Essays on Heidegger and Others.* Vol. 2 of *Philosophical Papers.* New York: Cambridge University Press, 1991.

——. "Habermas, Derrida, and the Functions of Philosophy." In *Truth and Progress.*

——. "Human Rights, Rationality, and Sentimentality." In *Truth and Progress.*

——. "Intellectuals in Politics." *Dissent* (fall 1991).

——. "Is Derrida a Transcendental Philosopher?" In *Essays on Heidegger and Others.*

——. *Objectivity, Relativism, and Truth.* Vol. 1 of *Philosophical Papers.* New York: Cambridge University Press, 1991.

——. "Philosophy As a Kind of Writing." In *Consequences of Pragmatism.* Minneapolis: University of Minnesota Press, 1982.

——. "Posties." *London Review of Books* (21 July 1983).

——. "Postmodern Bourgeois Liberalism." In *Objectivity, Relativism, and Truth.*

——. "The Priority of Democracy to Philosophy." In *Objectivity, Relativism, and Truth.*

——. "Religion As a Conversation-Stopper." *Common Knowledge* 3, no. 1 (spring 1994).

——. "Reply." *Dissent* (spring 1992).

——. *Truth and Progress.* Vol. 3 of *Philosophical Papers.* New York: Cambridge University Press, 1998.

Rosenblum, Nancy. *Membership and Morals*. Princeton: Princeton University Press, 1998.

Rothenberg, Randall. "Philosopher Robert Nozick vs. Philosopher John Rawls: Give Me Liberty or Give Me Equality." *Esquire*, March 1983.

Rouse, Joseph. "Power/Knowledge." In *The Cambridge Companion to Foucault*, Gary Gutting, ed.

Ryan, Alan. "John Rawls." In *The Return of Grand Theory in the Human Sciences*. Quentin Skinner, ed.

———. "Republican Nostalgia." *Dissent* (winter 1997).

Ryan, Michael. *Marxism and Deconstruction*. Baltimore: Johns Hopkins University Press, 1982.

Sachs, David. "How to Distinguish Self-Respect from Self-Esteem." *Philosophy and Public Affairs* 10, no. 4 (fall 1981).

Sandel, Michael. *Democracy's Discontent*. Cambridge: Harvard University Press, 1996.

———. *Liberalism and the Limits of Justice*. Second edition. New York: Cambridge University Press, 1998.

———. "Morality and the Liberal Ideal." *The New Republic*, 7 May 1988.

de Saussure, Ferdinand. *Course in General Linguistics*. Charles Bally and Albert Sechehaye, eds., Roy Harris, trans. La Salle, Ill.: Open Court, 1986.

Scanlon, T. M. "Contractualism and Utilitarianism." In *Utilitarianism and Beyond*, Amartya Sen and Bernard Williams, eds.

———. "Nozick on Rights, Liberty, and Property." *Philosophy and Public Affairs* 6, no. 1 (fall 1976).

Schaller, Walter. "Rawls, the Difference Principle, and Economic Inequality." *Pacific Philosophical Quarterly* 79, no. 4 (Dec. 1998).

Schneewind, J. B. "Book Review of *Sources of the Self*." *The Journal of Philosophy* 88, no. 8 (Aug. 1991).

———. "Natural Law, Skepticism, and Methods of Ethics." *The Journal of the History of Ideas* 52, no. 2 (April-June 1991).

Schor, Juliet. "The New Politics of Consumption." *The Boston Review* 24, no. 3-4 (summer 1999).

Schwartz, Adina. "Moral Neutrality and Primary Goods." *Ethics* 83 (1973).

Scruton, Roger. *The Meaning of Conservatism*. Second edition. London: Macmillan, 1984.

Sen, Amartya, and Bernard Williams, eds. *Utilitarianism and Beyond*. New York: Cambridge University Press, 1982.

Shklar, Judith. *The Faces of Injustice*. New Haven: Yale University Press, 1990.

Shwartzenbach, Sybil. "Rawls, Hegel, and Communitarianism." *Political Theory* 19, no. 4 (Nov. 1991).

Sidgwick, Henry. *The Methods of Ethics*. Seventh edition. Indianapolis: Hackett, 1981.

Simons, Jon. *Foucault and the Political*. New York: Routledge, 1995.

Singer, Peter. "Sidgwick and Reflective Equilibrium." *The Monist* 58, no. 3 (July 1974).

Skinner, Quentin, ed. *The Return of Grand Theory in the Human Sciences*. New York: Cambridge University Press, 1985.

Smith, Paul. "Incentives and Justice: G. A. Cohen's Egalitarian Critique of Rawls." *Social Theory and Practice* 24, no. 2 (summer 1998).

Stevick, Philip. "Literature." In *The Postmodern Moment*, Stanley Trachtenberg, ed.

Stolzenberg, Nomi Maya. "'He Drew a Circle That Shut Me Out': Assimilation, Indoctrination, and the Paradox of Liberal Education." *Harvard Law Review* 106 (1993).

Strauss, Leo. *Natural Right and History*. Chicago: University of Chicago Press, 1953.

Strong, Tracy, and Frank Andreas Sposito. "Habermas's Significant Other." In *The Cambridge Companion to Habermas*, Stephen White, ed.

Sturrock, John, ed. *Structuralism and Since*. New York: Oxford University Press, 1979.

Tännsjö, Torbjörn. *Conservatism for Our Time*. New York: Routledge, 1990.

Taylor, Charles. "Atomism." In *Philosophy and the Human Sciences*. Vol. 2 of *Philosophical Papers*. New York: Cambridge University Press, 1985.

——. "Cross-Purposes: The Liberal-Communitarian Debate." In *Philosophical Arguments*. Cambridge: Harvard University Press, 1995.

——. *Hegel and Modern Society*. New York: Cambridge University Press, 1979.

——. *Sources of the Self*. Cambridge: Harvard University Press, 1989.

——. "What Is Human Agency?" In *Human Agency and Language*. Vol. 1 of *Philosophical Papers*. New York: Cambridge University Press, 1985.

Teitelman, Michael. "The Limits of Individualism." *The Journal of Philosophy* 69, no. 18 (Oct. 1972).

Temkin, Larry. "A Continuum Argument for Intransitivity." *Philosophy and Public Affairs* 25, no. 3 (summer 1996).

Tomasi, John. "Individual Rights and Community Virtues." *Ethics* 101, no. 3 (April 1991).

Trachtenberg, Stanley. Introduction to *The Postmodern Moment*, Stanley Trachtenberg, ed.

——, ed. *The Postmodern Moment*. Westport, Conn.: Greenwood Press, 1985.

Van Parijs, Philippe. "Why Surfers Should Be Fed: The Liberal Case for an Unconditional Basic Income." *Philosophy and Public Affairs* 20, no. 2 (spring 1991).

Venturi, Robert, Denise Scott Brown, and Steven Izenour. *Learning from Las Vegas*. Revised edition. Cambridge: MIT Press, 1977.

Waldron, Jeremy. "John Rawls and the Social Minimum." In *Liberal Rights*.

——. *Liberal Rights*. New York: Cambridge University Press, 1993.

——. "The Plight of the Poor in the Midst of Plenty," *London Review of Books* 21, no. 14 (15 July 1999). <http://www.lrb.co.uk/v21/n14/wald2114.htm>.

——. *The Right to Private Property*. New York: Oxford University Press, 1988.

——. "Theoretical Foundations of Liberalism." In *Liberal Rights*.

——. "When Justice Replaces Affection: The Need for Rights." In *Liberal Rights*.

Walzer, Michael. "The Communitarian Critique of Liberalism." *Political Theory* 18, no. 1 (Feb. 1990).

——. *The Company of Critics*. New York: Basic Books, 1988.

——. "In Defense of Equality." In *Radical Principles*. New York: Basic Books, 1980.

——. *Interpretation and Social Criticism*. Cambridge: Harvard University Press, 1987.

——. "Philosophy and Democracy." *Political Theory* 9, no. 3 (Aug. 1981).

——. "The Politics of Michel Foucault." In *Foucault: A Critical Reader*, David Hoy, ed.

——. "Response." In *Pluralism, Justice, and Equality*, David Miller and Michael Walzer, eds.

——. *Spheres of Justice*. New York: Basic Books, 1983.

——. "'Spheres of Justice': An Exchange." *New York Review of Books*, 21 July 1983.

——. *Thick and Thin*. South Bend, Ind.: University of Notre Dame Press, 1994.

Warren, Virginia. "Guidelines for Non-Sexist Use of Language," *Proceedings and Addresses of the APA* 59, no. 3 (Feb. 1986). Reprint by the American Philosophical Association.

Weber, Max. *The Protestant Ethic and the Spirit of Capitalism.* Talcott Parsons, trans. Boston: Unwin Hyman, 1930.

Wellbank, J. H., Denis Snook, and David Mason. *John Rawls and His Critics: An Annotated Bibliography.* New York: Garland Publishing, 1982.

White, Hayden. "Michel Foucault." In *Structuralism and Since.* John Sturrock, ed.

White, Stephen, ed. *The Cambridge Companion to Habermas.* New York: Cambridge University Press, 1995.

——. *Political Theory and Postmodernism.* New York: Cambridge University Press, 1991.

Williams, Andrew. "Incentives, Inequality, and Publicity." *Philosophy and Public Affairs* 27, no. 3 (summer 1998).

——. "The Revisionist Difference Principle." *The Canadian Journal of Philosophy* 25, no. 2 (June 1995).

Williams, Bernard. *Ethics and the Limits of Philosophy.* Cambridge: Harvard University Press, 1985.

——. "A Fair State." *London Review of Books*, 13 May 1993.

——. "Internal and External Reasons." In *Moral Luck.* New York: Cambridge University Press, 1981.

Wills, Garry. *Reagan's America.* Garden City, N.Y.: Doubleday, 1987.

Wolff, Jonathan. "Fairness, Respect, and the Egalitarian Ethos." *Philosophy and Public Affairs* 27, no. 2 (spring 1998).

Wolff, Robert Paul. *The Poverty of Liberalism.* Boston: Beacon, 1968.

——. *Understanding Rawls: A Reconstruction and Critique of "A Theory of Justice."* Princeton: Princeton University Press, 1977.

Young, James. *Reconsidering American Liberalism.* Boulder, Colo.: Westview, 1996.

Index

Ackerman, Bruce, 5, 83
Adorno, Theodor, 254-255
Alejandro, Roberto, 21n17, 81-82
Alexander, Larry, 134n95
Allegheny County v. ACLU, 160n21
Althusser, Louis, 222
Anderson, Elizabeth, 147n122, 148n125
Amdur, Robert, 4n11
Americans with Disabilities Act of 1990, 133-134
apartheid, 229-230
archaeology, 234-239, 247. *See also* care, perspective of; Foucault, Michel; genealogy
Archimedean point, 31
Arneson, Richard, 94n9, 134n95, 145n115, 146, 176
Arrow, Kenneth, 138-139
atomism, *see* individualism
Austin, J. L., 224
autonomy, 75, 108, 270-271

background justice, *see* basic structure of society
Baier, Kurt, 41n58
Baker, C. Edwin, 168n41, 203n147
Barber, Benjamin 173, 281
Barry, Brian, 38n55, 45n69, 87n153, 150, 168n41, 177, 181, 185, 186n84, 188n95, 203n147, 205, 207
basic liberties, 82n142, 91-97, 109, 114-116, 119-124, 134-136, 161, 271-272, 280. *See also* freedom of speech; justice, mixed conceptions of; justice, principles of; political liberties, fair value of; primary goods; religion; utilitarianism; voluntarism
basic structure of society, 23-30, 38-45, 58-59, 66, 70-72, 76, 80, 85, 93, 101-104, 116-118, 122, 125n74, 129, 135-136, 139n103, 154-155, 164-

166, 169-170, 188, 294. *See also* justice, procedural
Baynes, Kenneth, 273
Beardsworth, Richard, 226
Beckley, Harlan, 72n123, 84n151
Beiner, Ronald, 11-12, 201n142, 288
Bell, Daniel, 215
Bellah, Robert, 10-11
Benhabib, Seyla, 83, 98, 111n38, 189-190
Berlin, Isaiah, 19, 35, 102, 271n188
Berman, Marshall, 217, 292
Berman, Paul, 5-6, 14n42, 222n33
Bernardin, Cardinal Joseph, 79-80
Bernstein, Richard, 226-229, 232-233
Best, Steven, 215
Bird, Colin, 35n39
Bloom Allan, 21n14, 98n15
Bork, Robert, 21n15
Boxill, Bernard, 40
Bradley, Gerard, 72n123
Brandt, Richard, 49-51
Braybrooke, David, 19n7
Brighouse, Harry, 104n28
Brown, Denise Scott, 216n13
Buchanan, Allen, 34n37, 59n105, 156n7
Buckley v. Valeo, 280
burdens of judgment, 34-35, 74-76, 79, 88. *See also* civility, duty of; justice, political conception of; pluralism; reasonable, the
Burke, Edmund, 153, 187, 194-200, 204, 210, 289. *See also* conservatism

Calhoun, John, 208-209
Callinicos, Alex, 24, 214n4, 217-218, 222, 230, 292
Caney, Simon, 156n7
Cantwell v. Connecticut, 160
care, perspective of, 171, 188-190, 234, 247-249. *See also* conservatism; Foucault, Michel; justice, as a

313

About the Author

Jon Mandle is an Assistant Professor of Philosophy at the University at Albany–SUNY. He received his B.A. *magna cum laude*, from the University of Pennsylvania in 1988. In 1994, he completed his Ph.D. in philosophy from the University of Pittsburgh, working under the direction of Kurt Baier. His publications have appeared in *Social Theory and Practice, The Canadian Journal of Philosophy, The Pacific Philosophical Quarterly, The Journal of the History of Philosophy, Socialist Review, Challenge,* and *The Annals of the American Academy of Political and Social Science,* among others.